Freud, Psychoanalysis, and Symbolism

Freud, Psychoanalysis, and Symbolism offers an innovative general theory of symbolism, derived from Freud's psychoanalytic theory and relocated within mainstream scientific psychology. It is the first systematic investigation of the development of Freud's treatment of symbolism throughout his published works, and discovers in those writings a broad theory which is far superior to the widely accepted, narrow, 'official' view. Agnes Petocz argues that the treatment of symbolism must begin with the identification and clarification of a set of logical contraints and psychological requirements which any general theory of symbolism must respect, and that these requirements have been neglected by existing accounts across a number of disciplines. Her newly proposed 'Freudian Broad' theory of symbolism, by contrast, does meet these requirements, but only after it has been rehabilitated within a revised psychoanalytic context. An important contribution to the ongoing development of a coherent and scientifically acceptable version of psychoanalytic theory, *Freud, Psychoanalysis, and Symbolism* also offers a radical reconceptualisation of the unconscious and repression and of the role of language.

AGNES PETOCZ is a lecturer in the Department of Psychology at the University of Western Sydney Macarthur, Australia. She has degrees in classics and psychology and has published in the areas of psychoanalysis and philosophy of mind.

Freud, Psychoanalysis, and Symbolism

Agnes Petocz

CAMBRIDGE
UNIVERSITY PRESS

PUBLISHED BY THE PRESS SYNDICATE OF THE UNIVERSITY OF CAMBRIDGE
The Pitt Building, Trumpington Street, Cambridge, United Kingdom

CAMBRIDGE UNIVERSITY PRESS
The Edinburgh Building, Cambridge, CB2 2RU, United Kingdom
http://www.cup.cam.ac.uk
40 West 20th Street, New York, NY 10011-4211, USA   http://www.cup.org
10 Stamford Road, Oakleigh, Melbourne 3166, Australia

First published 1999

Printed in the United Kingdom at the University Press, Cambridge

Typeset in Monotype Plantin 10/12 pt. [WV]

A catalogue record for this book is available from the British Library

Library of Congress cataloguing in publication data

Petocz, Agnes
  Freud, psychoanalysis, and symbolism / Agnes Petocz.
    p. cm.
  Includes bibliographical references and index.
  ISBN 0 521 59152 X
  1. Freud, Sigmund, 1856–1939. 2. Symbolism (Psychology).
3. Psychoanalysis. I. Title.
BF109.F74P48 1999
150.19′52 – dc21   98-39047 CIP

ISBN 0 521 59152 X hardback

For Anna and Dani
non omnino moriemini

Contents

Figures

Preface

This book had its origins in two questions related to symbolism, and in my dissatisfaction with the existing answers. Firstly, given the central place of symbolism and symbolic activity in human behaviour and mental life, is it possible to have a general, unified theory of the symbol? Secondly, if symbolism is so obviously important, why has it been almost completely neglected by the very discipline which claims to be concerned with human behaviour and mental life – psychology, especially *scientific* psychology? At present, the answers to these two questions may be found in the extensive *non*-psychological literature on symbolism. In this literature, which spans many different fields – philosophy, sociology, anthropology, hermeneutics, semiotics, aesthetics, and so on – and which is, perhaps not surprisingly, full of controversies, one observation which is made time and time again is that symbolism is *inherently* elusive; that the complex and multifaceted nature of the symbol rules out not just a coherent scientific treatment, but any kind of general theory. Thus, the answer to the first question is: 'no'; and the answer to the second question is: 'because symbolism is beyond the reach of science'.

In this book I challenge those answers. I do so by bringing together three lines of argument, none of which, to my knowledge, has previously been proposed. The first line of argument reverses the typical treatment of symbolism. Rather than survey the multitudinous manifestations of the symbol in human life, and conclude that a general theory is out of the question, my own treatment focuses the discussion about symbolism onto what should be the primary task, that of identifying the *criteria* for an adequate general theory. It seems to me that any unified theory of the symbol must respect certain logical constraints (one of which, significantly, is that it be a *psychological* theory) and must, thereby, meet certain *psychological* requirements. When these requirements are spelled out (as they are in the final chapter of the book), it becomes clear that it has been the lack of awareness of them, and the consequent failure to meet them, rather than the infinite variability and complexity of the symbol, which is responsible for so much of the confusion and disorganisation in the field. The second line of argument concerns Freud's psychoanalytic theory, and is a response to Ricoeur's comment, made three decades ago, that a systematic investigation of Freud's notion of the symbol remained to be done. That investigation is undertaken here (in the first part of the book), with surprising results. The picture which emerges is quite different from the narrow and easily dismissible position which has been taken (even by Freud himself) to be Freud's theory of symbolism. As a result of this new picture, it becomes evident that psychoanalysis contains the foundations for a general theory of the symbol, a theory which does appear to meet the logical and psychological requirements, albeit only when it is consolidated via a number of modifications and revisions to Freud's general theory (these revisions are developed in the second half of the book). The third line of argument (which runs through the whole book) presents an unlikely (to some, no doubt, inconceivable) combination: the symbol, psychoanalysis, and science. However, my particular combination is made possible because it is based on an approach to the symbol which is not found elsewhere in the literature, on a modified version of psychoanalysis, and on a view of science which does not accept the contemporary, largely postmodernist, (mis)characterisations. In weaving together these three lines of argument, my aim is to show that, when the logical and psychological criteria for an adequate account of symbolism are identified, when an investigation of Freud's treatment of symbolism *is* undertaken, and when a number of conceptual weaknesses are removed from psychoanalytic theory, then we have the ingredients for a scientifically coherent, general, psychological theory of the symbol.

The question of symbolism began to occupy me when I took my first degree in Classics during the 1970s at the University of Sydney. With a growing interest in philosophy and psychoanalysis, I eventually became diverted into psychology. Most of the work for the book was done over the ten years that I taught (while also completing my doctorate) in the history and philosophy of psychology, psychological theory, and personality theory, in the Department of Psychology at the University of Sydney. During that time, I was fortunate enough to come into contact with John Maze, whose rigorous but open-minded approach to psychological theory in general, and to psychoanalytic theory in particular, and whose own contributions in those areas, became a continuing source of inspiration to me, as they have been to many others.

During the early 1990s, the administrative demands of my additional role as Coordinator of First Year Studies made it almost impossible to find the time to work on this project, and I am particularly grateful to the Deputy Head of Department, Ian Curthoys, for his unfailing support 'from above' through these difficult times. I am also grateful to my assistants during that period, Agi O'Hara and Sandra Rickards, both of whom took on much more than their fair share of the workload, despite heavy teaching and research commitments of their own. A number of other colleagues at the University of Sydney have made numerous contributions in the form of discussions and critical comments on parts of the manuscript – my thanks especially to Olga Katchan, Doris McIlwain, Terry McMullen, Joel Michell, and George Oliphant. My debts to Joel and George are particularly great, for they accompanied me on every step of this long journey: Joel also gave me the use of his office and computer, and his loyal support sustained me through many difficult times; George proofread and commented on every draft of every chapter of the book; each brought to many hours of discussion his keen insight and clarity of thought.

I am grateful also to a number of people whose respective areas of technical expertise contributed towards the smooth preparation of the manuscript: John Holden, Noel Hunt, Cyril Latimer, and Les Petocz. Catherine Max, of Cambridge University Press, has throughout been extremely patient and supportive, not only in negotiating reviews of the manuscript, but in responding readily to my questions and concerns. I have also been encouraged by comments on the manuscript from Jim Hopkins and Nigel Mackay, whose suggestions have allowed me to fine-tune some of my arguments, and extend them in directions I would not otherwise have taken.

Finally, I would like to give special thanks to two people: firstly, to my current Head of Department in Psychology at the University of Western Sydney Macarthur, Jim McKnight, not just for his support during the last difficult year of completing the manuscript, but, what is much rarer these days, for his steadfast promotion of the value of critical conceptual inquiry in psychology, and for his readiness to back it up by providing the kind of environment which is conducive to conducting theoretical research; secondly, to Glenn Newbery, for all those things to which mere public acknowledgement could never do justice.

Introduction

In the Western philosophical tradition, the human being has been characterised variously as *animal politicum*, and as *animal rationale*. Fifty years ago, Cassirer (1944) proposed another characterisation: *animal symbolicum*. Just as we humans are community-living creatures, and just as we are creatures endowed with the ability to reason, so, too – and this has long been acknowledged – we are symbol-producing, symbol-using and, often, symbol-dominated beings; the creation and use of symbols is central and distinctive in our behaviour and in our mental life.

Human behaviour and mental life being the specific concerns of psychology, it would seem reasonable to look to that discipline for an account of symbolism. But mainstream psychology has disappointingly little to say about the subject. As Bertalanffy (1981) observes, 'In spite of the fact that symbolic activity is one of the most fundamental manifestations of the human mind, scientific psychology has in no way given the problem the attention it deserves' (p. 42). In contrast, outside mainstream psychology there is no shortage of material on symbolism. Leaving aside psychoanalysis (for the moment), the humanist, phenomenological and existentialist movements, on the periphery of mainstream psychology because of their opposition to science, devote considerable attention to symbolism, and their contributions are joined by an even more extensive body of literature which spans the whole range of the social sciences: general philosophical treatments of the symbol, hermeneutics, sociology, anthropology, semiotics, aesthetics, and so on, each either appropriating symbolism as its own proper subject matter, or, at least, claiming to reveal valuable insights into symbolism.

This vast literature, however, is disorganised, confusing, and riddled with disagreements. Perhaps we should not be surprised by this, given the enormous range of phenomena encompassed by the concept of 'symbol', from the consciously formed and completely transparent symbols of, say, logic and mathematics, to the unconsciously formed and quite opaque symbols of the dream. But almost all of the controversial

1

literature on symbolism is concerned with only one end of this continuum; in general, the use of mathematical symbols is not regarded as contentious, or as posing interesting and difficult psychological questions, whereas what *is* contentious, what has been disputed for hundreds of years, is the explanation of symbols in myths, fairy tales, dreams, ritual, religion, art, psychopathological symptoms, and so on. In these areas consensus appears to be limited to two points: firstly, that the lack of a general, unified theory of the symbol, though regrettable, is an inevitable result of the nature of the symbol, which is 'intrinsically complex', 'infinitely varied', 'multifaceted'; and, secondly, that the contribution of scientific psychology (including psychoanalysis) to theories of symbolism is necessarily limited, because the symbol is not amenable to scientific investigation; only a broader social-science perspective, a perspective whose eclecticism and opposition to 'psychologism' and to 'psychological reductionism' can accommodate the complexity of the symbol, holds any promise for the eventual emergence of a unified theory.

If these claims were true, they would indeed explain why mainstream scientific psychology has neglected the subject, and why there is no general theory of the symbol. But inspection of the literature reveals both claims to be unjustified. For one thing, the disorganisation and lack of unity in the existing treatments of symbolism are attributable less to the 'complexity' of the symbol than to conceptual confusions and other flaws in the various treatments. Any theory of symbolism, it seems to me, is obliged to respect certain logical constraints and meet certain psychological requirements. The contributions from the various areas which purport to deal with symbolism, or offer insights into it, show little awareness of these requirements, and so fail to meet them. For another thing, although symbolism does belong generally to the social sciences, nevertheless, when the logical constraints are identified, it is clear that the rejection of psychology is misguided. Since symbolisation is a three-term relation, one term of which is a cognising subject, one of the logical constraints on any theory of symbolism is that it *must* be a *psychological* theory. Not only must psychology play a part, that part is fundamental. As for the nature of the required psychological theory, symbolism *is* (as it must be) amenable to scientific investigation. Having said that, however, let me quickly add that, by 'scientific', I do not mean 'positivist' or 'behaviourist' (despite the widespread contrary misconception in contemporary psychological theory), but rather, realist, empiricist, and determinist. Unfortunately, these terms are themselves today much misunderstood. The history of psychology is not just a history of recurrent themes, it is a history of recurrent conceptual confusions. Psychology's attempts to extricate itself from its philosophical roots have long resulted in the neglect of important theoretical issues. Critical thinking and conceptual analysis have been abandoned as esoteric and irrelevant exercises, and looked upon with suspicion and contempt, rather than acknowledged as necessary tools for conducting any kind of scholarship, including scientific inquiry. Today there are signs that theoretical issues in psychology are beginning, again, to receive the attention they deserve. But the signs are far from uniformly encouraging. As part of the broader intellectual *Zeitgeist*, the directing of the critical spotlight in contemporary psychology onto questions of conceptual clarity and coherence is too often advocated only by those who are opposed to science, and welcomed only because it is thought to go hand in hand with 'marginalizing facts' and with recognising that 'the very idea of an "independent" world may itself be an outgrowth of rhetorical demands' (Gergen 1991, p. 23). This attitude is combined with an appeal for psychology to move beyond the sterile, outmoded 'Rhetoric of Scientific Truth' (Ibañez 1991, p. 187), and to embrace instead the post-empiricist, postmodernist 'turn', whose key achievements have been to expose the fallacy of objective science, and to unmask all theory as mere ideology. Similarly, what is identified (and rejected) as 'empiricism' is the supposed scientific aim of discovering indubitable truths, an aim which is illegitimately conflated in contemporary theory with objectivity (realism). This conflation has resulted in the proclaiming of the 'waning of empiricist foundationalism' (Gergen 1991, p. 13), and of the victory of relativism, that is, the victory of 'traditions marginalized within this century by the empiricist hegemony, metatheories of long-standing intellectual currency removed from common consciousness by the prevailing practices' (ibid., p. 16). Consequently, having been told almost three decades ago that 'Philosophically, the heyday of realism is receding into the past' (Palmer 1969, p. 221), those who take the presently unfashionable step of supporting realism find that they have to make an unusual effort to justify that step.

It is not my purpose here to mount a detailed defence of philosophical realism. But, briefly, there is no question that the 'demise' of realism has had much to do with the mistaken equating of it with some kind of self-proclaimed path to the indubitable, and with aspects of positivism and behaviourism. Greenwood (1992) shows how social constructionists, for example, misrepresent scientific realism by assimilating to it a number of features (e.g., operationalism, verificationism, instrumentalism) that are supposed to be associated with empiricism, and he presents realism as a choice of theoretical stance which has been misunderstood, and which, *properly* understood, offers much more than has recently been appreciated. Stove (1991) goes further, suggesting that realism, properly understood, is not even an *option*; it is not contingent, not a scientific *theory*, but a *precondition* of discourse and understanding, the only apparent alternative, solipsism, being unworthy of serious consideration. As for determinism, that is perhaps less controversial. 'Without a causal structure', says Hart (1982), 'the mind should probably be denied to have a nature; and if the mind had no nature, there would be precious little for a scientific psychology to discover' (p. 193). Conversely, anything which has a nature must be bound by the constraints of that nature. As Anderson (1936) points out, 'it is a condition of a thing's existence that it determines and is determined by other things, and . . . to investigate or "give an account of" it involves consideration of such determinations' (p. 123). Therefore, 'Those who are interested in mind's workings will naturally take up a determinist position . . . Theoretical concern with what is the case is, it seems to me, coextensive with determinism' (ibid., p. 125). Furthermore, any attempt to import a partial non-determinism via the postulation of a particular version of the free-will/determinist 'interactionist' position effectively denies *any* determinism; if the same set of physical antecedents leads, on one occasion, to a certain set of physical consequents, and, on another occasion (that of the intervention of a free agent), to a different set of physical consequents, then it is clear that 'there can be no physical uniformity' (ibid., p. 124). This illustrates Anderson's insistence that the strongest defence of a particular theoretical position consists in demonstrating that the opposition must implicitly assume it in the process of explicitly rejecting it, and so can be shown to hold a view which 'amounts to the same as contradicting the possibility of discourse' (ibid., p. 123). Arguments such as these suggest that many contemporary anti-scientific movements are self-contradictory – they are logically dependent on the realism and determinism which they explicitly deny. In the case of symbolism, then, only a theory which is realist, empiricist, and determinist will be genuinely explanatory. I am well aware that many readers would not be satisfied by this all too brief nod towards a defence of the philosophical realism of my position. I can only request them to reserve final judgement until the end of the book, for many of the discussions throughout the rest of the book serve as developments of the points I have made here.

Bearing these points in mind, then, let me return to the unjustified claims made in the literature on symbolism. Not only is the disorganisation there *not* the result of the complexity of the symbol, and not only must a general theory of the symbol be both psychological and scientific, but the material for such a theory is in fact available. That material is to be found in Freud's writings. There, as I shall show, the groundwork for a scientific treatment of symbolism has been laid, in that respect confirming Badcock's (1980) observation that 'the relative failure of the human sciences to provide convincing and exact explanations of cultural phenomena is in large part to be attributed to their failure to take account of Freud' (p. 2). There are two reasons why Freud's contribution to a general theory of the symbol has gone unrecognised. Firstly, as Ricoeur (1970) points out, 'a systematic study of Freud's notion of symbol remains to be done' (n. p. 97). *A fortiori*, there has been no critical evaluation of Freud's writings (direct and indirect) on symbolism. Secondly, as a psychological theory, psychoanalysis is caught between two hostile movements in psychology, each rejecting it, but each, ironically, locating it in the other camp. On one side are the humanist, idealist, phenomenological, and existentialist psychologists, united by an anti-scientific stance, an insistence that symbolism cannot be studied scientifically, and the claim that psychoanalysis – classical psychoanalysis, at least – is hampered by its 'scientistic' restrictions and misconceptions: its narrow determinism, outmoded realism, and 'reductionist' bias. On the other side are the mainstream, largely 'experimental', psychologists, united by their scientific stance, and by the rejection of psychoanalysis (including any psychoanalytically based theory of the symbol) as 'unscientific'. Little wonder that, on the one side Freud alone, and on the other side Freud and symbolism together, have not been given the attention they deserve.

It is my contention, then, that a general theory of the symbol derived from Freud's psychoanalytic theory *is* possible, and that the resulting theory *is* scientific. Investigation of Freud's writings reveals that, in those writings, there is a genuine foundation for such a theory. Admittedly, the identification of that foundation requires considerable extraction and critical textual exegesis, to show that what is of value is not what is usually identified (even by Freud himself) as his theory of symbolism (i.e., the narrow view onto which his ideas converged during the years 1914–17), but, rather, a broader view, for which a schema is discernible in his earlier writings, and whose individual themes were elaborated later, although Freud, for various reasons, did not recognise the unifying role of those themes. Those aspects of the narrow view which are conceptually flawed, and which have left (what is generally regarded as) Freud's theory of symbolism open to easy dismissal, must of course be rejected, but the rest are assimilable into the broader view. As it stands, however, that broader theory will not do. A coherent and defensible general theory of the symbol does not appear until a number of major issues in Freud's writings have been revised and clarified. These revisions are required not only to safeguard the theory from certain potentially damaging criticisms, criticisms which have caused concern to Freud's defenders, but also for establishing the soundness of the theoretical basis of psychoanalysis, upon which the broad theory of the symbol rests. The direction of these revisions is towards maintaining Freud's explicit commitments to realism, empiricism, and determinism, commitments in which he sometimes wavers in his metapsychological treatment of the central concepts of his theory. Those commitments underlie his contribution to one of the major concerns of twentieth-century psychology and philosophy of mind, that of human action and its explanation by means of the traditional 'desire plus belief' model, a model which is currently popular in the 'folk psychological' treatment of humans as 'intentional systems', but which has also come in for much (often justified) criticism. Some of the sounder aspects of Freud's contribution along these lines have been brought out recently by, for example, Maze (1983), Hopkins (1988), Wollheim (1993), and Gardner (1993). But the revisions which I am proposing here are particularly relevant to a successful consolidation of the general theory of the symbol. Once that consolidation has been achieved, I shall be able to show that the theory does meet the logical and psychological requirements which constrain any theory of symbolism, and that its meeting these criteria contrasts with the failure of other approaches, which are left unable to offer any serious challenge, either in the form of a successful alternative, or in the form of valid criticisms of the psychoanalytic approach.

Exegesis and Extraction

My main concern in Part One is to show, via chronological exegesis of Freud's published writings, that what is of value in those writings for a general theory of the symbol is not what is commonly identified as his contribution to symbolism. I shall first present in detail (in Chapter 2) that 'standard' picture of Freud's position, a position whose easy rebuttal reveals why his contribution has been underestimated. In Chapter 3, I begin the chronological investigation by demonstrating that Freud's early writings, typically dismissed as irrelevant to his theory of symbolism, contain the foundations for a different, much broader, approach to the symbol. Chapters 4 to 6 trace the development of those early themes in Freud's subsequent work, showing how they were continued and elaborated, albeit in a scattered and unsystematic fashion, and alongside the 'standard' narrow view. Before turning to Freud's material, however, let me depict the scene which first confronted me, and which would confront anyone approaching this field with the question: can there be a general theory of the symbol?

1   From disorder towards the focus of inquiry

The problem of definition

'There is something very curious in semantics', says Lévi-Strauss (1978), 'that the word "meaning" is, probably, in the whole language, the word the meaning of which is the most difficult to define' (p. 12). Perhaps because of its intimate connection with the concept of meaning, the term 'symbol', despite an extensive literature devoted to the subject, is almost as difficult. Derived from the Greek verb συμβάλλειν (literally, 'to throw together'), the noun σύμβολον (a 'tally') referred originally to each of the two corresponding pieces of some small object which contracting parties broke between them and kept as proof of identity (Liddell and Scott 1968). That meaning subsequently expanded to include a diversity of meanings (other kinds of token, seal, contract, sign, code, etc.), which today has mushroomed even further. Many contemporary definitions reflect the mystique originally associated with symbols, and which prompted Whitehead (1927) to comment on the 'unstable mixture of attraction and repulsion' (p. 60) in our attitude towards symbolism. But the most frequent observation is that it is impossible to find a general, unifying definition. Bertalanffy (1981), for instance, complains that 'in spite of the fact that symbolic activity is one of the most fundamental manifestations of the human mind . . . there is no generally accepted definition of "symbolism" ' (pp. 41–2), and Safouan (1982) warns that 'anyone who tries to study symbolism in all its generality is liable to discover that there is no unity at all that underlies these different uses of the word' (p. 84). To underscore the point, we are faced with such vacuities as 'whatever has meaning is a symbol, and the meaning is whatever is expressed by the symbol' (Radcliffe-Brown, in Skorupski 1976, p. 117), or, worse, 'wherever we look around us, everything can be expressed by the concept of symbol' (Ver Eecke 1975, p. 28). Even amongst those who bring some rigour to their treatment of the topic, there is considerable disagreement: disagreement, for example, about how to classify signs and symbols – what is the difference (if any) between the two, which is the broader term, and to which does language belong; disagreement also about the nature of symbolism – what constitutes symbolism, what activity may properly be described as 'symbolic', what are its origins, development, role, effects, and so on.

But this picture of disorder should not lead us to agree too readily that there can be no general theory of symbolism. Instead, by considering the definitions of symbolism from two different perspectives in turn, the first an overview both of the scope of the subject matter and of the extent of the disorder, the second allowing a convergence on the real centres of controversy, we shall find ourselves on a journey which leads through the disorder towards a focus of inquiry.

Perspective one: the broad to narrow continuum

The more obvious perspective is to regard the enormous range of definitions of symbolism as lying along a continuum, from very broad definitions to extremely narrow ones. At the broad extreme we find the **symbol as superordinate category**. Here are located the 'Bibles' of symbolism (as Bertalanffy (1981) calls them): Cassirer's *The Philosophy of Symbolic Forms* (1953, 1955, 1957 [orig. 1923, 1925, 1929]), and Langer's *Philosophy in a New Key* (1942). Each of these works is neo-Kantian in spirit; philosophical concern with the question of 'meaning' intersects with the treatment of symbols from a strongly phenomenological, constructivist perspective. Cassirer's Kantian debt is the more marked; for him, the 'symbolic' is equated with 'structure' or 'form', and it is the symbolic concept, not the semantic, that is truly universal. Thus, 'the conceptual definition of a content goes hand in hand with its stabilization in some characteristic sign. Consequently, all truly strict and exact thought is sustained by the *symbolics* and *semiotics* on which it is based' (1953, p. 86). Langer also says that symbolisation is the *essential* act of thought, and that 'The symbol-making function is one of man's primary activities, like eating, looking or moving about. It is the fundamental process of his mind, and goes on all the time' (1942, p. 41). Unlike Cassirer, however, Langer combines this broad definition with a more modern information-processing view of thinking, according to which 'the human brain is constantly carrying on a process of symbolic transformation of the experiential data that come to it' (ibid., p. 43). This notion is still, of course, popular, especially with those involved in computer applications in psychology and artificial intelligence. McCorduck, for instance (in Graubard 1988), suggests that artificial intelligence might be the best hope for discovering that 'universal symbolic code', that 'set of universal concepts', which 'underlies all human symbolic expression' (p. 82). Others who appear to follow the general Cassirer–Langer broad approach include: Rapoport (in Royce 1965), for whom symbols are 'products of the human abstracting process' (p. 97), Hayakawa (ibid.), for whom symbolism is 'that which shapes the entire psychic life of man' (p. 92), and Whitehead (1927), for whom symbolism 'is inherent in the very texture of human life' (p. 60). Piaget too, though he is not consistent, occasionally treats symbolic behaviour as being almost as broad as what he terms 'operational intelligence', and his philosophical perspective is similarly neo-Kantian and constructivist. In general, what characterises these very broad definitions of symbolism is the view that the 'symbolic' is universal because it is somehow fundamental to the thinking process.

At a little distance from the broad end of the definitional continuum are treatments of the **symbol as a kind of sign**; the sign is the generic term and the symbol is the special case, albeit special in different ways for different theorists. This view is typical of semiologists or semioticians. As Todorov (1982) says, 'if one gives the word "sign" a generic meaning through which it encompasses that of symbol (the symbol then becomes a special case of the sign), one may say that studies of the symbol belong to the general theory of signs or semiotics' (pp. 9–10). Eco (1973) defines a sign as 'anything that can be taken as "significantly substituting" for something else . . . a sign is something (whether a natural or an artificial object) which stands in place of something which is absent' (p. 1149). Hawkes (1977) points to the culmination of the historical development of a general theory of signs in Jakobson's synthesis of the work of Peirce and Saussure – a curious combination, given the radically different views on the concept of 'symbol' held by these two. For Peirce, the American 'founder' of semiotics, the tripartite division of signs produces the icon, the index, and the symbol, the last being the case where the relation between signifier and signified is arbitrary; thus the major systematic manifestation of symbols is in language. Saussure, on the contrary, held that it is the *sign* which is arbitrary, and the *symbol* which is non-arbitrary or 'motivated', and so does not properly belong to the field of semiology (which, of course, locates Saussure's position further along our definitional continuum, in a region where the symbol is no longer a *kind* of sign, and where 'affect' plays a crucial role). In Jakobson's synthesis, the Saussurean fundamental dimensions of language – the syntagmatic and the paradigmatic – will be found in *any* symbolic process or system of signs. Bertalanffy (1965) follows Peirce; for him also the sign is the broader term, deriving from the general notion of 'meaning' (i.e., representation), and symbols are *kinds* of signs (other kinds are signals, schemata, etc.) which are characterised by being arbitrary, i.e., 'freely created', there being no biologically enforced connection between symbol and symbolised. Within this general position, there are other views on what kind of sign a symbol is which do not depend on the arbitrary/non-arbitrary distinction. For Skorupski (1976), symbols can be characterised as 'designators which *represent* what they stand for' (p. 12), as opposed to those which *indicate* what they stand for:

> the symbol substitutes for the thing symbolised . . . it . . . is treated for the purposes of symbolic action as being what is symbolised. On this picture, the structure of a symbolic action is clear: it represents or enacts an action, event or state of affairs in which the thing represented by the symbol plays a part analogous to that which the symbol plays in the symbolic action itself. (ibid., p. 123)

One major contribution made by these theorists is their recognition of, and emphasis on, the fact that symbolisation (like any representation) is a *relational* phenomenon, a fact which should not be overlooked in the concern with the entities involved in the relation. So Peirce's tripartite classification is made in terms of the *relation between* signifier and signified. Morris (in Eco 1973) also insists that 'something is a sign only because it is interpreted as a sign of something by some interpreter . . . semiotic, then, is not concerned with the study of a particular kind of object, but with ordinary objects insofar (and only insofar) as they participate in semiosis' (p. 1149). Skorupski emphasises the same point:

> While a symbol may often have some natural appropriateness which fits it to the object represented, this characteristic is not constitutive of its semantic status *as* a symbol: what is essential for this is simply that it is taken as standing for an object, as when the pepperpot is taken to represent a car involved in an accident . . . The relation between symbols and things is that of conventional identification: symbols are *taken to be* their objects. (1976, p.139)

Still further along the definitional continuum we find treatments of the **symbol as vehicle of indirect expression**. Here, typically, the symbol is taken to be something which *does* have some qualities analogous to, or some natural association with, what is symbolised, and many of those whose views are located here claim that the primary form of symbolism is metaphor. But the situation at this point is not clear; sometimes the symbol is still classified as a kind of sign; sometimes it is opposed to the sign; sometimes the symbol is 'indirect' *only* in the sense that it is merely a vehicle for saying what a sign *cannot* say; almost always, however, 'affect' is seen to be an important characteristic of symbolism. Amongst those who see the symbol as a vehicle of indirect expression, Ricoeur's position is probably the broadest, and he explicitly locates it somewhere between the 'Cassirer' position and the 'metaphor' view:

I give a narrower sense to the word 'symbol' than authors who, like Cassirer, call symbolic any apprehension of reality by means of signs, from perception, myth, and art to science; but I give it a broader sense than those authors who, starting from Latin rhetoric or the neo-Platonic tradition, reduce the symbol to analogy. *I define 'symbol' as any structure of signification in which a direct, primary, literal meaning designates, in addition, another meaning which is indirect, secondary and figurative and which can be apprehended only through the first.* (Ricoeur 1965, p. 245, italics in original)

To mean something other than what is said – this is the symbolic function . . . it presupposes signs that already have a primary, literal manifest meaning. Hence I deliberately restrict the notion of symbol to double or multiple-meaning expressions whose semantic texture is correlative to the work of interpretation that explicates their second or multiple meanings. (Ricoeur 1970, pp. 12–13)

There is a similar emphasis on the *indirect* nature of the symbol in the neo-classical view. Todorov (1982) notes that, in Augustine's theory of signs, 'signs (in the restricted sense) are opposed to symbols as the proper is to the transposed, or, better yet, as the direct is to the indirect' (p. 57). What is important here, and what marks off the neo-classical view from the romantic, is that the symbol is 'indirect' only in the sense that it is a different way to say what the sign says.

Further along the continuum, the romantic conception treats the **symbol as vehicle of the ineffable**. Indeed, the concept of the symbol is central to romanticism: 'without exaggerating, we could say that if we had to condense the romantic aesthetic into a single word, it would certainly be the word "symbol" ' (Todorov 1982, p. 198). This approach combines an emphasis on the proper/transposed distinction with an insistence on the importance of affective/motivational factors, following the Jung/Silberer idealist position. The affect which lies at the heart of symbolism is the affect of idealism, the 'spiritual', the affect which accompanies the expression of something which could never be expressed by the sign. In Jaffé's words: 'the symbol is an object of the known world hinting at something unknown; it is the known expressing the life and sense of the inexpressible' (1964, pp. 309–10). In the romantic approach, above all, the notorious mystique associated with symbols is created and maintained: symbols are intransitive, intuitive, ineffable; they 'involve the progressive, typological elaboration of feelings and impulses which are ineffable and incapable of literal description' (Munz 1973, p. 78); and this is as it must be, for 'reality that is strictly metaphysical . . . can be approached in no other way than through myths and symbols' (Eliade, in Fingesten 1970, p. 136). On this view, symbols are characterised as 'progressive' or 'anagogic' – they are indicators of the forward-moving, spiritual, religious aspects of human nature.

In opposition, further towards the narrow end of the continuum, but also with an emphasis on affect, is the treatment of the **symbol as unconsciously produced substitute**. This approach is often characterised as 'regressive', and belongs to the realm of classical psychoanalysis. What is important here is the unconscious nature of the symbolic process, and the 'primary' nature of what is symbolised. While many later psychoanalysts support a position nearer the broad end of the continuum, arguing that the term 'symbolism' should be used generically to cover both conscious *and* unconscious productions, the classical psychoanalytic position, as expressed by Freud, and supported by Jones, restricts the term 'symbolism' to cases where the substitutive process operates largely unconsciously and in the service of defence. On this view, symbolism and symbolic activity is the result of a compromise between repressed and repressing forces. Thus Jones (1916) explicitly rejects the view of Jung and Silberer, that metaphor is the symbol *par excellence*, on the grounds that metaphor does not necessarily involve unconscious affective and repressed forces. According to Jones's defence of the psychoanalytic position, 'only what is repressed is symbolised; only what is repressed needs to be symbolised' (1916, p. 116). How far this view is from that of the linguists and semioticians can be seen from Grünbaum's (1986) reminder that 'symptoms, as compromise formations, have traditionally been viewed as "symbols", but they are "symbols" in the nonsemantic sense of being substitutive formations affording replacement satisfactions or outlets, not linguistic representatives of their hypothesized unconscious causes' (p. 219).

At the narrow end of the definitional continuum, we find Freud's later (1914a, 1916/17) treatment of the symbol as unconscious, phylogenetically inherited universal code. Here the word is reserved for those 'universal' symbols which appear in dreams (and also in myths and folklore), and have three characteristics which distinguish them from all other forms of 'indirect representation': firstly, constancy of meaning, i.e., the relation between symbol and symbolised provides a 'fixed' meaning in the unconscious; secondly, these symbols are 'mute' – or, rather, the dreamer (or subject) becomes mute in the face of them, being unable to produce any associations to them as he or she can to other repressed material; and thirdly, the meanings of these symbols are not learned, but inherited. As will later be seen, this peculiar restricted view is at odds with Freud's treatment of symbols elsewhere, and there are, I shall argue, compelling reasons for agreeing with those who reject it.

Limitations of perspective one

Surveying the range of definitions of 'symbol' along this broad/narrow continuum provides a general overview of the subject, and gives us some indication of the number and variety of views on symbolism. But this perspective is limited in two ways. Firstly, many theorists or theories, especially those with a broader approach, occupy more than one location on the continuum, also supporting a narrower definition in the case of *some* symbols. So, for example, Langer characterises only *some* symbols (e.g., a cross) as 'charged with affect', and only *some* symbols (the 'non-discursive' ones) as indicating a different realm of reality and truth. Sapir (1959) treats *one* kind of symbolism ('condensation' symbolism) in a manner akin to the narrow psychoanalytic approach; such symbolism 'strikes deeper and deeper roots in the unconscious and diffuses its emotional quality to types of behaviour and situations apparently far removed from the original meaning of the symbol' (pp. 492–3). Again, we find those at the narrow end of the continuum occasionally making pronouncements which properly belong to the broad end. The psychoanalyst Rycroft (1956) asserts that 'symbolisation is a general capacity of the mind, which is based on perception and can be used by the primary or secondary process, neurotically or realistically, for defence or self-expression' (pp. 142–3). Even Freud often uses 'symbol' in the sense of metaphor (e.g., the 'sweet taste of the bread' is 'symbolic' of the happy life that might have been led with a particular girl (1899, p. 315)), and he allows that 'the concept of a symbol cannot at present be sharply delimited: it shades off into such notions as those of a replacement or representation, and even approaches that of an allusion' (1916/17, p. 152). Secondly, and more crucially, this perspective draws no distinction between those cases of symbolism which, for psychologists as well as for everyone else, are uncontroversial and uninteresting, and about which there is general agreement, and those cases which are controversial and which have for centuries been sources of dispute. A second perspective allows this distinction to be made.

Perspective two: 'conventional' versus 'non-conventional' symbols

This second perspective identifies a fundamental distinction between two kinds of symbol, and allows us to move swiftly towards the focus of inquiry. Since, logically, anything can symbolise anything else (more accurately, anything can be used or taken to symbolise anything else), it seems reasonable to ask what the grounds are for claiming, in any particular case, that a symbol means one thing and not another. In the case of, for example, the symbols of logic, mathematics or language, the meanings of the symbols have been established by agreement or convention. In such cases, naturally, what the symbol stands for must be learned, is not generally in dispute, and so is not held to pose interesting psychological questions. But there are other phenomena, which are considered to contain symbols, or deal with them, or be symbolic, or have some kind of symbolic force, in the areas of dreams, art, literature, rituals, myths, fairy tales, folklore, psychopathological symptoms, and so on. Because the interpretation of *these* symbols is *not* set by convention, the explanations of the occurrence, and the meanings, of such symbolic phenomena are contentious, and have in fact been investigated, discussed, and disputed at enormous length.

Now, perhaps not surprisingly, given its central importance, this distinction between what may be termed 'conventional' and 'non-conventional' symbols is one which seems to emerge naturally from the general confusion of definitions and classifications, cutting across the broad versus narrow approaches discussed above, and also cutting across the various terminological, classificatory divisions to be found in the different subject areas in the literature on symbolism – in philosophy, semiotics, anthropology, psychology, etc. Thus, sometimes, the distinction is made between two different kinds of symbol (e.g., Langer's (1942) and Bertalanffy's (1981) 'discursive' versus 'non-discursive' symbols, Sapir's (1959) 'referential' versus 'condensation' symbols, Turner's (1968) 'logical' versus 'non-logical' symbols). On other occasions, the distinction is made between signs and symbols, the former representing conventional, the latter non-conventional, symbols. Here the distinction is characterised as 'arbitrary' versus 'transitive', or 'direct' versus 'indirect'. But, whatever the terminology, and whatever the disagreements, there appears to be a major (albeit often only implicit) agreement that it is the non-conventional symbols which are the psychologically interesting and controversial ones. Further, there is notable cross-domain generality in the grounds on which the non-conventional symbols are separated from the conventional ones. For Langer, the 'non-discursive' symbols, the non-scientific, controversial ones, point to a radically different symbolic 'mode', the two 'modes' having important ontological and epistemological implications: 'truth is so intimately related to symbolism that if we recognise two radically different types of symbolic expression we should logically look for two distinct meanings of truth' (1942, p. 260). Sapir distinguishes between 'referential' symbols, such as writing, speech, code, and other conventional devices for the purpose of reference, and 'condensation' symbols, which are 'highly condensed forms of substitutive behaviour, allowing for release of emotional tension', the essential difference between the two groups being that 'while referential symbolism grows with formal elaboration in the conscious, condensation symbolism strikes deeper and deeper roots in the unconscious . . . and . . . diffuses its emotional quality to types of behaviour and situations apparently far removed from the original meaning of the symbol' (1959, pp. 492–3). For Turner (1968), 'logical' symbols 'are conceived in the conscious mind, as Pallas was in Zeus' head', whereas 'nonlogical' symbols 'represent the impress on consciousness of factors external or subliminal to it' (p. 579). Saussure too, though excluding symbols from semiology, does so on the grounds that they are 'motivated' and 'involuntary'. Bertalanffy supports Langer's distinction between discursive and non-discursive symbols; for him, discursive symbols convey facts, but non-discursive symbols (also called 'experiential' or 'existential' symbols) convey values. In romanticism, symbols (as opposed to signs) have the characteristics of Bertalanffy's 'existential' symbols; they are intuitive, transcendent, ineffable, belong to a 'higher' reality, and act as vehicles for the expression of the spiritual and 'progressive' aspects of human beings.

As for the question of the *relationship between* these two kinds of symbolism, this is rarely addressed, although, amongst the few speculations which are offered, there seems to be some agreement that the controversial non-conventional symbols enjoy an ontogenetic priority over the conventional symbols, the latter developing from the former via a gradual diminishing of affect coupled with an increasing contribution of conscious, as compared with unconscious, processes, although it is not clear how this transition is supposed to occur. Sapir (1959) suggests that it is likely that most referential symbolism evolved from condensation symbolism, and that the essential feature of this development was the gradual erosion of the emotion, so that 'the less primary and associational the symbolism, the more dissociated from its original context, the less emotionalized it becomes, the more it takes on the character of true reference' (p. 493). Balkányi (1964) agrees: 'I still would assume that the difference between verbal symbol and verbal conventional sign is an evolutionary one . . . the combination of the sound-image with the thing-presentation alone makes possible that wearing down of the sensual value which leads to abstraction. This combination is the word' (p. 72). Langer, too, argues that 'denotation is the essence of language, because it frees the symbol from its original, instinctive utterance and marks its deliberate *use*, outside of the total situation that gave it birth' (1942, p. 75). Even Bertalanffy (1981), though not explicitly supporting this position, comes close to it in his view that the so-called Freudian symbols, because of their biologically determinate or obsessive nature, are not yet genuine symbols, but are best seen as 'pre-symbols', as unconscious associative formations which provide the raw materials from which true symbols arise. A radical version of this evolutionary view came from the Swedish philologist Hans Sperber, who suggested (1912) that much of the origin of speech is concerned with sexual issues – a suggestion which was embraced by Freud and Jones, and which has, in modified form, found some favour with more recent psychoanalytic supporters. Baker (1950), for example, after an extensive survey of etymological linguistic connections in the Polynesian languages, concludes that Sperber's views deserve some respect, for:

primary experiences of pleasure-giving bodily functions – oral, anal, urethral and genital – serve to bequeath to the individual a series of unconscious images which he never throws off. These images form the associative bases for all his later conquests of reality. Since language is one of the main instruments for this conquest, one can scarcely be surprised to find that it bears multitudinous traces of man's infantile fantasies. (Baker, 1950, p. 178)

Whatever the relationship between the two classes of symbols, it is clear that the focus of our inquiry here must be on the non-conventional symbols.

Sources of confusion and centres of dispute

One major source of confusion in the literature on symbolism, and the reason for the disorder along the broad/narrow continuum, is that, when the controversial (i.e., non-conventional) symbols are under discussion, most theorists neglect to maintain clearly and consistently the distinction between the two types of symbol, slipping back and forth between them. This contributes to a second source of confusion, the question of the specific nature of the symbols which belong to the non-conventional group. There are two, closely connected, centres of controversy: the first is the question of the conscious or unconscious nature of the symbolic processes and productions, including the question of the *relative* contributions of conscious and unconscious processes; and the second, related, question is that of the 'progressive' or 'regressive' nature of symbolism, and whether there is any connection between these two. As mentioned earlier, the conventional symbols are unproblematic; almost all writers on the subject consider them to be entirely conscious productions. They do not all agree, however, that the *non*-conventional symbols are *un*conscious; nor do they agree on the degree to which unconscious processes contribute to the symbolic productions, or on the origin and function of these unconscious processes. It is perhaps no surprise that this area is rife with inconsistencies. The resulting tensions encourage theorists to speak (albeit uncertainly) of the 'double aspect' of symbolism; 'logos' versus 'mythos', 'demystification' versus 'remystification', 'transparent' versus 'opaque', 'concealing' versus 'revealing', and so on. The tensions also fuel the disputes and confusions surrounding the 'progressive' versus 'regressive' vectors of symbolism. For the supporters of the 'progressive' or 'anagogic' view, symbols either have nothing to do with regressive, biological instinctual drives and their gratification, or they somehow 'accomplish liberation from the slavery of the biologically imposed' (Hacker 1965, p. 82), while still having ' "natural", biological, quasi-instinctual origins and vicissitudes' (p. 87). For the supporters of the regressive view, on the other hand, the 'anagogic' approach, with its idolisation of the mystical 'opacity' of the symbol, and its celebration of the freedom and creativity of the human spirit, is merely an attempt to disguise the formation of symbols, and 'divert interest from their instinctual roots' (Freud 1919a, p. 524), and grows out of idealism, the 'philosophical brand of escapism' (Reichenbach 1951, p. 254). It will become clear how both the failure (of which Freud is also guilty) to draw clearly and maintain consistently the distinction between conventional and non-conventional symbols, and the tensions produced by vacillations concerning the conscious/unconscious and progressive/regressive aspects of non-conventional symbols, serve as foci from which many difficulties and confusions arise.

The aim of this brief journey was to give some idea of the great number and variety of different approaches to, and pronouncements about, symbolism, to narrow the focus onto the subject matter of the inquiry, and to point to some of the sources of confusion and centres of controversy which have rendered problematic various approaches to symbolism – in short, to indicate why it is that there is a widespread belief that no unified theory is possible. But, as I have said, I do not share that belief. The general theory of symbolism which I am proposing in this book is derived from a *particular version* of Freud's theory, so my next step is to present and develop an account of that particular version. This, as I indicated earlier, will require a detailed, chronological examination, exegetical and critical, of Freud's published writings, tracing the development of his treatment of symbolism from the early years, through many additions and modifications, to a major shift and its consequences. In particular, the problems with which he is faced as a result of his changes will be examined, and I shall argue that those changes were neither warranted nor tenable. That will clear the way for consolidating the theory via revision of some of the important aspects of

Freud's theory which relate to symbolism, and for defending it by assessing its ability to meet certain logical and psychological requirements, requirements which any theory of symbolism must meet.

2 The 'Freudian Narrow' (FN) theory of symbolism

In Freudian scholarship it is notoriously difficult to give a substantial account of any important topic, other than perhaps the most general underlying theses, which may confidently be claimed to be a faithful representation of Freud's own views. Freud himself is largely responsible for this. The revolutionary nature of his theory, and the fact that it evolved over a long period, meant inevitable changes in his ideas. Freud complained of the 'no-win' situation in which he was left by his critics as a result of these changes: 'Some people have taken no notice whatever of my self-corrections and continue to this day to criticize me for hypotheses which have long ceased to have the same meaning for me. Others reproach me precisely for these changes and regard me as untrustworthy on their account' (1916/17, pp. 245–6). In addition, while Freud considered himself a scientist, always insisting that his work was an empirical search for truth, and thus part of the scientific *Weltanschauung*, his language is frequently imbued with more literary qualities, often displaying, as Cheshire and Thomä (1991) observe, an artist's tolerance for looseness and ambiguity. Of course, this is partly because he lacked an accepted 'technical' terminology in which to express his new ideas, and partly because the typically austere, precise, 'scientific' prose style was not yet commonplace. But it is also clear that Freud realised how unfamiliar and initially unpalatable many of these ideas would be, and, like the Roman poet-philosopher Lucretius, he understood that when the aim was to 'tell of important discoveries, set free the mind from the tangles of superstition, and uncover what has for long been hidden', there was considerable value in 'touching everything with the sweet charm of the muse – just as doctors, when trying to entice children to drink foul-tasting medicine, seduce them with sweet honey applied around the rim of the cup' (Lucretius, *De Rerum Natura* I, lines 931–9).

These reasons are sufficient to make the task of accurate representation of Freud's ideas a daunting one. Fortunately, however, except perhaps for the historian, that task would also be futile. For the psychologist, the really fruitful, albeit difficult, work of Freudian scholarship consists in extracting from Freud's writings the valuable contributions to a genuinely explanatory account of human behaviour which are to be found there. For those who are prepared to sift through the tangled web of developing ideas, to look for the sense behind often obscure metaphorical expressions, and to draw together the diverse lines of argument and evidence, the effort is well repaid: in the case of many central ideas, Freud did more than just lay the groundwork; he also provided a wealth of additional detailed, though scattered, material. But the time and effort required to piece together those details, and the demanding nature of Freudian scholarship in general, have made it altogether too tempting to take various short cuts. Freud himself complained of the apparent arbitrariness of the typical process of selection from his work:

a sort of buffer-layer has formed in scientific society between analysis and its opponents. This consists of people who allow the validity of some portions of analysis and admit as much, subject to the most entertaining qualifications, but who on the other hand reject other portions of it, a fact which they cannot proclaim too loudly. It is not easy to divine what determines their choice in this. It seems to depend on personal sympathies. One person will take objection to sexuality, another to the unconscious; what seems particularly unpopular is the fact of symbolism. Though the structure of psycho-analysis is unfinished, it nevertheless presents, even today, a unity from which elements cannot be broken off at the caprice of whoever comes along: but these eclectics seem to disregard this. I have never had the impression that these half- or quarter-adherents based their rejection on examination of the facts. (1933, p. 138)

This comment contains two important points, albeit only implied, on the question of the *selection* of material from Freud. Firstly, the nomination of the particular themes of sexuality, the unconscious, and symbolism – themes without which psychoanalysis would not *be* psychoanalysis – suggests that Freud did not mean that *no elements at all* may be broken off, but that those which either form the core of the theory, or are necessary consequences of that core, cannot be discarded without discarding the entire theory. In combination with the second implicit point, that the rejection of any particular element would be acceptable only if based on 'examination of the facts', Freud is here hinting that the crucial task of selecting and rejecting requires a clear understanding of valid criteria for such selection or rejection. The absence of the required understanding, to which Freud here is referring, is one reason why many of Freud's supporters and critics have failed to come properly to grips with his material; indeed, it would not be an exaggeration to suggest that every topic of importance has suffered as a consequence.

The theory of symbolism is a case in point. Few scholars have explored Freud's writings in the detail which is required to see that, on this topic, he offered much more than the simplistic contribution usually attributed to him. Consequently, there is a widespread lack of recognition both of the unifying explanatory nature of that theory, and of the lack of genuine novelty in many of the 'additions', 'revisions', and 'modifications' which have been offered in the name of psychoanalysis since Freud. Nowhere do we find a clear, systematic account of what Freud's theory of symbolism is and of what it offers; instead, it is either presented (and then dismissed) in the briefest of sketches, or it is distorted and is assimilated into theories whose fundamental tenets are opposed to those on which Freud's theory is built.

As a result, it is difficult, for example, to make proper use of the entry for 'symbolism' in the dictionary of psychoanalytic concepts, *The Language of Psychoanalysis* (Laplanche and Pontalis 1985). The discussion here begins by distinguishing between a broad sense of the term (in which any substitutive formation can be held to be symbolic) and a more restricted sense (in which there is a constant relation in the unconscious between symbol and symbolised). It then continues:

> The notion of symbolism is nowadays so closely tied to psycho-analysis, the words 'symbolic', 'symbolise' and 'symbolisation' are used so often – and so variously – and the problems surrounding symbolic thought and the creation and utilisation of symbols fall within the scope of so many disciplines (psychology, linguistics, epistemology, history of religions, anthropology, etc.), that it is particularly hard in this case to mark off a specifically psycho-analytic use of these terms and to distinguish their various senses. The following remarks aim to do no more than help the reader get his bearings in the psycho-analytic literature. (p. 442)

But the text which follows, consisting of a sequence of disconnected points, some descriptive, some critical, some useful, some vague, is informative only for the reader who already *has* his or her bearings.

While Laplanche and Pontalis do at least appeal to several of Freud's own claims, many modern conceptions of the psychoanalytic contribution to the theory of symbolism (or the 'symbolic function', as it is more often called) typically submerge Freud's insights into the contemporary fashionable *Zeitgeist* of confused and incoherent relativism and constructivism, with the result that his genuine contributions have become distorted and swamped by wave after wave of subjectivist philosophy quite inimical to the spirit of the Freudian enterprise. This modern movement has spawned a profusion of literature professing allegiance to 'psychoanalysis and . . .' (usually 'language'), in which there is subsequently very little which is even remotely recognisable as psychoanalytic theory, and in which the nature of the Freudian support for a major 'thesis' such as the 'impossibility of the world of "facts" and "persons" in the absence of a symbolic potential to form significant relationships' (Corradi Fiumara 1992, pp. 9–10) is left a complete mystery to the reader. Worse still, in a kind of anti-Freudian humanistic spirit, what Freud unearthed as symbolic is labelled merely 'pseudo-symbolic' because 'rather than construct reality, it constructs a "neurotic" substitute for reality' (ibid., pp. 84–5). Clearly, a return to Freud, and a new start from there with respect to the theory of symbolism is needed.

There are, as Laplanche and Pontalis indicate, two discernible positions on symbolism in Freud's writings: the first, which may be referred to as the 'Freudian Narrow' (FN) position, restricts the use of the term 'symbol' to a special technical sense, in which symbols are the elements of an unconscious, universal, phylogenetically inherited code; the second, which may be referred to as the 'Freudian Broad' (FB) position, is a much less restricted view, in which the term 'symbol' usually refers to any unconsciously produced defensive substitute, while nevertheless retaining certain specifiable connections with conscious, non-defensive productions.

The theory which is to be developed here is largely a synthesis of these two positions, producing what was described earlier as the classical psychoanalytic position, although it is also in harmony with some post-Freudian formulations. The synthesis involves assimilating the acceptable aspects of the FN into the FB position, and arguing that this can be achieved (a) with very little loss or distortion, and (b) by appealing to Freud's own writings, rather than by combining externally derived criticisms with what are unjustifiably claimed to be 'neo'-Freudian conceptions. There has been widespread agreement among psychoanalysts that any revival of 'classical' Freudian theory will depend for its viability and explanatory power on important post-Freudian developments. However, at least in the case of symbolism, many of those supposedly 'neo'-Freudian contributions are in fact part of Freud's original theory, and others are conceptually untenable, inimical to the fundamental tenets of Freud's theory, and so, rather than contributing to a Freudian 'revival', serve to place those advocating them firmly in the anti-Freudian camp.

The post-Freudian climate

After Freud's own work, together with Jones's supportive (1916) paper on 'The Theory of Symbolism', there was comparative silence on the topic until the 1950s. Forty years after the publication of Jones's paper, Rodrigué (1956) writes, with some truth, that:

Symbolism has had a strange and disappointing fate in the development of psychoanalytical thought. At a time in which the social sciences were becoming 'symbol-conscious', analysts lost interest in the subject. After a promising start, about 1909–11, when the subject was tackled by Freud and the best analytical minds, the initial impetus faded away. After the far-reaching discovery that the same symbolic motifs which appeared in dreams and insanity were also present in art, religion and folklore, later work mainly consisted in finding new symbols or in venturing alternative meanings for old ones. Practically no theoretical work has been done since then on the nature and function of symbols. In fact, the theory took its final shape in the surprisingly short period of less than ten years. Little has been added since Jones wrote his comprehensive essay . . .

Why have we failed to be stimulated by a notion which, apart from being our true legacy, has proved to be so fruitful in the social sciences? I think that the answer lies in the limitations of our basic theoretical assumptions on symbolism . . . these have remained unchallenged for so long, in spite of the revolutionary changes taking place everywhere in psycho-analytical theory . . . A revision is needed, particularly on account of a very recent revival of interest in symbolism, chiefly excited by the work of Melanie Klein. (p. 147)

Rodrigué's paper was one of a number of contributions (e.g., H. Segal 1950, 1952, 1958; Milner 1952; Kubie 1953; R. Fliess 1973; Rycroft 1956; N. Segal 1961) whose authors were concerned to revive the theory of symbolism. Several of these authors criticised the classical Freudian theory of symbolism, and offered 'new' contributions of their own. The criticisms were directed first against the narrow FN position; but they were subsequently directed against the broader FB position as well – for various reasons, *both* positions were charged with being too narrow. Many theorists, following particularly the work of Melanie Klein (e.g., Klein 1930), saw the classical theory as limited and undeveloped, and argued that the light thrown on it by post-Freudian developments would help to produce a revised and more acceptable approach to symbolism and symbolic activity. Thus they saw their initial task as one of pointing out those 'limitations of our theoretical assumptions' to which Rodrigué refers.

But, as I suggested, these critics were, to a large extent, misguided – at least in their overall attack, if not in all of its details. They were wrong both about the supposed limitations of Freud's theory and about the novelty of many of their own contributions. On the first point, the classical Freudian theory *does* allow for an adequately broad conception of symbolism, since it can be shown, using Freud's own writings, that the FN position, minus its conceptually untenable aspects, is simply part of the FB position, and that when the FB position is properly understood, any charges of 'narrowness' can be seen to rest on confusions, misconceptions, and misrepresentations. On the second point, many of the critics' 'additions' and 'modifications' are already to be found in Freud's own writings, even though, as pointed out earlier, it is by no means an easy task to extract them and organise them into a coherent whole.

These conclusions will be reached using the following steps. Firstly, the FN position, as understood by post-Freudian psychoanalysts, will be set out, and the criticisms and objections made by Rodrigué and others will be presented. In order to reply to the objections, and to illustrate the FB position as able to accommodate the acceptable parts of the FN position, the remaining chapters of Part One contain a detailed, chronological account and critical examination of the development of Freud's ideas on symbolism. In Part Two, the FB theory will be consolidated via a number of revisions to the Freudian material which, as it stands, would otherwise be faced with certain problems. Once these problems have been cleared away, and the FB theory fully presented, it will be time to consider what truly *are* the limitations of current theoretical work on symbolism, to identify the logical constraints and psychological requirements which, it will be argued, *any* theory of symbolism must respect, and to show that, of all the approaches to symbolism, only the FB theory meets these requirements.

Characteristics of the 'Freudian Narrow' (FN) position

In the literature, generally, the commonly presented standard Freudian position is the FN one. Freud's ideas on symbolism, it is usually claimed, gradually converged (after some fits and starts, and despite continued looseness here and there) onto an extremely narrow view, which began to be stated explicitly around 1910/11, and was given a complete formulation in a new section on symbolism inserted into the fourth (1914a) edition of *The Interpretation of Dreams* (Ch. VI, section E), and Lecture X of the (1916/1917) *Introductory Lectures on Psycho-Analysis*. The FN position consists of a *general* claim, together with the detailing of certain *specific characteristics* of symbols. According to the general claim, the term 'symbol' is reserved for use in a special technical sense, to refer to certain elements which occur in dreams (but which also crop up in myths, fairy tales, folklore, etc.), and which are distinguished from all other unconscious, indirect, substitutive, representational material used in the service of defence. In Freud's words, 'representation by a symbol is among the indirect methods of representation, but . . . all kinds of indications warn us against lumping it in with other forms of indirect representation' (1914a, p. 351). In fact, Freud asserts that symbols are distinguished from other forms of indirect representation by three specific characteristics, each of which has one or more consequences.

Firstly, **symbols are 'mute' or 'silent'** – or, rather, the dreamer/ patient is silent or mute in the face of them, being unable to produce any 'associations' to them as he or she can to all other elements. In Freud's words:

As a rule, the technique of interpreting according to the dreamer's free associations leaves us in the lurch when we come to the symbolic elements in the dream content. (1914a, p. 353)

symbolism in the language of dreams was almost the last thing to become accessible to me, for the dreamer's associations help very little towards understanding symbols. (1914c, p. 19)

it does sometimes really happen that nothing occurs to a person under analysis in response to particular elements of his dream . . . cases in which an association fails to emerge . . . we are tempted to interpret these 'mute' elements ourselves. (1916/17, pp. 149–50)

it is strange . . . that if a symbol is a comparison it should not be brought to light by an association. (ibid., p. 152)

It must theoretically always be possible to have an association . . . Yet there is one case in which in fact a breakdown occurs with absolute regularity. (1925d, p. 42)

The consequence of this 'muteness' of the symbol is that it leads to a sharp dichotomy in the technique of dream interpretation into (i) the interpretation of associations, and (ii) the translation of symbols:

The . . . extremely frequent use of symbols . . . make[s] us able to some extent to translate the content of dreams without reference to the associations of the individual dreamer. (1913e, p. 176)

we are tempted to interpret these 'mute' dream elements ourselves, to set about translating them with our own resources. (1916/17, p. 150)

[The two complementary techniques of dream interpretation are (i)] . . . calling up ideas that occur to the dreamer till you have penetrated from the substitute to the genuine thing . . . [and (ii)] . . . on the ground of your own knowledge, replacing the symbols by what they mean. (ibid., p. 170)

This assertion that our method of interpreting dreams cannot be applied unless we have access to the dreamer's associative material requires supplementing: our interpretative activity is in one instance independent of these associations – if, namely, the dreamer has employed *symbolic* elements in the content of the dream. In such cases we make use of what is, strictly speaking, a second and auxiliary method of dream interpretation. (1925a, n. p. 241)

Secondly, **symbols have constant meanings**, unlike all other elements:

we obtain constant translations for a number of dream elements – just as popular 'dream books' provide them for *everything* that appears in dreams ... [whereas] ... when we use our *associative* technique, constant replacements of dream elements never come to light ... A constant relation of this kind between a dream-element and its translation is described by us as a 'symbolic' one, and the dream-element itself as a 'symbol' of the unconscious dream-thought. (1916/17, p. 150)

We noticed at an early stage that it is always in connection with the same elements that this [i.e., failure of associations] happens; they are not very numerous, and repeated experience has taught us that they are to be regarded and interpreted as *symbols* of something else. As contrasted with the other dream elements, a fixed meaning may be attributed to them. (1933, p. 13)

The consequence of this characteristic is that there are no 'individual' symbols:

it is strange ... that the dreamer should not be acquainted with it but should make use of it without knowing about it. (1916/17, p. 152)

it is a question of ... unconscious pieces of knowledge, of connections of thought, of comparisons between different objects ... These comparisons are not freshly made on each occasion; they lie ready to hand and are complete, once and for all. This is implied by the fact of their agreeing in the case of different individuals – possibly, indeed, agreeing in spite of differences of language. (ibid., p. 165)

Thirdly, **symbols are phylogenetically inherited**, and this explains their constant, universal meanings. Knowledge of symbolic connections and of the meanings of symbols is not acquired by learning, but is part of an unconscious, phylogenetically transmitted 'archaic heritage', a universal code which may be found in dreams, myths, fairy tales, folklore, etc. In Freud's words:

the dreamer has a symbolic mode of expression at his disposal which he does not know in waking life and does not recognise. This is as extraordinary as if you were to discover that your housemaid understood Sanskrit, though you know that she was born in a Bohemian village and never learnt it ... it is a question of unconscious pieces of knowledge. (1916/17, p. 165)

It seems to me ... that symbolic connections, which the individual has never acquired by learning, may justly claim to be regarded as a phylogenetic heritage. (ibid., p. 199)

analytic experience has forced on us a conviction that even particular psychical contents, such as symbolism, have no other sources than hereditary transmission. (1937, p. 240)

According to Freud, there are three consequences of (or corollaries to) this particular characteristic. Firstly, it leads to the inevitable acceptance of Lamarckism, so that 'I cannot do without this factor in biological evolution' (1939, p. 100). Secondly, symbolism becomes an essential part of the 'language of the unconscious' – an inherited, archaic, primitive, regressive mode of expression (and thus a 'primary process' phenomenon), in which the constancy of the relation can be traced back to an original identity between word and thing:

We have seen that hysterical compulsion originates from a peculiar kind of $Q\dot{\eta}$ motion (symbol-formation), which is probably a *primary process*, since it can easily be demonstrated in dreams. (1895b, pp. 352–3)

Things that are symbolically connected today were probably united in prehistoric times by conceptual and linguistic identity. The symbolic relation seems to be a relic and a mark of former identity. (1914a, pp. 352)

One gets the impression that what we are faced with here is an ancient but extinct mode of expression, of which different pieces have survived in different fields . . . a 'basic language' of which all these symbolic relations would be residues. (1916/17, p. 166)

The symbolic relation would be the residue of an ancient verbal identity. (ibid., p. 167)

Symbols . . . seem to be a fragment of extremely ancient inherited mental equipment. The use of a common symbolism extends far beyond the use of a common language. (1923a, p. 242)

symbolism is not a dream problem but a topic connected with our archaic thinking – our 'basic language', as it was aptly called by the paranoic Schreber. (1925b, p. 135)

Thirdly, symbolism is not the work of the 'censorship', nor the construction of the 'dream-work', since symbols are *already present* in the unconscious, and are merely 'used by' (not 'formed by') the censorship. Thus, symbolisation is not only separate from the other dream-work 'mechanisms' (condensation, displacement, pictorial representation); it also constitutes a fourth kind of relation between manifest and latent content (alongside that of part-to-whole, allusion, and plastic portrayal):

there is no necessity to assume that any peculiar symbolizing activity of the mind is operating in the dream-work, but that dreams make use of any symbolizations which are already present in unconscious thinking. (1900, p. 349)

We must not suppose that dream-symbolism is a creation of the dream-work; it is in all probability a characteristic of unconscious thinking which provides the dream-work with the material for condensation, displacement and dramatization. (1911b, p. 685)

There is a fourth kind of relation between the manifest and latent elements, which I must continue to hold back from you until we come upon its key-word in considering technique. (1916/17, p. 122)

even if the dream censorship was out of action we should still not be in a position to understand dreams. (ibid., p. 149)

symbolism is a second and independent factor in the distortion of dreams, alongside of the dream-censorship. It is plausible to suppose, however, that the dream-censorship finds it convenient to make use of symbolism. (ibid., p. 168)

Critics' objections to the 'Freudian Narrow' (FN) position

Although Rodrigué and the others do not document the FN position as systematically and extensively as I have done here, they do identify the three distinctive characteristics of symbols according to that narrow view, support them with one or two illustrative quotes from Freud, and then proceed to present a number of criticisms and objections. These objections may be divided into general ones (in reply to the general formulation of the position) and specific ones, directed at the specific characteristics outlined above.

On the general claim, Freud's convergence on the FN position amounts to a too 'drastic narrowing' of the concept of symbolism, and there is little evidence to support the three distinctive characteristics which are supposed to separate symbols from other forms of indirect representation (Rodrigué 1956). This narrowing is conceptually untenable, 'not only intrinsically fallacious, but also irreconcilable with the implicit requirements of psychoanalytic psychology' (Kubie 1953, p. 73). To some extent Freud should not be blamed, since the problems surrounding the narrowing are indicative of 'some of the difficulties created by the immaturity of psychoanalytical theory at the time' (Rycroft 1956, p. 164). Rodrigué argues that Freud was (cautiously) attracted to oneiromancy, and this explains his abandoning of the conceptually sound earlier use of the term 'symbol' in connection with hysterical symptoms, and as described in the *Project*. According to that description, says Rodrigué:

the symbol takes the place of a traumatic object or event, owing to the fact that both objects had been coupled in a past experience . . . In this conception, the relation object-symbol has taken place in the subject's lifetime. The meaning of the symbol can be understood only if the original context . . . is traced. In this use of the word, symbols are not items to be translated following a given code, but need to be interpreted to fit each instance. I consider this earlier conception of symbolism to be more fruitful than the later. (1956, p. 149)

In addition, suggests Rodrigué, the narrow view was perhaps the result of the fact that Freud discovered the importance of symbolism relatively late, after he had already worked out the basic structure of his dream theory, so that 'by the time Freud discovered the significance of dream symbolism, he had already described three main forms of dream distortion and representation; symbolism then took its place side by side with them. This did not lead to a reformulation of the dream as a symbolic structure' (ibid., p. 150). Finally, these objections are supported by the observation that Freud is in any case not completely committed to his narrow view, and warns against assigning definite limits to the concept of a symbol. As Todorov (1982) remarks, in some passages Freud seems 'almost aware that he was describing the forms of all symbolic processes, not those of an unconscious symbolism' (pp. 248–9).

There are also a number of objections made to the three supposedly distinctive characteristics of symbols according to this narrow view. Firstly, Rodrigué suggests that the 'muteness' or 'silence' of the symbol was probably the 'artificial outcome of the way dreams were interpreted at the time. The method of splitting the dream into several parts and of asking or even pressing the dreamer to associate to each item, very likely stirred and altered the natural fabric in which dreams were meaningfully related to their context' (1956, p. 148). Further, the silence of the symbol could also result from the fact that 'the analyst's inquisitive attitude could easily arouse persecutory anxiety and be felt by the patient as a dangerous intrusion into his inner world' (ibid.). Thus associations fail when the defence or repression is sufficiently severe. Next, Freud's assertion that symbols have constant meanings is objected to on the grounds that it simply constitutes another 'fixed-key' code approach of a kind which Freud himself explicitly rejected, but to which he was cautiously attracted. After all, 'the difference between Freud's symbolics and popular keys to dreams . . . does not lie in their logical form but in the source that is tapped in the search for latent meanings' (Todorov 1982, p. 250). Indeed, since Freud's time, many new meanings of symbols have been discovered. 'This fact', Rodrigué admits, 'does not disprove the theory of their having a few fixed meanings, but it considerably weakens it' (1956, p. 148). He goes on to point out that in 1916 Jones had commented that there are probably more symbols of the male organ than all other symbols put together, and that, in the same year, Freud in his *Introductory Lectures* was 'almost apologetic when including symbols for the breast', but that 'Today, breast symbols are considered to play a role almost equal to the phallic ones'. Therefore, the discovery of new symbols and new meanings undermines this putative distinctive characteristic: 'Each analytical discovery has brought about new meanings for old symbols and new objects deserving to be "meant" symbolically. This suggests that symbols are not fixed relics, but extremely plastic items' (ibid., p. 149). Of course, the argument continues, Freud may have been misled into this view because he was influenced by the prevailing theory of signs, which considered 'meaning' to be a property, thus allowing it to be intrinsic to the symbol. However, says Rodrigué, 'a considerable amount of work on the nature of meaning has been done since then. As a result of it, meaning is no longer considered a quality, but a *function* of a term related with at least one other term and with the subject who uses it. By virtue of their relation one term can "mean" another' (1956, p. 150). Rodrigué is here appealing to the work of Langer (1942) which, he feels, 'provides a much-needed logical framework for a psychoanalytical theory of symbols'. Freud's adherence to this characteristic, therefore, may well have been the result of the drawbacks of an 'obsolete logical theory [of signs] underlying our analytical approach to symbols' (Rodrigué 1956, p. 150). Finally, once again, Freud's inconsistency is noted: 'Although Freud never officially rescinded or corrected this narrow definition, the customary practice in psychoanalysis (including that of Freud) has been to recognise the personal, shifting, idiosyncratic meaning of symbols, which necessitates the complex, technical procedure of interpretation' (Hacker 1965, pp. 78–9). Indeed, according to Rycroft (1956), some of the examples in Freud's list of typical symbols are 'only compatible with Jones's view that each individual re-creates his symbolism anew by perception' (p. 144). As for the third specific characteristic of symbols, Rycroft notes some unclarity in the statement that symbolism is inherited. If what is meant is that the *propensity* to form and use symbols is inherited, then that is true but 'of no especial significance, since all propensities are presumably in some sense inherited' (p. 144). But if it means that the mode of acquiring symbols is inherited, then the claim is untrue since 'either (a) it implies that acquired knowledge can be inherited, i.e. it is Lamarckian, or (b) it is self-contradictory, since the essence of a symbol is that it acquires its significance by displacement from something else, while the essence of an inherited idea is that its significance is intrinsic' (ibid.). In general, the critics appear to agree that neither the notion of the inheritance of acquired knowledge, nor that of a 'collective unconscious' is acceptable, but that the postulation of phylogenetic inheritance is in any case unnecessary to explain the constancy and universality of some symbolic meanings, since there are many more obvious factors which can account for the occurrence of typical, universal symbols. Rycroft (1956) argues that 'The so-called universality of symbols is better explained by reference to (a) "the uniformity of the fundamental and perennial interests of mankind", to use Jones's phrase, (b) the uniformity of the affects and sensations accompanying instinctual acts . . . and (c) the uniformity of the human mind's capacity for forming Gestalts and seeing resemblances between them' (p. 144). In a similar vein, Rodrigué argues that:

> The fact that the same symbolic motifs keep recurring in the patient's phantasies and dreams and that they also appear in myths, jokes, etc., can be explained without the need to postulate a palaeological tie. I think that these features can be explained by the effect of several complementary factors. First, by the similar nature of our phantasies and basic conflicts, which direct our interests towards the same primary objects, organs and bodily needs. Secondly, that we deal with at least one type of symbolic material that is the same for all of us, namely, the parts of our body. Our symbolic possibilities are both determined and limited by the immediate nature of our corporeal surroundings. Finally, that nature presents many shapes and phenomena that lend themselves ideally to acquiring quite unequivocal meanings due to their likeness with our primary objects. The more 'iconic' and striking the symbol, the more widespread its use. (1956, p. 149)

Another objection made to this characterisation of symbolism is that it suggests that symbolism is merely a useless relic – the 'useless repetition of an archaic tie' (Rodrigué 1956, p. 151), whereas, in fact, since symbolism has the primary function of dealing with anxiety, it plays an important role in healthy ego development (Klein 1930; H. Segal 1950). This particular objection to the FN view is also made against the FB view, and will be treated in more detail later. Finally, if some of the earlier arguments are accepted – if, for instance, the silence of the symbol is the result of the patient's feeling threatened – then symbolism is *not* always independent of the censorship. Rodrigué draws the following overall conclusion: 'To sum up: there is small evidence for considering symbols as having a "silent", constant, and archaic meaning. Consequently, "true symbols" do not basically differ from other representational forms, and more is lost than gained by trying to set them apart' (p. 150).

Response to Freud's critics

It is clear that these criticisms are a very mixed bag. A number, for example, are not criticisms of the theory at all, but speculations about what might have led Freud to adopt a particular view – speculations which do not, of course, invalidate that view. Some of the objections are incomplete: of these, some are simply general assertions that the FN position is 'too narrow', or 'unfruitful', or 'intrinsically fallacious', without any supporting arguments or evidence, while others offer alternative explanations, without indicating why they are required, or in what way the particular explanations offered are superior. Finally, several objections amount to pointing out that Freud is inconsistent, in the sense that he contradicts himself; yet, while one of two contradictory assertions must be false if the other is true, the inconsistency itself does not tell us which; again, independent evidence and arguments are required to establish that.

Despite these shortcomings, the criticisms do succeed in raising a number of questions and concerns. Did Freud indeed abandon the earlier, broader conception of symbolism which was introduced in the *Project* and in his discussion of hysterical symptoms? Is there really a sharp division between those earlier formulations and the FN position? Is it true that Freud 'discovered symbolism' relatively late? Was he misled by an obsolete theory of signs? What are his views on the concepts of 'meaning' and 'signification'? Does the FN position amount to a 'fixed-key' code approach? What are Freud's explicit objections to such an approach, and does he, as accused, commit himself to a view which he explicitly rejects? Are the suggested 'alternatives to Freud' actually to be found in Freud's own writings? Does he himself, for instance, offer alternative explanations for universal symbols, and does he provide any justification for those alternative explanations? Does he suggest anywhere that the symbol's 'muteness' may be the result of repression? Does he indeed neglect breast symbols? Does he recognise the symbol's role in dealing with anxiety? And so on. What does Freud *himself* say in answer to all of these questions?

Of course, the objections to the FN position assume that it is *the* 'classical' Freudian position on symbolism. An important preliminary question, therefore, must be: *is* that the case? Is the FN position really *the* Freudian theory? Before answering that question, however, it must first be properly understood. Since, as the critics themselves point out, Freud is inconsistent, what exactly is meant by identifying one of two (or more) inconsistent views as *the* Freudian position? Is it the one which Freud 'really' held (whatever that may mean)? Is it the one he expresses most often, the one to which he devotes the most material, or the one for which he provides the best evidence?

While these questions will be given some attention here, it may be repeated that the question of which view Freud himself 'really' held, while perhaps of concern to the historian, is not of central importance for the psychologist who is concerned to extract from Freud's writings the worthwhile contributions to an explanation of human behaviour. Rather, *the* Freudian theory of symbolism is that theory for which Freud provides (inconsistencies, vacillations and uncertainties notwithstanding) the best evidence and the strongest arguments. And a detailed examination of Freud's developing ideas on symbolism supplies the material from which to piece together such a theory.

3   The 'symbol' in Freud's early writings (1893–1899)

In Freud's early writings, there are two distinct usages of the term 'symbol'. The first plays a central part in Freud's account of conversion symptoms in hysteria, and the second is a wider application of the term, usually in the context of defence, but according to which symbol formation may be either pathological or normal.

Symbolism in hysteria

The first usage may be subdivided into (i) the concept of a '**mnemic symbol**' in hysteria, and (ii) the process of '**symbolization**' (spelled with a 'z' here to distinguish it as a technical term) in hysteria. The distinction between these two is that 'symbolization', unlike the 'mnemic symbol', is dependent on linguistic (particularly metaphorical) expressions, and is, in a sense, secondary to (and dependent on) the original formation of a mnemic symbol.

The concept of a 'mnemic symbol' first occurs in the Freud and Breuer 'Preliminary communication' (1893), in the *Studies on Hysteria* (1895a). The authors argue that, in hysteria, the affect which accompanies a traumatic experience, instead of being 'discharged', remains in a 'strangulated' state, and the memory of the experience to which it is attached is cut off from consciousness. Instead of there being an affectively-charged memory, then, the dissociated affect becomes 'converted' into a hysterical symptom, and this hysterical symptom may be regarded as a 'mnemic symbol', since it has replaced ('stands for') the repressed memory. Such a pathological process may result from one of two conditions: either the original traumatic experience occurred when the subject was in a peculiar 'hypnoid' (dissociated) state (as, for example, was suggested to have happened in the case of Anna O.); or the traumatic experience was regarded by part of the psyche (the ego) as 'psychically incompatible', and so was 'fended off'. While the mnemic symbol may be a hallucination (visual image or smell), more often it is a physical symptom, usually a pain or paralysis in some (psychologically delineated) part of the body, a pain which appears to have no real organic basis, although there *was originally* a genuine pain. Thus the hysteric is suffering from a memory, but without recognising it to be one – a memory of an original pain (or some other sensory experience), which has replaced and now stands for the traumatic experience which occurred simultaneously with that original pain.

So, for example, in the case of Frau Emmy von N. (first treated in the late 1880s), who suffered from, among other symptoms, a number of mysterious pains, Freud grants that some of these pains were indeed organically determined, but then adds:

Another set of pains were in all probability *memories* of pains – were mnemic symbols of the times of agitation and sick-nursing which played such a large part in the patient's life. These pains, too, may well have been originally justified on organic grounds but had since then been adapted for the purposes of the neurosis. (1895a, pp. 90–1)

A similar simultaneity of occurrence of symbol and symbolised is established in the somewhat unusual case of Miss Lucy R. This patient had entirely lost her sense of smell, but at the same time was constantly plagued by an olfactory hallucination of burnt pudding. Freud says of her symptom:

Thus I only needed to assume that a smell of burnt pudding had actually occurred in the experience which had operated as a trauma. It is very unusual, no doubt, for olfactory sensations to be chosen as mnemic symbols of traumas, but it was not difficult to account for this choice. (ibid., p. 107)

And Freud goes on to point to the hysterical conversion's occurring as a result of a traumatic event, which was experienced at a time when the smell of burnt pudding happened to be in the air. Moreover, Freud is aware that the particular *selection* of whatever is to become the mnemic symbol also requires explanation: 'It was still necessary to explain why, out of all the sense perceptions afforded by the scene, she had chosen this smell as a symbol' (ibid., p. 116). The answer (which, admittedly, goes only part of the way towards accounting for the selection) lay in the fact that, at the time, Miss Lucy R. had been suffering from such a bad cold that she had been unable to smell anything *except* the burnt pudding.

Still within the context of hysteria, Freud uses the term 'symbolization' to refer to a process which similarly results in the 'conversion' of a mental state into a physical symptom, but which now depends on a linguistic/metaphorical connection.

For example, in the case of Frau Cäcilie M., who showed 'the best examples of symbolization that I have seen' (Freud 1895a, p. 176), one of the patient's hysterical symptoms, a facial neuralgia, was produced via a mechanism which Freud describes as her taking literally a verbal/ metaphorical expression – the result of an insulting remark of her husband's which she had experienced as 'like a slap in the face'. 'There is no doubt', Freud continues, 'that what had happened had been a symbolization. She had felt as though she had actually been given a slap in the face' (ibid., p. 178). In fact, Freud claims to have 'examples at my disposal which seem to prove the genesis of hysterical symptoms through symbolization alone' (ibid., p. 179), the best example being Frau Cäcilie's sudden penetrating pain between the eyes when, at the age of fifteen, she felt the 'piercing look' of a suspicious grandmother. 'In this instance', says Freud, 'I can detect nothing other than the mechanism of symbolization' (ibid., p. 180). Freud's summary statement of this phenomenon is given in his paper 'On the psychical mechanism of hysterical phenomena':

> The determination of the symptom by the psychical trauma is not so transparent in every instance. There is very often only what may be described as a 'symbolic' relation between the determining cause and the hysterical symptom. This is especially true of pains . . . Symbolizations of this kind were employed by many patients for a whole number of so-called neuralgias and pains. It is as though there were an intention to express the mental state by means of a physical one; and linguistic usage affords a bridge by which this can be effected. (1893, pp. 33–4)

Freud's comment here that symbolization is observed where the determination of the symptom by the psychical trauma is 'not so transparent', hints at a relationship between mnemic symbol and symbolization which becomes apparent upon closer inspection: symbolization is not an alternative to the mnemic symbol; it is built onto it, reinforcing it via an additional, linguistic, connection.

This can be seen, for example, in the case of Fräulein Elisabeth von R., who suffered from hysterical pains in her legs, and from intermittent astasia and abasia. In struggling to trace her symptoms back to their origins, the patient describes a series of episodes during which she found it painful to think of the necessity to 'stand alone', and felt that she could not 'take a single step forward'. Freud duly comments here: 'I could not help thinking that the patient had done nothing more nor less than look for a *symbolic* expression of her painful thoughts' (1895a, p. 152) (meaning, of course, that the patient had used symbolization). However, Fräulein Elisabeth had in fact originally suffered from genuine pains in her legs – 'a mild rheumatic affection' (ibid., p. 147) – and these became the focus of a 'functional paralysis based on psychical associations' (ibid., p. 153) (i.e., a hysterical symptom as mnemic symbol), according to which 'the affect attaching to that [repressed erotic] idea was used to intensify or revive a physical pain which was present simultaneously or shortly before' (ibid., pp. 146–7). It is this original mnemic symbol which was subsequently reinforced by the mechanism of symbolization described above:

> This psychical mechanism of symbolization did not play a prominent part with Fräulein Elisabeth von R. It did not *create* her abasia. But everything goes to show that the abasia which was already present received considerable reinforcement in this way. Accordingly, this abasia, at the stage of development at which I came across it, was to be equated not only with a functional paralysis based on psychical associations but also with one based on symbolization. (1895a, pp. 152–3)

A similar reinforcement of the mnemic symbol by the mechanism of symbolization can be observed in Freud's analysis of Fräulein Rosalia H.'s hysterical symptoms of hand twitchings and prickling sensations in the fingers. While these formed a mnemic symbol based on her slamming down a piano lid and throwing away music at a time of traumatic conflict, when she was rejecting her aunt's suspicions about her (Rosalia's) relationship with her uncle, Freud adds: 'The movement of her fingers which I saw her make while she was reproducing this scene was one of twitching something away, in the way in which one literally and figuratively brushes something aside – tosses away a piece of paper or rejects a suggestion' (ibid., p. 173).

Even in the case of Frau Cäcilie M., who was initially presented as demonstrating the operation of the symbolization mechanism alone, it is revealed that the apparently independent symbolizations were built onto a mnemic symbol. Freud admits that, while it is true that 'for years insults, and particularly spoken ones, had, through symbolization, brought on fresh attacks of her facial neuralgia', nevertheless:

> ultimately we were able to make our way back to her first attack . . . Here there was no symbolization but a conversion through simultaneity. She saw a painful sight which was accompanied by feelings of self-reproach, and this led her to force back another set of thoughts. Thus it was a case of conflict and defence. The generation of the neuralgia at that moment was only explicable on the assumption that she was suffering at the time from slight toothache or pains in the face. (1895a, pp. 178–9)

Likewise, in the same patient, a pain which was traced back to a fear that she might not 'find herself on a right footing' needed *real* pains on which to be based:

> All that could be claimed on behalf of symbolization was that the fear which overcame the patient, as she took her first steps, picked out from among all the

pains that were troubling her at the time the one particular pain which was symbolically appropriate . . . and developed it into a psychical pain and gave it special persistence.

In these examples the mechanism of symbolization seems to be reduced to secondary importance, as is no doubt the general rule. (ibid., p. 179)

So, despite Freud's claim to have at his disposal 'examples which seem to prove the genesis of hysterical symbols by symbolization alone', attention should be directed at the word 'seem' here, for the evidence favours Freud's conclusion above; that, when symbolization occurs, it is able to be traced back to an original mnemic symbol; that symbolization does not occur *without* there having been an original mnemic symbol (although the latter may occur without the former); thus, that symbolization is, in this sense, of secondary importance, an elaboration on the original formation of the mnemic symbol, in which the associative connection can be strengthened by linguistic connections: 'Conversion on the basis of simultaneity, where there is also an associative link, seems to make the smallest demands on a hysterical disposition; conversion by symbolization, on the other hand, seems to call for the presence of a higher degree of hysterical modification' (ibid., p. 176).

The 'symbol' as general substitute produced by displacement

In addition to the concepts of 'mnemic symbol' and 'symbolization' in hysteria, the second of Freud's earliest uses of the term 'symbol' involves the more general notion of the symbol as a substitutive formation produced by displacement, whether that displacement occurs pathologically or normally (although Freud reserved the term 'displacement' for the pathological process). The difference between a pathological and a normal use of symbols is not always clearly indicated, but it seems to turn on whether the process of substitution is unconscious or conscious (with various modifications to this rule, which will be examined later). In the case of the pathological process, Freud's discussion, not surprisingly, draws on examples from hysteria and from obsessional neurosis.

Thus, in the *Project for a Scientific Psychology*, Freud asserts that the *prima facie* unintelligibility of hysterical compulsion is due to 'symbol formation' (which, as Freud's editor Strachey notes, is used more broadly here – almost synonymously with 'displacement' (1895b, n. p. 349)), and he presents the following general account:

For there has been an occurrence which consisted of B+A. A was an incidental circumstance; B was appropriate for producing the lasting effect. The reproduction of this event in memory has now taken a form of such a kind that it is as though A had stepped into B's place. A has become a substitute, a *symbol* for B. Hence the incongruity: A is accompanied by consequences which it does not seem worthy of, which do not fit in with it. (1895b, p. 349)

Freud immediately goes on to distinguish this pathological formation of symbols from a normal one:

The *formation of symbols* also takes place normally. A soldier will sacrifice himself for a many-coloured scrap of stuff on a pole, because it has become a symbol of his fatherland, and no one thinks that neurotic.

But a hysterical *symbol* behaves differently. The knight who fights for his lady's glove *knows*, in the first place, that the glove owes its importance to the lady; and secondly, he is in no way prevented by his adoration of the glove from thinking of the lady and serving her in other respects. The *hysteric*, who weeps at A, is quite unaware that he is doing so on account of the association A–B, and B plays no part at all in his psychical life. The symbol has in this case taken the place of the thing entirely. The pathological process is one of *displacement*, such as we have come to know in dreams – a primary process therefore. (ibid., pp. 349–50)

Two points here are worthy of note. Firstly, 'no part at all in his psychical life' is to be taken as something like 'no part at all in his *conscious* psychical life', since the stable formation is maintained because of its *unconscious* significance. Secondly, Freud is using the word 'displacement' to denote the complete, stable, unconscious replacement of the symbolised by the symbol (in contrast to the 'partial', conscious, replacement in the case of the normal use of symbols), and this enables him to categorise displacement as 'pathological', and tie it in with dreams and the so-called 'primary process'; later, 'displacement' is to become the most important of the 'dream-work mechanisms', along with 'condensation' and 'pictorial representation', and Freud is to make much of displacement as one of the characteristics of the 'system *Ucs.*'. It might be observed that the restriction of the term 'displacement' to the pathological case produces more confusion than clarity. However, it testifies to Freud's recognition of the fundamental division of symbols into the conventional and non-conventional.

Freud's distinction between the pathological and the normal formation of symbols is reinforced by his distinction between pathological and normal 'defence'. In the latter, we simply 'manage to bring it about that the incompatible [idea] B seldom emerges in our consciousness, because we have so far as possible kept it isolated, yet we never succeed in forgetting B in such a way that we could not be reminded of it by a fresh perception' (1895b, pp. 351–2).

In pathological defence, on the other hand: 'while . . . an arousal of this kind cannot be precluded . . . the difference consists only in the fact that then, instead of B, A always becomes conscious . . . that is, is cathected. Thus it is *symbol formation* of this stable kind which is the function that goes beyond normal defence' (ibid., p. 352).

In keeping with this more general usage, it is not surprising that the terms 'displacement' and 'substitution' appear to be indispensable in any discussion of symbol formation:

> Hysterical repression evidently takes place with the help of *symbol-formation*, of *displacement* onto other neurones. We might think, then, that the riddle resides only in the mechanism of this displacement, that there is nothing to be explained about repression itself. We shall hear, however, in connection with the analysis of, for instance, obsessional neurosis, that there *repression without* symbol-formation occurs, and indeed that there repression and substitution are chronologically separated. Accordingly, the process of repression remains as the core of the riddle. (ibid., p. 352)

It is clear from what Freud says elsewhere that he is not here denying the process of symbol formation in obsessional neurosis; rather, symbol formation (for which 'substitution' is used as a synonym) is chronologically separated from repression. Indeed, Freud often replaces the sequential process of 'repression and substitution' with 'repression and symbol-formation', thus using 'symbol-formation' to mean 'substitution'; and, in the case of pathology, the process is not restricted to hysteria. In both hysteria and obsessional neurosis 'the incompatible idea is not admitted to *association*'; whereas in hysteria the content is cut off and the affect 'converted' into the somatic sphere, in obsessional neurosis the content is 'replaced by a substitute' (1895c, p. 212). There is no question that in the phrase 'replaced by a substitute' Freud is talking of symbol formation, for he immediately proceeds to comment on its non-pathological use, using exactly the same examples as appear later in *The Interpretation of Dreams* when he is talking explicitly about symbolism:

> The mechanism of substitution is also a normal one. When an old maid keeps a dog or an old bachelor keeps snuff-boxes, the former is finding a substitute for her need for a companion in marriage and the latter for his need for – a multitude of conquests. Every collector is a substitute for a Don Juan Tenorio, and so too is the mountaineer, the sportsman and such people. These are erotic equivalents . . . This normally operating mechanism of substitution is abused in obsessional ideas – once again for purposes of *defence*. (1895c, pp. 209–10)

The supposed discontinuity between early and later uses of 'symbol'

A typical observation made by Freudian scholars, usually in the form of a passing comment, is that Freud's early notion of the symbol rarely appears later and plays little part in his more developed views on symbolism. In the case of the mnemic symbol and symbolization in hysteria, the observation is usually that these were particular, restricted, technical usages, peculiar to Freud's early work on hysteria, and unrelated to his later concept of the symbol. In the case of the more general notion of the symbol as substitute produced by displacement, the observation (at least from some of the post-Freudians) is that this broader view is more acceptable than the later, narrower, FN position. Rodrigué, it will be recalled, remarked that 'I consider this earlier conception of symbolism to be more fruitful than the later' (1956, p. 149). In either case, however, the observations involve a judgement of discontinuity between the early and the later views, regardless of which of the early views is being considered. Even Freud's editor, Strachey, makes a comment to this effect on the use of the term 'symbol' in the *Project*:

> In this discussion Freud seems for the most part to be using 'symbolization' in the very general sense of 'displacement'. In his contribution to *Studies on Hysteria* . . . he had used the term in the more restricted sense of the 'conversion' of mental states into physical sensations . . . These uses are only loosely connected with those found more often in Freud's later writings, especially in connection with dreams. (n. on Freud 1895b, p. 349)

Consistent with this judgement, those who discuss Freud's theory of symbolism tend to pay very little attention to these early views, alluding to them, if at all, only briefly, and quickly dismissing them as of little interest or value.

Freud himself, on the other hand, seemed to feel that there was a continuity between his early and his later work on symbolism (although, characteristically, he is inconsistent on this point). In the preface to the second (1908) edition of the *Studies on Hysteria*, he writes: 'The attentive reader will be able to detect in the present book the germs of all that has since been added to the theory of catharsis: for instance, the part played by psychosexual factors and infantilism, the importance of dreams and of unconscious symbolism' (1895a, p. xxxi). Clearly, in 1908, not long before the introduction of some of the distinctive characteristics of the FN position, Freud saw these early views as germinal to the later important work on symbolism in dreams.

As a matter of fact, Freud is correct; but Strachey and other Freudian scholars may be forgiven for not recognising this, since the conditions responsible for producing their misjudgement are partly created by Freud himself; in his failure to set out explicitly the conceptual schema into which his early work on the symbol fits, and in his failure to bring out clearly the themes common both to the early and to the later work on symbolism. Admittedly, there are three ways in which the early views were indeed left behind by Freud. The first is that in later discussions of symbolism the mere fact of temporal contiguity is insufficient for playing the role of the *tertium comparationis* ('third [element] of comparison') between symbol and symbolised; the second is the rarity with which any explicit discussion using the terms 'mnemic symbol' and 'symbolization' is to be found in Freud's later writings; and the third is the explicit narrowing of the term 'symbol' in the FN position on symbolism. Closer inspection, however, reveals that each of these is somewhat misleading in its implications of discontinuity.

The question of the *tertium comparationis*, as will be seen, is complex, and it is by no means true that the similarity of symbol and symbolised is not considered in these early views. Besides, little apparent consideration is given to this matter by those who dismiss Freud's earlier views. The burden of responsibility, therefore, falls onto the second and third points. Now, one of the differences between the FN and the FB position on symbolism is that the FN position can be documented easily with the handful of specific and explicit supportive claims which may be found in Freud's writings. This was shown in the previous chapter. It has not been appreciated, however, that these specific FN claims are embedded in a much larger number of statements about symbolism which make up the FB position. But the difficulty in documenting the FB position is that, often, statements about symbolism which belong to this broader position are only *indirectly* supportive; for example, after a direct connection has been made between, say, 'symbol' and 'substitute' (where 'symbol formation' is used interchangeably with 'substitution'), this process of 'substitution' is then discussed at a later stage, but without use of the term 'symbol' or its cognates. Thus, only if the original connection has been noted will the later discussion be recognised to be one concerning symbolism; and only if the initial connection has been documented will there be manifest evidence for the claim that the later discussion *is* about symbolism.

It is hardly surprising, then, given the difficulty of identifying and tracing such connections, that there has been no attempt to document what I have called the FB position on symbolism in Freud's writings, and a corresponding preference for presenting the more easily documented FN position as *the* Freudian theory of symbolism. And, in that FN position, there is indeed no explicit reference to symbolism in hysteria, or to the more general notion of the symbol as substitute via displacement.

Nevertheless, indirect supportive connections to the FB position do appear in Freud's early writings on the symbol, and together they contribute to a number of common themes which are picked up and developed later, and which are central to the FB position. These common themes are more easily extracted when they are seen to emerge from a general conceptual schema on symbolism, one which, unfortunately, is not explicitly set out by Freud, and which is obscured by the chronological relationship between the treatment of the symbol in hysteria and the more general account of symbolism which appears in the *Project*.

The foundations of continuity: a general conceptual schema

Freud's early work on symbolism, therefore, can be seen to incorporate a hierarchical schema (see Figure 1), in which the 'mnemic symbol' and 'symbolization' of hysteria are special cases of the more general process of symbol formation as defensive substitution. Using this schema, it becomes easier to identify certain themes which are important in the FB position on symbolism. These six themes are listed at the foot of Figure 1.

The first of these themes is the **normal/pathological dimension**. Within the conceptual schema, the term 'symbol' is not restricted to the pathological case; symbol formation may occur normally or pathologically, and in both cases the symbolised is displaced/replaced by the symbol (although Freud usually uses 'displacement' to refer to the pathological process). Thus Freud allows that symbol formation may be pathological *or* normal, unconscious *or* conscious, non-conventional *or* conventional. In other words, to use the jargon of the post-Freudian critics, Freud does *not* deny the continuity of the symbolic function through primary and secondary processes. The main difference between the normal and the pathological formation of symbols seems to turn on the extent to which the person remains aware both of the process itself, and of what the symbol has replaced. In the case of normal symbol formation, the substitutive process appears to be *either* conscious (e.g., the soldier who sacrifices himself for a flag is aware of why he does so; the knight who fights for his lady's glove knows that the glove stands for her), *or* it may be unconscious and even defensive, but nevertheless socially acceptable and not regarded as neurotic. Freud himself does not say this, but clearly the old maid *may* be unaware that her pet is a companion substitute, and she *may* have reasons for not wishing to realise this; nevertheless, Freud categorises this as normal. Such examples suggest that the dividing line between normal and pathological depends, at least in some cases, simply on social acceptability. This is supported by Freud's comment, quoted earlier, that a soldier might sacrifice himself for a scrap of stuff on a pole 'because it has become a symbol of his fatherland, *and no one thinks that neurotic*' (my emphasis).

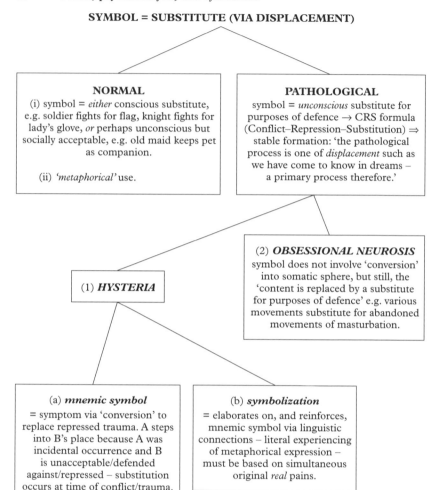

SYMBOL = SUBSTITUTE (VIA DISPLACEMENT)

NORMAL

(i) symbol = *either* conscious substitute, e.g. soldier fights for flag, knight fights for lady's glove, *or* perhaps unconscious but socially acceptable, e.g. old maid keeps pet as companion.

(ii) *'metaphorical'* use.

PATHOLOGICAL

symbol = *unconscious* substitute for purposes of defence → CRS formula (Conflict–Repression–Substitution) ⇒ stable formation: 'the pathological process is one of *displacement* such as we have come to know in dreams – a primary process therefore.'

(1) *HYSTERIA*

(2) *OBSESSIONAL NEUROSIS*
symbol does not involve 'conversion' into somatic sphere, but still, the 'content is replaced by a substitute for purposes of defence' e.g. various movements substitute for abandoned movements of masturbation.

(a) *mnemic symbol*

= symptom via 'conversion' to replace repressed trauma. A steps into B's place because A was incidental occurrence and B is unacceptable/defended against/repressed – substitution occurs at time of conflict/trauma.

(b) *symbolization*

= elaborates on, and reinforces, mnemic symbol via linguistic connections – literal experiencing of metaphorical expression – must be based on simultaneous original *real* pains.

COMMON THEMES

(i)   The normal/pathological dimension.
(ii) Centrality of CRS (Conflict–Repression–Substitution) formula: symbol as defensive substitute.
(iii) The role of language.
(iv) The *tertium comparationis* and the individual/universal distinction.
(v)   The ontogenesis of symbols in the individual's past experience.
(vi) Symbols are already available in the unconscious.

Figure 1 The 'symbol' in Freud's early writings

There is, of course, much more that could be explored in such cases (and indeed *is* explored later in Freud's writings); for example, the flag as symbol of the fatherland may be conscious and socially acceptable, but it is worth examining whether the fatherland itself does not symbolise something more intimate, and perhaps repressed. Such questions are discussed at length by Jones in his 1916 paper on 'The theory of symbolism'. In addition, the FB position on symbolism includes the categorisation by Freud as 'normal' not only of conventional symbols, but also of symbols produced by the process later to be called 'sublimation', which seems to be an unconscious, defensive process. For many reasons, then, the equation of pathological with unconscious and of normal with conscious is inaccurate. Not surprisingly, however, Freud devotes most of his attention to what he labels the 'pathological' cases. These clearly belong to the category of the 'non-conventional' symbols, which was identified in Chapter 1 as being the major focus of interest and controversy in the literature on symbolism.

The second common theme may be identified as the **symbol as defensive substitute and the centrality of the CRS (Conflict–Repression–Substitution) 'formula'**. The function of symbol formation and use in the service of defence, via the cutting off of a memory or idea which is unacceptable to some part of the psyche, and the substitution in its place of something which *is* acceptable to that part of the psyche, is without question the most important theme which emerges from Freud's early writings on symbolism. This central theme is encapsulated in what may be called the CRS (Conflict–Repression–Substitution) 'formula', expressed in Freud's statement:

The process which we see here at work – conflict, repression, substitution involving a compromise – returns in all psychoneurotic symptoms and gives us the key to understanding their formation. (1899, p. 308)

It will be recalled that in the Breuer and Freud 'Preliminary communication', the authors identified two possible conditions from which symbol formation might arise: either from the defensive 'fending off' by the ego of a psychically incompatible idea, or because the subject happened at the time to be in a peculiar 'hypnoid' state. Freud's recognition of, and insistence on, the centrality of defence is revealed very early, in his preference for the first of these two accounts, and in his eventual dispute with Breuer, who favoured the second. It is clear from the examples discussed earlier that Freud invariably points to defence as the motivating cause of symbol formation. Thus hysteria 'originates through the repression of an incompatible idea from a motive of defence' (1895a, p. 285), and, via the process of 'conversion', 'the ego succeeds in freeing itself from the contradiction [with which it is confronted]' (1894, p. 49). Elisabeth von R., for instance, protected herself from experiencing a conscious love/moral guilt conflict regarding her brother-in-law, by loving him *unconsciously* – 'she was in the peculiar state of knowing and at the same time not knowing – a situation, that is, in which a psychical group was cut off' (1895a, p. 165). Freud realises, furthermore, that what is necessary for this defence is that whatever becomes 'cut off' must, initially, have been experienced:

Consciousness, plainly, does not know in advance when an incompatible idea is going to crop up. The incompatible idea which, together with its concomitants, is later excluded and forms a separate psychical group, must originally have been in communication with the main stream of thought. Otherwise, the conflict which led to their exclusion could not have taken place. It is these moments, then, that are to be decribed as 'traumatic': it is at these moments that conversion takes place, of which the results are the splitting of consciousness and the hysterical symptom. (1895a, p. 167)

Obsessional neurosis, similarly, involves the replacement of the content of a psychically unacceptable idea by a substitute, thus producing the obsessional symptom (whether idea or action). For instance, Freud writes, in a letter to Fliess: 'It has become clear to me that various obsessional movements have the meaning of a substitute for the abandoned movements of masturbation' (1897, p. 267). This theme of the symbolic function of obsessional ideas and actions is taken up and developed in detail in Freud's later writings.

Given Freud's frequent interchanging of 'substitution' and 'symbol-formation', the importance of the CRS formula in his theory of symbolism is evident. Freud never abandoned this formula; it was firmly established in these early views, which are unfortunately so often ignored or dismissed, and it continued to form the core of the FB position on symbolism.

The third common theme which emerges from the general conceptual schema is the **role of language**. A number of Freudian scholars (e.g., Ricoeur 1970; Forrester 1980; Todorov 1982) have commented on Freud's penchant for philological speculation, and on the importance which he gradually gave, in his discussions of symbolism, to the role of language. In the later FN position, he constantly appeals to linguistic parallels to support his interpretations of symbols, often resorting to somewhat far-fetched, and at times bizarre, linguistic reasoning, in preference to drawing attention to more obvious connections.

However, Freud's interest in language is not revealed only in his later writings; and a consideration of his earlier linguistic speculations can shed a good deal of light on the extent to which some of the later, rather obscure, manoeuvres in this area were the confused result of attempts to accommodate quite sound theoretical premises.

As we have seen, the mechanism of symbolization involves a linguistic, metaphorical expression, taken literally. But, despite being apparently autonomous, this process can always be traced back to the existence of an original pain or physical state. In further support of this, Freud asserts that, in general, the linguistic expression (which is now taken metaphorically by current language-users) was originally a literal description of an appropriate accompanying physiological state. In summing up his treatment of Frau Cäcilie M., Freud assures us that the phenomenon of symbolization is not as strange and inexplicable as it might seem:

It is my opinion . . . that when a hysteric creates a somatic expression for an emotionally-coloured idea by symbolization . . . in taking a verbal expression literally and in feeling the 'stab in the heart' or the 'slap in the face' after some slighting remark as a real event, the hysteric is not taking liberties with words, but is simply reviving once more the sensations to which the verbal expression owes its justification . . . What could be more probable than that the figure of speech 'swallowing something', which we use in talking of an insult to which no rejoinder has been made, did in fact originate from the innervatory sensations which arise in the pharynx when we refrain from speaking and prevent ourselves from reacting to the insult? All these sensations and innervations . . . may now for the most part have become so much weakened that the expression of them in words seems to us only to be a figurative picture of them, whereas in all probability the description was once meant literally; and hysteria is right in restoring the original meaning of the words in depicting its unusually strong innervations. Indeed, it is perhaps wrong to say that hysteria creates these sensations by symbolizations. It may be that it does not take linguistic usage as its model at all, but that both hysteria and linguistic usage alike draw their material from a common source. (1895a, pp. 180–1)

In the case of hysteria, such connections *do* touch the relationship between the mnemic symbol and what that symbol stands for, albeit only indirectly, insofar as they touch the relationship between expression (e.g., 'I cannot stand alone') and physical symptom (astasia), in a mechanism which is a reinforcing elaboration on the mnemic symbol. More significantly, however, there is in these early views a foreshadowing of two characteristic concerns with respect to language which become more focused in Freud's later writings on symbolism.

Firstly, the observation that symbolization involves a metaphorical expression which, once again, as it was originally, is taken literally, is a precursor of Freud's later connection between universal symbols and the origins of language. As Forrester (1980) has maintained, Freud's gradually increasing attention to linguistic speculations, his drawing of linguistic parallels, and his appealing to the origins of language, were all made in an effort to undercut a possible charge of arbitrariness in his interpretations of symbols. While the appreciation of the unacceptability of such arbitrariness, and the effort to find something which would undercut it, were both sound, the particular means by which Freud attempted to do this were less sound. These culminated in his attempt to justify the constant meanings of universal symbols by tracing the linguistic term for the symbol back to an original identity between word and thing – a manoeuvre which, it will be argued, was confused and unnecessary.

Secondly, Freud's explanation of symbolization in terms of the revival of the literal meaning of a metaphorical expression is an example of a theoretically sound lifelong commitment to linguistic realism. His constant attempts to ground the linguistic in the prior, non-linguistic, testify to his appreciation that language, ultimately, being a referential system, must have something to which it refers. This commitment is seen in his later rejection of the idealist and constructivist tendencies in the approach to language of his opponents (particularly Jung), which inevitably marred their theories of symbolism.

An additional usage, which is not unconnected with the mechanism of symbolization, is that of the term 'symbol' in a more loose sense to mean 'metaphor'. Scattered examples of this usage crop up in all periods of Freud's writings. An early instance comes in Freud's discussion of an analysis of a particular 'screen memory' of a friend (whom Strachey, following Jones (1953, p. 28), identifies as Freud himself). Freud says, of the 'friend's' reported memory of the sweet taste of bread:

It seems clear that this idea, which amounted almost to a hallucination, corresponded to your phantasy of the comfortable life you would have led if you had stayed at home and married this girl – or in symbolic language, of how sweet the bread would have tasted for which you had to struggle so hard in your later years. (1899, p. 315)

The parallel between this kind of loose metaphorical interpretation, and the linguistic connection which is the basis of symbolization, is obvious, although it is less obvious where it should appear in the conceptual schema. Freud does not mark off this use as 'pathological', and for this reason it has been categorised with the normal use of symbols, although often the examples are to be found in the context of a discussion of pathological phenomena.

The fourth common theme is the **'tertium comparationis' and the individual/universal distinction.** Later in his writings on symbolism Freud (following others) adopts the phrase *tertium comparationis* to refer to the 'third [term] of comparison', i.e., that element shared by symbol and symbolised which accounts for the symbol's standing for, or substituting for, the symbolised. Most often, the *tertium comparationis* is identified as 'iconicity' (similarity of shape or form); less often it is identified as similarity of function. Furthermore, the similarities which are identified are typical, universally occurring ones (upright poles, sticks, knives as phallic symbols; cupboards, rooms, containers as female sexual symbols, etc.).

In Freud's later discussion of symbols, hardly ever is *mere* temporal/spatial contiguity sufficient to act as the connecting link; yet it does seem to be sufficient in the early accounts of the mnemic symbol. The smell of burnt pudding, the toothache, the rheumatic pains in the legs – these, according to Freud, became mnemic symbols simply because they occurred simultaneously with the traumatic event. There is no similarity of form or function between the smell of burnt pudding and the repressed erotic impulses of Miss Lucy R. Nor is there anything either typical or universal about the smell of burnt pudding, or its occurrence simultaneously with a traumatic event. So too with the relationship between toothache and the repressed erotic ideas of which Frau Cäcilie's grandmother might have been suspicious. The 'symbol' becomes a symbol simply because it is an incidental, simultaneous occurrence.

It is not surprising that this early position is seen as irrelevant to the later one, for, although one might take James Mill's view of contiguity as a legitimate (in fact the *only*) law of association, or appeal to the *associator* as the crucial connecting link, or speculate about some further connecting link, not apparent to the observer, in the mind of the hysteric, there is a clear difference between an object's substituting for something else because it resembles it, and an object's standing for something else simply because it was present at the time. The two different kinds of connecting link are significant for the later development of the CRS formula. In the case of the mnemic symbol, the *tertium comparationis* of temporal contiguity coincides with the fact that, while the symbol does stand as a substitute, it does not provide substitute satisfaction, whereas for those symbols in which the connecting link is some kind of similarity, the notion of substitute *satisfaction* is (especially later in Freud's writings) important.

Yet there are two respects in which the concept of similarity between symbol and symbolised is already part of Freud's early views. The first has been hinted at above – in the similarity between the metaphorical expression and the physical state depicted literally by that expression in the phenomenon of symbolization – the similarity, in other words, which lies at the heart of metaphor and is made use of in one kind of symbol formation. The metaphorical expressions 'piercing glance', 'unable to stand alone', 'cannot swallow', and so on, are to be taken literally in uncovering this kind of symbolism. Where this particular similarity comes into play, so too, significantly, do typicality and universality (as contrasted, for example, with the mnemic symbol of the burnt pudding). In tracing the metaphorical expressions back to their original literal meanings, Freud is pointing to a connection which goes beyond the individual, in the sense that the experiencing of a 'lump in the throat', the inability to swallow, when one has been insulted and refrains from replying, is presented as a common, typical physiological reaction, not peculiar to certain individuals only. There is no question that the convergence of these concerns (i.e., linguistic parallels, similarity, typicality, and universality) plays an important role in Freud's writings; he returns to them again and again, and in the later FN position on symbolism they become central, where they are combined with the notion of the 'muteness' of symbols. At this early stage, admittedly, free association is necessary for the interpretation of symbolic phenomena, for only this method reveals 'an uninterrupted series, extending from the unmodified *mnemic residues* of affective experiences and acts of thought to the hysterical symptoms, which are the *mnemic symbols* of these experiences and thoughts' (1895a, p. 297). However, in the typicality of the bases of symbolization, there are already signs of the later break from a dependence on individual associations.

The second respect in which a *tertium comparationis* of similarity begins to creep in is in the discussions of symbolism in obsessional neurosis, and of normal symbol formation. Although Freud does not spell this out in the case of conscious symbol formation, the examples are clearly not based on mere temporal contiguity. The pet who is a companion-substitute for an old maid, the lady's glove for which the knight fights, owe their selection not to some accidental simultaneous presence: the pet is cuddly and may respond with affection and loyalty; the lady's glove belongs to her (and so is a part of her – perhaps symbolising a more intimate part of her, with which it shares some characteristic). Likewise, the symbol formation in obsessional neurosis owes something to similarity – recall Freud's comment that various obsessional movements have the meaning of a substitute for the abandoned movements of masturbation. These movements no doubt bear some resemblance to the movements which would have been made during masturbation (e.g., repetitiveness). The *tertium comparationis* of similarity in obsessive ideas, acts, and rituals, is developed extensively by Freud in his later discussions of such phenomena.

The fifth theme which emerges from this general schema of Freud's early views is **the ontogenesis of symbols in the individual's past experience** – mnemic symbols, obsessional substitutes, symbolizations, normal symbols. Not only is there no appeal to phylogenetic inheritance, there is a substantial basis for a theory of symbolism *without* it. The closest Freud comes at this early stage to any notion of phylogenetic inheritance is in his assertion that the linguistic expressions of symbolization may be traced back to an original non-metaphorical, literal meaning – but there is no need, of course, to see this (as Freud does later) as being based on any kind of inheritance. There is also Freud's observation that 'the assertion that a psychical intensity can be displaced from one presentation (which is then abandoned) on to another (which thenceforth plays the psychological part of the former one) is as bewildering to us as certain features of Greek mythology' (1899, pp. 308–9). Again, much is later to be made by Freud of such parallels with mythological and philological material. But at this stage all symbol formation is accounted for by tracing the symptom back in the individual's past experience and discovering an original occasion of psychical substitution.

Finally, the sixth common theme is the treatment of **symbols as already available in the unconscious**. In his later writings on symbolism Freud on several occasions claims that symbolism is neither the work of the 'censorship' nor one of the 'dream-work mechanisms' whose aim is distortion and disguise in the service of defence. Symbols, Freud asserts, are *already present* in the unconscious, and are *used by* the censorship, seized on as convenient, readily available material with which to effect the necessary disguise.

At first glance, it would seem that this contradicts, and so threatens to undermine, the sequence of events identified by the central CRS formula. In that sequence, symbolic substitution is the last step – the *result* of repression, which itself follows the initial internal psychical conflict. This apparent contradiction crops up a number of times later, and contributes to a certain amount of obscurity and confusion. It is not difficult to see, for instance, how the claim that symbols are already present in the unconscious lends itself to Freud as support for his subsequent claims that symbols are phylogenetically inherited, that psychoanalysis did not invent them, that they are part of the inherited, archaic 'language of the unconscious', and so on. As has already been shown, these are claims which are central to the later FN position on symbolism, and if they *did* succeed in undermining the CRS formula, that would be a serious problem for the broader FB position.

Now, while this point is not examined by Freud in these early writings, nevertheless there is material available which serves to clarify the issue. This is largely because it is only in these early writings that Freud presents two different kinds of symbolism with respect to the *tertium comparationis*: one kind (the mnemic symbol) in which the connecting link is mere temporal simultaneity, and the other kind (symbolization, symbolism in obsessional neurosis, normal symbol formation) in which the connecting link is similarity.

The assertion of the symbol's *a priori* existence in the unconscious is only ever made in the latter case, where the *tertium comparationis* is similarity. It is not claimed for mnemic symbols, such as the smell of burnt pudding; since the selection of the mnemic symbol depends on its occurring simultaneously with a traumatic event, it would obviously be false to claim that the symbol was *already present*. On the other hand, where the connecting link is some kind of similarity, that similarity is not (usually) a temporary characteristic, and so is perceived (in fact, *must* be perceived) *before* it is made use of by whatever produces the substitute. It is this fact of the similarity having been noted which is the appropriate sense in which symbols may be claimed to be already present in the unconscious, and it should not be confused with the actual substitution itself, which, of course, takes place later.

Clearly, this theme requires elaboration – *why* such similarities are noticed and remembered, *what* does the noticing, and so on – which is certainly provided by the later developments in Freud's theory. But, for the time being, it is at least evident that the CRS formula is not undermined, for it is the *perception of similarity* which has already taken place, and not the last step in the formula, the *actual substitution*. There is no need, then, to conclude that symbols are phylogenetically inherited.

Summary and conclusions

Although Freud's early work on symbolism is often ignored or dismissed as irrelevant and of little value, the material presented in this chapter shows that such dismissals are unjustified. While it *is* true that the early writings include a particular case (that of the mnemic symbol) in which the *tertium comparationis* is mere simultaneity, that explicit discussion of the 'mnemic symbol' and of 'symbolization' rarely occurs later, that there is, as yet, no detailed discussion (although there are hints) of the substitute *satisfaction* provided by the symbol, and that there is no obvious anticipation of what is usually taken to be 'the' Freudian theory of symbolism (the FN position), nevertheless, to conclude from these facts that Freud abandoned his earlier views, and that there is little of value anyway to be found in them for the Freudian theory of symbolism, is a serious mistake.

The early views are usually rejected either because they are seen (in the case of the mnemic symbol and symbolization) as being too narrow, or, ironically, because they are seen (in the more general case of the symbol as substitute) as being too broad. What is not recognised, however, is (a) the conceptual hierarchical connection between these two cases, as I have set out in Figure 1, and (b) the continuity between the treatment of the symbol in Freud's early writings and the later FB theory of symbolism. This continuity is provided by the six common themes which emerge from the conceptual schema; but, like the FB position itself, of which the themes are an important part, they are not easily documented, for what is required is a tracing of indirect connections with constant contextual considerations. When this is done, it can be seen that the groundwork for the FB theory of symbolism was laid in the early years of Freud's work, and an examination of subsequent writings reveals the extent to which these common themes were later taken up and developed.

4   Continuation and elaboration (1900–1913)

Despite Freud's claim, in the preface to the second (1908) edition of the *Studies on Hysteria*, that the germs of his theory of symbolism were already present in the first (1893–5) edition of that work, he himself contributed to the myth of a discontinuity between his early and later writings on symbolism; on a number of occasions he asserted that it was only late in his work that he had come to a 'discovery' of unconscious symbolism and to an appreciation of its important role. This assertion, apart from contradicting the above claim, is belied by what was shown in the previous chapter, i.e., that in Freud's early writings there is already a substantial basis for a theory of symbolism, including a number of important themes which were never subsequently abandoned. It is also at odds with evidence from an examination of the development of Freud's treatment of symbolism in the writings which followed this earliest period, evidence which indicates that the continuity with his earlier writings was maintained by the retention and elaboration of those general themes. However, the examination also allows some insight into why Freud made the assertion.

Firstly, it is not that a theory of symbolism *per se* came late; what came late was an explicit statement of the narrow FN position (see Chapter 2), the core years for this being 1914–17, with the completely new chapter on symbolism added to the fourth (1914a) edition of *The Interpretation of Dreams*, and with the tenth lecture of the 1916/1917 *Introductory Lectures on Psycho-Analysis*, which was devoted entirely to the topic of symbolism. Freud's writings up to 1914 show a gradual convergence onto the FN position, accompanied by an increase of interest in, and discussion of, the subject of symbolism. Secondly, Freud appeared not to recognise the unifying role of the conceptual schema and themes related to symbolism which are present in his earliest writings, so, not surprisingly, he made no attempt to systematise this material into what is called here the FB position. Yet the identifiable expansion of material on symbolism is by no means restricted to the narrow FN view. Despite the fact that the years 1914–17 are identifiable as the 'core' years for an explicit statement of the FN position, neither during these years, nor in any other period, however short, is there an unambiguous commitment to that position. In fact, there is far more supportive material for the FB position. As I pointed out in the previous chapter (and will illustrate in the next), the handful of explicit statements of the FN position are embedded in a much greater number of statements pointing (albeit often only indirectly) to the broader FB approach. Furthermore, statements of the FN position, even in the core years, are accompanied by uncertainty, inconsistency and vacillation. Thirdly, because of Freud's failure to locate the common themes within the particular unifying conceptual schema outlined, or even to recognise them as common themes, they were isolated from the schema and disconnected from each other; consequently, some became largely divorced from any explicit discussion of symbolism; others, by contrast, were selected for exclusive focus when the matter at hand was symbolism, and, left in isolation, encouraged Freud in his mistaken belief that the FN position was inevitable.

The steps in the convergence onto the FN position

The movement towards the FN position seems to have followed certain chronologically ordered steps, and to have been facilitated by a number of converging factors, these being a combination of theoretical considerations, empirical discoveries, methodological requirements, and practical manoeuvres. While the development was not at all smooth and uncluttered, the following general sequence can be identified:

Step 1. Initially, in *The Interpretation of Dreams*, and elsewhere, Freud identified particular elements which 'stand for' other elements, and whose 'translation' helps render an apparently nonsensical event intelligible in the context of the dreamer's psychic life. The only requirement was that there be contextual checks on any such translation, although, on occasions, the resulting intelligibility was treated by Freud as itself sufficient check. However, strong support for the claim that these elements are indeed symbols, and for the particular translations offered, was considered to be provided by the fact that they also appear in other areas – myths, folk tales, legends, popular customs, etc.

Step 2. This led to an increased interest in symbols and symbolism, since the search for, and study of, symbols became a relatively isolatable conceptual and practical task, and a convenient 'tool' with which to bring psychoanalysis into the fields of mythology and philology. This increased interest was shared by Freud's fellow workers, especially Stekel, who enthusiastically plunged into studies of symbolism (with, as Jones tells us, considerable flair and success), mainly discovering new symbols and offering new translations, but still treating symbolism almost as if it were independent of the rest of the theoretical structure of psychoanalysis. This isolation of the topic of symbolism was reinforced by the implicit focus on the 'symbol' as substantive entity, and neglect of the adjectival notion of 'symbolic', which can be applied to events, actions, relations, and other phenomena more complex than the singular entity. Freud continued to support the latter in his writings, but without making explicit the connection between the two.

Step 3. Freud himself, then, in contrast to those such as Stekel who were dealing with symbolism in isolation, can be seen to vacillate on the issue. On the one hand, there was increasing pressure to treat symbolism as a separate phenomenon, since by so doing apparently successful discoveries and contributions were being made. But there was also a realisation on Freud's part that, without the theoretical structure and methodological principles of psychoanalysis, such 'discoveries' and 'translations' of symbols remained arbitrary and without firm foundational support – amounting, indeed, to exactly the kind of approach which he had initially rejected in *The Interpretation of Dreams.* Not surprisingly, this was also recognised by Freud's critics. Freud found himself repeatedly having to defend his approach to symbolism, expressing surprise at the criticism and 'resistance' which psychoanalytic pronouncements on symbolism had attracted, pointing to the existence of symbolism long before psychoanalysis 'discovered' it, and so on. Partly as a reaction to the criticisms, then, Freud himself continued to stress the importance of contextual checks, individual variations, personal experiential justifications of different translations, and the place of symbolism generally in the 'language of the unconscious', as an 'archaic', primitive mode of expression typical of unconscious thinking.

Step 4. The increased interest in symbolism led, inevitably, from the recognition of the universality of certain symbols, to their taking centre stage in the psychoanalytic theory of symbolism. That the same symbols, with apparently the same meanings, crop up repeatedly in mythology and so on had already been noticed, but it eventually led to a focus on symbolism as a universal language. While the individual use of symbolism was still acknowledged, Freud clearly believed that there was much to be gained in explanatory power by focusing interest on the general finding of a universal symbolism.

Step 5. It was a relatively small and understandable step from the notion of universality to that of fixity, and thence to the possibility of a fixed-key code approach to the interpretation of symbols. This was encouraged by the mutually supporting nature of the combination of fixity with the failure of associations (the 'muteness' of symbols). However, the danger of potential arbitrariness of the interpretations was to be obviated (as always) by 'converging evidence' from other areas. There is no need for associations if these universal symbols are part of some general, archaic language of the unconscious; they can be understood immediately by anyone familiar with myths, rituals, fairy tales, folklore, and so on. The restriction of the term 'symbolism' to these universal, fixed elements became the next step, thus completing the divorce between individual and universal symbols. Indeed, since there are no associations to symbols, and since individual symbols, by definition, do not occur in these other broad, cultural products (and so cannot be confirmed), there is no obvious place for them in the psychoanalytic theory of symbolism.

Step 6. Finally, if associations fail, this raises again the question of the ontogenesis of symbols. The presence of unconscious symbols already in the psyche, and their universal fixed meanings, allows not only for the relatively painless acceptance of the lack of associations, but also for the move to the view that symbols are not acquired in the same way as other unconscious ideas. Obviously, if there are no associations which can take us backwards through various connections to the original meaning (an unfailing indicator in the case of individually acquired connections) then symbols are not individually acquired. This took Freud to the final step in the FN position – the claim that symbols are phylogenetically inherited.

The steps described above relate almost wholly to the movement towards the FN position on symbolism, and the description of those steps has been achieved by extracting certain elements from Freud's writings. In reality, those steps and the elements concerned are almost completely submerged in the rest of Freud's work. Therefore, Freud's writings up to 1914 do more than illustrate the gradual convergence onto the FN position, including the factors which contributed to it, and the sequence of steps via which the convergence occurred. They also illustrate two further points: firstly, the continuation, elaboration, and consolidation of the common themes introduced in the early writings, resulting in an adherence (albeit more often implicit than explicit) to the broader FB position on symbolism, in which the FN position was to become embedded; and, secondly, the resulting contradictions, tensions, and uncertainties (sometimes explicit, more often unrecognised) with respect to the narrow FN position, and the availability of material adequate for the kind of synthesis which would give to the FB position a range and explanatory power in harmony with the rest of the theoretical structure of psychoanalysis.

It might be simpler to illustrate these three points in turn, rather than as they appear in Freud's writings when considered chronologically. But to do so would give a misleading impression of order, and would raise the question why Freud himself did not see the obvious tensions, and the possibility of their resolution. The most significant feature of Freud's writings on symbolism is the disordered, unsystematic nature of the material devoted to it, mingled as it is with material on various other subjects. The extent of this disorganisation was not accurately reflected in the previous chapter, since the aim there was to impose structure and order so as to bring out certain important, and hitherto unacknowledged, themes in Freud's early writings on symbolism. But that lack of structure and order appears to have been the main reason for the failure of Freud (and others after him) to recognise that the material from which a clear and coherent FB theory of symbolism may be constructed is available in his writings. And, of course, it is much more difficult to collate the material for the FB position, drawing together many indirectly supportive strands and connections, than it is to extract the few relatively straightforward and explicit statements constituting the FN approach, the position which is usually presented as 'the' Freudian theory of symbolism. Thus, it is important that the unsystematic and often confused character of the material on symbolism be accurately portrayed, and this is achieved by allowing that material to speak for itself, in the way, and in the order, in which it was produced.

The Interpretation of Dreams

A general overview

Freud's most famous work, *The Interpretation of Dreams*, spans a period of thirty years, from the first edition in 1900 (actually published in 1899, but post-dated) to the eighth edition in 1930. Since it was one of only two works (the other was *Three Essays on the Theory of Sexuality*) which Freud kept up-to-date through subsequent editions, and since most of the additions and revisions were concerned with symbolism, this work offers a miniature picture, as it were, of Freud's developing views on symbolism, with the first three editions reflecting the gradual convergence onto the FN position, culminating in the insertion of a completely new chapter on symbolism in the fourth edition of 1914, and with that and subsequent editions illustrating the resulting uncertainties and unclarities. Shortly after the publication of the first edition, Freud was persuaded to produce a summary version in the form of an essay entitled 'On dreams' (1901a). Naturally, this contained nothing new. However, a second edition of this essay was published in 1911, and the juxtaposition of the two editions gives an illuminating, condensed illustration of the extent to which Freud's views on symbolism had developed over the intervening decade.

From one perspective, it is less a matter of genuine change than of confused continuation and elaboration. Ernest Jones plays down the changes through the successive editions of *The Interpretation of Dreams*, claiming that they involved merely 'a more adequate account of the important theme of symbolism, one which Freud admitted he was late in properly appreciating' (1953, p. 396). As a matter of fact, Jones's own (1916) paper on symbolism reveals a more perceptive appreciation than Freud's of the unity of Freud's material on symbolism, both in the implicit assumption that the FB position is the one which Freud developed, and in the belief, indicated by glossing over one or two unacceptable and less easily accommodated aspects of the FN position, that the distinction between the two positions is not sharp enough to disallow a synthesis.

However, much supporting material for the FB position, and for the continuation into Freud's later work of the common themes in his earlier writings, can be found in his other works, and, in accordance with the arguments presented above, I shall consider here only the first edition of *The Interpretation of Dreams*.

Approaches to symbolism rejected by Freud

In that first edition, Freud's major concern is to present his revolutionary approach to the interpretation of dreams as the only viable alternative to existing approaches, all of which had been rejected (and deservedly, according to Freud) by the scientific community. Thus Freud begins by considering, evaluating, and dismissing those other views, and part of that process involves his rejecting the particular usages to which the notion of 'symbolic' has been put. He does admit a point of agreement between his own and lay approaches to interpreting a dream: it lies in the process of 'assigning a "meaning" to it' (1900, p. 96). However, he rejects the different ways in which that assignment of meaning is traditionally made.

The first procedure is labelled the method of 'symbolic' dream-interpreting, and refers to the replacing of the whole content of the dream with another content, a kind of translation *en masse*, such as was used in the allegorical interpretations of the ancients. The obvious objection to this, which Freud is quick to make, is the unreliable and speculative nature of the interpretations. In commenting on Stumpf's approach, Freud says: 'He effects his interpretations, however, by means of a symbolism of an allegorical character without any guarantee of the general validity of his procedure' (ibid., n. p. 100).

The second method which Freud rejects, although he allows that his own approach has some affinity with it, is the so-called 'decoding' method. Instead of symbolic translation *en masse*, this involves a kind of piecemeal translation of different elements in accordance with some supposed cryptography, and is used when the dream is disconnected and confused and so not amenable to the holistic 'symbolic' method. The problem with this second method, according to Freud, is that 'everything depends on the trustworthiness of the "key" – the dream-book, and of this we have no guarantee' (ibid.). Freud singles out for particularly extensive consideration the views of Scherner, whom he later nominates as 'the true discoverer of symbolism in dreams' (1911a, p. 359). Scherner claimed that the central force in every dream is the 'symbolizing activity' of the imagination, which typically produces symbolisations of bodily activities and internal bodily sensations occurring during sleep. According to Scherner, the bodily organ, the substance contained in it, the nature of the excitement it produces, the object it desires, and so on, may all be symbolically represented. Some of Scherner's symbolic interpretations are remarkably close to Freud's own later suggestions (e.g., house = human body, pipe = penis), but his explanatory schema is quite different from Freud's. Later in the discussion, when Freud is considering the material and sources of dreams, in his section on somatic sources, he again turns to Scherner, who:

believed, too, that he had discovered the principle according to which the mind deals with the stimuli presented to it. On his view, the dream-work, when the imagination is set free from the shackles of daytime, seeks to give a *symbolic* representation of the nature of the organ from which the stimulus arises and of the nature of the stimulus itself. Thus he provides a kind of 'dream-book' to serve as a guide to the interpretation of dreams, which makes it possible to deduce from the dream images inferences as to the somatic feelings, the state of the organs and the character of the stimuli concerned . . . As will have been seen [this theory] involves a revival of dream-interpretation by means of *symbolism* – the same method that was employed in antiquity, except that the field from which interpretations are collected is restricted within the limits of the human body. (1900, pp. 225–6)

Freud goes on to list a number of objections to Scherner's theory. Firstly, it lacks 'any technique of interpreting that can be grasped scientifically', so that it 'seems to leave the door open to arbitrary interpretations' (ibid., p. 226). Secondly, as Freud had remarked earlier, 'there is no utilitarian function attached to Scherner's symbolizing imagination. The mind plays in its sleep with the stimuli that impinge upon it' (ibid., p. 87). Thus it appears that 'the mind is saddled with the dream-work as a useless and aimless function', since it 'is content with making phantasies about the stimulus with which it is occupied, without the remotest hint at anything in the nature of *disposing* of the stimulus' (ibid., p. 226). Thirdly, and perhaps most damningly, since bodily stimuli are always present, 'it is difficult to understand, then, why the mind does not dream continuously all through the night, and, indeed, dream every night of all the organs' (ibid.). Finally, any attempt to answer this by appealing to special motives which might direct attention under certain conditions to certain visceral sensations 'carries us beyond the scope of Scherner's theory' (ibid.). Thus, Freud's overall judgement is that behind Scherner's attempt at interpretation 'there is an element of reality, though it has only been vaguely perceived and lacks the attribute of universality which should characterise a theory of dreams' (ibid., p. 87).

Freud also considers Silberer's views on the 'functional symbolism' of dreams: some self-observing agency in the dreamer represents abstract mental processes and thoughts by concrete visual images. For example, the feeling of approaching consciousness just before waking up is replaced by the image of stepping across a brook. While Freud allows that this may form part of the true picture, he warns that: 'This very interesting functional phenomenon of Silberer's has, through no fault of its discoverer's, led to many abuses; for it has been regarded as lending support to the old inclination to give abstract and symbolic interpretations to dreams' (ibid., p. 505). The term 'symbolic' here is being used in the typically Jungian sense. The 'old inclination to give abstract and symbolic interpretations' became epitomised in Jung's later 'anagogic' or 'progressive' approach to symbolism, and was rejected by Freud and vehemently attacked by Jones in his 1916 paper, which was basically an extended polemic against the Jung/Silberer view.

Freud's alternative: continuation of earlier FB themes

When considering Freud's proposed alternative, two points require emphasis. Firstly, while Freud explicitly rejects what he calls the 'symbolic' method of dream interpretation, he nevertheless uses that term and its cognates in his own theory, so it is important to ascertain the difference between his use of the term and that of others, especially since, with the later (FN) position, the question arises whether there is indeed any gap between Freud's theory and those which he rejects. Secondly, each of the common themes which have been identified as emerging from the conceptual schema in Freud's early approach to symbolism are shown to have been taken up and given further support. In those themes the peculiarly Freudian use of the term 'symbolic' is clearly revealed.

Recall that the general schema treats the symbol as substitute produced via displacement, and used consciously or unconsciously, normally or pathologically. Within this schema, which accommodates both conventional and non-conventional symbols, the psychoanalytic focus is on the controversial, non-conventional symbols, in which the theme of the symbol as defensively produced substitute and the CRS (conflict–repression–substitution) formula play a central role. This theme is continued in Freud's discussion of dreams, and its generality accounts for the lack of any attempt, as yet, to separate symbols from other material categorised by him as 'forms of indirect representation'. Thus, for the dream interpreter, the translation of the 'manifest' into the 'latent' content requires concentrating on the 'symbolic', as opposed to the 'pictorial' (i.e., literal) value of the dream 'characters': 'The dream-content . . . is expressed as it were in a pictographic script, the characters of which have to be transposed individually into the language of the dream thoughts. If we attempted to read these characters according to their pictorial value instead of according to their symbolic relation, we should clearly be led into error' (1900, p. 277).

When discussing the dream as distorted and disguised wish-fulfilment, resulting from censorship, Freud identifies displacement as an important mechanism of the so-called 'dream-work', and he repeats the examples which are familiar from his earlier discussion of symbol formation, introducing the relationship between displacement and the normal/pathological continuum:

Displacements of this kind are no surprise to us where it is a question of dealing with quantities of *affect* or with motor activities in general. When a lonely old maid transfers her affection to animals, or a bachelor becomes an enthusiastic collector, when a soldier defends a scrap of coloured cloth – a flag – with his life's blood . . . all of these are instances of psychical displacements to which we raise no objection. (1900, p. 177)

However, the displacement which leads to symbol formation may also be other than normal:

But when we hear that a decision as to what shall reach our consciousness and what shall be kept out of it . . . has been arrived at in the same manner and on the same principles, we have an impression of a pathological event . . . the psychical process which we have found at work in dream displacement, though it cannot be described as a pathological disturbance, nevertheless differs from the normal and is to be regarded as a process of a more primary nature. (ibid., p. 177)

The other themes belonging to the general schema – the individual/ universal distinction, the ontogenesis of symbols in the individual's past experience, the role of language, and the *a priori* availability of symbols in the unconscious – are also again taken up and elaborated. For example, Freud hints at universality in symbolism: 'A dream-symbolism of universal validity has only emerged in the case of a few subjects, on the basis of generally familiar allusions and verbal substitutes. Moreover a good part of this symbolism is shared by dreams with psychoneuroses, legends and popular customs' (ibid., p. 345).

At the same time, he acknowledges individual variations and insists on contextual checks, singling out the ancient Greek Artemidorus as the only one who appreciates the need for this: while Artemidorus' piecemeal decoding approach must be rejected, he is nevertheless to be commended for allowing that 'the same dream element will have a different meaning for a rich man, a married man or, let us say, an orator, from what it has for a poor man, a bachelor or a merchant' (ibid., pp. 98–9). Consistent with this recognition of individuality, Freud gives an example of one of his own dreams, in which he was riding a grey horse, and 'the horse acquired the symbolic meaning of a woman patient' (ibid., p. 231). Freud is thus at pains to emphasise this important difference between his own and existing approaches to dream interpretation: 'My procedure is not so convenient as the popular decoding method which translates any given piece of a dream's content by a fixed key. I, on the contrary, am prepared to find that the same piece of content may conceal a different meaning when it occurs in different people or in various contexts' (ibid., p. 105).

Further caution is suggested by the fact that it is not invariably the case that any particular element must be interpreted 'symbolically', since 'a dream never tells us whether its elements are to be interpreted literally or in a figurative sense' (1900, p. 341).

In addition, Freud locates the formation (via displacement) of the original symbolic equation in the individual's early life:

the displacement which replaces psychically important by indifferent material (alike in dreaming and in thinking) has in these cases already taken place at the early period of life in question and since then become fixed in the memory. These particular elements which were originally indifferent are indifferent no longer, since taking over (by means of displacement) the value of psychically significant material. (ibid., p. 182)

The theme of language is also elaborated, with an increased focus on its role in avoiding arbitrariness in the interpretations of symbols (the term 'symbolic' here being used as a label for the method of the opposition):

The distinction between dream-interpretation of this kind and interpretation by means of symbolism can still be drawn quite sharply. In the case of symbolic dream-interpretation the key to the symbolization is arbitrarily chosen by the interpreter; whereas in our cases of verbal disguise the keys are generally known and laid down by firmly established linguistic usage. (ibid., pp. 341–2)

Nor has the special connection, which Freud had earlier identified, between the phenomenon of symbolization in hysteria and the metaphorical uses of language been abandoned. Of a particular dream in which a servant girl hurls animals at the dreamer, Freud says: 'This dream achieved its purpose by an extremely simple device: it took a figure of speech literally and gave an exact representation of its wording. "Monkey", and animals' names in general, are used as invectives; and the situation in the dream meant neither more nor less than "hurling invectives" ' (ibid., p. 406).

Similarly, in the many examples of dream interpretations which occur in this work, Freud often uses 'symbolism' in a very loose sense. For example, a man standing on a high tower is interpreted by Freud as representative of his 'towering above' the dreamer (ibid., p. 342).

Finally, the theme of symbols as already available in the unconscious is strengthened by Freud's observations:

Indeed, when we look into the matter more closely, we must recognize the fact that the dream-work is doing nothing original in making substitutions of this kind. In order to gain its ends – in this case the possibility of a representation not hampered by censorship – it merely follows the paths which it finds already laid down in the unconscious. (1900, pp. 345–6)

The existence of 'paths' which are 'already laid down in the unconscious' is evidence for a universal 'language' of the unconscious, discoverable in myths and rituals no less than in dreams, and preempts any need for the mind to bring to dreams a separate symbolising activity. In giving some support to Scherner's emphasis on the ubiquity of the body as symbolised, Freud notes how common is sexual symbolism, for which 'the way has been well prepared by linguistic usage, itself the precipitate of imaginative similes reaching back to remote antiquity' (ibid., p. 346). In addition, the exaggeration by neurotics of, for instance, the natural human dread of snakes, illustrates the point that:

'wherever neuroses make use of such disguises they are following paths along which all humanity passed in the earliest periods of civilization – paths of whose continued existence to-day, under the thinnest of veils, evidence is to be found in linguistic usages, superstitions and customs' (ibid., p. 347). Thus: 'It all leads to the same conclusion, namely that there is no necessity to assume that any peculiar symbolizing activity of the mind is operating in the dream-work, but that dreams make use of any symbolizations which are already present in unconscious thinking' (ibid., p. 349).

In summary, in 1900, Freud rejects 'symbolic' methods of dream interpretation, whether they be of the wholesale allegorical kind or the piecemeal fixed-key kind, not because the key to which they appeal is fixed, but rather because they have no theoretical structure, independent of those interpretations, which would provide some guarantee of the trustworthiness of the key to the code. This objection extends to Scherner's approach, again because there is no theoretical justification of the particular translations offered, and also to Silberer's 'functional' symbolism, although the attack on Silberer will not be worked out until several years later, when the Jung/Silberer position becomes a more obvious threat. While one or two of Freud's later claims do appear to come very close to these earlier rejected approaches, his objections point to that single crucial difference. And, to the extent that it can be demonstrated that Freud did offer a theory which served to ground independently his symbolic interpretations, and which made unnecessary such dubious appeals as appear in his later talk of phylogenetic inheritance, his approach to symbolism is quite different from those which he is here rejecting. He is clearly struggling with the attempt to provide the kind of theoretical underpinnings to symbolism which were lacking in other accounts. What is also obvious is the undeniable place of symbolism within the general structure of his theory, especially in the continuation and elaboration of the themes common to the FB approach. At the same time, however, there is a tendency of some of those common themes to be extracted and isolated from that general structure.

The writings from 1901 to 1908

Broad and narrow treatments of symbolism

Between 1900 and 1909, when the second edition of *The Interpretation of Dreams* appeared, there were a number of publications in which Freud continued, in a characteristically sporadic and unfocused way, to treat symbolism in much the same manner as he had earlier, but with signs of an increasing recognition of the promising material to be gleaned from mythology and philology, and of an increasing tendency to isolate those themes which would lead eventually to a commitment to the FN position. Most significantly, typical of Freud's writings in this period is a mixture of a broad and a narrow treatment of symbolism. The broad approach includes both a general metaphorical notion, and the application of the theme of the symbol as defensively produced substitute (via the CRS formula) to the adjectival notion of the 'symbolic' nature of more complex actions, events, relations, etc. The narrow approach is exemplified by appeals to simple translations of discrete substantive elements.

For example, in 1901, in *The Psychopathology of Everyday Life*, there is little explicit discussion of symbolism, although Freud does talk of related issues, of unconscious substitution via the mechanism of displacement in the service of defence, thus picking up the earlier general theme of symbol as unconsciously produced substitute. As with *The Interpretation of Dreams*, it is only in later editions (in numerous footnotes added in 1910 and 1912) that Freud brings out more strongly the general sense of symbolism in which 'symbol' and 'symptom' are used interchangeably; a symptomatic act expresses symbolically something which is meant to be hidden. On the other hand, in a footnote added in 1904, there is a more specific treatment of symbolism; Freud refers to a dream from which it appears that:

ice is in fact a symbol by antithesis for an erection: i.e. something that becomes hard in the cold instead of – like a penis – in heat (in excitation). The two antithetical concepts of sexuality and death are frequently linked through the idea that death makes things stiff. (1901b, n. p. 49)

Several years later Freud was to publish 'The antithetical meaning of primal words' (1910d), in which he elaborates extensively on this point and on its relationship to the *tertium comparationis* in symbol formation. There is a similar juxtaposition of a broad, almost metaphorical use of the term 'symbolism' with discussion of particular symbols, in Freud's famous Dora case study (1905a). Although Dora suffered from hysteria, Freud mentions neither 'mnemic symbol' nor 'symbolization'; however, he labels his interpretation 'symbolic' in the following passage:

Dora's aphonia, then, allowed of the following symbolic interpretation. When the man she loved was away she gave up speaking; speech had lost its value since she could not speak to *him*. On the other hand, writing gained in importance, as being the only means of communication with him in his absence. (1905a, p. 40)

Clearly, the use of 'symbolic' here is extremely broad, since Freud is merely pointing to the symptom of aphonia as the result of speech having lost for Dora its *raison d'être*. Another example suggests a position mid-way between broad and narrow approaches. In discussing what came to be known as 'transference', Freud says in his analysis of Dora's dream: 'Just as Herr K. had stood beside her sofa, so her father had often done in her childhood. The whole trend of her thoughts could be most aptly symbolized by her substitution of her father for Herr K. in that situation' (ibid., p. 89).

Alongside this is the narrow treatment of symbolism, anticipating the later focus on specific symbols. On the theme of locking her bedroom door, in Dora's first dream, Freud observes:

I suspected, though I did not as yet say so to Dora, that she had seized upon this element on account of a symbolic meaning which it possessed. *'Zimmer'* ['room'] in dreams stands very frequently for *'Frauenzimmer'* [a slightly derogatory word for 'woman'] . . . The question whether a woman is 'open' or 'shut' can naturally not be a matter of indifference. It is well known, too, what sort of 'key' effects the opening in such a case. (ibid., n. p. 67)

A continuity between these approaches, however, is established in Freud's discussion of a symptomatic act, in which 'symptomatic' is used synonymously with 'symbolic'. A symptomatic act is 'one which people perform . . . automatically, unconsciously . . . to which people would like to deny any significance . . . [but which] . . . gives expression to unconscious thoughts and impulses' (ibid., p. 76). That this refers to symbolism is indicated by Freud's following promise:

On some other occasion I will publish a collection of these symptomatic acts as they are to be observed in the healthy and in neurotics . . . *There is a great deal of symbolism of this kind in life*, but as a rule we pass it by without heeding it . . . He that has eyes to see and ears to hear may convince himself that no mortal can keep a secret. If his lips are silent, he chatters with his finger-tips; betrayal oozes out of him at every pore. (1905a, pp. 77–8, italics mine)

Similarly, in *Jokes and their Relation to the Unconscious* (1905b), the continuity of the broad and the narrow treatments of symbolism is underscored by Freud's constant shifting between assimilating the notion of symbolism to the general notion of defensive substitution, and treating it as a special case (alongside other products) of such substitution. In the former case, Freud is concerned to uncover the similarity between the process underlying the joke technique and that of dream formation – both instances of the general formula of the formation of substitutes:

The interesting process of condensation accompanied by the formation of a substitute, which we have recognised as the core of the technique of verbal jokes, points towards the formation of dreams, in the mechanism of which the same psychical processes have been discovered . . . Indirect representation – the replacement of a dream-thought by an allusion, by something small, a symbolism akin to analogy – is precisely what distinguishes the mode of expression of dreams from that of our waking life. So far-reaching an agreement between the methods of the joke-work and those of the dream-work can scarcely be a matter of chance. (1905b, pp. 88–9)

In the latter case, the connection is supported by a number of comments which Freud makes on the role of displacement, and its importance in indicating the operation of repression and the attempt to evade the censorship. Here, symbolism is treated as a particular version or form of displacement:

Among displacements are to be counted not merely diversions from a train of thought but every sort of indirect representation as well, and in particular the replacement of an important but objectionable element by one that is indifferent and that appears innocent to the censorship, something that seems like a very remote allusion to the other one – substitution by a piece of symbolism, or an analogy, or something small. (ibid., p. 171)

Freud goes on:

It cannot be disputed that portions of such indirect representation are already present in the dreamer's preconscious thoughts – for instance, representation by symbols or analogies – because otherwise the thought would not have reached the stage of preconscious expression at all. (ibid., pp. 171–2)

Moreover:

Indirect representations of this kind and allusions whose reference to the thing intended is easy to discover, are indeed permissible and much used methods of expression in our conscious thinking as well. The dream-work, however, exaggerates this method of indirect expression beyond all bounds. Under the pressure of the censorship, any sort of connection is good enough to serve as a substitute by allusion, and displacement is allowed from any element to any other. (ibid., p. 172)

A number of significant points emerge from this passage. Firstly, symbolism is not synonymous with displacement, which is more general; symbolism is one kind of displacement. Secondly, in the comment that representation by symbols is already present in the dreamer's preconscious thoughts, we have again the suggestion of two separate uses of the concept of displacement – one in which symbolism has its core in displacement (affect, say, or attention, or interest, is 'displaced' from one object to another, from the symbolised to the symbol), and the other which refers to a general mechanism of the 'dream-work', and which selects the already existing symbol because of the need to disguise something objectionable so that it may pass the censorship. Freud's account of this distinction is unclear, and is responsible for much subsequent confusion. Thirdly, Freud here reiterates the theme of the normal/pathological dimension with its implications of a continuity of symbolism through conscious and unconscious processes. However, since symbolism is not peculiar to unconscious thinking, the difference cannot be one of kind of mechanism or operation, but simply whether it is used consciously or unconsciously. Freud, unfortunately, does not spell out this implication; had he done so, he might have avoided his later somewhat confused theorising about the 'characteristics of the system *Ucs*.' (see Chapter 7).

Conscious and unconscious symbolism

This recognition of the existence of both conscious and unconscious use of symbolism is a theme which cuts across the broad (often metaphorical) and narrow treatments of symbols. Once again, what is most marked is the lack of any systematic treatment of these themes; Freud's focus is often elsewhere, and his treatment of symbolism peripheral. For example, in his analysis of Jensen's *Gradiva* (1907a), Freud introduces his oft-repeated 'archaeology' analogy for repression, the burial of Pompeii, the 'symbolism of which the hero's delusion made use in disguising his repressed memory. There is, in fact, no better analogy for repression, by which something in the mind is at once made inaccessible and preserved' (1907a, p. 40). When Norbert Hanold, the hero of Jensen's novel, draws a parallel between his childhood and the classical past, using the 'digging up' motif, Freud says: 'In this he was employing the same symbolism that the author makes the girl use consciously towards the conclusion of the story. "I told myself I should be able to dig out something interesting here even by myself" ' (ibid., p. 51); or again, this time unconsciously, 'she made her neatest use of her symbolism when she asked: "I feel as though we had shared a meal like this once before, two thousand years ago; can't you remember?" ' (ibid., p. 85). This discussion deals with the interweaving of the author's conscious use of symbolism, with that (both conscious and unconscious) of his characters. The treatment is of no major consequence, but it illustrates Freud's readiness to accept and use the term symbolism in the broadest sense.

There are many other examples of Freud's acknowledgement of the multiple layers provided by conscious and unconscious symbolism, and of their assimilation into both broad and narrow treatments of symbolism. In a technical paper, 'Obsessive actions and religious practices' (1907b), Freud says that one of the main differences between religious practices and obsessive actions lies in their ostensible meaning – 'while the minutiae of religious ceremonial are full of significance and have a symbolic meaning, those of neurotics seem foolish and senseless' (1907b, p. 119). But it is clear that Freud is here contrasting the apparent senselessness of obsessive actions with the overt, conscious, 'rationalised' 'symbolism' of religious ritual, for he goes on to argue that this merely masks an underlying unconscious symbolism which is shared by both phenomena:

> it is precisely this sharp difference between neurotic and religious ceremonial which disappears when, with the help of the psychoanalytic technique of investigation, one penetrates to the true meaning of obsessive actions . . . it is found that obsessive actions are perfectly significant in every detail, that they serve important interests of the personality and that they give expression to experiences that are still operative and to thoughts that are cathected with affect. They do this in two ways, either by direct or by symbolic representation; and they are consequently to be interpreted either historically or symbolically. (ibid., pp. 119–20)

Thus, despite the overt symbolism of one, and the seeming lack of symbolism of the other, each is based on an unconscious symbolism, and each can only be explained by unmasking the unconscious symbolism involved. 'In all believers', says Freud, 'the motives which impel them to religious practices are unknown to them or are represented in consciousness by others which are advanced in their place' (ibid., pp. 122–3). Once again, it is displacement which lies at the heart of the move from the unconscious to the conscious symbolism: 'their symbolism and the detail of their execution are brought about by a displacement from the actual, important thing on to a small one which takes its place' (ibid., p. 126).

The focus on the unconscious production of the symbol lies at the core of the theme of the ontogenesis of symbols in the individual's early experience. For example, in *Three Essays on the Theory of Sexuality* (1905c), after emphasising the crucial role of early sexual impressions for the development of fetishism, Freud adds:

> In other cases the replacement of the object by a fetish is determined by a symbolic connection of thought, of which the person concerned is usually not conscious. It is not always possible to trace the course of these connections with certainty. (The foot, for instance, is an age-old sexual symbol which occurs even in mythology; no doubt the part played by fur as a fetish owes its origin to an association with the hair of the *mons Veneris*.) None the less even symbolism such as this is not always unrelated to sexual experiences in childhood. (1905c, p. 155)

This passage is a good example of Freud's typical method, later to

become very familiar; it is a particularly mixed approach to the interpretation of symbols which Freud uses over and over again, and it consists
of the following ingredients: a translation is suggested; the subject is
claimed to be unconscious of the connection; an appeal is then made
to supportive instances in other cultural products, usually mythology,
often language; finally, a return is made to the individual with a tentative
suggestion as to how the connection might have been made earlier in
his/her life. As will be seen, while the order of presentation is not always
the same, the ingredients themselves rarely vary.

Intimations of the FN position

In 1908 Freud published a short paper, 'Character and anal erotism',
which was clearly inspired by his 'Rat Man' analysis, successfully completed late in the same year. In this paper Freud develops his hint,
expressed more than a decade earlier (in a letter to Fliess), of the association between money and faeces. What is interesting here is not so much
that connection as Freud's drawing on a wealth of support from mainly
philological and mythological material, and intimations of the use to
which he will put such analyses and such material in his later explicit
statements of the FN position:

> It might be supposed that the neurosis is here only following an indication of
> common usage in speech, which calls a person who keeps too careful a hold on
> his money 'dirty' or 'filthy'. But this explanation would be far too superficial.
> In reality, whatever archaic modes of thought have predominated or persist – in
> the ancient civilizations, in myths, fairy tales and superstitions, in unconscious
> thinking, in dreams and in neuroses – money is brought into the most intimate
> relationship with dirt. We know that the gold which the devil gives his para-
> mours turns into excrement after his departure, and the devil is certainly nothing
> else than the personification of the repressed unconscious instinctual life. We
> also know about the superstition which connects the finding of treasure with
> defaecation, and everyone is familiar with the figure of the 'shitter of ducats
> [Dukatenscheisser]'. Indeed, even according to ancient Babylonian doctrine, gold
> is 'the faeces of Hell' [Mammon = ilu manman]. Thus in following the use of
> language, neurosis, here as elsewhere, is taking words in their original, signifi-
> cant sense, and where it appears to be using a word figuratively it is usually
> simply restoring its old meaning.
>   It is possible that the contrast between the most precious substance known
> to men and the most worthless, which they reject as waste matter ('refuse'), has
> led to this specific identification of gold with faeces. (1908a, pp. 173–4)

It will be recalled that, in his account of the mechanism of symbolization
in hysteria, Freud appeals to linguistic parallels in a move which anticipates his later speculations about a linguistic link between universal

symbols and their constant, fixed meanings. Freud is here applying that kind of analysis to what is to become one of his list of typical universal symbols, and he is doing so in the context of the notion of a universal, primitive, 'archaic' language which ties together disparate cultural phenomena.

1909: further expansion

Continuation of earlier themes

For the development of Freud's theory of symbolism, 1909 is a year of productivity and increasing focus, although, not surprisingly, the expansion of the material on symbolism, and the more obvious signs of the convergence onto an FN position, are, characteristically, accompanied by vagueness and uncertainty, especially concerning the boundaries of the phenomenon. This was the year of the publication of two of Freud's most famous case studies ('Little Hans' and the 'Rat Man'), the writing of 'Five lectures on psycho-analysis' (published in the following year) and, significantly, the publication of the second edition of *The Interpretation of Dreams*, heralding a sequence of four new editions in which supplements to the theory of symbolism constituted the most prominent additions.

Although the issue is not explicitly addressed, in neither the Little Hans case study nor the Rat Man analysis is there any indication that the ontogenesis of symbolism is to be explained in any way other than by appealing to the past experience of the individual concerned. Of two of Hans's phantasies (forcing his way into a forbidden space, and smashing a railway carriage window – in each of which his father appeared as accomplice), Freud says:

Some kind of vague notion was struggling in the child's mind of something that he might do with his mother by means of which his taking possession of her would be consummated; for this elusive thought he found certain pictorial representations, which had in common the qualities of being violent and forbidden, and the content of which strikes us as fitting in remarkably well with the hidden truth. We can only say that they were symbolic phantasies of intercourse. (1909a, pp. 122–3)

A little later Freud goes on to make a number of symbolic equations (*lumpf* = baby; all furniture, vans, carts, stork-boxes, etc. = the womb; if the latter are heavily laden, they constitute a symbolic representation of pregnancy; falling down = childbirth, and so on). As for the Rat Man's central complex, Freud comments that 'rats had acquired a series of symbolic meanings, to which, during the period which followed, fresh ones were continually being added' (1909b, p. 213). However, he also says:

It was only then that it became possible to understand the inexplicable process by which his obsessional idea had been formed. With the assistance of our knowledge of infantile sexual theories and of symbolism (as learnt from the interpretation of dreams) the whole thing could be translated and given a meaning. (ibid., p. 217)

In other productions at this time, intimations of the FN position are more marked. In September, Freud delivered five lectures on psychoanalysis at Clark University in Worcester, Massachusetts, lectures which were published in the following year. In addition to reiterating the earlier views that the symptoms of hysteria are mnemic symbols of particular traumatic experiences, and that we also make use of conscious mnemic symbols (the Monument in London as a memorial to the Great Fire), and after describing again the operation of the repressed wishful impulse 'sending into consciousness a disguised and unrecognizable substitute for what has been repressed', in which we can trace 'the remains of some kind of indirect resemblance to the idea that was originally repressed' (1910a, p. 27), Freud gives expression to the beginnings of a splitting of symbolism into the individually learned and modified, and the *a priori* laid down, fixed and inherited:

I should like you to notice, too, that the analysis of dreams has shown us that the unconscious makes use of a particular symbolism, especially for representing sexual complexes. This symbolism varies partly from individual to individual; but partly it is laid down in a typical form and seems to co-incide with the symbolism which, as we suspect, underlies our myths and fairy tales. It seems not impossible that these creations of the popular mind might find an explanation through the help of dreams. (ibid., p. 36)

Freud had used this phrase 'laid down' on several earlier occasions when referring to symbolism and the language of the unconscious, always without any clarification of what is meant by 'laid down in a typical form'. Obviously, it lends itself to different interpretations, ranging from the conservative (simply that certain symbols occur universally), to the radical (that some symbolic connections are part of every person's *innate* equipment). Freud, as we know, came eventually to embrace the latter view.

Symbolism as an isolated area of research

At about this time, Stekel, one of the members of Freud's 'Vienna Group', was becoming prominent in his investigations of, and (largely, according to Jones) speculations on, symbolism, an area in which, on the admission of Freud and others, he was to gain considerable success. Jones (1955) observes that Stekel was naturally gifted, with an 'unusual flair for detecting repressed material', and that:

> his contributions to our knowledge of symbolism, a field in which he had more intuitive genius than Freud, were in the earlier stages of psycho-analysis of very considerable value. Freud freely admitted this. In a letter to Jung (Nov. 11, 1909) he said that he had often contradicted Stekel's interpretation of a given symbol only to find that Stekel had been right the first time. (pp. 151–2)

However, Jones tells us, Stekel was uncritical and lacking in judgement, wildly speculative, with 'no scientific conscience'. Whether for this or for other reasons Freud remained cautious. In his comments on the Minutes of the Vienna Psycho-Analytical meeting of 10 November 1909, Freud says: 'Dream symbols that do not find any support in myths, fairy tales, popular usages etc., should be regarded as doubtful' (in Jones 1955, p. 493).

There are two points to note here. Firstly, the topic of symbolism is now beginning to be treated as if it were a separate area, in which the task is to isolate and translate certain elements, using as supportive material similar instances in other cultural products. There is, of course, nothing incompatible between such an approach and the FB position on symbolism; the hermeneutical question of what does a particular element in a dream, say, stand for is perfectly intelligible and respectable, and as deserving of examination as the questions of what does this more complex event or activity symbolise, how has it come about, why, etc. However, it is not difficult to appreciate the temptation which the simple hermeneutical question might produce to encourage the view that the phenomenon itself is psychically isolated, just because its investigation is isolatable. Secondly, if Freud believes that dream symbols which are not supported in myths, fairy tales, etc. are doubtful, then he is moving away from the acknowledgement of individually formed symbols, and adumbrating the later restriction of the term 'symbol' to those universally occurring elements which crop up in parallel in dreams, myths, folklore, and so on.

Additions to The Interpretation of Dreams

In his preface to the second (1909c) edition of *The Interpretation of Dreams*, Freud says: 'I am glad to say that I have found very little to change in it.' However, while it is true that there are very few alterations, several additions, mainly on symbolism, strengthen the intimations of the FN position, and show Freud to be hovering, as it were, between the two positions. For example, he is now much more willing to allow his position to come close to that of the fixed-key code approach which in 1900 he rejected:

When we become familiar with the abundant use made of symbolism for representing sexual material in dreams, the question is bound to arise of whether many of these symbols do not occur with a permanently fixed meaning, like the 'grammalogues' in shorthand; and we shall feel tempted to draw up a new dream-book on the decoding principle. On that point there is this to be said: this symbolism is not peculiar to dreams, but is characteristic of unconscious ideation, in particular among the people, and it is to be found in folklore, and in popular myths, legends, linguistic idioms, proverbial wisdom and current jokes, to a more complete extent than in dreams. (1909c, p. 351)

Of course, Freud's answer to the question he poses is not really an answer at all, but his response is typical, appealing once again to the existence of the same symbols in many different cultural areas as sufficient to rebut the charge of arbitrariness in his list of dream symbol meanings, and suggesting that, once they were shown to be part of some universal and archaic 'language of the unconscious', their status could not reasonably be questioned.

Yet Freud goes on to allow both for universality and for individuality in these symbols:

Dreams make use of this symbolism for the disguised representation of their latent thoughts. Incidentally, many of the symbols are habitually or almost habitually employed to express the same thing. Nevertheless, the peculiar plasticity of the psychical material [in dreams] must never be forgotten. Often enough a symbol has to be interpreted in its proper meaning and not symbolically; while on other occasions a dreamer may derive from his private memories the power to employ as sexual symbols all kinds of things which are not ordinarily employed as such. Moreover, the ordinarily used sexual symbols are not invariably unambiguous. (ibid., p. 352)

Significantly, the last sentence of this paragraph was allowed to remain in the third (1911) edition, but is absent in the fourth (1914) edition, the edition in which the FN position receives its most complete statement. Again, however, there is nothing here which is incompatible with the FB approach. At this stage, despite intimations of the narrow position, Freud appears more concerned to warn against the overtaking of the method of free association by that of the translation of symbols, although it is also notable that he is beginning to emphasise these as two distinct methods:

I should like to utter an express warning against over-estimating the importance of symbols in dream interpretation, against restricting the work of translating dreams merely to translating symbols and against abandoning the technique of making use of the dreamer's associations. The two techniques of dream interpretation must be complementary to each other; but both in practice and in theory the first place continues to be held by the procedure which I began by describing and which attributes a decisive significance to the comments made by the dreamer, while the translation of symbols, as I have explained it, is also at our disposal as an auxiliary method. (1909c, pp. 359–60)

In summary, 1909 gives increasingly stronger intimations of the FN position, but no definitive support for that view, and nothing which constitutes a serious threat to the FB approach. And Freud is still insisting that universal, fixed symbols are not to be interpreted by a fixed-key code approach, because there is converging evidence for their meanings in mythological and other material outside of dreams; nor is translation of symbols to be undertaken as a substitute for the central psychoanalytic technique of interpreting associations, for it is at best an adjunct. The area of symbolism, however, is beginning to be set apart from other material. This is not surprising, given the activities of Stekel and others, and Freud's own personal interest in broader cultural areas in which he gradually came to believe that his theory had an important stake and would make valuable contributions. At the same time there is an insistence on individual variation, contextual checks, and converging evidence, and caution regarding wild and unsupported speculation. None of this, finally, is presented in any organised or systematic way.

The years 1910 and 1911

Freud's writings continue to illustrate the same combination of themes: the retention of the FB schema, the simultaneous contribution of various factors in a gradual convergence onto the FN position, and the resulting tensions and inconsistencies. Overall, there is little change in terms of organisation or clarity; indeed, some of the inconsistencies are thrown into sharper relief. Freud is still seen alternately isolating the area of symbolism and then, faced with criticism, defending his approach by pointing to connections between symbolism and other aspects of his theory. Of the three distinctive characteristics of symbols according to the FN theory, universality has already been touched on several times, but muteness and phylogenetic inheritance have not yet been introduced – although a number of comments (i.e., that collecting associations and translating symbols are two complementary dream interpretation techniques, and that some symbols are 'laid down in typical form') have foreshadowed those characteristics. Now, gradually, hints of the muteness and of the phylogenetic inheritance of symbols are becoming stronger. Still, however, these hints are mitigated by reservations, and by the weight of supporting material favouring the FB position.

Plans for a collective study of symbolism

In 1910 the degree of interest and activity in the field of symbolism increased. In March of this year Jones wrote to Freud suggesting that a collective study of symbolism be undertaken, and, on Freud's recommendation, Stekel raised the matter at the Second International Psycho-Analytical Congress at Nuremberg in April. As a consequence, a committee (consisting of Abraham, Maeder, and Stekel) was appointed under Stekel's instigation. Although, as Jones tells us, little actually came of this, there seems to have been a general consensus that such a study was both overdue and worthwhile. Forty-five years later, Jones says: 'I still consider that much could be learned from such a comparative study from all sources, dreams, jokes, myths and so on, so as to ascertain the precise points of resemblance on which symbols are constructed' (1955, pp. 75–6). Symbolism was undoubtedly being marked out as a relatively new and promising field of inquiry. Commenting on Freud's address before that Congress, 'On the future prospects of psycho-analytic therapy', Jones declares that 'The knowledge of typical symbols had been a recent addition' (1955, p. 75). Certainly, Freud presents the field of symbolism as an area in which new discoveries are being made:

Let me now touch upon one or two fields in which we have new things to learn and do in fact discover new things every day. Above all, there is a field of symbolism in dreams and in the unconscious – a fiercely contested subject as you know. It is no small merit in our colleague, Wilhelm Stekel, that, untroubled by all the objections raised by our opponents, he has undertaken a study of dream symbols. There is indeed still much to learn here; my *Interpretation of Dreams*, which was written in 1899, awaits important amplification from researches into symbolism. (1910b, p. 142)

Continuation of the familiar method

Nevertheless, on scrutiny, it is evident that Freud's method of treating symbols has not really changed. For example, a little later in that address, he says:

We began to turn our attention to the appearance of steps, staircases and ladders in dreams, and were soon in a position to show that staircases (and analogous things) were unquestionably symbols of copulation. *It is not hard to discover the basis of the comparison*: we come to the top in a series of rhythmical movements and with increasing breathlessness and then, with a few rapid leaps, we can get to the bottom again. Thus the rhythmical pattern of copulation is reproduced in going upstairs. Nor must we omit to bring in the evidence of linguistic usage. (1910b, p. 143, italics mine)

Here follow various supportive German and French terms linking 'climbing' with 'intercourse', after which Freud concludes: 'The dream material from which these newly recognised symbols are derived will in due time be put before you by the committee we are about to form for a collective study of symbolism' (ibid.). It is perhaps significant that the *tertium comparationis* of the symbolic equation which links climbing stairs with sexual intercourse is treated here as unmysterious, whereas only a year later Freud suggests that the connection is completely obscure if we try to rely only on individual experience. However, this passage illustrates, once again, Freud's standard method when faced with the task of interpreting symbols: an appeal to observable similarities and to individual experiences which might have furnished the connections, supplemented by linguistic and/or mythological parallels which are considered to provide converging evidence and strengthen the case for the interpretation offered.

Even Freud's more extended interpretations usually contain these ingredients, although he occasionally changes the order of presentation. In 'Leonardo da Vinci and a memory of his childhood' (1910c), Freud begins by suggesting the 'translation' (as with a dream) of Leonardo's 'memory' (phantasy) of a vulture striking him in the mouth with its tail – 'The translation is then seen to point to an erotic content. A tail, "coda", is one of the most familiar symbols and substitutive expressions for the male organ, in Italian no less than in other languages' (1910c, p. 85). Then (and here the famous mistranslation of *nibbio* as 'vulture' rather than as 'kite' is irrelevant to the point) Freud's method is first to reason from a wealth of philological and mythological evidence for the 'vulture = mother' equation (though at the same time musing on 'how it could be that the ancient Egyptians came to choose the vulture as a symbol of motherhood'). This is followed by the suggestion that, ultimately, the equation for Leonardo must be accounted for in terms of his own experience, and that, quite possibly, 'Leonardo was familiar with the scientific fable which was responsible for the vulture being used by the Egyptians as a pictorial representation of the idea of mother' (ibid., p. 89).

Language and the 'idioticon' of the unconscious

The connection between philological 'evidence' for symbolic interpretations and the notion of a primitive, archaic language is elaborated in
Freud's paper 'The antithetical meaning of primal words' (1910d).
Jones tells us that late in 1909 Freud came across Abel's *Der Gegensinn
der Urworte*, in which it is claimed that in many languages (e.g., Old
Egyptian, Sanskrit, Arabic, and Latin) opposites are designated by the
same word. Freud draws on this material for his theory of the 'language
of the unconscious' with its regressive, archaic *modus operandi* (it
encompasses no negation, fuses opposites, etc.), and he anticipates the
later explicit connection which he is to make between symbols and the
origins of language:

> In the correspondence between the peculiarity of the dream-work . . . and the
> practice discovered by philology in the oldest languages, we may see a confir-
> mation of the view we have formed about the regressive, archaic character of
> the expression of thought in dreams. And we psychiatrists cannot escape the
> suspicion that we should be better at understanding and translating the language
> of dreams if we knew more about the development of language. (1910d, p. 161)

Freud had earlier noted the importance for symbolism of representation
by the opposite. In a letter to Pfister (18 March 1909), when commenting on a dream of one of Pfister's patients, Freud says that being
born can be symbolised both by coming out of water and by entering
water, and he adds:

> Because of the ease of 'representation by its opposite' the symbolisms of giving
> birth and being born are often exchanged. In the well-known exposure myths
> of Sargon, Moses, Romulus, etc., the exposure in a basket or in water signifies
> the same as the subsequent rescuing out of the water. Both refer to birth.
> (Basket is box, casket, genitals, womb – from there we get to the flood sagas.)
> (in Jones 1955, p. 490)

When Freud uses the terms 'primitive' and 'archaic' in his discussions
of symbolism and language, it is often unclear whether he is referring to
ontogeny or phylogeny. His observations on ancient languages in 'The
antithetical meaning of primal words' seem to point to the latter. Sometimes, however, it appears that the language to which symbolism is tied
is 'primitive' only in terms of the ontogenesis of the individual. For
example, in a footnote added in 1910 to the *Three Essays on the Theory
of Sexuality*, Freud says that the case of Little Hans:

> made it possible to gain direct insight into infantile psycho-sexuality . . . [and]
> . . . has taught us much that is new for which we have not been prepared by
> psycho-analysis: for instance the fact that sexual symbolism – the representation

of what is sexual by non-sexual objects and relations – extends back into the first years of possession of the powers of speech. (1905c, n. pp. 193–4)

Freud clearly felt that connecting his theory of symbolism to a language of the unconscious gave him a vantage-point from which he might criticise the views of people such as Stekel. In a letter to Pfister on 6 November 1910, he writes: 'I am entirely in accord with your treating with suspicion every new symbol you hear of until your experience forces it on you. I do the same in regard to Stekel. But the best tool of psychoanalysis is still a knowledge of the peculiar idioticon of the unconscious' (in Jones 1955, p. 498).

The word 'idioticon' was in frequent use in Germany, signifying a dictionary of words and phrases confined to a particular region or dialect. The 'dictionary' of the words and phrases in the language of the unconscious must be collated, then, by waiting until 'experience forces it on' us.

Finally, Freud continues during this period to maintain the broadest, metaphorical use of the term 'symbolic'. For instance, in a footnote added in 1910 to the *Psychopathology of Everyday Life*, during a discussion of the meaning of the symptomatic act, Freud gives the following sketch:

A man overburdened with worries and subject to occasional depressions assured me that he regularly found in the morning that his watch had run down whenever the evening before life had seemed to be altogether too harsh and unfriendly. By omitting to wind up his watch he was giving symbolic expression to his indifference about living till the next day. (1901b, p. 215)

It is in examples such as this that we are reminded of the potential problems of a forced distinction between the 'symbol' as single entity or element, and 'symbolic' as descriptive of more complex states, actions, events, etc.

The following year, 1911, was an important one for the development of Freud's writings on symbolism. In particular, it was the year of publication of the third edition of the *Interpretation of Dreams*, to which much new material on symbolism was added, and also of the second edition of the summary version 'On dreams'. Additionally, during that year, several papers which included extensive discussions of symbolism were published. In general, what is illustrated in all of this material is the growing commitment to aspects of symbolism which become important in the FN position, alongside the retention and continuation of the general themes which are part of the FB view, supplemented, as usual, with the occasional use of 'symbolic' to mean simply 'metaphorical'.

The third edition of The Interpretation of Dreams

In the preface to the third edition of the *Interpretation of Dreams*, Freud writes:

> My own experience, as well as the works of Wilhelm Stekel and others, have since taught me to form a truer estimate of the extent and importance of symbolism in dreams (or rather in unconscious thinking). Thus in the course of these years much has accumulated which demands attention. I have endeavoured to take these innovations into account by making numerous interpolations in the text and by additional footnotes. (1911a, p. xxvii)

Needless to say, these 'innovations' are generally further examples in support of themes already examined. For instance, some of the interpolations attest to Freud's ever enthusiastic appeal to linguistic parallels for supporting evidence, while at the same time they illustrate an increasing tendency to isolate the theme of language from the rest of the FB schema. In a footnote to a discussion of the popular decoding method of interpretation, after briefly examining the part played by word resemblance in terms of phonological similarity (e.g., Alexander the Great's dream of a satyr (σάτυρος = σὰ Τύρος = 'Tyre is yours')), Freud comments: 'Indeed, dreams are so closely related to linguistic expression that Ferenczi [1910] has truly remarked that every tongue has its own dream language' (1911a, p. 99).

Many other additions are simply translations of particular symbols, or introductions of new ones:

> In men's dreams, a necktie often appears as a symbol for the penis. No doubt this is not only because neckties are long, dependent objects and peculiar to men, but also because they can be chosen according to taste – a liberty which, in the case of the object symbolized is forbidden by nature. (ibid., p. 356)

> A quite recent symbol of the male organ in dreams deserves mention: the airship, whose use in this sense is justified by its connection with flying as well as sometimes by its shape. (ibid., p. 357)

> For it is a fact that the imagination does not admit of long, stiff objects and weapons being used as symbols of the female genitals, or of hollow objects, such as chests, cases, boxes, etc., being used as symbols for the male ones. It is true that the tendency of dreams and of unconscious phantasies to employ sexual symbols bisexually betrays an archaic characteristic; for in children the distinction between the genitals of the two sexes is unknown. (ibid., p. 359)

> The frequency with which buildings, localities and landscapes are employed as symbolic representations of the body, and in particular (with constant reiteration) of the genitals, would certainly deserve a comprehensive study, illustrated by numerous examples. (ibid., n. p. 366)

These examples, and many more, are offered 'with the idea of showing how impossible it becomes to arrive at the interpretation of a dream if one excludes dream-symbolism, and how irresistibly one is driven to accept it in many cases' (ibid., p. 359).

That demonstration aside, two important points are illustrated in these examples. Firstly, Freud's method of justifying the meanings of the symbols is to point to observable, learnable similarities of form or function (sometimes both). That is, the *tertium comparationis* is something which is experienced by the individual in terms of perceptible similarities between symbol and symbolised. This is a theoretically sound idea, consistent with Freud's earlier notions and with the broader FB position. Secondly, it is clear that the 'archaic' nature of symbolism does not entail anything phylogenetic – it is an ontogenetic archaism, since Freud accounts for his use of the term by appealing to the ignorance of the individual in infancy. This too is sound theorising; had Freud used the word 'infantile' to replace 'archaic', he might perhaps have resisted the temptation later to bring in appeals to phylogenetic inheritance – although he did gradually come to believe that this latter mechanism was being suggested by additional findings.

Intermingled with such examples of standard symbol interpretations are several cases which call to mind the broader metaphorical use of 'symbol', and how Freud connected that with language, and with his method of analysing the mechanism of 'symbolization' in hysteria. For instance, a man dreamt that his uncle gave him a kiss in an automobile, and this 'meant auto-erotism' (1911a, pp. 408–9).

In addition, Freud remains cautious: 'A number of other symbols have been put forward, with supporting instances, by Stekel, but have not yet been sufficiently verified' (ibid., p. 357). Freud does not say what would constitute sufficient verification, given that Stekel had provided 'supporting instances'.

The isolation of the topic of symbolism as a separate phenomenon appears to have been responsible for much of the negative criticism which it drew. It is not difficult to understand how many theorists would have seen the enterprise as an exercise in arbitrary code-translation, and, accordingly, we find Freud making several allusions to 'resistance' against the fact of symbolism. His standard response is to emphasise how necessary it is to examine the symbolism in order to 'complete the picture' in any interpretation, and how stringent must be the methods of investigation and verification. In a footnote to the 1911 introduction of the hat as a symbol of a man or the male genitals, Strachey refers to a paper published by Freud in 1911, which began with the following paragraphs which were never reprinted in German:

Of the many objections that have been raised against the procedure of psycho-analysis, the strangest, and, perhaps, one might add, the most ignorant, seems to me to be doubt as to the existence of symbolism in dreams and the uncon-scious. For no one who carries out psycho-analysis can avoid assuming the pres-ence of such symbolism, and the resolution of dreams by symbols has been practised from the earliest times. On the other hand, I am ready to admit that the occurrence of these symbols should be subject to particularly strict proof in view of their great multiplicity.

In what follows I have put together some examples from my most recent experience: cases in which a solution by means of a particular symbol strikes me as especially revealing. By this means a dream acquires a meaning which it could otherwise never have found; it falls into place in the chain of the dreamer's thoughts and its interpretation is recognised by the subject himself.

On a point of technique I may remark that a dreamer's associations are apt to fail precisely in connection with the symbolic elements of dreams. (1911a, n. p. 360)

In this last sentence is the first hint of what was soon to become one of the three distinctive features of symbols in the FN view – their 'mute-ness' (i.e., the failure of the subject's associations with respect to them). But here it seems not to be a necessary condition; the associations are merely 'apt to fail', something which, according to Freud, happens often with other material as well, is a mark of resistance, and can be overcome via patience and insistence on the part of the analyst.

The second edition of 'On dreams'

In 1911 Freud's condensed version of the *Interpretation of Dreams* was published in a second edition, into which an extensive section on sym-bols was inserted. Freud begins this new section by pointing to the con-tingent fact (as opposed to theoretical necessity) of the repression of sexuality, and its subsequent importance as a motivating force in dreams, and proceeds to present an account in which 'symbolic' is almost synonymous with 'indirect representation', which, as will be seen, lies at the heart of the FB theory of symbolism.

There is only one method by which a dream which expresses erotic wishes can succeed in appearing innocently non-sexual in its manifest content. The mater-ial of the sexual ideas must not be represented as such, but must be replaced in the content of the dream by hints, allusions and similar forms of indirect representation. But, unlike other forms of indirect representation, that which is employed in dreams must not be immediately intelligible. *The modes of represen-tation which fulfil these conditions are usually described as 'symbols' of the things which they represent.* (1911b, pp. 682–3, italics mine)

This definition of symbolism is clearly not the FN one – there is no reference to the three distinctive characteristics of symbols. Freud continues:

> Particular interest has been directed to them since it has been noticed that dreamers speaking the same language make use of the same symbols, and that in some cases, indeed, the use of the same symbols extends beyond the use of the same language. Since dreamers themselves are unaware of the meanings of the symbols they use, it is difficult at first sight to discover the source of the connection between the symbols and what they replace and represent. The fact itself, however, is beyond doubt, and it is important for the technique of dream-interpretation. For, with the help of a knowledge of dream-symbolism it is possible to understand the meaning of separate elements of the content of a dream or separate pieces of a dream or in some cases even whole dreams, without having to ask the dreamer for his associations. Here we are approaching the popular ideal of translating dreams and on the other hand are returning to the technique of interpretation used by the ancients, to whom dream-interpretation was identical with interpretation by means of symbols. (ibid., p. 683)

Here we have a confident insistence on the crucial role played by symbolism. Symbolism cannot be denied or ignored. It sometimes allows us to understand a whole dream without having to ask the dreamer for associations.

Freud goes on to say that, while the study of dream symbols is far from complete, certain general statements can be made, and certain special information is available. For instance, 'there are some symbols which bear a single meaning almost universally' (e.g., king and queen for parents, rooms for women, entrances/exits for openings of the body):

> The majority of dream-symbols serve to represent persons, parts of the body and activities invested with erotic interest; in particular, the genitals are represented by a number of often very surprising symbols, and the greatest variety of objects are employed to denote them symbolically [For instance, long stiff objects = male genitals, hollow objects = female genitals, etc.] . . . In such cases as these the *tertium comparationis*, the common element in these substitutions, is immediately intelligible; but there are other symbols in which it is not so easy to grasp the connection. Symbols such as a staircase or going upstairs to represent sexual intercourse provoke our unbelief until we can arrive at an understanding of the symbolic relation underlying them by some other means. (1911b, pp. 683–4)

Here there are clear signs of vacillation on Freud's part. Staircase symbols now 'provoke our unbelief', whereas a year earlier he had said that 'it is not hard to discover the basis of the comparison'. Yet, in his identification of the *tertium comparationis*, Freud is still pointing to obvious, perceptible similarities. Furthermore, he is quite explicit in his acknowledgement of both universal and individual symbols:

> Some symbols are universally disseminated and can be met with in all dreamers

belonging to a single linguistic or cultural group; there are others which occur only within the most restricted and individual limits, symbols constructed by an individual out of his own ideational material. Of the former class we can distinguish some whose claim to represent sexual ideas is immediately justified by linguistic usage. (ibid., p. 684)

In fact, Freud takes pains to point out that the existence of individual symbols serves to check any tendency on the part of the interpreter simply to apply stock translations. He also reiterates the importance of individual associations, since even the 'universal' symbols are not necessarily fixed and independent of individual influence:

It would, incidentally, be a mistake to expect that if we had a still profounder knowledge of dream-symbolism (of the 'language of dreams') we could do without asking the dreamer for his associations to the dream and go back entirely to the technique of dream interpretation of antiquity. Quite apart from the individual symbols and oscillations in the use of universal ones, one can never tell whether any particular element in the content of a dream is to be interpreted symbolically or in its proper sense, and one can be certain that the *whole* content of the dream is not to be interpreted symbolically. (ibid., p. 684)

It seems that, having established how important a role is played by symbolism, which can even 'help us to understand the meaning . . . of the whole content of a dream', Freud must now modify that claim in the interests of caution and of highlighting the ways in which his own method differs from the inadequate 'decoding' method. Thus:

A knowledge of dream-symbolism will never do more than enable us to translate certain constitutents of the dream content, and will not relieve us of the necessity for applying the technical rules which I gave earlier. It will, however, afford the most valuable assistance to interpretation precisely at points at which the dreamer's associations are insufficient or fail altogether.

Dream-symbolism is also indispensable to an understanding of what are known as 'typical' dreams, which are common to everyone, and of 'recurrent' dreams in individuals . . .

Dream-symbolism extends far beyond dreams: it is not peculiar to dreams, but exercises a similar dominating influence on representation in fairy tales, myths and legends, in jokes and in folk-lore. It enables us to trace the intimate connections between dreams and these latter productions. We must not suppose that dream-symbolism is a creation of the dream-work; it is in all probability a characteristic of the unconscious thinking which provides the dream-work with the material for condensation, displacement and dramatization. (1911b, pp. 684–5)

The whole of the new section on symbolism added to the second edition of 'On dreams' is notable for its tensions and fluctuations. Yet it also illustrates the extent to which the FN consideration of 'universal' symbols can be accommodated within an FB position which also recognises individual symbols. As mentioned earlier, Freud's vacillation appears to be the result of his shifting emphasis in response to (real or imagined) criticism. When he is responding to the charge that symbolism is a useless and unsupported piece of excess baggage for psychoanalysis, he is at pains to point out how indispensable it is – it is ubiquitous, universal, able to provide the key to otherwise uninterpretable parts of dreams, can sometimes help us to understand the whole dream, can be applied where associations fail, is indispensable in the case of typical or recurrent dreams, is an essential part of the 'language of the unconscious' which extends to various diverse cultural phenomena and serves to tie them together, is already in evidence in those other areas and so is not the invention of Freud or the 'dream-work', and so on. On the other hand, when he is responding to the charge of the apparent arbitrariness of interpretations of symbols, of its betrayal of psychoanalytic theory and technique, then Freud is at pains to point out that it can never stand alone, that it is at best only a technique additional to the major one, that the latter forms the ultimate justification, for symbols can be formed and varied individually, despite the existence of universal symbols, and so on.

Other writings

The uncertainties and fluctuations which are evident in Freud's 1911 section on symbolism in his 'On dreams' are also evident in other publications of that year. In his paper 'The handling of dream-interpretation in psycho-analysis', after discussing the need to follow the 'technical rules' (i.e., collecting and interpreting the dreamer's associations), he adds:

Another situation to be considered is one which has arisen since we have acquired more confidence in our understanding of dream symbolism, and know ourselves to be more independent of the patient's associations. An unusually skilful dream-interpreter will sometimes find himself in a position of being able to see through every one of a patient's dreams without requiring him to go through the tedious and time-absorbing process of working over them. (1911c, p. 94)

Here, the ability to translate symbols makes us independent of associations, thus reinforcing the distinction between the two techniques. But, presumably, the reason that such a process requires 'unusual skill' is that the interpreter is not just required to identify and then cavalierly 'translate' typical symbols, but rather must be able to judge, from knowledge of the individual and the context, whether particular elements in the dream are to be taken symbolically, and, if so, whether they are straightforward cases or not. Freud insists, however, that the situation in which a dream interpretation can be effected solely via symbol-translation is a rare one.

Again, in a short paper jointly written with Oppenheim, 'Dreams in folklore', there is an extensive discussion of symbolism in folklore dreams where, Freud notes, the translation or interpretation of symbols is often added unashamedly (but conveniently) because the whole thing may be dismissed as 'just a story'. 'These stories', says Freud, 'delight in stripping off the veiling symbols' (1911d, p. 181), with the result that, 'we have been able to establish the fact that folklore interprets dream-symbols in the same way as psycho-analysis' (ibid., p. 203). Once again, however, the interesting factor is Freud's method of giving reasons for suggesting (where they are not provided) particular meanings of symbols, his caution, his comment on the amount of supporting evidence, and so on. For example:

The lottery ... could perhaps be understood as a symbolic reference to marriage. This symbol has not yet been identified with certainty in psychoanalytic work, but people are in the habit of saying that marriage is a game of chance, that in marriage one either draws the winning lot or a blank. (ibid., p. 186)

And again:

This dream calls for a symbolic interpretation, because its manifest content is quite incomprehensible whereas the symbols are unmistakably clear. Why should the dreamer really feel frightened at the sight of a water-jug rocking on the tip of a minaret? But a minaret is excellently suited to be a symbol for the penis, and the rhythmically moving water-vessel seems a good symbol of the female genitals in the act of copulation. (ibid., p. 199)

Here, quite simply, it is observed similarity to which Freud appeals in order to justify, in the absence of the dreamer's associations, the suggested symbolic equations.

Freud's familiar method of combined appeals to typical symbol translations, individual variations and associations, supportive linguistic and mythological material, and general psychoanalytic principles, is well illustrated in his Schreber analysis, also published in 1911, in which there are several suggestions for symbolic translations (some individual, some universal) of certain elements in Schreber's florid delusions and phantasies:

If the 'miracled' birds, which have been shown to be girls, were originally forecourts of Heaven, may it not be that the *anterior* realms of God and the forecourts of Heaven are to be regarded as a symbol of what is female, and the *posterior* realms of God as a symbol of what is male? (1911e, p. 53)

On the other hand:

> The sun . . . is nothing but another sublimated symbol for the father; and in pointing this out I must disclaim all responsibility for the monotony of the solutions provided by psycho-analysis. (ibid., p. 54)

In Schreber's delusions about the sun, and in his ability to stare at it without being dazzled, Freud finds several parallels in mythology (e.g., the eagle which puts its young to the test of staring unblinkingly into the sun, before it recognises them as its legitimate offspring, etc.), and then concludes:

> when Schreber boasts that he can look into the sun unscathed and undazzled, he has rediscovered the mythological method of expressing his filial relation to the sun, and has confirmed once again in our view that the sun is a symbol of the father. (ibid., pp. 81–2)

Apart from illustrating Freud's mixed approach, what is of particular significance in the Schreber analysis is that in it we have the first hint of what is later to become one of the distinctive characteristics of symbols in the FN position, and what is more generally to occupy Freud's thoughts in his later writings – the notion of the phylogenetic inheritance, along Lamarckian lines, of an 'archaic heritage', of which symbolism is a central part:

> Jung had excellent grounds for his assertion that the mythopoeic forces of mankind are not extinct . . . And I am of opinion that the time will soon be ripe for us to make an extension of a thesis which has long been asserted by psychoanalysts, and to complete what has hitherto had only an individual and ontogenetic application by the addition of its anthropological counterpart, which is to be conceived phylogenetically. 'In dreams and in neuroses', so our thesis has run, 'we come once more upon the *child* and the peculiarities which characterize his modes of thought and his emotional life.' 'And we come upon the *savage* too,' we may now add, 'upon the *primitive* man, as he stands revealed to us in the light of the researches of archaeology and of ethnology.' (1911e, p. 82)

Despite this hint, Freud retains, at this stage, what must be regarded as a sound principle with respect to questions of the ontogenetic versus phylogenetic explanation of symbolism or, indeed, of any other phenomenon. At the 1911 Congress at Weimar, Jung had presented a paper on symbolism in the psychoses and mythology. In the Minutes of 8 November Freud writes:

> As for the possibility of a phylogenetically acquired memory content (Zurich school) which could explain the similarity between the constructions of a neurosis and those of ancient cultures one should bear in mind another possibility. It could be a matter of identical physical conditions which must then lead to identical results . . . The inference of a phylogenetic inborn store of memories

is not justified so long as we have the possibility of explaining these things through an analysis of the psychical situations. What remains over after this analysis of the psychical phenomena of regression could then be conceived of as a phylogenetic memory. (in Jones 1957, pp. 330–1)

A few weeks later, on 11 December, in a letter to Jung, Freud was also suggesting caution in Jung's own favoured field of investigation, with respect to the confidence with which one is entitled to claim supportive evidence from mythological material – something Freud was able to recognise in Jung's case, but tended to overlook in his own:

> my objection to exploiting mythological material at its surface value ... the manifest forms of mythological material cannot without further investigation be used for purposes of comparison with our psycho-analytical conclusions. One has first to ascertain their latent original forms by tracing them back through historical comparative work so as to eliminate the distortions that have come about in the course of the development of the myth. (in Jones 1955, p. 501)

Freud versus Jung on symbolism

Freud's disgreements with Jung, which came to a head in 1911/1912, concerned, among other things, a radically different approach to the concept of symbolism. Jung's famous essay on 'Symbols of the libido' appeared in two parts (1911 and 1912), and it was, as Jones tells us, in the second that Jung's divergence from Freud's theories became evident. While it is obvious, notes Jones, that the revival of Freud's interest in religion (which led to the publication in the following year of *Totem and Taboo*) 'was to a considerable extent connected with Jung's excursion into mythology and mysticism', nevertheless:

> They brought back opposite conclusions from their studies: Freud was more confirmed than ever in his views about the importance of incestuous impulses and the Oedipus complex, whereas Jung tended more and more to regard these as not having the literal meaning they appeared to, but as symbolizing more esoteric tendencies in the mind. (Jones 1955, p. 110)

Jones goes on to say that the second part of Jung's essay:

> was the part where the idea of incest was no longer to be taken literally but as a 'symbol' of higher ideas. Other divergences, such as the belief in 'prospective tendencies' and the need for 'psycho-synthesis', dated from 1909 ... Freud ... wrote saying he could tell me the very page where Jung went wrong; having discovered that, he lost further interest ... In May of that year [1912] Jung had already told Freud that in his opinion incest wishes were not to be taken literally but as symbols of other tendencies; they were only a phantasy to bolster up morale. (ibid., p. 162)

This is the Jung/Silberer 'anagogic' or 'progressive' approach to symbolism, which Freud was to attack two years later in 'On the history of the psycho-analytic movement' (1914c). Freud himself was in no doubt about Jung's motivation in taking this path. As Jones relates:

On Jung's return from America he sent Freud a long account of his experiences and of how successful he had been in making psychoanalysis more acceptable by leaving out the sexual themes. To which Freud tersely replied that he could find nothing clever in that: all one had to do was to leave out more still and it would become still more acceptable. (ibid., pp. 162–3)

There are a number of aspects of Freud's rejection of Jung's position which, as will be shown later, are both theoretically sound and important contributions in the FB theory of symbolism.

At about this time, in a climate of unrest and dissension amongst Freud's 'inner circle', Freud also quarrelled with Stekel on the grounds of the latter's lack of care in his approach to the interpretation of symbols. As Jones describes the episode:

Stekel was on his high horse and would not give way. His success in the field of symbolism made him feel he had surpassed Freud. He was also fond of expressing this estimate of himself half-modestly by saying that a dwarf on the shoulder of a giant could see farther than the giant himself. When Freud heard of this he grimly commented: 'That may be true, but a louse on the head of an astronomer does not'. (1955, p. 154)

The years 1912 and 1913

Continuation of earlier themes

In Freud's publications in 1912, and a number of the minor publications in 1913, the little that is of relevance to his theory of symbolism simply picks up the common, broader themes of earlier works, illustrating again a somewhat unsystematic, mixed approach, in which 'symbolic' is used almost synonymously with 'symptomatic', and which continues the theme of the symbol as defensively produced substitute. In 'Contributions to a discussion on masturbation' (1912a), Freud argues that the 'actual neuroses' (i.e., neurasthenia and anxiety neurosis) are different from the 'psycho-neuroses' because:

their symptoms cannot be analysed. That is to say, the constipation, headaches and fatigue of the so-called neurasthenic do not admit of being traced back historically or symbolically to operative experiences and cannot be understood as substitutes for sexual satisfaction or as compromises between opposing instinctual impulses, as is the case with psychoneurotic symptoms. (1912a, p. 249)

When Freud talks of tracing something back 'historically', he is not

referring simply to the identification of antecedent causal conditions;
Freud was an uncompromising determinist, and he would certainly not
be suggesting that neurasthenic symptoms have no causes, or that their
causes cannot be discovered. For Freud, tracing a symptom back 'historically' requires identifying the *psychological* causes, usually the conditions of motivational conflict, which have produced the symptom. As
for tracing the symptom back 'symbolically', this means finding answers
to the hermeneutical question of what does this action (or its elements)
'represent' or 'substitute for' in the mind of the patient. Thus, in
combination:

Psycho-analysis has shown us that when the original object of a wishful impulse
has been lost as a result of repression, it is frequently represented by an endless
series of substitutive objects none of which, however, brings full satisfaction.
(1912b, p. 189)

This general theme allows the application of the psychoanalytic theory
of symbolism to broader cultural areas. With its material on symbolism,
psychoanalysis even extends to the field of art, which 'is a conventionally
accepted reality in which, thanks to artistic illusion, symbols and substitutes are able to provoke real emotions' (1913e, p. 188).

In addition, understanding symbols is not simply a matter of knowing
the meaning of the symbol as soon as the symbol has been identified;
symbols vary in their 'transparency' according to certain conditions,
either of the interpreter or of the symbol producer. In a second-hand
dream analysis, 'An evidential dream' (1913a), Freud points out that
the lady's interpretation of the nurse's dream was incomplete because
the former:

suffered from an obsessional neurosis, a condition which, from what I have
observed, makes it considerably harder to understand dream symbols, just as
dementia praecox makes it easier.
    Nevertheless, our knowledge of dream-symbolism enables us to understand
uninterpreted portions of this dream . . . the nurse who threw herself into the
Rhine out of mortification found a sexual-symbolic consolation for her despair
of life in the mode of her death – by going into the water. The narrow footbridge
on which the apparition met her was in all probability also a genital symbol,
although I must admit that here we lack as yet more precise knowledge. (1913a,
pp. 275–6)

Once again, we see a mixture of the confident appeal to knowledge of
symbolism, and caution in proposing uncorroborated translations.

In another paper, 'The occurrence in dreams of material from fairy
tales' (1913b), Freud points to the support for his theory of symbolism
gained from a close examination of how and when the dreamer incor-

porates such material into his/her dream. For instance, a young married woman's dream contains such similarities to the tale of Rumpelstiltskin that one can confidently affirm the equations room = vagina, little man = penis, short-cut hair = castration, and so on. Freud takes another example from the case of the Wolf Man (a case on which he was engaged at the time, but which was not published until four years later). The Wolf Man's dream contains connections to Grimm's 'The wolf and the seven little goats' and to 'Little Red Riding Hood', and the wolf (which eats up the little goats) is a symbol for the father. Other symbolic equations are offered in Freud's favourite essay 'The theme of the three caskets' (1913c), in his discussion of *The Merchant of Venice* – a discussion which reinforces both the general psychoanalytic stance, and the more specific approach to symbolism:

we do not share the belief of some investigators that myths were read in the heavens and brought down to earth; we are more inclined to judge with Otto Rank that they were projected onto the heavens after having arisen elsewhere under purely human conditions. (1913c, p. 292)

If what we were concerned with were a dream, it would occur to us at once that caskets are also women, symbols of what is essential in woman, and therefore of a woman herself – like coffers, boxes, cases, baskets, and so on. If we boldly assume that there are symbolic substitutes of the same kind in myths as well . . . (ibid.)

Symbolism as connecting religion, ritual and obsessive acts

One of the two major publications of 1913 was *Totem and Taboo*, an examination of primitive religion, in which Freud continues with the general theme of the symbol as defensively produced substitute via the CRS formula. Once again, this time in the context of a discussion of religion, ritual and obsessive acts, though usually without using the term 'symbolism', Freud presents a general account of the vicissitudes of the instinctual drives in their search for substitutes, and concludes that obsessive acts are both defences against, and substitutes for, forbidden (repressed) desires: 'The instinctual desire is constantly shifting in order to escape from the *impasse* and endeavours to find substitutes – substitute objects and substitute acts – in place of the prohibited ones' (1913d, p. 30). The compromise acts which result are both 'efforts at expiation' and 'substitutive acts to compensate the instinct for what has been prohibited' (ibid.). Taboo is of the same nature as obsessive prohibition: 'The obsessional act is ostensibly a protection against the inhibited act; but *actually*, in our view, it is a repetition of it. The "ostensibly" applies to the *conscious* part of the mind, and the "actually" to the unconscious part' (ibid., pp. 50–1).

In his discussion of animal phobias in childhood, Freud argues that the real fear, which is of the father, is displaced onto an animal (as in the case of Little Hans). According to Freud, this has implications for the origins of totemism, since the ambivalence (fear and hostility in conflict with affection and need) is relieved when the hostile, fearful feelings can be displaced onto a substitute. To understand totemism, then, we substitute father for totem animal (as primitives do, in describing their totem as a common ancestor and primal father). Thus the totemic formula becomes an injunction against the two crimes of Oedipus, and the two primal wishes of children. The ritual killing and eating of the totem, followed by festive rejoicing, is a clear manifestation that 'A festival is a permitted, or rather, an obligatory, excess, a solemn breach of a prohibition' (ibid., p. 140). The equation of totem animal with the father explains the fact that, while killing the totem is as a rule forbidden, it is also an occasion for rejoicing (as well as mourning). Freud appeals to Frazer's *Golden Bough* as providing support for his theory that the original animal sacrifice was already a substitute for human sacrifice – for the ceremonial killing of the father – and he adduces material from mythology to support his famous claim that 'the beginnings of religion, morals, society and art converge in the Oedipus complex' (1913d, p. 156). Finally, universality is illustrated in the fact that incest, in which the original object (for the male) is the mother or sister, forms the material for the most common theme in art and creative writing. The whole of Freud's account in *Totem and Taboo* rests on the alleged symbolic substitution of totem animal for father. From that single equation, several others, concerned with actions, wishes, and events, follow. This account shows how symbolism is woven into the whole theoretical structure of psychoanalysis. Further, in his reasons for rejecting Wundt's claim that taboo is based on fear of 'demonic' power, Freud reveals an important aspect of his theoretical justification for any interpretation of symbols: 'Neither fear nor demons can be regarded by psychology as "earliest" things, impervious to any attempts at discovering their antecedents. It would be another matter if demons actually existed' (1913d, p. 24). In other words, what is symbolised is always, ultimately, primary, for anything secondary will admit of further breakdown. This method is very similar to Freud's later (1915a) analysis of instinctual drives, in which he escapes the problem of the potential arbitrary proliferation of instinctual drives by insisting that we must ask about any particular supposed 'drive' whether it will admit of further analysis into a more primitive drive.

The return to language

The second major publication of 1913 was Freud's paper 'The claims of psycho-analysis to scientific interest'. In a section headed 'The philological interest of psycho-analysis', Freud returns to one of his favourite themes, language, and talks of the characteristics of the 'language of dreams', a language which 'forms part of a highly archaic system of expression' (1913e, p. 176). He then elaborates:

Another striking feature of our dream-language is its extremely frequent use of symbols, which make us able to some extent to translate the content of dreams without reference to the associations of the individual dreamer. Our researches have not yet sufficiently elucidated the essential nature of these symbols. They are in part substitutes and analogies based upon obvious similarities; but in some of these symbols the *tertium comparationis* which is presumably present escapes our conscious knowledge. It is precisely this latter class of symbols which must probably originate from the earliest phases of linguistic development and conceptual construction. In dreams it is above all the sexual organs and sexual activities which are represented symbolically instead of directly. (1913e, pp. 176–7)

Once again, it is unclear whether Freud means these 'earliest phases of linguistic development' to be understood ontogenetically or phylogenetically; but this time it is the latter which he seems to favour, because he immediately brings in Sperber's (1912) views on the origins of language, in particular that 'words which originally represented sexual activities have, on the basis of analogies of this kind, undergone an extraordinarily far-reaching change in their meaning' (1913e, p. 177). Freud then likens the dream to a pictographic script, and insists on the dependence of the psychoanalytic enterprise on philology: 'If this conception of the method of representation in dreams has not yet been followed up, this, as will be readily understood, must be ascribed to the fact that psycho-analysts are entirely ignorant of the attitude and knowledge with which a philologist would approach such a problem as that presented by dreams' (ibid.). Despite such disclaimers, the appeal to linguistic connections continues to form part of Freud's method in the interpretation of specific symbols. For example, in his paper 'Observations and examples from analytic practice', Freud says: 'In women's dreams an overcoat [German *'Mantel'*] is unquestionably shown to be a symbol for a man. Linguistic assonance may perhaps play some part in this' (1913f, p. 196).

Summary and concluding remarks

Freud's writings from 1900 to 1913, leading up to the 'core' years for the expression of the FN theory of symbolism, reveal the continuation and elaboration of themes which were introduced in his early writings, themes which lie at the heart of the FB position. The steps leading to the convergence onto the FN position gradually become more pronounced, indicated both by the isolation of symbolism as a separate area of research and by its being brought explicitly into connection with only one or two of the FB themes, namely, the role of language and the *a priori* availability of symbols in the unconscious. Because of this, Freud's stance consists of defending the psychoanalytic emphasis on the importance of symbols, while at the same time repeatedly voicing warnings about premature interpretations which lack supportive material, neglect of individual and contextual factors, and so on. His typical approach to the interpretation of symbols is mixed, consisting of offering translations, noting the unconscious nature of the symbolic equation, appealing to mythological and/or philological parallels, and pointing to the individual's experience of perceptible similarities between symbol and symbolised.

The obvious tensions, obscurities, and inconsistencies seem to be the result of a lack on Freud's part of a clear overall vision about symbolism, consistent with a similar failure in his earliest writings. He seems not to have recognised that the whole picture can be presented systematically without incurring any of the losses which he feared. Firstly, the fact that there are symbols which are ubiquitous and which occur with much the same meanings everywhere does not negate the importance of individual factors, both for the formation of those symbols, and for the possibility of individual variations in the use of them. Of course, to the extent that universal symbols may be identified and corroborated by other material, it is possible to place less emphasis on the need for individual associations. But that will never be a matter of complete certainty; the interpreter may be confident about the suggested interpretations, but must always be open to the possibility that this is not a typical case. Secondly, if similarities of form or function have been noted by the mind, then it is clear in what sense symbols are 'already present' in the unconscious, clear in what sense the dream-work does not 'create' symbolism, but makes use of it. Thirdly, that language reflects these facts is no surprise at all, but it does not, of course, necessitate the step which Freud would finally take – justification of the constant meanings of universal symbols by tracing the linguistic term for the symbol back to an original identity between word and thing. When all is considered, then, it is notable that there is little material which is explicitly contradictory to the FB theory, and in fact little which cannot be easily assimilated into that theory.

5 The 'core years' for the FN theory (1914–1917)

The FN theory, according to which symbols are distinguished from all other material by the three characteristics of constant meaning, 'muteness', and phylogenetic inheritance, is typically regarded both by supporters and by critics of psychoanalysis as *the* Freudian theory of symbolism. In Chapter 2, I presented that theory in detail by extracting from Freud's writings all of his explicit statements of the FN view. Noticeably, most of those statements are in material published during the period 1914 to 1917 (in particular, the fourth edition of *The Interpretation of Dreams*, and the tenth lecture in the *Introductory Lectures on Psycho-Analysis*). Accordingly, this period may be identified as the 'core' years for the FN theory. In Chapters 3 and 4, I documented certain significant features of the Freudian material on symbolism leading up to these core years. Freud's earliest writings contain the basis for a much broader (FB) theory of symbolism, consisting of a general conceptual schema and a number of important unifying themes. Subsequent writings show much continuity with the earlier work, and, while a slow convergence onto the FN view is discernible, this is relatively weak compared with the FB themes which emerge from the rest of Freud's material, and which are progressively elaborated and consolidated. However, Freud himself did not organise his material explicitly according to the FB schema and its themes, and he did not appear to recognise the value of much of that material. Instead, he came gradually to isolate symbolism as a separate area, and to justify that separation by focusing, in any explicit discussion of symbolism, on the distinctively FN view of symbols. As a result, his overall treatment of symbolism is characterised by tension, uncertainty, and disorganisation.

These characteristics are evident also in Freud's writings during the core years for the FN theory. Even during this period there is by no means an unambiguous commitment to the narrow view, and, indeed, the context from which the FN statements may be extracted continues to support the FB position. However, because we now have an explicit presentation, instead of mere hints, of the FN theory, and because this presentation is embedded in the broader FB context, two further points are illustrated by material from these core years: firstly, the FN theory can be assimilated into the FB theory with very little loss; and, secondly, it is Freud himself who, in expressing his uncertainty and well-founded reservations, shows the way to achieve that assimilation.

The Interpretation of Dreams

The fourth edition of *The Interpretation of Dreams* (1914a) contains, in Chapter VI, an entirely new section on symbolism, as well as numerous additional paragraphs and footnotes in the rest of the text.

Symbolism versus 'other forms of indirect representation'

In the new section on symbolism, Freud's uncertainty about how to define symbolism is evident. He isolates symbolism as a separate phenomenon in dreams, yet recognises its connection with other material. Three years earlier, in the second edition of 'On dreams', he had marked off symbolism from what he called 'other forms of indirect representation' simply by the requirement that it 'must not be immediately intelligible' (it must effect the disguise necessary to escape the censorship), and he had concluded that 'the modes of representation which fulfil these conditions are usually described as "symbols" of the things which they represent' (1911b, p. 683). Now, however, Freud wishes to separate symbolism more definitely, but is uncertain how that might be achieved:

representation by a symbol is among the indirect methods of representation, but . . . all kinds of indications warn us against lumping it in with other forms of indirect representation without being able to form any clear conceptual picture of their distinguishing features. (1914a, pp. 351–2)

Then, rather than specify the 'all kinds of indications', Freud singles out those symbols for which the *tertium comparationis* is obscure, and suggests that these must provide the key to the nature of symbolism in general:

In a number of cases the element in common between a symbol and what it represents is obvious; in others it is concealed and the choice of the symbol seems puzzling. It is precisely these latter cases which must be able to throw light upon the ultimate meaning of the symbolic relation, and they indicate that it is of a genetic character. Things that are symbolically connected to-day were probably united in prehistoric times by conceptual and linguistic identity. The symbolic relation seems to be a relic and a mark of former identity. (ibid., p. 352)

Once again, the two FB themes of the role of language and of the *a priori* availability of symbols in the unconscious form the bedrock for the characterisation of symbols. But Freud's argument here is confused. While it may be true that the *tertium comparationis* in some symbols is more obscure than in others, Freud gives no reason why we should focus on the obscure cases to find 'the ultimate meaning of the symbolic relation'. Nor is there any indication whence it follows that this 'ultimate meaning' is 'of a genetic character'. What, indeed, does that mean? Apparently, the symbol and the symbolised were 'united in prehistoric times by conceptual and linguistic identity'. But what exactly does that tell us?

'Conceptual' identity, as contrasted with factual identity, must mean that two things are thought to be identical when they are not in fact identical; this is true (in fact, must be true – at least for one part of the mind) of all unconscious, defensive substitution of the kind dealt with by Freud in the context of the FB schema. There are, of course, profound questions raised by this idea, but there is no justification for restricting such 'conceptual identity' to prehistoric times. 'Linguistic' identity, on the other hand, can only mean that the same word is used both for the symbol and for the symbolised. That this may be true in some ancient languages, and is true in other, present-day languages (Baker 1950), indicates nothing more than that the same labels may be used for things which share certain perceptible characteristics relevant to the interests of the language users. Again, important questions are raised here, but they do not concern the conventional nature of language as a symbolic system, or the fact that the perception of similarities is logically prior to their reflection in the linguistic terms chosen. Thus, appealing to (speculations about) an ancient language (even if the speculations are correct, and even if some of the language's features could be transmitted via heredity) simply pushes any problems back one step. As I shall show later (in Chapter 8), Freud's linguistic hypothesis concerning the genesis of symbolism is, however well-motivated, conceptually confused, and cannot do the job for which he misguidedly recruited it.

Freud is also inconsistent about aspects of the 'language of symbolism'. It is a general, universal language: 'In this connection we may observe how in a number of cases the use of a common symbol extends further than the use of a common language' (1914a, p. 352). But its vocabulary is not, after all, entirely ancient: 'A number of symbols are as old as language itself, while others (e.g. "airship", "Zeppelin") are being coined continuously down to the present time' (ibid., p. 352). In view of the emphasis which Freud gives to the phylogenetically archaic genesis of symbolism, an adequate account would require him to clarify the connection between the original, ancient language and current coinages – a connection which, once made (see again Chapter 8), provides support for the FB, rather than for the FN, theory of symbolism.

Individual variations

Freud has hitherto always acknowledged individual symbols and individual variations with respect to universal symbols, and, hence, the importance of contextual checks on alleged symbol translations. Now he continues this, but with subtle modifications in favour of a greater emphasis on what is typical and universal. On examination, however, this attempted shift is not managed at all successfully.

For instance, in the second (1909c) edition of *The Interpretation of Dreams*, Freud had acknowledged the existence of individual symbolism, saying that a dreamer 'may derive from his private memories the power to employ as sexual symbols all kinds of things which are not ordinarily employed as such' (1909c, p. 352). Immediately following this is the statement: 'Moreover the ordinarily used sexual symbols are not invariably unambiguous.' This last sentence was allowed to remain in the third (1911) edition, but now, in 1914, is removed and replaced by:

If a dreamer has a choice open to him between a number of symbols, he will decide in favour of the one which is connected in its subject-matter with the rest of the material of his thoughts – which, that is to say, has individual grounds for its acceptance in addition to the typical ones. (1914a, pp. 352–3)

Thus, Freud is suggesting, the symbol may have individual justification, provided it also has typical justification. But this conflicts with the sentence (quoted above) which now immediately precedes it (i.e., a dreamer 'may derive from his private memories . . . '), which is a much greater concession to individuality, and which, curiously, was allowed to remain.

Further, while Freud once again connects the presence of symbolism with the failure of the dreamer's associations, he still has to admit that contextual converging evidence must be found in order to avoid the charge of the arbitrary nature of symbol interpretation:

As a rule, the technique of interpreting according to the dreamer's free associations leaves us in the lurch when we come to the symbolic elements in the dream-content. Regard for scientific criticism forbids our returning to the arbitrary judgment of the dream-interpreter, as it was employed in ancient times and seems to have been revived in the reckless interpretations of Stekel. We are thus obliged, in dealing with those elements of the dream content which must be recognised as symbolic, to adopt a combined technique, which on the one hand rests on the dreamer's associations and on the other hand fills the gaps from the interpreter's knowledge of symbols. We must combine a critical caution in resolving symbols with a careful study of them in dreams which afford particularly clear instances of their use, in order to disarm any charge of arbitrariness in dream-interpretation. The uncertainties . . . spring in part from our incomplete knowledge . . . but in part from certain characteristics of dreamsymbols themselves. They frequently have more than one or even several meanings, and, as with Chinese script, the correct interpretation can only be arrived at on each occasion from the context. (1914a, p. 353)

Here, associations do not fail invariably, but only 'as a rule', the translation of symbols must be made with regard to their place in the context of the latent dream material produced by the dreamer's associations, and the symbols themselves are not characterised by constant meanings.

Individual variation is also conceded in that the sliding scale of the opaqueness of the symbol's meaning is a direct result of the degree of repression involved. This is an observation which Freud makes on several occasions. Here, partly in reply to Havelock Ellis's claim that dream symbolism occurs only in neurotics, Freud includes a section on symbolism in the dreams of normal persons, in which he reiterates his general stance that 'psycho-analytic research finds no fundamental, but only quantitative, distinctions between normal and neurotic life' (ibid., p. 373). He then adds:

The naive dreams of healthy people actually often contain a much simpler, more perspicuous and more characteristic symbolism than those of neurotics; for in the latter, as a result of the more powerful workings of the censorship and of the consequently more far-reaching dream-distortion, the symbolism may be obscure and hard to interpret. (ibid., p. 374)

If this is true, then, while it makes sense within the FB approach to symbolism (in which the strength of repression affects the choice of symbols no less than the choice of any other material), it points to a lacuna in the FN theory; something needs to be added to the claim that symbols have a constant meaning, and that repression makes use of already existing symbols.

The combination of the broad (metaphorical) and the narrow usage

Finally, Freud continues to treat symbolism both from a broad perspective and more narrowly, sometimes combining the two approaches in a single interpretation. For example: 'A man dreamt that he was an officer sitting at a table opposite the Emperor. This meant that he was putting himself in opposition to his father' (1914a, p. 409). In this example, the Emperor = father is the stock universal symbol, while 'sitting opposite' is interpreted metaphorically, along the lines suggested by the mechanism of symbolization in hysteria (but without the conversion of the meaning into a physical symptom). The broader approach, which identifies symbolism with unconscious substitution, is also supported in Freud's paper, 'Some reflections on schoolboy psychology' (1914b), in which he argues that a child's emotional attitudes to other people are based on his or her feelings towards his parents and siblings – 'All those whom he gets to know later become substitute figures for these first objects of his feelings' (1914b, p. 243).

The history of the psychoanalytic movement

Probably the most important single publication of 1914 was Freud's 'On the history of the psycho-analytic movement', which deals with, among other topics, two important aspects of the Freudian treatment of symbolism. This paper was written in large part to make explicit Freud's disagreements with Adler and Jung, and it contains Freud's account of the discovery and development of the field of symbolism, and his reasons for rejecting Jung's approach to symbolism.

The discovery of the importance of symbolism

According to Freud, the recognition of the true importance of symbolism came relatively late in the development of psychoanalysis, because Freud himself was held back by the discovery of, and subsequent reliance on, the technique of free-association, a technique which does not help in the case of symbolism. Thus:

> it followed that the *symbolism* in the language of dreams was almost the last thing to become accessible to me, for the dreamer's associations help very little towards understanding symbols. I have held fast to the habit of always studying things themselves before looking for information about them in books, and therefore I was able to establish the symbolism of dreams for myself before I was led to it by Scherner's work on the subject [1861]. It was only later that I came to appreciate to its full extent this mode of expression of dreams. This was partly through the influence of the works of Stekel, who at first did such very creditable work but afterwards went totally astray. (1914c, p. 19)

I pointed out before that this assessment is true only if the FN view is 'the' Freudian theory of symbolism, as Freud himself is implying here. Earlier, Freud had a great deal to say about symbolism, but it was in the FB context, in which he took pains to distance his own theory of symbolism in dreams from the arbitrary decoding method of the ancients. Now, however, in his readiness to draw parallels, Freud closes the gap between his (FN) approach and the approaches which he had initially strongly rejected: 'The close connection between psycho-analytic dream-interpretation and the art of interpreting dreams as practised and held in such high esteem in antiquity only became clear to me much later' (1914c, pp. 19–20). Freud then identifies symbolism as central in the spread of psychoanalysis to the normal mind and to other mental products such as myths, fairy tales, etc.: 'Further investigation into dream-symbolism led to the heart of the problems of mythology, folklore . . . and the abstractions of religion' (ibid., p. 36).

Freud's rejection of Jung's approach

This paper also contains the famous polemic against Jung's 'anagogic' or 'progressive' approach to the interpretation of symbols. In directing his attack both at Jung's rejection of the Freudian treatment of sexuality and repression, and at Jung's attempt to contrast what is 'symbolic' with what is 'real', important aspects of Freud's own (FB) theory of symbolism are revealed.

Freud argues that there is no support for Jung's views, which are obviously motivated by a desire to eliminate from psychoanalytic theory that which is objectionable to so many of its critics – the focus on sexuality. Jung and his followers are behaving like the *parvenu* who boasts of being descended from a distant noble family, and, when faced with the evidence that his parents live somewhere locally and are quite humble people, insists that they are of noble lineage but have come down in the world. Thus, for Jung:

If ethics and religion were not allowed to be sexualized but had to be something 'higher' from the start, and if nevertheless the ideas contained in them seemed undeniably to be descended from the Oedipus and family-complex, there could be only one way out: it must be that from the very first these complexes themselves do not mean what they seem to be expressing, but bear the higher 'anagogic' meaning (as Silberer calls it) . . .

All the changes that Jung has proposed to make in psycho-analysis flow from his intention to eliminate what is objectionable in the family complexes, so as not to find it again in religion and ethics. (1914c, p. 62)

The result is that in Jung's hands:

the Oedipus complex has merely a 'symbolic' meaning: the mother in it means the unattainable, which must be renounced in the interests of civilization; the father who is killed in the Oedipus myth is the 'inner' father, from whom one must set oneself free in order to become independent . . . The truth is that these people have picked out a few cultural overtones from the symphony of life and have once more failed to hear the mighty and primordial melody of the instincts. (ibid., p. 62)

Although Freud does not elaborate on his last point here, there are clear indications of the nature of his own theoretical commitments concerning what is 'symbolic' – in particular, that the justification of the symbolised is to be founded on a theory of the distinction between what is 'primary' and what is 'derivative', and on the ways in which these two are related. This is supported by his claim that part of Jung's error lies in his rejection of the Freudian unconscious and of repression:

When Jung tells us that the incest-complex is merely 'symbolic', that after all it has no 'real' existence, that after all a savage feels no desire towards an old hag but prefers a young and pretty woman, we are tempted to conclude that 'symbolic' and 'without real existence' simply mean something which, in virtue of its manifestations and pathogenic effects, is described by psychoanalysis as 'existing unconsciously'. (ibid., p. 64)

In other words, Jung's denial of the 'reality' of the 'symbolic' amounts, on examination, simply to a denial of the reality of the unconscious. His confusion, according to Freud, arises from the false contrast between 'symbolic' and 'real' – 'The opposites', Freud wrote to Jung, 'are actually fantastic-real, not symbolic-real' (in Forrester 1980, p. 101).

Another of Jung's errors, according to Freud, is his rejection of the Freudian concept of sexuality. In Freud's response, the nature of the contingent connection in his own theory between symbolism and sexuality is highlighted. For instance, he accuses Jung and Adler of playing down sexuality in much the same way as had Breuer, who claimed, for example, that the element of sexuality was undeveloped in Anna O. However:

Anyone who reads the history of Breuer's case now in the light of the knowledge gained in the last twenty years will at once perceive the symbolism in it – the snakes, the stiffening, the paralysis of the arm – and, on taking into account the situation at the bedside of the young woman's sick father, will easily guess the real interpretation of her symptoms. (1914c, pp. 11–12)

Of course, Freud's concern here is to point to the unmistakable role of sexuality, but it is significant that he appeals to the context of Anna O.'s symptoms for his interpretation of the symbolism in them. And this context includes the existence of repression, another concept now rejected by Jung. 'The theory of repression', says Freud, 'is the cornerstone on which the whole structure of psycho-analysis rests' (ibid., p. 16).

Continuation of FB themes

Other writings produced by Freud during the years 1914–16 reveal a continuation of the FB schema, particularly in the assimilation of symbolism and 'substitutive formation', and in the connection between 'symbolic' and 'symptomatic'.

To begin with, some symbols are formed during the individual's early life. Jones (1955) reports that in an unpublished 1914 paper, 'A case of foot fetishism', Freud gives some background details to the case, and then comments: 'The perversion was evidently fixed by his seventh year, when he fell in love with his governess's foot. By then it had acquired the symbolic meaning of a male genital organ' (in Jones 1955, p. 343).

Then, in 1915, Freud published three of the five 'metapsychological' papers which he had written in that year (the other two were published in 1917). These papers were orginally intended to form a book which would provide the theoretical foundations of psychoanalysis. Each contains further supporting material for the FB theory, particularly in the notion of the symbol as defensively formed substitute, in which 'substitutive formations' are treated as 'symbols'. In 'Instincts and their vicissitudes' (1915a), Freud emphasises the mobility and lability of the instinctual drives (especially the component sexual instincts), characteristics which enable them to find satisfaction in substitute objects. In 'Repression' (1915b), Freud observes that the patient's 'associations' are simply derivations from the repressed unconscious which 'in consequence either of their remoteness or of their distortion, can pass the censorship of the conscious' (1915b, pp. 149–50), and he goes on to point to the variable amount of distortion necessary, an aspect which he has on a number of earlier occasions connected to the variable degree of obscurity in symbolism. Freud also suggests that any substitutive formation (such as the symptom in anxiety hysteria, or the phobic animal object (the wolf in the case of the Wolf Man) which replaces the father) 'has come about by *displacement* along a chain of connections' (ibid., p. 155).

These points are developed more extensively in 'The unconscious' (1915c). Again, symbols are individually formed substitutive formations which are derivatives of the 'system *Ucs.*'. Freud introduces his notion of the 'systematic' unconscious (as compared with the 'descriptive' unconscious), according to which certain ideas etc. are characterised by 'inclusion in particular systems and possession of certain characteristics' (1915c, p. 172). The characteristics of this 'system *Ucs.*' are: absence of negation, exemption from mutual contradiction, primary process (mobility of cathexes), timelessness, and replacement of external by psychical reality. However, despite these distinctive characteristics, the unconscious is also 'continued into what are known as its derivatives' (1915c, p. 190), which may be highly organised, free from self-contradiction, and so on. Symbolism falls into this category – but the connection is provided indirectly. Freud begins by characterising substitutive formations: 'Substitutive formations, too, are highly organized derivatives of the *Ucs.* of this kind; but they succeed in breaking through into consciousness when circumstances are favourable' (ibid., p. 191).

Against this background, Freud treats 'symbol' and 'substitutive formation' interchangeably. He assimilates the concept of symbolism to the substitutive formations of hysteria, obsessional neurosis, and schizophrenia, arguing that schizophrenics employ symbols in a peculiar way. He alludes to a current schizophrenic patient of his, who is 'playing out his castration complex upon his skin' (ibid., p. 199), by persistently squeezing out all the blackheads on his face, first experiencing satisfaction at the squirting out, and then feeling punished by the cavities which he has created:

Pressing out the contents of the blackheads is clearly to him a substitute for masturbation. The cavity which then appears owing to his fault is the female genital, i.e. the fulfilment of the threat of castration . . . This substitutive formation has, in spite of its hypochondriacal character, considerable resemblance to a hysterical conversion. (ibid., p. 200)

Yet, Freud goes on, there is an important distinction between symbolism in hysteria and symbolism in schizophrenia:

and yet we have a feeling that something different must be going on here, that a substitutive formation such as this cannot be attributed to hysteria, even before we can say in what the difference consists. A tiny little cavity such as a pore of the skin would hardly be used by a hysteric as a symbol for the vagina, which he is otherwise ready to compare with every imaginable object that encloses a hollow space. Besides, we should expect the multiplicity of these little cavities to prevent him from using them as a substitute for the female genital. (ibid.)

A similar example, Freud continues, can be seen in one of Tausk's apparently obsessional patients, who was disturbed at the prospect of pulling apart the stitches in his stockings: 'the holes, and to him every hole was a symbol of the female genital aperture. This again is a thing which we cannot attribute to an obsessional neurotic' (ibid., p. 200).

Having established the general (FB) equation of 'symbol' and 'substitutive formation', Freud then appeals to one of the FB themes to provide the solution to the mystery of the difference between schizophrenia and other types of pathology in the use of symbolism. The solution lies in the role of language:

If we ask ourselves what it is that gives the character of strangeness to the substitutive formation and the symptom in schizophrenia, we eventually come to realize that it is the predominance of what has to do with words over what has to do with things. As far as the thing goes, there is only a very slight similarity between squeezing out a blackhead and an emission from the penis, and still less similarity between the innumerable shallow pores of the skin and the vagina; but in the former case there is, in both instances, a 'spurting out', while in the latter the cynical saying 'a hole is a hole', is true verbally. What has dictated the substitution is not the resemblance between the things denoted but the sameness of the words used to express them. Where the two – word and thing – do not coincide, the formation of substitutes in schizophrenia deviates from that in the transference neuroses. (ibid., pp. 200–1)

Although the examples themselves are not very convincing, Freud is pointing to a commonly observed characteristic of schizophrenic thinking – its confusion of words and things. His last comment is well illustrated by an example from Hanna Segal (1950), whose schizophrenic patient one day brought in a canvas stool and offered it to her with great embarrassment, behaving 'as if he had offered me an actual faecal stool. It was not merely a symbolic expression of his wish to bring me his stool. He felt that he had actually offered it to me' (Segal 1950, p. 269).

Symbols and symptoms are almost as closely interconnected in the FB theory as are symbols and substitutive formations; Freud often describes a symptom as symbolic in itself, as well as being built up out of separate symbols. In a short paper 'A connection between a symbol and a symptom' (1916a), Freud discusses the 'symptom', common among obsessionals, of waiting for an acquaintance met in the street to be the first to raise his hat. Using the symbolic equation hat = head = penis, Freud brings this into connection with another 'symptom' – the horror of beheading:

Experience in the analysis of dreams has sufficiently well established the hat as a symbol of the genital organ, most frequently of the male organ. It cannot be said, however, that the symbol is an intelligible one. In phantasies and in numerous symptoms, the head too appears as a symbol of the male genitals, or, if one prefers to put it so, as something standing for them. (1916a, p. 339)

It may be that the symbolic meaning of the hat is derived from that of the head, in so far as a hat can be regarded as a prolonged, though detachable, head. (ibid., pp. 339–40)

The horror of beheading, then, comes from 'treating being beheaded as a substitute for being castrated' (ibid., p. 339), and in the obsessive symptom of waiting for the other's hat to be raised first, 'the source of this excess of feeling might easily be found in its relation to the castration complex' (ibid., p. 340).

The *Introductory Lectures on Psycho-Analysis*

These lectures were delivered by Freud in two successive winter terms (1915–16 and 1916–17), and were published in 1916/17. Although the tenth lecture is devoted entirely to symbolism, there are scattered comments on symbolism throughout the others. The material is a mixture of FB and FN themes; in the case of the latter, which have now become relatively prominent, the comments in which Freud expresses his own reservations and uncertainties often show the way to an assimilation of the FN into the FB theory.

In the second lecture, on parapraxes, Freud harks back to his now familiar emphasis on the psychical significance of opposites, which has formed the basis earlier for a number of interpretations of symbols:

The most usual, and at the same time the most striking kind of slips of the tongue . . . are those in which one says the precise opposite of what one intended to say. Here . . . we can appeal to the fact that contraries have a strong conceptual kinship with each other and stand in a particularly close psychological association with each other. (1916/17, pp. 33–4)

Notably, however, the focus here is on the broader conceptual or psychological kinship of opposites, as contrasted with the emphasis earlier on the linguistic kinship.

In the sixth lecture, Freud mentions once again the failure of the dreamer's associations in the case of symbols, but his account is more suggestive here:

When the dreamer is questioned about the separate elements of the dream he may reply that nothing occurs to him. There are some instances in which we let this reply pass, and you will later hear which these are; strangely enough, they are instances in which definite ideas may occur to us ourselves. But in general, if the dreamer asserts that nothing occurs to him we contradict him; we bring urgent pressure to bear on him, we insist that something must occur to him – and we turn out to be right. He will produce an idea – some idea, it is a matter of indifference to us which. (ibid., p. 105)

Now, a number of significant points emerge from this passage. Firstly, the failure of associations is not a response restricted to symbols; it is a more general response, resulting, as Freud tells us elsewhere, from the censorship and resistance. Such resistance may be overcome by the persistence of the analyst. Secondly, in the case of symbols, it is not that the analyst tries, and fails, to overcome the resistance; rather, he does not attempt to do so, since he recognises the elements as symbols and understands their meanings without needing to bother to collect the dreamer's associations – 'we let this reply pass', says Freud. Thus the status of the dreamer's associations to symbols is no different from the status of the associations to other material against which the dreamer is defending – they are initially not forthcoming. What this passage suggests is something which Freud has hinted at on earlier occasions – that the interpreter can bypass the troublesome task of collecting and interpreting associations in those cases where the meaning (the 'translation') of the material is obvious because it has been confirmed so often elsewhere.

In the FB theory, resistance and the failure of associations are also connected to the degree of obscurity in the choice of symbol (i.e., the obscurity of the *tertium comparationis*). In the seventh lecture, when discussing the 'latent' and 'manifest' contents of the dream, Freud reiterates his earlier suggestions that the 'sliding scale' of clarity/opaqueness in symbolism is a result of the strength of the repression involved: 'If the resistance is small, the substitute cannot be far distant from the unconscious material; but a greater resistance means that the unconscious material will be greatly distorted and that the path will be a long one from the substitute back to the unconscious material' (1916/17, p. 117).

In this lecture, also, Freud adumbrates his identification of symbolism as a 'fourth kind of relation between the manifest and the latent elements, which I must continue to hold back from you until we come upon its key-word in considering technique' (ibid., p. 122). This separates symbolism from the relations of part-to-whole, allusion and plastic portrayal. But, as will be seen, Freud is unable to maintain that separation consistently.

Lecture X: symbolism in dreams

According to Strachey, 'the present lecture has claims to being regarded as the most important of all Freud's writings on symbolism' (n. in Freud 1916/17, p. 149). Because this lecture is devoted entirely to symbolism, and contains Freud's most explicitly developed discussion of the topic, it is naturally the work to which anyone dealing with the Freudian theory of symbolism immediately turns. The lecture certainly contains statements of the FN theory, but also, significantly, of the FB theory.

Freud begins by commenting that censorship is not the sole factor responsible for the distortion in dreams, so that 'even if the dream cen-

sorship was out of action we should still not be in a position to understand dreams' (1916/17, p. 149). We discover what is responsible for
this when we are faced with the failure of associations:

it does sometimes really happen that nothing occurs to a person under analysis
in response to particular elements in his dream. It is true that this does not
happen as often as he asserts; in a great many cases, with perseverance, an idea
is extracted from him. But nevertheless there remain cases in which an association fails to emerge. (ibid., p.149)

Freud goes on to suggest that sometimes, during analysis, this is the
result of resistance from unconscious transference, but that this failure
of associations also occurs in the interpretation of normal people's
dreams: 'If we convince ourselves that in such cases no amount of pressure is of any use, we eventually discover that this unwished-for event
regularly occurs in connection with particular dream elements' (ibid.,
p. 150).

Clearly, Freud has become more committed now, suggesting that
symbols are identified only after pressure and insistence have been tried,
and have failed. Despite this commitment, nowhere in Freud's writings
is there a single illustration of the phenomenon which he is describing
here: instead, typically, symbolic interpretations either follow the collection of associations, or, in those cases where the meaning of the symbol
is thought to be beyond dispute, are simply given without bothering
with associations. Freud continues: 'we are tempted to interpret these
"mute" dream-elements ourselves, to set about translating them with
our own resources' (ibid.). We are justified in such a move by two facts:
firstly, when we do this, we find that the dream 'makes sense' where it
would otherwise have been senseless; also:

An accumulation of many similar cases eventually gives the necessary certainty
to what began as a timid experiment . . . In this way we obtain constant translations for a number of dream-elements – just as popular 'dream-books' provide
them for *everything* that appears in dreams. You will not have forgotten, of
course, that when we use our *associative* technique constant replacements of
dream elements never come to light. (ibid.)

Freud immediately anticipates that this will appear arbitrary and
insecure (in contrast with interpretations made from using free
associations). He reassures his audience with the promise that it will
soon become clear that we already know the meanings of these elements
from other sources – which is his familiar, standard response to the
charge of arbitrariness.

Freud then gives a summary statement of the second distinctive
characteristic of symbols in the FN view:

A constant relation of this kind between a dream-element and its translation is described by us as a 'symbolic' one, and the dream-element itself as a 'symbol' of the unconscious dream-thought. (1916/17, p. 150)

Therefore:

Symbolism is perhaps the most remarkable chapter of the theory of dreams. In the first place, since symbols are stable translations, they realize to some extent the ideal of the ancient as well as of the popular interpretation of dreams, from which, with our technique, we had departed widely. They allow us in certain circumstances to interpret a dream without questioning the dreamer, who indeed would in any case have nothing to tell us about the symbol. (ibid., p. 151)

Freud has now identified two of the distinctive characteristics of symbols in the FN view. However, just as, in the case of muteness, he fails to provide convincing evidence or arguments in favour of the claim that a dreamer would not (under any conditions) have associations to symbols, so there is no convincing support for this second characteristic. Freud offers no reasons for his suddenly restricting the term 'symbol' to those elements which he has hitherto identified as 'universally occurring symbols', nor does he give any indication that all previous discussion of individual symbols and individual variations in universal symbols must now be ignored, or, at least, that the terms 'symbol' and 'symbolic' are no longer to be applied in those cases. In fact, Freud seems to sense the weakness of his position, and finds it necessary to emphasise the subordinate nature of the translation of symbols as a dream-interpretation technique: 'Interpretation based on a knowledge of symbols is not a technique which can replace or compete with the associative one. It forms a supplement to the latter and yields results which are only of use when introduced into it' (ibid.). Freud then comments on the opposition to his theory of symbolism:

it is quite specially remarkable . . . that the most violent resistances have been expressed once again to the existence of a symbolic relation between dreams and the unconscious. Even people of judgement and reputation, who, apart from this, have gone a long way in agreeing with psycho-analysis, have at this point withheld their support' (ibid., pp. 151–2)

Of course, if Freud is now referring to the narrow FN approach to symbolism, then the 'resistance' is understandable and anything but 'quite specially remarkable'. Although he must have been aware of the reasons for the criticisms, instead of acknowledging these, he answers them in his usual way:

This behaviour is all the stranger in view, first, of the fact that symbolism is not peculiar to dreams alone and is not characteristic of them, and, secondly, that

symbolism in dreams is by no means a discovery of psycho-analysis, however
many surprising discoveries it has made. (1916/17, p. 152)

Before launching into a more detailed discussion of symbolism, Freud
admits 'I must confess that our understanding of it does not go as far
as we should like' (ibid.). His uncertainty, and his failure to mark off
clearly this apparent fourth relation between latent and manifest content, are all evident in what follows: 'The essence of this symbolic
relation is that it is a comparison, though not a comparison of any sort.
Special limitations seem to be attached to the comparison, but it is hard
to say what these are' (ibid.). Freud is almost as silent on these 'special
limitations' as he was earlier on the 'all kinds of reasons' which prevent
us from classifying symbolism together with other forms of indirect representation. He does suggest, however, that not everything is symbolised, and not everything appears as a symbol. He continues: 'We
must admit, too, that the concept of a symbol cannot at present be
sharply delimited: it shades off into such notions as those of a replacement or representation, and even approaches that of an allusion' (ibid.).
   If this is true, then 'symbolic' as a particular relation between manifest
and latent content is not clearly separate from one of the other three
nominated relations, that of 'allusion'. Also, Freud is hinting that the
difficulties in demarcating symbolism are but temporary; it cannot be
sharply delimited 'at present', he says, implying that time will clear up
this 'problem'. He then attempts, once again, to locate the uniqueness
of the symbolic relation in its 'muteness':

With a number of symbols the comparison which underlies them is obvious.
But again there are other symbols in regard to which we must ask ourselves
where we are to look for the common element, the *tertium comparationis*, of the
supposed comparison ... It is strange, moreover, that if a symbol is a comparison it should not be brought to light by an association, and that the dreamer
should not be acquainted with it but should make use of it without knowing
about it: more than that, indeed, that the dreamer feels no inclination to
acknowledge the comparison even after it has been pointed out to him. You
see, then, that a symbolic relation is a comparison of a quite special kind, of
which we do not as yet clearly grasp the basis. (1916/17, pp. 152–3)

This passage contains a notable addition to Freud's argument. What
makes the symbolic relation 'a comparison of a quite special kind' is
not just the obscurity of the *tertium comparationis* in some cases, but the
curious fact that the dreamer is not 'acquainted with' the symbol, uses
it 'without knowing about it'. Of course, the meaning of the symbol is
unconscious, since it would not serve its purpose if it were conscious;
but, in view of the wealth of earlier material in which Freud has been
quite willing to acknowledge the existence and causal efficacy of uncon-

scious processes, it is significant that he expresses discomfort at the possibility of unconscious knowledge of symbols. The reasons for Freud's discomfort will become clear shortly.

For the time being, Freud's attention turns to a consideration of the discrepancy between the number of things which are typically symbolised and the number of symbols for them: 'The range of things which are given symbolic representation in dreams is not very wide: the human body as a whole, parents, children, brothers and sisters, birth, death, nakedness – and something else besides' (ibid., p. 153). Here follows a list of some of Freud's most familiar universal symbols. Then:

there is another field in which the objects and topics are represented with an extraordinarily rich symbolism. This field is that of sexual life . . . . The very great majority of symbols in dreams are sexual symbols. And here a strange disproportion is revealed. The topics I have mentioned are few, but the symbols for them are extremely numerous, so that each of these things can be expressed by numbers of almost equivalent symbols. The outcome, when they are interpreted, gives rise to general objection. For, in contrast to the multiplicity of the representations in the dream, the interpretations of the symbols are very monotonous, and this displeases everyone who hears of it; but what is there that we can do about it? (ibid., pp. 153–4)

The answer, obviously, is to provide a theory which explains this 'strange disproportion' by justifying the claims that what is symbolised is primary, and that the small number of primary objects, through repression and unavailability, are represented during development by an ever-widening range of substitutes. This is exactly what Freud does provide, although not explicitly. It is tempting to conclude that he did not recognise the significance of his general theory for his specific theory of symbolism, and this conclusion is supported by the fact that Freud's own response to the problem was to attempt repeatedly to ground his symbols in linguistic parallels.

Freud then presents an extensive list of common symbols, together with elaboration on the *tertium comparationis* in a number of cases; for example, the most striking sexual symbols are the ones in which the shared feature is shape, then function, and so on. Even in the case of symbols whose meanings are obscure, 'where the common element in the comparison is not understood' (1916/17, p. 157), Freud attempts to identify and give an explanation of the *tertium comparationis*, often appealing to the obvious basis of the comparison. The staircase crops up again here: '*Ladders, steps* and *staircases*, or, more precisely, walking on them, are clear symbols of sexual intercourse. On reflection, it will occur to us that the common element here is the rhythm of walking up them – perhaps, too, the increasing excitement and breathlessnesss the higher one climbs' (ibid., p. 158).

Having introduced the apparently obscure symbols, Freud then moves on to the question of how 'we in fact come to know the meaning of these dream-symbols, upon which the dreamer himself gives us insufficient information or none at all' (ibid.). The answer (by now familiar), which is to meet any criticism of arbitrariness, is:

> that we learn it from very different sources – from fairy tales and myths, from buffoonery and jokes, from folklore (that is, from knowledge about popular manners and customs, sayings and songs) and from poetic and colloquial linguistic usage. In all these directions we come upon the same symbolism, and in some of them we can understand it without further instruction. If we go into these sources in detail, we shall find so many parallels to dream-symbolism that we cannot fail to be convinced of our interpretations. (ibid., pp. 158–9)

Freud gives numerous examples, calling on converging evidence from mythology, philology, jokes, slang, etc., and emphasising that, in view of the obvious connection between psychoanalysis and these areas, there is a need for contributions from the experts: 'you may imagine how much richer and more interesting a collection like this would be if it were brought together, not by amateurs like us, but by real professionals in mythology, anthropology, philology and folklore' (ibid., p. 165).

He then turns to the important question of the ontogenesis of symbolism, once again remarking on the mysterious unconscious nature of the dreamer's knowledge of symbols. This time, however, Freud attempts to explain his discomfort:

> In the first place we are faced by the fact that the dreamer has a symbolic mode of expression at his disposal which he does not know in waking life and does not recognise. This is as extraordinary as if you were to discover that your housemaid understood Sanskrit, though you know that she was born in a Bohemian village and never learnt it. It is not easy to account for this fact by the help of our psychological views. We can only say that the knowledge of symbolism is unconscious to the dreamer, that it belongs to his unconscious mental life. But even with this assumption we do not meet the point. *Hitherto it has only been necessary for us to assume the existence of unconscious endeavours –* endeavours, that is, of which, temporarily or permanently, we know nothing. *Now, however, it is a question of more than this, of unconscious pieces of knowledge,* of connections of thought, of comparisons between different objects which result in its being possible for one of them to be regularly put in place of the other. These comparisons are not freshly made on each occasion; they lie ready to hand, and are complete, once and for all. This is implied by the fact of their agreeing in the case of different individuals – possibly, indeed, agreeing in spite of differences of language. (1916/17, p. 165, italics mine)

There are a number of interesting points in this passage. Symbolism is like a language, but one which, curiously, the dreamer has not learned. Knowledge of the language is unconscious, but this, according to Freud, is more problematic than unconscious 'endeavours' (presumably, wishes and impulses). Despite the fact that Freud earlier referred to unconscious psychical conflict as leaving the patient 'in the peculiar state of knowing and at the same time not knowing' (1895a, p. 165), here, unconscious *knowledge* presents a problem. If we put these two together, as Freud himself does, then Freud's concern about the problematic nature of the unconscious knowledge of symbolism can be explained as a result of the confusion generated by his over-extension of the analogy between symbolism and language. A more detailed analysis of this confusion is presented later (in Chapter 8), but it might be noted here that it is based on two factors: firstly, Freud's failure to recognise the implications of the difference between a conventional symbolic system such as language, and non-conventional symbolism such as appears in dreams, myths, etc.; and, secondly, Freud's use of 'learned' in the sense of 'acquired via instruction', which is appropriate in the case of language, rather than in the more general sense of 'acquired as a result of experience', which encompasses also the formation of non-conventional symbols.

In his misguided belief that appeals to language are the best way to avoid the potential arbitrariness of the translation of symbols, Freud frequently over-extends the analogy between symbolism and language. This leads him into some bad theorising. To begin with, the occurrence of symbols in many different areas is taken as evidence for their belonging to a universal, archaic language:

The multiplicity of parallels in other spheres of knowledge are mostly unknown to the dreamer . . . these symbolic relations are not something peculiar to dreamers or to the dream-work . . . This same symbolism, as we have seen, is employed by myths and fairy tales, by the people in their sayings and songs, by colloquial linguistic usage and by the poetic imagination. The field of symbolism is immensely wide, and dream-symbolism is only a small part of it: indeed, it serves no useful purpose to attack the whole problem from the direction of dreams. Many symbols which are commonly used elsewhere appear in dreams very seldom or not at all. Some dream symbols are not to be found in all other fields but only, as you have seen, here and there. One gets the impression that what we are faced with here is an ancient but extinct mode of expression of which different pieces have survived in different fields, one piece only here, another only there, a third, perhaps, in slightly modified forms in several fields. And here I recall the phantasy of an interesting psychotic patient [Schreber], who imagined a 'basic language' of which all these symbolic relations would be residues. (1916/17, p. 166)

The next, curious, observation which Freud makes is that symbols in these other areas are not as exclusively sexual as they are in dreams. The introduction of this point seems to be made so that Freud can then launch into a discussion supporting the philologist Sperber's (1912) theory of the sexual origins of language: original sounds were made to summon the sexual partner; then words enunciated during work denoted sexual acts, so that work was thereby made acceptable. Finally, this is brought into connection with dreams:

> If the hypothesis I have here sketched out is correct, it would give us a possibility of understanding dream-symbolism. We should understand why dreams, which preserve something of the earliest conditions, have such an extraordinarily large number of sexual symbols, and why, in general, weapons and tools always stand for what is male, while materials and things that are worked upon stand for what is female. The symbolic relation would be the residue of an ancient verbal identity; things which were once called by the same name as the genitals could now serve as symbols for them in dreams. (1916/17, p. 167)

It is surprising that Freud feels that there is a need for Sperber's speculations in order to justify both the predominance of sexual symbols, and the particular things chosen as symbols. In addition, if dreams are now to be identified as more primitive and archaic than myths, folklore, fairy tales, and so on, then the parallelism on which the notion of converging evidence has hitherto been based is lost. Freud clearly believes that connecting symbolism with Sperber's philological thesis, via the notion of a 'primal language', forges links between psychoanalysis and mythology, philology, folklore, social psychology and religion. This contrasts with earlier discussions of the dream's 'preserving something of the earliest conditions', in which the reference was seemingly to childhood, rather than to the infancy of the human species.

Finally, Freud returns to the earlier claim that, even without the censorship, the dream would not be easily intelligible because of the presence of symbols:

> Thus symbolism is a second and independent factor in the distortion of dreams, alongside of the dream-censorship. It is plausible to suppose, however, that the dream-censorship finds it convenient to make use of symbolism, since it leads towards the same end – the strangeness and incomprehensibility of dreams. (ibid., p. 168)

What is of interest here is the relationship between the incomprehensibility of dreams, the use of symbolism, and the dream censorship. The use of symbolism makes sense if the aim is disguise, and that indeed is the aim of the censorship. While the censorship may not necessarily create the symbols, in the sense of being responsible for the original comparison, it certainly would not make sense for symbols to appear where there is no need for disguise. Thus far, Freud has not provided supportive evidence for his claim that, even without the censorship, symbols would appear in dreams, and that the dreams would consequently be obscure (in fact, in his examples of straightforward, undisguised dreams, there are no symbols). Without censorship, there would be no justification for the presence of symbols. Freud's account would hardly be more acceptable than Scherner's, which Freud himself rejects precisely on this basis, that there is no 'utilitarian function' attached to dreams. Freud appears to feel constrained to make these claims in order to underscore the independence of symbolism from the rest of the dream-work, its *a priori* existence in the unconscious, and its connection with the manifestations of the 'language of the unconscious' in many other areas.

In summary, this lecture, generally regarded as a *tour de force* on symbolism, is a mixture of FN and FB views, in which the confusions and weaknesses of Freud's arguments have tended to go unrecognised, masked perhaps by the interesting content and by Freud's persuasive style.

Additional support for FB themes from the remaining lectures

In Lecture XI, Freud identifies the two complementary techniques of dream interpretation as (i) 'calling up ideas that occur to the dreamer till you have penetrated from the substitute to the genuine thing', and (ii) 'on the ground of your own knowledge, replacing the symbols by what they mean' (1916/17, p. 170). Given that the words 'symbol' and 'substitute' are so often used interchangeably in Freud's writings, these instructions, in the FB theory of symbolism, may be combined into: 'use the dreamer's associations to penetrate to the meaning of the substitute, unless that substitute is one of the typical, universal ones, whose meaning has been confirmed by converging evidence from other sources – in which case you may tentatively assume that meaning, provided that it fits with the dreamer's associations, other contextual material, and so on. And be prepared, always, to change the interpretation.' These are the instructions, indeed, which would be derived by anyone who simply reads Freud's own case studies and observes his *modus operandi*.

In Lecture XII, Freud presents analyses of some sample dreams, in which he restricts his analyses to parts of dreams, saying that 'easiest to demonstrate are dream symbols and, after them, some characteristics of the regressive representation in dreams' (1916/17, p. 185). On one occasion, Freud ponders: 'Where could there possibly be a *tertium comparationis* between the tooth and his father, to make the condensation possible?' (ibid., p. 188). Not only is the tooth = father equation not a case of universal symbolism, but also the technical term for the element of comparison, typically associated with symbolism, is here explicitly associated with the mechanism of condensation. By this stage, Freud is so confident about symbolism that he expressly uses the 'piling up' of symbolic interpretations as persuasive evidence for other aspects of the theory:

I have a particular reason for piling up instances of the use of symbols in dreams . . . the different theses of psycho-analysis are so intimately connected that conviction can easily be carried over from a single point to a larger part of the whole . . . No one, even, who has accepted the explanation of parapraxes can logically withhold his belief from all the rest. A second, equally accessible position is offered by dream-symbolism. (ibid., p. 193)

This seems to be simply an example of Freud's ingenuity: since psychoanalytic pronouncements on symbolism have met with such criticism and resistance, why not boldly assume the opposite, and appeal to the irresistibly incontrovertible evidence of symbolism as able to extend its persuasive power to other aspects of psychoanalytic theory!

But Freud's vacillation on the theme of symbolism is still evident. In Lecture XV, 'Uncertainties and criticisms', he returns to anticipating, once again, the charge of arbitrariness:

You will argue . . . that in the first place one never knows whether a particular element of the dream is to be understood in its actual sense or as a symbol, since the things employed as symbols do not cease on that account to be themselves. If, however, one has no objective clue for deciding this, the interpretation must at that point be left to the arbitrary choice of the interpreter. (ibid., p. 228)

However:

What in other ways gives an impression of arbitrariness – in for instance, the interpretations of symbols – is done away with by the fact that as a rule the interconnection between the dream-thoughts, or the connection between the dream and the dreamer's life, or the whole psychical situation in which the dream occurs, selects a single one from among the possible determinations presented and dismisses the rest as unserviceable. (ibid., p. 229)

The implication here is that the symbol is not immune from the need to be closely interconnected with its context. Needless to say, Freud continues, the interpretation of symbols still requires skill, and if such skill is absent, the technique may, of course, be abused. But this is a potential problem for any scientific endeavour. Then, without mentioning symbolism explicitly, but in the context of the formation of 'substitutive structures', Freud identifies displacement as:

the most powerful instrument of the dream-censorship. With the help of displacement the dream-censorship creates substitutive structures which we have described as allusions. But they are allusions which are not easily recognizable as such, from which the path back to the genuine thing is not easily traced, and which are connected with the genuine thing by the strangest, most unusual, external associations. In all these cases it is a question, however, of things which are *meant* to be hidden, which are condemned to concealment, for that is what the dream censorship is aiming at. (ibid., p. 233)

This passage is not out of place as a description of the major theme in the FB schema, that of the symbol as defensively produced substitute via the CRS formula.

The FB themes are continued. In Lecture XVII, 'The sense of symptoms', Freud appeals to knowledge of dream symbolism as providing support for his interpretation of an obsessional symptom:

We must agree that the bed and the sheet were replaced by the table and the tablecloth. This might seem arbitrary, but surely we have not studied dream-symbolism to no purpose. In dreams too we often find a table which has to be interpreted as a bed. Table and bed together stand for marriage, so that the one can easily take the place of the other. (ibid., p. 262)

In another case, Freud confirms both a connection between symbolism and associations, and a variability in the symbol's meaning, which contradicts the FN theory. Having collected the patient's associations, he offers various interpretations, with the result that:

Our patient gradually came to learn that it was as symbols of the female genitals that clothes were banished from her equipment for the night. Clocks and watches – though elsewhere we have found other symbolic interpretations for them – have arrived at a genital role owing to their relation to periodic processes and equal intervals of time . . . The ticking of a clock may be compared with the knocking or throbbing in the clitoris during sexual excitement . . . Flower-pots and vases, like all vessels, are also female symbols. Taking precautions against their falling and being broken at night was thus not without its good sense. We know the widespread custom of breaking a vessel or plate at betrothal ceremonies. Each man present gets hold of a fragment, and we may regard this as a sign of his resigning the claims he had upon the bride in virtue of a marriage regulation dating from before the establishment of monogamy. In connection with this part of her ceremonial the girl produced a recollection and several associations. (ibid., pp. 266–7)

It would be hard to believe, for anyone taking the FN view seriously, that this passage occurs during the core years for that position. Here we have Freud's familiar mixed method: the interpretation of the symbols, the appeal to an ancient custom, and the return to the individual, this time with specific acknowledgement of her associations – associations which, on the FN theory, should not exist.

The question of phylogenetic inheritance

It is in Lecture XIII that Freud commits himself explicitly to the most controversial of the characteristics of symbols in the FN theory – that they are phylogenetically inherited. However, once again, Freud can be seen to vacillate on the extent of his commitment. As already mentioned, in his earlier writings it is unclear whether the term 'archaic' is meant in an ontogenetic or in a phylogenetic sense, and it is perhaps significant that the title of this lecture is 'The archaic features and infantilism of dreams'. Here, Freud treats the issue in more detail than before. Having pointed to the 'archaic' or 'regressive' mode of expression of dreams, he says:

The prehistory into which the dream-work leads us back is of two kinds – on the one hand, into the individual's prehistory, his childhood, and on the other, in so far as each individual somehow recapitulates in an abbreviated form the entire development of the human race, into phylogenetic prehistory too. Shall we succeed in distinguishing which portion of the latent mental processes is derived from the individual prehistoric period and which portion from the phylogenetic one? It is not, I believe, impossible that we shall. It seems to me, for instance, that symbolic connections, which the individual has never acquired by learning, may justly claim to be regarded as a phylogenetic heritage. (1916/17, p. 199)

Later in the same lecture Freud reinforces this idea:

the regression of the dream-work is not only a formal but also a material one. It not only translates our thoughts into a primitive form of expression; but it also revives the characteristics of our primitive mental life – the old dominance of the ego, the initial impulses of our sexual life, and even indeed, our old intellectual endowment, if symbolic connections may be regarded as such. (ibid., p. 211)

However, Freud makes no secret of the fact that such claims 'signify the beginnings of fresh enigmas and fresh doubts' (ibid.), which he examines in the later lectures.

In Lecture XVII, 'The sense of symptoms', Freud explores the parallels and differences between typical or universal symptoms (whose connection with symbols has been made on several earlier occasions), and individual ones. This material is important in the consideration of the question whether the FN theory of symbolism can be incorporated into the FB theory, or whether there is an impassable gulf between the two:

The sense of a symptom lies . . . in some connection with the patient's experience. The more individual is the form of the symptom the more reason we shall have for expecting to establish this connection . . . But there are – and they are very frequent – symptoms of quite another character. They must be described as 'typical' symptoms of an illness; they are approximately the same in all cases, individual distinctions disappear in them or at least shrink up to such an extent that it is difficult to bring them into connection with the patient's individual experience . . . The sleep ceremonial of our second patient already has much that is typical about it, though at the same time it has enough individual traits to make what I might call a 'historical' interpretation possible. But all these obsessional patients have a tendency to repeat, to make their performances rhythmical and to keep them isolated from other actions. The majority of them wash too much. Patients who suffer from agoraphobia . . . often repeat the same features in their symptoms with wearisome monotony . . . On this similar background different patients nevertheless display their individual requirements . . . In the same way, hysteria, in spite of its wealth of individual traits, has a superfluity of common, typical symptoms, which seem to resist any easy historical derivation . . . Suppose, in a case of hysteria, we have really traced a typical symptom back to an experience or a chain of similar experiences – a case of hysterical vomiting, for instance, to a series of disgusting impressions – then we are at a loss when the analysis in a similar case of vomiting reveals a series of a quite different kind of ostensibly effective experiences. It looks, then, as though for unknown reasons hysterical patients are bound to produce vomiting and as though the historical precipitating causes revealed by analysis were only pretexts which, if they happen to be there, are exploited by this internal necessity.

So we are now faced by the depressing discovery that, though we can give a satisfactory explanation of the individual neurotic symptoms by their connection with experiences, our skill leaves us in the lurch when we come to the far more frequent typical symptoms . . . I will try to console you, therefore, with the reflection that any fundamental distinction between one kind of symptom and the other is scarcely to be assumed. If the individual symptoms are so unmistakably dependent on the patient's experience, it remains possible that the typical symptoms may go back to an experience which is in itself typical – common to all human beings. (ibid., pp. 270–1)

Here, despite Freud's explicit uncertainty, he is willing to draw the stronger (FN) distinction between what is individual and what is typical, although by the end of the passage he describes the 'typical' as what is simply 'common to all human beings', which leaves open the temporal question.

In Lecture XXII, however, Freud answers that question in an FB way, suggesting that the individual and the typical are not sharply distinct. When talking of the two courses of development of the ego and the libido, he says:

both of them are at bottom heritages, abbreviated recapitulations of the development which all mankind has passed through from its primaeval days over long periods of time. In the case of the development of the libido, this *phylogenetic* origin is, I venture to think, immediately obvious . . . Among animals one can find, so to speak in petrified form, every species of perversion of the sexual organization. In the case of human beings, however, this phylogenetic point of view is partly veiled by the fact that *what is at bottom inherited is nevertheless freshly acquired in the development of the individual, probably because the same conditions which originally necessitated its acquisition persist and continue to operate upon each individual.* I should like to add that originally the operation of these conditions was creative but that it is now evocative. (1916/17, pp. 354–5, later italics mine)

Of course, it is clear that Freud is here wanting to have it both ways. But what is more important is that he himself provides a fairly sensible alternative to the phylogenetic inheritance of universal symbols: they are freshly acquired by each individual because the same conditions obtain for all individuals at all times.

Freud was at this time very much preoccupied with the notion of the recapitulation of phylogeny by ontogeny, and there are many hints of this preoccupation in the later lectures. For instance, in Lecture XXIII, he explains the monotony and universality of 'primal phantasies' (i.e., early childhood seduction phantasies) as being 'a phylogenetic endowment' (ibid., p. 371). As Strachey notes, this discussion was based largely on Freud's findings in the Wolf Man case study, which was completed two or three years earlier, but not published until 1918. When Freud did finally publish it, he added two long passages to his original draft, referring back to the present discussion. Jones comments on Freud's preoccupation with a study which he and Ferenczi were jointly undertaking on the bearing of Lamarckism on psychoanalysis. Freud sent Abraham the following summary: 'Our intention is to place Lamarck entirely on our basis and to show that his "need" which creates and transforms organs is nothing other than the power of unconscious ideas over the body, of which we see relics in hysteria' (in Jones 1955, p. 219). Again, in Lecture XXV, on the topic of anxiety, Freud says:

It must be admitted, subject to the necessary qualifications, that among the contents of phobias there are a number which, as Stanley Hall insists, are adapted to serve as objects of anxiety owing to phylogenetic inheritance. It tallies with this, indeed, that many of these anxiety-objects can only establish their connection with danger by a symbolic tie. (1916/17, p. 411)

Here Freud is reinforcing the dependence of 'symbolic' on 'phylogenetically inherited connection', something which, as will be seen, he turns to in his later writings.

Summary and conclusions

When all of Freud's material on symbolism during the 'core' years for the FN theory is considered, the picture of symbolism which emerges is very different from that which emerges when only the explicit statements of the FN position are considered. In general, three points are illustrated.

Firstly, there is a clear continuation of the broader FB schema and its themes, particularly in the continuing support for the concept of the symbol as defensively produced substitute via the CRS (conflict–repression–substitution) formula. This formula connects symbols, symptoms, and substitutive formations generally, and there are many additional indications in Freud's material (for example, in his reasons for rejecting Jung's approach) of the extent to which the theory of symbolism is not independent of the rest of the theoretical structure of psychoanalysis. Secondly, since we are now faced with the fullest exposition of the FN theory, what is revealed in Freud's material of this period is his own uncertainty on that position. To begin with, the material in which Freud identifies the three distinctive characteristics of symbols according to the FN view is embedded in the broader FB context, and thus mitigated by that context. In addition, Freud is inconsistent in his commitment to the implicit claim that the three FN characteristics are the necessary and sufficient conditions for the presence of symbolism. The more explicitly Freud commits himself to that view, the more its weakness (in terms of lack of supportive evidence or argument) is highlighted. Finally, in his reservations and expressions of uncertainty about muteness, constant meaning, and phylogenetic inheritance, and in his answers to potential objections to defining symbolism in terms of those characteristics, it is Freud himself who shows the way in which the FN theory can be assimilated into the FB theory without loss of those genuine insights which motivated the narrower view.

6   The treatment of symbolism in Freud's later writings (1918–1940)

Given the treatment of symbolism in Freud's writings leading up to, and during, the core years for the presentation of the FN theory, it is not surprising that, in his later writings, the mixture of themes which I have documented in the previous three chapters continues essentially unchanged. In particular, in spite of the relative concentration of FN statements during the years 1914 to 1917, there is no subsequent attempt by Freud to consolidate the FN theory. In this respect, the writings of the last two decades of Freud's life continue in the same vein as before, and illustrate three, by now familiar, points. Firstly, the explicit statements of the FN theory are repeated, particularly when the topic of discussion is specifically symbolism. Secondly, these statements are still accompanied by reservations and uncertainty, and there is still visible wavering on Freud's part with respect to the extent to which he is willing to commit himself to the FN position. Thirdly, the FN statements are, as usual, embedded in material which belongs to the broader FB theory, and which continues the FB schema and themes, and Freud continues to show the way to a synthesis of the two theories. The illustrations of these three points are typically to be found in scattered comments rather than in extended discussions.

On one point, however, there are notable developments: in his later writings, Freud's attention turns increasingly to the general question of the recapitulation of phylogeny by ontogeny, and to the elaboration of the theme of an 'archaic heritage'. Accordingly, of the three distinctive characteristics of symbols in the FN view, particular attention is devoted to that of phylogenetic inheritance. Not surprisingly, the development of this theme is characterised by tension, reservations, a lack of strong supportive arguments or evidence, and the same uncertainties which Freud had displayed earlier. On the one hand, he declares that symbolism is part of a phylogenetically transmitted 'archaic heritage' which is more than a mere 'predisposition' (i.e., it is inherited *content*), it is not 'learned', and it takes over where individual experience is lacking. On the other hand, he mitigates these claims by insisting that the only methodologically sound approach is to seek an ontogenetic explanation before resorting to appeals to phylogenetic inheritance, and by the weakness of the arguments which he himself offers to justify his proposed phylogenetic explanation.

The years 1918 and 1919

The Wolf Man and phylogenetic inheritance

In 1918, Freud finally published his famous case study of the 'Wolf Man' ('From the history of an infantile neurosis'), which he had written four years earlier, but whose publication had been delayed. Although, for Freud, the main significance of this case study was its confirmation (particularly welcome in the face of opposition from Adler and Jung) of infantile sexuality, the work is also significant in that, in 1918, Freud inserted two long passages on the theme of phylogenetic inheritance, in which he discusses the hypothesis of the inheritance of the mental content of primal phantasies. On the question of whether the Wolf Man's primal scene was phantasy or reality, Freud's initial response is:

These scenes of observing parental intercourse, of being seduced in childhood, and of being threatened with castration are unquestionably an inherited endowment, a phylogenetic heritage, but they may just as easily be acquired by personal experience ... All that we find in the prehistory of the neuroses is that a child catches hold of this phylogenetic experience where his own experience fails him. He fills in the gaps in individual truth with prehistoric truth; he replaces occurrences in his own life by occurrences in the life of his ancestors. I fully agree with Jung in recognising the existence of this phylogenetic heritage. (1918, p. 97)

However, Freud reiterates his earlier caution, a caution missing from Jung's account:

but I regard it as a methodological error to seize on a phylogenetic explanation before the ontogenetic possibilities have been exhausted. (ibid.)

Of course, Freud's attention here is not on the theory of symbolism, but rather on rejecting Jung's approach, in which the phylogenetic view completely replaces the ontogenetic one. It is significant, however, that Freud both recognises that phylogenetic inheritance itself requires explanation, and is prepared to locate that explanation, at least for some cases, in experience at the individual level:

I cannot see any reason for obstinately disputing the importance of infantile prehistory while at the same time freely acknowledging the importance of ancestral prehistory. Nor can I overlook the fact that phylogenetic motives and pro-

ductions themselves stand in need of elucidation, and that in quite a number
of instances this is afforded by factors in the childhood of the individual. And,
finally, I cannot feel surprised that what was originally produced by certain circumstances in prehistoric times and was then transmitted in the shape of a
predisposition to its re-acquirement should, since the same circumstances persist, emerge once more as a concrete event in the experience of the individual.
(ibid., p. 97)

Freud's notion of the inheritance of a 'predisposition' here appears to
be very similar to Jung's stance on the transmission of the so-called
'archetypes'. In response to the objection that mental contents cannot
be inherited, Jung accuses his critics of *ignoratio elenchi*, on the grounds
that it is not the archetypes or 'primordial images' *per se* which are subject to phylogenetic inheritance, but rather 'the tendency to form them'
(1964, p. 57); in fact, archetypes themselves have earlier been described
by Jung as 'living dispositions, ideas in the Platonic sense' – 'the arche-
type in itself is empty and purely formal, nothing but a *facultas praeform-
andi*, a possibility of representation which is given a priori' (1954, p.
79). There are, of course, problems with this notion, so it is doubtful
whether Jung has strengthened his position with this argument. Freud,
on the other hand, connects (albeit vaguely) the inheritance of predispositions with his theory of instincts, but he feels himself forced to com-
pass the inheritance of more than mere dispositions. This has been
hinted at earlier in his discomfort at the unconscious knowledge of
unlearned symbolic connections, and it is to be given fuller expression
later in *Moses and Monotheism* (1939).

At this point, at the end of his discussion of the Wolf Man case, Freud
takes up the basic theme, claiming that two problems have been raised
by the case. The first, in which Freud likens the function of the 'archaic
heritage' to that of the Kantian categories, is:

the phylogenetically inherited schemata, which, like the categories of philosophy, are concerned with the business of 'placing' the impressions derived from
actual experience. I am inclined to take the view that they are precipitates from
the history of human civilization. The Oedipus complex . . . is, in fact, the best
known member of the class. Wherever experiences fail to fit in with the hereditary schema, they become remodelled in the imagination . . . It is precisely such
cases that are calculated to convince us of the independent existence of the
schema. We are often able to see the schema triumphing over the experiences
of the individual; as when in our present case the boy's father became the castr-
ator and the menace of his infantile sexuality in spite of what was in other
respects an inverted Oedipus complex. (ibid., p. 119)

The second problem takes Freud a step closer to a more extreme commitment, this time in his attempt to grapple with the apparent involve-
ment of innate knowledge in the inherited 'schema':

The second problem is not far removed from the first, but it is incomparably more important . . . it is hard to dismiss the view that some sort of hardly definable knowledge, something, as it were, preparatory to an understanding, was at work in the child at the time. We can form no conception of what this may have consisted in; we have nothing at our disposal but the single analogy – and it is an excellent one – of the far-reaching *instinctive* knowledge of animals. (ibid., p. 120)

Further exploration of this analogy is not undertaken until a decade later; here, Freud merely reiterates his caution:

I am aware that expression has been given in many quarters to thoughts like these, which emphasize the hereditary, phylogenetically acquired factor in mental life. In fact, I am of the opinion that people have been far too ready to find room for them and ascribe importance to them in psycho-analysis. I consider that they are only admissible when psycho-analysis strictly observes the correct order of precedence, and, after forcing its way through the strata of what has been acquired by the individual, comes at last upon traces of what has been inherited. (ibid., p. 121)

Although Freud's motive for emphasising this point probably lies in his desire to distance himself from Jung, his caution is conceptually and methodologically sound; the problem for Freud lay only in execution – in his mistaken belief that, in certain cases of attempted explanations, he had indeed exhausted the ontogenetic possibilities.

Alongside these speculations about phylogenetic inheritance, Freud's method in the Wolf Man attests to his continuing belief that, just as with other material, where the interpretation of symbols is concerned, it is still context which is the important factor. For example:

But what can have been the meaning of the fact that this veil, which was now symbolic but had once been real, was torn at the moment at which he evacuated his bowels after an enema, and that under this condition his illness left him? The *context* enables us to reply. (ibid., p. 100, italics mine)

The Interpretation of Dreams

In 1919, Freud published the fifth edition of *The Interpretation of Dreams*. In a new section, 'The feeling of reality and the representation of repetition', he offers interpretations of the symbolism in a dream reported by the dreamer to have occurred when he was four years old – 'The failure of the dreamer's associations gave us a right to attempt an interpretation by symbolic substitution' (1919a, p. 372) – and he concludes: 'It is most remarkable, of course, that symbolism should already be playing a part in the dream of a four-year-old child. But this is the rule and not the exception. It may safely be asserted that dreamers have symbolism at their disposal from the very first' (ibid., p. 373). It is not clear whether Freud is referring here simply to the availability of symbols in the unconscious prior to the construction of the dream, or whether he is making a stronger commitment to the presence, via heredity, of knowledge of certain symbols. If the latter, then the illustration which immediately follows is neither convincing nor faithful to Freud's commitment to exhaust ontogenetic possibilities before turning to a phylogenetic explanation. He gives an example of a woman's childhood memory, which 'shows at what an early age symbolism is employed outside dream-life as well as inside it' (1919a, p. 373). When this woman was between three and four years of age, she asked a cousin: 'Have you got a purse too? Walter's got a little sausage; I've got a purse.' Her cousin replied: 'Yes, I've got a purse too.' Freud's example here can easily be explained in terms of the young child's ability to recognise similarities, and to use the name of a familiar object as comparison. That Freud calls this 'symbolism' is supportive of the FB view, since this is not yet necessarily symbolism in the defensive sense, and it also provides indirect support for Freud's idea that symbolism is not a product of the dream-work: this is the kind of connection via similarity which may later become unconscious, and thus available for dream symbolism. But, if Freud is intending that his example be support for the FN theory of the innate presence of symbolism in the infant, it is unconvincing.

In another paragraph added in 1919, Freud once again supports the FB approach in pointing to the variability in the ease of interpreting symbols: 'Ferenczi (1917) has justly pointed out that the meaning of symbols and the significance of dreams can be arrived at with particular ease from the dreams of precisely those people who are uninitiated into psycho-analysis' (ibid., p. 377).

But probably the most significant addition in 1919 is yet another attack on the Jung/Silberer 'anagogic' interpretation of symbols:

I cannot confirm the opinion, first stated by Silberer . . . that all dreams (or many dreams, or certain classes of dreams) require two different interpretations, which are even stated to bear a fixed relation to each other. One of these interpretations, which Silberer calls the 'psycho-analytic' one, is said to give the dream some meaning or other, usually of an infantile-sexual kind; the other and more important interpretation, to which he gives the name of 'anagogic', is said to reveal the more serious thoughts, often of profound import, which the dream-work has taken as its material . . . In spite of what he says, the majority of dreams require no 'over-interpretation' and, more particularly, are insusceptible to an anagogic interpretation. As in the case of many other theories put forward in recent years, it is impossible to overlook the fact that Silberer's views are influenced to some extent by a purpose which seeks to disguise the fundamental circumstances in which dreams are formed and to divert interest from their instinctual roots. (ibid., pp. 523–4)

In his analysis of the motivation behind such views, Freud reveals his own implicit commitment to the FB connection between a theory of symbolism as defensively produced substitution and the central tenets of psychoanalytic theory.

Finally, Freud is still grappling with the question of phylogenetic inheritance. In the context of dreaming as regression and revival of childhood, he says:

Behind this childhood of the individual we are promised a picture of a phylogenetic childhood – a picture of the development of the human race, of which the individual's development is in fact an abbreviated recapitulation influenced by the chance circumstances of life. We can guess how much to the point is Nietzsche's assertion that in dreams 'some primaeval relic of humanity is at work which we can now scarcely reach any longer by a direct path'; and we may expect that the analysis of dreams will lead us to a knowledge of man's archaic heritage, of what is psychically innate in him. Dreams and neuroses seem to have preserved more mental antiquities than we could have imagined possible; so that psycho-analysis may claim a high place among the sciences which are concerned with the reconstruction of the earliest and most obscure periods of the beginnings of the human race. (ibid., pp. 548–9)

The years 1920 to 1932

Continuations and repetition

None of Freud's writings between 1920 and 1932 is devoted to symbolism; rather, a number of works, one or two of them major, but most relatively minor, contain various comments on, or indirect illustrations of, points already elaborated in more detail earlier. The general effect of these scattered offerings is simply to continue the same mixture as before.

For instance, indirect support for Freud's focus on the necessity, in the case of symbol formation, of individual experience is found in *Group Psychology and the Analysis of the Ego* (1921), in his rejection of the concept of a 'group mind' to which one can attribute mental processes independent of the mental processes of the individual. In this work, Freud also returns to the broader conception of 'symbolic', exploring the importance of the leader (God, captain, etc.) as a substitute father, and moving on to an examination of the heroic myth as dealing with the slayer of the father, the latter appearing originally as a totemic monster: 'As Rank has observed . . . we often find that this hero can carry out his task only by the help of a crowd of small animals, such as bees or ants. These would be the brothers in the primal horde, just as in the same way in dream symbolism insects or vermin signify brothers and sisters' (1921, p. 136).

Amongst the shorter writings of 1920 to 1922, in a piece called 'Associations of a four-year-old child' (1920a), Freud says, of a child who made the association between having a baby and a tree growing in the ground: 'She was not expressing this knowledge directly, but symbolically, by replacing the mother by Mother Earth. We have already learnt from numerous incontestable observations the early age at which children know how to make use of symbols' (1920a, p. 266). Here, symbolism is indirect, analogical representation, albeit perhaps unconscious.

In his paper 'Dreams and telepathy' (1922), when discussing the symbolic representation of birth both by rescuing from water and by immersing in water, Freud points to a feature of the language of symbolism: 'The language of symbolism, as you are aware, knows no grammar; it is an extreme case of a language of infinitives, and even the active and passive are represented by one and the same image' (1922, p. 212).

Here, Freud has returned to the theme of language to explain the representation of the same thing by opposites; initially, this had been explained by the antithetical meaning of primal words, later by the psychological kinship of opposites.

In 1923, Freud contributed two encyclopaedia articles. In the first of these, he restates, in very condensed form, his position on symbolism:

In the course of investigating the form of expression brought about by the dream-work, the surprising fact emerged that certain objects, arrangements and relations are represented, in a sense directly, by 'symbols', which are used by the dreamer without his understanding them and to which as a rule he offers no associations. Their translation has to be provided by the analyst, who can himself only discover it empirically by experimentally fitting it into the context. It was later found that linguistic usage, mythology and folklore afford the most ample analogies to dream symbols. Symbols, which raise the most interesting and hitherto unsolved problems, seem to be a fragment of extremely ancient inherited mental equipment. The use of a common symbolism extends far beyond the use of a common language. (1923a, p. 242)

Once again, that symbols are part of 'ancient inherited mental equipment' is supposedly supported by the facts that (i) they are not understood by the dreamer, (ii) the dreamer 'as a rule' offers no associations to them, (iii) they are found in areas outside dreams, and (iv) they are cross-cultural and cross-linguistic.

In this same article, Freud relates how Jung defected from psychoanalysis: 'evidently with the object of mitigating its repellent features . . . in an endeavour to conform to ethical standards, [he] divested the Oedipus complex of its significance by giving it only a *symbolic* value (ibid., p. 248). In this Jungian sense of 'symbolic', there is a double divergence from Freudian theory. Firstly, for Jung the Oedipus complex is not real (what is 'symbolic' being opposed to what is 'real'), and secondly, reality is accorded, not to the incestuous impulses, but to the 'higher' spiritual aspirations which the 'Oedipus complex' supposedly symbolises.

The technique of symbol translation is still separated from that of interpreting associations. In 'Remarks on the theory and practice of dream-interpretation', Freud points out that, if the patient's resistance is very high, there will be little point in bothering too much with dream-interpretation; instead, 'one is content to put before him a few translations of symbols that seem probable' (1923b, p. 110).

Occasionally, earlier themes recur with some elaboration. The symbolism of the mythological Medusa's head is discussed again in 'The infantile genital organization'. Here, Freud comments on the degree to which:

depreciation of women, horror of women, and a disposition to homosexuality are derived from the final conviction that women have no penis. Ferenczi (1923) has recently, with complete justice, traced back the mythological symbol of horror – the Medusa's head – to the impression of the female genitals devoid of a penis. (1923c, p. 144)

And in a footnote:

I should like to add that what is indicated in the myth is the *mother's* genitals. Athene, who carries Medusa's head on her armour, becomes in consequence the unapproachable woman, the sight of whom extinguishes all thought of a sexual approach. (n., ibid.)

Other themes are repeated with no elaboration. In 'The dissolution of the Oedipus complex', Freud talks of the girl's ability to tolerate renunciation of the desire for a penis by slipping 'along the lines of a symbolic equation, one might say – from the penis to a baby' (1924a, pp. 178–9).

The broader view of symbols as substitutes (as in the FB schema) is also retained, this time with some apparent awareness of its divergence from the FN position. In 'The loss of reality in neurosis and psychosis', Freud argues that, with respect to the part played by phantasy in neurosis and psychosis, the difference is that:

whereas the new, imaginary external world of a psychosis attempts to put itself in the place of external reality, that of a neurosis, on the contrary, is apt, like the play of children, to attach itself to a piece of reality – a different piece from the one against which it has to defend itself – and to lend that piece a special importance and a secret meaning which we (not always quite appropriately) call a *symbolic* one. Thus we see that both in neurosis and psychosis there comes into consideration the question not only of a *loss of reality* but also of a *substitute for reality*. (1924b, p. 187)

This is the only occasion on which Freud gives any acknowledgement of the inconsistency between this and the FN use of 'symbolic'.

In 1925, the eighth edition of *The Interpretation of Dreams* was published, enlarged and revised, with a number of additional comments on symbolism. For example, writing of the need to collect the dreamer's associations, Freud adds the following footnote:

This assertion that our method of interpreting dreams cannot be applied unless we have access to the dreamer's associative material requires supplementing: our interpretative activity is in one instance independent of these associations – if, namely, the dreamer has employed *symbolic* elements in the content of the dream. In such cases we make use of what is, strictly speaking, a second and auxiliary method of dream-interpretation. (1925a, n. p. 241)

On the history of the development of his theory of symbolism, Freud says: 'I recognized the presence of symbolism in dreams from the very beginning. But it was only by degrees and as my experience increased that I arrived at a full appreciation of its extent and significance, and I did so under the influence of the contributions of Wilhelm Stekel (1911)' (ibid., p. 350).

The question of experimental evidence for dream symbolism is also addressed. Freud comments on the work of Betlheim and Hartmann in 1924, and he uses their observations to back up his own conclusions. For example: 'The authors attach special importance to the appearance of the symbol of a staircase, for, as they justly observed, "no conscious desire to distort could have arrived at a symbol of such a kind" ' (ibid., p. 384).

Freud also published in 1925 a short paper, 'Some additional notes on dream-interpretation as a whole', in which he claims that: 'dream-interpretation ... without reference to the dreamer's associations, would in the most favourable case remain a piece of unscientific virtuosity of very doubtful value' (1925b, p. 128).

Nevertheless, symbolism is not insignificant:

for instance, symbolism is not a dream problem, but a topic connected with our archaic thinking – our 'basic language', as it was aptly called by the paranoic Schreber. It dominates myths and religious rituals no less than dreams, and dream symbolism can scarcely even claim that it is peculiar in that it conceals more particularly things that are important sexually. (ibid., p. 135)

The connection for Freud between symbolism and language, and the lack of distinction between conventional and non-conventional symbolism, finds another expression in his paper 'Negation' (1925c). Here Freud introduces a somewhat obscure usage – 'the symbol of negation'. By this, he seems to be attempting to capture the verbal form of rejection (i.e., saying 'no'), since he contrasts it with the 'fact that in analysis we never discover a "no" in the unconscious' (1925c, p. 239).

Freud's *An Autobiographical Study* (1925d) is another account of the evolution of his ideas, which overlaps with the 1914 paper on the history of the psychoanalytic movement, but, as Strachey notes, is less entangled in embittered controversies than was the earlier account. This account contains a more extensive treatment of symbolism than most of the other productions of this period, but the material consists largely of repetitions. Freud once again claims the method of interpretation of symbols to be independent of associations:

Another advantage of the method is that it need never break down. It must theoretically always be possible to have an association, provided that no conditions are made as to its character. Yet there is one case in which in fact a breakdown occurs with absolute regularity; from its very uniqueness, however, this case too can be interpreted. (1925d, p. 42)

It is worth noting here the explicit FN statements: the failure of associations is described as occurring invariably, and as being unique to the presence of symbols. In addition, symbolism is independent of the dream-work processes (condensation, displacement, dramatisation and secondary revision), and is labelled 'archaic':

The dream work is an excellent example of the processes occurring in the deeper, unconscious layers of the mind, which differ considerably from the familiar normal processes of thought. It also displays a number of archaic characteristics, such as the use of a *symbolism* (in this case of a predominantly sexual kind) which it has since also been possible to discover in other spheres of mental activity. (ibid., p. 45)

Freud also comments on the hostility with which his observations on symbolism have been met, and reiterates his insistence that symbolism was neither invented nor even discovered by psychoanalysis:

Symbolism has brought psycho-analysis many enemies; many enquirers with unduly prosaic minds have never been able to forgive it the recognition of symbolism, which followed from the interpretation of dreams. But analysis is guiltless of the discovery of symbolism, for it has long been known in other regions of thought (such as folklore, legends and myths) and plays an even larger part in them than in the 'language of dreams'. (ibid., p. 69)

A year later Freud published a booklet, 'The question of lay analysis' (1926b), in which his difficulties with separating symbolism from 'other forms of indirect representation' are again reflected. After discussing the dependence on the 'personal contribution' of the analyst, Freud says that one need not pessimistically resign oneself to inevitable subjectivism – for there are facts which can be agreed upon: 'And, moreover, even in the interpretative art of analysis there is much that can be learnt like any other material or study: for instance, in connection with the peculiar method of indirect representation through symbols' (1926b, p. 220).

In his contribution to the twelfth edition of the *Encyclopaedia Britannica*, Freud mentions 'the part played by symbolism' (along with sublimation and ambivalence) as being among the 'matters of the greatest interest' which he has been unable to cover in the small space allotted to him (1926c, p. 268).

In the following year, in his book *The Future of an Illusion*, Freud likens the truth contained in religious doctrines in distorted and systematically disguised form to 'what happens when we tell a child that new-born babies are brought by the stork. Here, too, we are telling the truth in symbolic clothing, for we know what the large bird signifies' (1927, p. 44).

Sometimes Freud uses the term 'symbolic' in a sense which he rejects elsewhere. In a letter to Maxime Leroy on 'Some dreams of Descartes' ', Freud asserts that only a meagre result can be given without the dreamer's associations, and that in any case Descartes' dreams are 'from above', i.e., not much derived from the deep unconscious. He concludes: 'That is why these dreams offer for the most part a content which has an abstract, poetic or symbolic form' (1929, p. 203). Freud is clearly here returning to the use of the term 'symbolic' in the Jungian sense, the sense in which Jung applied it to the Oedipus complex.

In 1932, Freud published a short paper entitled 'The acquisition and control of fire', whose theme is the connection between fire, sexuality and micturation – reflected in the myth of Prometheus. This myth involves the same distortions as are revealed in daily reconstructions of repressed childhood experiences from the dreams of patients: 'The mechanisms employed in the distortions I have in mind are symbolic representation and turning into the opposite' (1932, p. 187). In the ensuing account, Freud appeals to similarities of experiences, and, in pointing to the survival of the symbolic relation in the metaphors of language, he seems almost to be returning to the 'symbolization' of hysteria, without, however, its 'conversion' into physical symptoms:

primitive man was bound to regard fire as something analogous to the passion of love – or, as we should say, as a symbol of the libido. The warmth that is radiated by fire calls up the same sensation that accompanies a state of sexual excitation, and the shape and movements of a flame suggest a phallus in activity . . . when we ourselves speak of the 'devouring fire' of love and of 'licking' flames

... – we have not moved so very far away from the mode of thinking of our primitive ancestors. (ibid., p. 190)

But, of course, there is no justification for limiting any such experience to 'primitive man', and Freud's account suggests that our ancestors made exactly the same connections as we do today; the use of fire symbolism to indicate the passion of love was no less metaphorical then than it is now. Thus we cannot be said to have moved any distance 'away from the mode of thinking of our ancestors'. Freud calls this metaphor a 'symbolic analogy', and goes on to talk of further elements of the myth as 'bearing the significance of', which he appears to be using synonymously with 'symbolising'.

The archaic heritage revisited

The only work published during the period 1920 to 1932 in which Freud says anything new on the topic of symbolism is *Inhibitions, Symptoms and Anxiety* (1926a). Here, in his treatment (reminiscent of Darwin's) of affective states as archaic vestiges, Freud takes up again the theme of phylogenetic inheritance:

Anxiety is not newly created in repression; it is reproduced as an affective state in accordance with an already existing mnemic image ... affective states have become incorporated in the mind as precipitates of primaeval traumatic experiences, and when a similar situation occurs they are revived like mnemic symbols. I do not think I have been wrong in likening them to the more recent and individually acquired hysterical attack and in regarding them as its normal prototype ... biological necessity demands that a situation of danger should have an affective symbol. (1926a, pp. 93–4)

It is not clear what Freud means here by 'in accordance with an already existing mnemic image'. Biological necessity certainly demands that the emotion of fear, say, be provoked by situations of danger – thus that the fear response is not learned. But Freud sees this as analogous to the replacement of a hidden trauma by a mnemic symbol in hysteria – and is thus led to label what is inherited (presumably, the fear response) an affective 'symbol'. However, it is not merely analogy, for these 'affective symbols' are the 'prototype' of hysterical attacks. These vague hints, as will be seen, are expanded a little later to clarify the relationship between universal symbols and the mnemic symbols of hysteria.

A further development can be seen in Freud's placing the discussion of this archaic heritage, in terms of the existence of 'inborn traces', into the context of the broader FB approach to symbolism. For example, he reflects on the case of Little Hans:

what made it a neurosis was one thing alone: the replacement of his father by a horse. It is this displacement, then, which has a claim to be called a symptom . . . such a displacement is made possible or facilitated at 'Little Hans's' early age because the inborn traces of totemic thought can still be easily revived. (ibid., p. 103)

Here, despite the relatively new connection of symbolism with inherited traces, a 'substitute' is clearly no different from what is elsewhere called a 'symbol'. This fact is further supported by the allusion to 'displacement', and by Freud's summary statement that symptoms in obsessional neurosis 'are either prohibitions, precautions and expiations – that is, negative in character – or they are, on the contrary, substitutive satisfactions which often appear in symbolic guise' (ibid., p. 112).

Unless one separates, simply by stipulation, Freud's use of the term 'symbolic' here, which is clearly general and part of the FB approach, from the narrower use of the term 'symbol', there is no reason why the FN view cannot be accommodated by the FB theory. This is supported by Freud's account of some of the defence mechanisms. In the case of the defensive ego activity of 'undoing', there is a kind of 'negative magic', in which the person endeavours to 'blow away' an experience 'by means of motor symbolism' (ibid., p. 119). So, too, in the case of the defence mechanism of 'isolation': 'when a neurotic isolates an impression or an activity by interpolating an interval, he is letting it be understood symbolically that he will not allow his thoughts about that impression or activity to come into associative contact with other thoughts' (ibid., p. 122). A little further on, Freud considers and rejects the possibility that anxiety is a 'symbol of separation', since birth, a separation from the mother's body, is also the first experience of anxiety. In this context, Freud returns to the earlier discussion of mnemic symbols and the archaic heritage. The mnemic symbols of hysteria are individually acquired; affects are their innate, universal analogues:

This does not imply that anxiety occupies an exceptional position among the affective states. In my opinion the other affects are also reproductions of very early, perhaps even pre-individual, experiences of vital importance; and I should be inclined to regard them as universal, typical and innate hysterical attacks, as compared to the recently and individually acquired attacks which occur in hysterical neuroses and whose origin and significance as mnemic symbols have been revealed by analysis. (ibid., p. 133)

This clarifies Freud's earlier talk of the inheritance of 'affective symbols': affects are the innate, universal counterparts of the individually acquired mnemic symbols of hysteria.

The years 1933 to 1940

The New Introductory Lectures

In 1933 Freud published the *New Introductory Lectures on Psycho-Analysis*, lectures which were not designed to be delivered, nor, according to Freud himself, intended to stand alone; they are supplements to the *Introductory Lectures*, and are numbered continuously with them. Once again, most of the scattered material on symbolism consists of repetitions of earlier statements.

In the first lecture, Lecture XXIX, 'Revision of the theory of dreams', Freud restates the basic FN position:

If in general and primarily we are dependent, in interpreting dreams, on the dreamer's associations, yet in relation to certain elements of the dream's content we adopt a quite independent attitude, chiefly because we have to, because as a rule associations fail to materialize in their case. We noticed at an early stage that it is always in connection with the same elements that this happens; they are not very numerous, and repeated experience has taught us that they are to be regarded and interpreted as *symbols* of something else. As contrasted with the other dream elements, a fixed meaning may be attributed to them, which, however, need not be unambiguous and whose range is determined by special rules with which we are unfamiliar. Since *we* know how to translate these symbols and the dreamer does not, in spite of having used them himself, it may happen that the sense of a dream may at once become clear to us as soon as we have heard the text of the dream, even before we have made any efforts at interpreting it, while it still remains an enigma to the dreamer himself. But I have said so much to you in my earlier lectures on symbolism, our knowledge of it and the problems it poses us, that I need not repeat it today. (1933, pp. 12–13)

Further, the 'archaic' nature of symbolism is reinforced: 'The copious employment of symbols, which have become alien to conscious thinking, for representing certain objects and processes is in harmony alike with the archaic regression in the mental apparatus and with the demands of the censorship' (ibid., p. 20). This time, however, there is some attempt to address the question of empirical evidence for symbolism. In response to the charge that psychoanalysis is non-scientific 'on the grounds that it did not admit of experimental proof', Freud says:

Nevertheless, some Viennese investigators have actually made a beginning with experimental confirmation of our dream symbolism. As long ago as in 1912 a Dr Schrötter found that if instructions to dream of sexual matters are given to deeply hypnotized subjects, then in the dream that is thus provoked the sexual material emerges with its place taken by the symbols that are familiar to us. For instance, a woman was told to dream of sexual intercourse with a female friend.

In her dream this friend appeared with a travelling-bag on which was pasted the label 'Ladies Only'. Still more impressive experiments were carried out by Betlheim and Hartmann in 1924. They worked with patients suffering from what is known as Korsakoff confusional psychosis . . . [They told patients grossly sexual stories and] . . . observed the distortions which appeared when the patients were instructed to reproduce what they had been told. Once more there emerged the symbols for sexual organs and sexual intercourse that are familiar to us – among them the symbol of the staircase which, as the writers justly remark, could never have been reached by a conscious wish to distort. (ibid., pp. 22–3)

There are also examples of appeal to converging evidence:

There are some which we believed we recognized but which nevertheless worried us because we could not explain how *this* particular symbol had come to have *that* particular meaning. In such cases confirmations from elsewhere – from philology, folklore, mythology or ritual – were bound to be especially welcome. (ibid., pp. 23–4)

Appeal to converging evidence is also found in specific instances of Freud's mixed method of interpreting symbols. In the case of the symbolic equation overcoat (or cloak) = man, Freud appeals to (i) the German word *Mantel,* and (ii) Theodor Reik's (1920) discovery that during the bridal ceremony of the Bedouin, the bridegroom covers the bride with a special cloak known as an *Aba,* and speaks the ritual words: 'Henceforth none save I shall cover thee.' In addition, although the word 'symbolic' is not used, interpretation is seen to depend on uncovering 'original interests', i.e., to be connected with the central tenets of psychoanalytic theory:

In the manifest content of dreams we very often find pictures and situations recalling familiar themes in fairy tales, legends and myths. The interpretation of such dreams thus throws light on the original interests which created these themes . . . Our work of interpretation uncovers, so to speak, the raw material. (1933, p. 25)

This broader connection is retained in Lecture XXXII, 'Anxiety and instinctual life', where Freud talks of symbols and associations in the same context:

If one is not aware of these profound connections, it is impossible to find one's way about in the phantasies of human beings, in their associations, influenced as they are by the unconscious, and in their symptomatic language. Faeces – money – gift – baby – penis are treated as though they meant the same thing, and they are represented too by the same symbols. (ibid., p. 101)

Similarly, in Lecture XXXIV, 'Explanations and applications', Freud talks of those critics who accept some parts of his theory but reject others, and he lists sexuality, the unconscious and symbolism as particularly popular targets for rejection, a rejection which is untenable because: 'Though the structure of psychoanalysis is unfinished, it nevertheless presents, even today, a unity from which elements cannot be broken off at the caprice of whoever comes along' (ibid., p. 138).

As I argued earlier (in Chapter 2), the nomination of the particular themes of sexuality, the unconscious and symbolism (themes which are central to Freud's theory) indicates that Freud does not mean that no elements at all may be broken off, but that those which either form the core of the theory, or are necessary consequences of that core, cannot be discarded without discarding the entire theory. The FB (but not, *pace* Freud, the FN) theory of symbolism is such an element.

In Lecture XXXV, 'The question of a *Weltanschauung*', Freud alludes to religion, in which a superman as creator (God) is 'undisguisedly called "father" ', and he adds that 'Psycho-analysis infers that he really is the father, with all the magnificence in which he once appeared to the small child' (ibid., p. 163).

Moses and Monotheism

In 1939 Freud published his last major work, *Moses and Monotheism*. This was written between 1934 and 1938, with the first draft completed in 1934, but Freud delayed its publication because of uncertainty about the content and the soundness of his arguments. As Strachey notes, the work is really a continuation of the earlier studies (in *Totem and Taboo* and *Group Psychology*) of the origins of human social organisation. With respect to symbolism, this work is of interest on two counts: firstly, the more general, broad use of 'symbolic' throughout; and, secondly, more importantly, Freud's attempt to elaborate the part played by symbolism in the 'archaic heritage'.

On the first point, in his discussion of the origin myth, Freud says:

Rank's researches have made us acquainted with the source and purpose of this myth . . . A hero is someone who has had the strength to rebel against his father and has in the end victoriously overcome him . . . The exposure in a casket is an unmistakable symbolic representation of birth: the casket is the womb and the water is the amniotic fluid. The parent-child relationship is represented in countless dreams by pulling out of the water or rescuing from the water . . . A child's earliest years are dominated by an enormous overvaluation of his father; in accordance with this a king and queen in dreams and fairy tales invariably stand for parents . . .

We may fairly say that these explanations make the widespread and uniform nature of myths of the birth of heroes fully intelligible. (1939, p. 12)

Significant here is that the universal king and queen symbols are given an ontogenetic justification inspired by psychoanalytic tenets – the over-valuation of the parents during the child's earliest years. In other examples, Amenophis is described as having worshipped the sun as 'the symbol of a divine being' (ibid., p. 22), Moses' breaking of the tables of the law 'is to be understood symbolically . . . as . . . "he has broken the law" ' (ibid., p. 48), and 'the sense and content of the old totem meal is repeated in the rite of the Christian communion, in which the believer incorporates the blood and flesh of his god in symbolic form' (ibid., p. 84).

On the second point, Freud here gives his fullest discussion of symbolism as a phylogenetically inherited part of the 'archaic heritage'. This passage is for that reason worth considering in its entirety:

a fresh complication arises when we become aware of the probability that what may be operative in an individual's psychical life may include not only what he has experienced himself but also things that were innately present in him at birth, elements with a phylogenetic origin – an *archaic heritage*. The questions then arise of what this consists in, what it contains, and what is the evidence for it.

The immediate and most certain answer is that it consists in certain [innate] dispositions such as are characteristic of all living organisms: in the capacity and tendency, that is, to enter particular lines of development and to react in a particular manner to certain excitations, impressions, and stimuli. (ibid., p. 98)

This, Freud goes on to say, represents the *constitutional* factor, insofar as there are differences between individuals. But, since all humans have largely the same very early experiences, they all react to these in much the same way, and stronger justification for the archaic heritage is required:

a doubt was therefore able to arise whether we should not include these reac-tions, along with their individual distinctions, in the archaic heritage. This doubt should be put on one side: our knowledge of the archaic heritage is not enlarged by the fact of this similarity.

Nevertheless, analytic research has brought us a few results which give us cause for thought. There is, in the first place, the universality of symbolism in language. The symbolic representation of one object by another – the same thing applies to actions – is familiar to all our children and comes to them, as it were, as a matter of course. We cannot show in regard to them how they have learnt it and must admit that in many cases learning it is impossible. It is a question of an original knowledge which adults afterwards forget. It is true that an adult makes use of the same symbols in his dreams, but he does not understand them unless an analyst interprets them to him, and even then he is reluctant to believe the translation. If he makes use of one of the very common figures of speech in which this symbolism is recorded, he is obliged to admit that its true sense has completely escaped him. Moreover, symbolism disregards differences of language; investigations would probably show that it is ubiquitous – the same for all peoples. Here, then, we seem to have an assured instance of an archaic heritage dating from the period at which language developed. But another explanation might still be attempted. It might be said that we are dealing with thought-connections between ideas – connections which had been established during the historical development of speech and which have to be repeated now every time the development of speech has to be gone through in an individual. It would thus be a case of the inheritance of an intellectual disposition similar to the ordinary inheritance of an instinctual disposition – and once again it would be no contribution to our problem. (1939, pp. 98–9)

Clearly, Freud feels that the inheritance of mere 'dispositions', whether intellectual or any other, would not justify the postulation of an archaic heritage, certainly not of the kind which he has in mind. However, he continues, there is a second source of evidence for such a heritage:

When we study the reactions to early traumas, we are quite often surprised to find that they are not strictly limited to what the subject himself has really experienced but diverge from it in a way which fits in much better with the model of a phylogenetic event and, in general, can only be explained by such an influence. The behaviour of neurotic children towards their parents in the Oedipus and castration complex abounds in such reactions, which seem unjustified in the individual case and only become intelligible phylogenetically – by their connection with the experience of earlier generations . . . Its evidential value seems to me strong enough for me to venture on a further step and to posit the assertion that *the archaic heritage of human beings comprises not only dispositions but also subject matter* – memory traces of the experiences of earlier generations. (ibid., p. 99, italics mine)

Freud here explicitly commits himself to the inheritance of content. Thus Jones is accurate in his summary that, whereas initially (in the *Introductory Lectures*) it is suggested that in humans there is *evocation* of an innate predisposition, Freud 'finally gave it as his opinion that not only specific predispositions could be inherited, but definite mental contents – the memory traces of prehistoric events as well as particular symbols' (Jones 1957, p. 351). But Freud is apologetic about the boldness of this move:

On further reflection I must admit that I have behaved for a long time as though the inheritance of memory-traces of the experience of our ancestors, independently of direct communication and of the influence of education by the setting of an example, were established beyond question. (1939, p. 99)

This apology was apparently prompted by persistent opposition from Jones, who complains that Freud was never willing to abandon his stance on phylogenetic inheritance, and clung to it obstinately, despite having commented, in the minutes of the meeting of the Vienna Psycho-analytic Society, 8 November 1911:

The inference of a phylogenetic inborn store of memories is not justified so long as we have the possibility of explaining these things through an analysis of the psychical situations. (in Jones 1957, pp. 330–1)

Jones claims to have found it extraordinary that Freud read Darwin but, instead of using him, supported the pre-Darwinian Lamarckian explanation of evolution: 'Freud remained from the beginning to the end of his life what one must call an obstinate adherent of this discredited Lamarckism. Over and over again he implied or explicitly stated his firm belief in it' (Jones 1957, p. 333). A little later, Jones says:

Freud never gave up a jot of his belief in the inheritance of acquired characters. How immovable he was in the matter I discovered during a talk I had with him in the last year of his life over a sentence I wished him to alter (in the Moses book) in which he expressed the Lamarckian view in universal terms. I told him he had of course the right to hold any opinion he liked in his own field of psychology, even if it ran counter to all biological principles, but begged him to omit the passage where he applied it to the whole field of biological evolution, since no responsible biologist regarded it as any longer tenable. All he would say was that they were all wrong and the passage must stay. And he documented this recalcitrance in the book with the following words. (ibid., p. 336)

Jones is referring here to the sentence which Freud adds at this point in his *Moses and Monotheism*:

My position, no doubt, is made more difficult by the present attitude of biological science, which refuses to hear of the inheritance of acquired characters by succeeding generations. I must, however, in all modesty confess that nevertheless I cannot do without this factor in biological evolution. (1939, p. 100)

Here, Freud explicitly commits himself to Lamarckism. Why does he feel that he 'cannot do' without this factor? Apparently, by assuming 'the survival of these memory-traces in the archaic heritage', we can achieve two things. The first is that:

we have bridged the gulf between individual and group psychology: we can deal with peoples as we do with an individual neurotic. Granted that at the time we have no stronger evidence for the presence of memory-traces in the archaic heritage than the residual phenomena of the work of analysis which call for a phylogenetic derivation, yet this evidence seems to us strong enough to postulate that such is the fact. If it is not so, we shall not advance a step further along the path we entered on, either in analysis or in group psychology. (ibid., p. 100)

However, it is unclear why, and in what ways, 'we shall not advance a step further', and Freud does not elaborate. The second 'achievement' is that 'we are diminishing the gulf which earlier periods of human arrogance had torn too wide apart between mankind and animals' (ibid.). Freud's argument here is weak; he has given no good reason why we 'cannot do without' the assumption of the archaic heritage. Even more illuminating is his concluding with:

a remark which brings up a psychological argument. A tradition that was based only on communication could not lead to the compulsive character that attaches to religious phenomena. It would be listened to, judged, and perhaps dismissed, like any other piece of information from outside; it would never attain the privilege of being liberated from the constraint of logical thought. (ibid., p. 101)

Once again, since the obvious response is that Freud's theory *does* allow explanation of such phenomena, his reasoning is unconvincing. The reference to the explanatory inadequacy of knowledge which is 'based only on communication' echoes his earlier comments on the inadequacy of postulating that symbols are 'learned', by which, as I suggested, he means 'acquired via instruction'. Freud seems unable or unwilling to connect symbolism and its unconscious, compulsive nature with his theory of the unconscious repression of instinctual drives, and proceeds as if the only choice available to him were between phylogenetic inheritance and learning via explicit communication.

Freud's commitment to this archaic heritage raises again the question of the similarity between his own views and those of his rival Jung. Freud, of course, rejected Jung's notion that symbolic productions indicate the mind's 'progressive', teleological tendencies, and both Freud and Jones appear to believe that there is no risk of Freud's being seen as subscribing to Jung's idea of a collective unconscious. According to Jones:

there is a world of difference between Freud's view of the inheritance of highly specific and limited mental processes, all to do with concrete ideas or situations, and Jung's wide-ranging views of an inherited collective unconscious replete with the most complicated, abstract, and spiritually-minded archetypes. (1957, p. 331)

And Freud himself says:

I do not think we gain anything by introducing the concept of a 'collective' unconscious. The content of the unconscious, indeed, is in any case a collective, universal property of mankind . . . we must finally make up our minds to adopt the hypothesis that the psychical precipitates of the primaeval period became inherited property which, in each fresh generation, called not for acquisition but only for awakening. In this we have in mind the example of what is certainly the 'innate' symbolism which derives from the period of the development of speech, which is familiar to all children *without their being instructed*, and which is the same among all peoples despite their different languages. (1939, p. 132, italics mine)

Again Freud uses 'unlearned' in the sense of 'not acquired via instruction'. He goes on to re-establish the connection between what is phylogenetically inherited and what is instinctive: 'We find that in a number of important relations our children react, not in a manner corresponding to their own experience, but instinctively, like the animals, in a manner that is explicable as phylogenetic acquisition' (ibid., pp. 132–3).

Although Freud combined his theory of the 'archaic heritage' with Lamarckism, the two are not necessarily mutually dependent. Jones, for example, feels that Freud could just as well have appealed to the Darwinian notion for his transmission of the archaic heritage: 'If further evidence should appear in favour of the inheritance of a few elemental images it is more than likely that it might be explicable on pure Darwinian lines, i.e. via Natural Selection' (Jones 1957, p. 336).

Regarding Freud's primal horde theory, Jones continues:

> Freud did, it is true, talk of impressions being burnt into the brains of the participants and then passed on to their descendants in a Lamarckian fashion. It is easy to criticize this, but there is no reason to suppose that the chain of events could not be described perfectly well in the more plausible terms of Natural Selection. (ibid., p. 352)

Finally, Jones says of Freud's *Moses and Monotheism*:

> As critics have been quick to point out, there are weak links in the chain of reasoning . . . The weakest of all, however, they have overlooked: Freud's theory of the unconscious transmission of historical events. This could certainly not have happened in the simple way he suggested, by the direct inheritance of traumatic impressions along Lamarckian lines . . . Nevertheless, there are alternative possibilities, e.g. along Darwinian lines, which would preserve the essence of his conclusions. (ibid., pp. 395–6)

Final statements

In 1937, Freud published 'Analysis terminable and interminable', in which he makes one of his final comments on the archaic heritage:

> we know that we must not exaggerate the difference between inherited and acquired characters into an antithesis; what was acquired by our forefathers certainly forms an important part of what we inherit. When we speak of an 'archaic heritage' we are usually thinking only of the id and we seem to assume that at the beginning of the individual's life no ego is as yet in existence. But we shall not overlook the fact that id and ego are originally one; nor does it imply any mystical overvaluation of heredity if we think it credible that, even before the ego has come into existence, the lines of development, trends and reactions which it will later exhibit are already laid down for it. The psychological peculiarities of families, races and nations, even in their attitude to analysis, allow of no other explanation. Indeed, more than this: analytic experience has

forced on us a conviction that even particular psychical contents, such as symbolism, have no other sources than hereditary transmission, and researches in various fields of social anthropology, make it plausible to suppose that other, equally specialized precipitates left by early human development are also present in the archaic heritage. (1937, pp. 240–1)

It is clear from the first part of this passage that Freud believes (in accordance with his later theory of the ego) that it is fine for the id to be part of the archaic heritage, because, unlike the ego, it is simply composed of the innate, biological instinctual drives, and is not capable of having knowledge (i.e. (for Freud here), of benefiting from 'instruction'). However, because Freud wishes to argue that knowledge of symbolism is both inherited and, at the same time, is of the kind which is usually acquired via instruction (and thus belongs to the ego), he reminds us of his formulation of the ego as a differentiated portion of the id.

In the unfinished *An Outline of Psycho-Analysis*, begun in 1938 and published in 1940 after his death, Freud discusses the 'abundant and convincing evidence of the share taken by the unconscious id in the formation of dreams', and amongst these pieces of evidence he includes, firstly:

Dreams make an unrestricted use of linguistic symbols, the meaning of which is for the most part unknown to the dreamer. Our experience, however, enables us to confirm their sense. They probably originate from earlier phases in the development of speech. (1940, p. 166)

And, secondly:

dreams bring to light material which cannot have originated either from the dreamer's adult life or from his forgotten childhood. We are obliged to regard it as part of the *archaic heritage* which a child brings with him into the world, before any experience of his own, influenced by the experiences of his ancestors. We find the counterpart of this phylogenetic material in the earliest human legends and in surviving customs. Thus dreams constitute a source of human prehistory which is not to be despised. (ibid., pp. 166–7)

It is worth repeating that there are no examples in Freud's writings of material brought to light by a dream, which is then shown by Freud not to have been able to have been capable of originating ontogenetically. There follows the by now familiar reminder:

it is of course justifiable to ask how it is at all possible to deduce the one [latent content] from the other [manifest content] and whether all we have to go on is a lucky guess, assisted perhaps by a translation of the symbols that occur in the manifest dream. (ibid., p. 169)

The problem can usually be solved, but only with the help of the dreamer's associations – 'Any other procedure is arbitrary and can yield no certain result' (ibid.).

Some indication of the way in which Freud saw the operation of what is phylogenetically inherited can be seen in his discussion of the primacy of the breast (and mother) as the infant's first and strongest love object, leading to her unparalleled importance in his later psychic life. Freud adds: 'In all this the phylogenetic foundation has so much the upper hand over personal accidental experience that it makes no difference whether a child has really sucked at the breast or has been brought up on the bottle' (ibid., p. 188).

Finally, Freud asserts that 'the blinding with which Oedipus punishes himself after the discovery of his crime is, by the evidence of dreams, a symbolic substitute for castration', and that:

The possibility cannot be excluded that a phylogenetic memory-trace may contribute to the extraordinarily terrifying effect of the threat – a memory trace from the prehistory of the primal family, when the jealous father actually robbed his son of his genitals if the latter became troublesome to him as a rival with a woman. (ibid., n. p. 190)

This comment harks back to the two 'achievements' which the postulation of an archaic heritage was supposed to produce. Here, it is the peculiar intensity of the productions which is supposedly explained by appeal to phylogenetic experiences. But, given the explanatory import of Freud's general theoretical formulations about the emotional impact of the long period of infantile dependence, this argument is no more necessary or convincing than the earlier ones.

Conclusions

It is clear that, apart from the shift in focus on to the question of phylogenetic inheritance, the treatment of symbolism in Freud's later writings is no different from the mixed approach evident in his earlier writings. The fact that there is no attempt to consolidate the FN theory, even though the core years for explicit statements of the FN view immediately precede these later writings, is not surprising, given that there was no consistent and unambiguous commitment to the FN position even during those core years. In addition, while there is less material devoted to extensive discussions of the theme of symbolism – Freud remarks on several occasions that he has already covered the topic adequately – in the scattered comments which do appear there is no abandoning of the FB approach. Any repetitions of earlier explicit FN statements, or summaries of the FN position, are found alongside assertions which continue the FB schema and its themes: the context is necessary for translating symbols, the *tertium comparationis* still consists of perceptible, learnable similarities, the connection between symbol, symptom and substitute formation is maintained, symbolism is present in the unconscious and is formed during the early life of the individual, translations of particular symbols or symbolic phenomena are still effected by Freud's familiar mixed method, and the theory of symbolism depends on the psychical importance of the initial primary objects of the instinctual drives. These factors demonstrate Freud's continuing implicit adherence to the FB theory, and to its connections with the rest of the theoretical structure of psychoanalysis.

As for the extension of Freud's treatment of symbolism into the field of phylogenetic inheritance, Jones repeatedly asserts that Freud was throughout his life subject to a conflict between his down-to-earth, scientific outlook and a more imaginative, speculative side to his nature, and that the older he became the less cautious and more daring were his speculations. While that may be so, several points are illustrated by the material on phylogenetic inheritance, some of which suggest internal reasons for Freud's speculations. Freud certainly does vacillate on the extent to which he is prepared to commit himself. However, he brings to this material his failure to distinguish clearly between conventional and non-conventional symbolism, and his resulting inability to see the theoretical choice as anything other than the choice between what is inherited and what is acquired via instruction. In addition, Freud's belief in the necessity and value of the assumption that symbolism is part of an archaic heritage is misguided; he provides no good reasons to support his claim that we 'cannot do without' such an assumption. Finally, Freud's own general theory, combined with his conceptually and methodologically sound insistence on the need to exhaust ontogenetic possibilities before turning to phylogenetic ones, renders the postulation of the phylogenetic inheritance of symbolism unnecessary.

Part Two

Consolidation and Defence

My aim in Part One was to extract from Freud's writings whatever valuable contributions to a general theory of symbolism (the FB theory) are to be found there, regardless of what is typically asserted, even by Freud himself, to be his position on symbolism (the FN theory). But simply piecing together that extracted material will not do. A coherent FB theory will not appear until we have addressed two major problems which arise in Freud's work and which, apart from their relevance to symbolism, have had significant implications for psychoanalytic theory in general. These involve fundamental concepts of psychoanalysis, such as the unconscious and repression. The inconsistent treatment each has received in Freud's writings has led to confusions which appear in elaborated and exacerbated form in more recent developments of psychoanalysis. The first problem stems from the notion of the unconscious as a separate 'system' with its own special characteristics, mechanisms, and modes of operation. In terms of its implications for the theory of symbolism, this notion has resulted in the proposition that symbolism is the natural mode of expression of the 'system unconscious'. In Chapter 7, I reject that proposition. The second problem is the question of the role of language, the unconscious as a language, and the evidential weight of philological material. This has resulted in the proposition that symbolism is a language whose universality is demonstrated by linguistic evidence. In Chapter 8, I reject that second proposition. Although the question of language has received the more critical attention, neither of these problems, I shall argue, has been properly appreciated, and both have become the object of much *un*critical attention. Freud himself is largely responsible; on each of these matters, he favours the less acceptable of two available interpretations (even where his motives are theoretically sound), and his account of symbolism is, in consequence, flawed in a number of ways. If the *more* acceptable interpretation is adopted, some important Freudian material can be clarified, and a number of criticisms of the FB theory nullified. In Chapter 9, I complete the clarification of the Freudian material with a new look at Jones's 1916 paper

'The theory of symbolism', a paper whose contribution understandably has been overlooked. This prepares the way (in Chapter 10) for presenting the FB theory, highlighting its major propositions, and illustrating its dependence on Freud's general theory. In the final chapter, I defend the FB theory by setting out the logical and psychological requirements which any theory of symbolism must meet, and showing how the FB theory, unlike its competitors, meets them.

7 The problem of the 'system unconscious'

The first of the propositions which are to be rejected is the more problematic, but is the one to which critics have given less attention; this is that symbolism is the natural mode of expression of the 'system unconscious', a system with its own characteristics, contents, and modes of operation.

The unconscious and repression are two central concepts in psychoanalytic theory. Freud insisted that the 'division of the psychical into what is conscious and what is unconscious is the fundamental premiss of psycho-analysis' (1923d, p. 13), he labelled the unconscious 'the true psychical reality' (1900, p. 613), and he identified repression as the 'cornerstone on which the whole structure of psycho-analysis rests' (1914c, p. 16). As is well known, the treatment of the unconscious in Freud's writings underwent a number of changes, changes which occurred over the course of the development of his ideas, particularly with the move from the 'topographical' to the 'structural' model of the mind. Anyone who attempts to present a systematic account of these changes, and to state exactly what is involved at any particular stage of that development, soon discovers how inconsistent and confusing is Freud's material, and how difficult it is to trace the tortuous paths of the changing classifications of the unconscious ('descriptive', 'dynamic', 'systematic'), and its relations to the conscious, the preconscious, the id, the ego, the superego, and so on. Such an attempt, however, is fortunately not necessary in order to identify and evaluate the intersection of the problems of symbolism with the theory of the unconscious. These problems, I shall argue, begin with a particular conception of the unconscious.

The qualitative ('systematic') view of unconscious mentality

While it is often remarked that Freud neither invented nor discovered the unconscious (see, e.g., Whyte 1960), it has been suggested by his supporters that the originality and importance of his contribution lay in his particular treatment of it – as a separate system, which obeys its own laws:

careful students have perceived that Freud's revolutionary contribution to psychology was not so much his demonstrating the existence of an unconscious, and perhaps not even his exploration of its content, as his proposition that there are two fundamentally different kinds of mental processes, which he termed primary and secondary respectively. The laws applicable to the two groups are so widely different. (Jones 1953, p. 436)

This qualitative or 'systematic' view of unconscious mentality is one to which Freud himself became increasingly and more explicitly committed, and which has received considerable support from others. According to this view, there is some essential, intrinsic difference between conscious and unconscious mental processes – unconscious processes differ from conscious processes *in kind*, and not simply by the epistemic fact of their being unavailable to consciousness. Thus Freud:

the laws of unconscious activity differ widely from those of the conscious . . .

Unconsciousness seemed to us only an enigmatical characteristic of a definite psychical act. Now it means more for us. It is a sign that this act partakes of the nature of a certain psychical category known to us by other and more important characters and that it belongs to a system of psychical activity which is deserving of our fullest attention. (1912c, p. 266)

analytic investigation reveals some of these latent processes as having characteristics and peculiarities which seem alien to us, or even incredible, and which run directly counter to the attributes of consciousness with which we are familiar. (1915c, p. 170)

we cannot escape the ambiguity of using the words 'conscious' and 'unconscious' sometimes in a descriptive and sometimes in a systematic sense, in which latter they signify inclusion in particular systems and possession of certain characteristics. (ibid., p. 174)

The distinction we have made between the two psychical systems receives fresh significance when we observe that processes in the one system, the *Ucs.*, show characteristics which are not met with again in the system immediately above it. (ibid., p. 186)

It is the observation that unconscious processes *exhibit a number of peculiar characteristics* that reveals that they belong to a separate 'system'. In his 1915 paper, 'The unconscious', Freud devotes a separate section to 'The special characteristics of the system *Ucs.*':

The cathectic intensities [in the *Ucs.*] are much more mobile. By the process of *displacement* one idea may surrender to another its whole quota of cathexis; by the process of *condensation* it may appropriate the whole cathexis of several other ideas. I have proposed to regard these two processes as distinguishing marks of the so-called *primary psychical process*. (1915c, p. 186)

To sum up: *exemption from mutual contradiction, primary process* (mobility of cathexes), *timelessness*, and *replacement of external by psychical reality* – these are the characteristics which we may expect to find in processes belonging to the system *Ucs.*. (ibid., p. 187)

To be sure, Freud eventually abandoned the 'system *Ucs.*' in favour of the 'id', a move (originally made in 1923, in *The Ego and the Id*) which he felt was necessary in order to accommodate his discovery that parts of the ego and the superego are also unconscious:

We perceive that we have no right to name the mental region that is foreign to the ego 'the system *Ucs.*', since the characteristic of being unconscious is not restricted to it. Very well; we will no longer use the term 'unconscious' in the systematic sense and we will give what we have hitherto so described a better name. (1933, p. 72)

However, this move did not involve abandoning the notion of a separate system, whose contents were unconscious, and which had its own characteristics. The 'special characteristics' and functions of the system *Ucs.* were now inherited by the id. In fact, Freud continued, on occasion, to use the terms 'unconscious' and 'id' synonymously:

We have found that processes in the unconscious or in the id obey different laws from those in the preconscious ego. We name these laws in their totality the *primary process*, in contrast to the *secondary process* which governs the course of events in the preconscious, in the ego. (1940, p. 164)

Implications for the concept of repression: the 'structural' approach

With respect to the concept of repression, the compatible complement of the qualitative (i.e., systematic) view of unconscious mentality is a 'structural' account of repression. According to this view, material which is in the repressed unconscious is there because of its distinctive characteristics. Rather than the unconscious being unconscious because it has been repressed, the repressed is repressed *because it is unconscious*. No censor, no blocking mechanism, no dynamic force is required to prevent the repressed from entering consciousness. It simply *cannot* become conscious because it lacks the attributes or qualities of conscious processes. This account of repression is not in fact the one favoured by Freud, yet it is required both by his support of the systematic unconscious, and by his treatment of repressed ideas as having undergone various dissociative processes which must be reversed if the ideas are to become conscious. This view of repression could hardly be avoided once the systematic view of unconscious mentality is adopted. Further, this implication of the systematic unconscious allows Jung (and others after him) to reject the distinctively Freudian dynamic concept of repression: 'The form that dreams take is natural to the unconscious

... Dreams do not guard sleep from what Freud called the "incompatible wish". What he called "disguise" is actually the shape all impulses take in the unconscious' (Jung 1964, p. 53). Indeed, one might suggest that this step is equivalent to demolishing completely the concept of repression.

The view of the unconscious as a separate system, with its structural account of repression, has been attractive, and has featured in a number of later developments of Freudian theory, developments explicitly devoted to elucidating the special characteristics of unconscious processes. There are three different versions of the attempt to reformulate the system unconscious, and each has been able to draw support from Freud's own material. The first is in terms of linguistic concepts, presenting the unconscious as a 'language', with its own syntactic and semantic rules (Edelson 1972; Foulkes 1978). The second is in terms of logico-mathematical concepts, presenting the unconscious as consisting of 'infinite sets' and operating according to its own 'logic' (Matte Blanco 1975). The third presents the unconscious as consisting of 'prepropositional' mental states, in contrast to the propositional mental states of the conscious system (Gardner 1993).

However, from Freud's original treatment onwards, the concept of the 'system unconscious' has led to serious theoretical difficulties and confusions which, apart from obscuring the insights which *are* to be found in Freud's material, have left the unconscious vulnerable to the kind of extreme verdict recently pronounced by Varela (1995); that we have no choice but to abandon the conception of the unconscious as a substantive, causal and lawful entity, and, together with it, any reconceptualisation which stems from the Freudian original. To make matters worse, many of the resulting tensions have spread so far into other material that their origins in the 'system unconscious' have gone unrecognised. This is particularly true in the case of symbolism; the anomalies in the Freudian material have been attacked by Freud's critics, and his supporters are left struggling in vain to answer the criticisms and to make sense of Freud's account.

Problems for the systematic unconscious and structural repression

The major criticism of Freud's formulation is that the putative peculiar 'mechanisms', 'characteristics' and 'contents' of the unconscious are *demonstrably not distinctive* of unconscious processes. To begin with, several scholars have pointed to the unsustainability of the notion that the modes of operation identified by Freud are peculiar to unconscious processes. They are, on the contrary, just as familiar in conscious mentality, in the form of the linguistic devices of metaphor and metonymy. As Forrester (1980) remarks: 'The processes he [Freud] conceived of as specific to the dream-work – condensation, displacement – have close affinities with strictly linguistic devices (metaphor, metonymy, tropes)' (p. 7). Todorov (1982) relates this observation specifically to symbolism, pointing out that 'the symbolic mechanism that Freud has described lacks specificity; the operations that he identifies are simply those of any linguistic symbolism, as they have been inventoried, most notably, by the rhetorical tradition' (p. 248). In support, Todorov points to a number of passages in *The Interpretation of Dreams* where the connection between symbolism and metaphor is closely drawn. Further, the ubiquity of condensation and displacement in conscious mentality has been used to attack Freud's restriction of the concept of symbolism to an unconscious mode of operation. This objection applies not just to the supposed mechanisms and characteristics of the unconscious, but also to its supposed 'contents'. They too are not different *in kind*. While certain thoughts, wishes, etc. may typically be found in the unconscious, the typicality of their occurrence there is attributable to the fact that those particular thoughts and wishes tend to become the object of social or moral censure, and so are more likely to be repressed. But if they are not repressed, or if the repression is 'lifted', there is no impediment to their being or becoming conscious.

Despite these criticisms in the literature, their implications have not been driven home: if the unconscious as a system cannot be distinguished from the conscious in terms of its 'characteristics', 'mechanisms' or 'contents', then the claim that any particular kind of material (in our case, symbolism) belongs to the peculiar mode of operation of the system unconscious cannot be upheld; there simply is no such peculiar mode.

This same objection likewise undermines the more recent attempts to elaborate or reformulate the systematic unconscious.

The unconscious is a language

The reformulation of the 'system unconscious' in linguistic terms is illustrated in Edelson's (1972) attempt, supported by Foulkes (1978), to assimilate Freudian dream theory (with its latent and manifest content) to Chomskyan linguistic structuralism (with its deep and surface structures). The starting point is Freud's comment that 'the dream content seems like a transcript of the dream thoughts into another mode of expression whose characters and syntactic laws it is our business to discover by comparing the original and the translation' (1900, p. 277). While it is taken for granted that the unconscious and the conscious are separate systems, the problem is that of their obvious interaction. This problem is particularly acute if the unconscious is conceived of as consisting of non-cognitive instinctual drives. As Foulkes remarks, 'so long as the unconscious is viewed as a repository of biological entities, its integration with thought or image justifiably will appear to contemporary cognitivists as exceedingly difficult' (1978, p. 22). The solution, according to Edelson and Foulkes, is to treat the unconscious as consisting of 'a finite set of underlying, personally significant propositions', which, in dreaming, are transformed into the 'infinitely various forms of dream imagery' (Foulkes 1978, p. 17) by 'a syntactic mechanism, a "parser" which . . . assigns visual constituents to verbally coded propositions' (ibid., p. 174). Thus, says Edelson, what distinguishes the unconscious from the conscious is that the former consists of the deep structures from which are generated the surface structures of the latter, the dream-work processes being analogous to generative transformational rules. As for repression, it is argued that the primary motive for dream distortion (i.e., for manifest content) is not censorship, but the intrinsic constraints of the representational medium in which that content is found. Distortion is a natural result of the characteristics of the system unconscious, for 'if the special characteristics of the dream can be explained by other considerations (necessary from the point of view of the nature of a symbolic system), such as economy and representability, without recourse to the postulation of a "censor" operating in the sleeping state . . . then it might be more parsimonious to accept such an explanation' (Edelson 1972, p. 268).

Now, while it is a considerable conceptual advance to recognise the *cognitive* nature of the unconscious (that amongst its 'contents' one may find, so to speak, unconscious knowings and unconscious believings), and it is thus legitimate to describe it as consisting of a set of 'personally significant propositions', it is not at all clear that such propositions (basically, *thoughts*) require *translation* in order to become conscious. The propositional nature of thinking does not, of course, make cognition *linguistic* in nature – but this confusion (which is addressed in the next chapter) is not relevant here. What *is* relevant is that, just as Chomsky's deep structures are not of a form which *cannot* appear in surface structures (e.g., the sentence 'the short happy boy who wanted to go to the store went with his mother' is supposedly derived from simpler underlying structures of the form 'the boy was short', 'the boy was happy', 'the boy wanted to go to the store', etc.), so latent or unconscious thoughts (such as the Rat Man's 'I hate my father') may, under certain conditions, appear consciously *in exactly the same form*. As for the version of structural repression, cast in terms of the constraints on possible representations, the obvious objection is that, whatever restrictions on the dream images arise from the peculiar nature of the representational medium, they cannot account for the conscious/unconscious distinction, because they cannot account for the *direction* of the substitution, for the occurrence of the manifest, in place of the latent, content. In a classic Oedipal dream, for instance, the presence of the queen might be a 'disguise' for the mother. But the conditions of pictorial representability are *equally* applicable to each of these; it is no more difficult to represent the mother via a visual image than it is to represent the queen. Why one image, then, and not the other, appears in the dream must be explained in some other way.

The unconscious has its own 'logic'

On occasion, Freud's characterisation of the system unconscious focused on the peculiar 'logic' of its operations:

The logical laws of thought do not apply in the id, and this is true above all of the law of contradiction . . . There is nothing in the id that could be compared with negation; and we perceive with surprise an exception to the philosophical theorem that space and time are necessary forms of our mental acts. (1933, pp. 73–4)

The governing rules of logic carry no weight in the unconscious; it might be called the Realm of the Illogical. (1940, pp. 168–9)

In accordance with these remarks, a reformulation of the Freudian unconscious in terms of 'logico-mathematical' concepts has been offered by Matte Blanco (1975) in *The Unconscious as Infinite Sets: An Essay in Bi-Logic*. The term 'Bi-Logic' is used to indicate that the mind operates according to two, radically different, systems of logic – conscious processes according to normal, 'asymmetrical', Aristotelian logical principles, and unconscious processes according to 'symmetrical logic' (whose two principles are 'generalisation' and 'symmetry'). Freud's 'system *Ucs.*' thus becomes renamed the 'symmetrical mode of being'. From 'symmetrical logic', in which asymmetrical relations are treated as if they were symmetrical, follow all the characteristics of the system to which Freud pointed. For example, if A follows B, the unconscious treats this as if the relation were symmetrical, and assumes that B also follows A. This means that it cannot recognise a succession of movements; hence, the unconscious is characterised by 'absence of time'. Symmetrical relations lie at the heart of symbolism, for symbolism involves a belief in the identity of symbol and symbolised. Now, because the unconscious *does not know individuals but only classes or propositional functions which define the class* (Matte Blanco 1975, p. 139, italics in original), whenever we desire anything, we desire the whole class of things which resemble the object of desire. In the case, for example, of the unconscious symbolic representation of the breast, this object, by virtue of the infinite number of objects which bear some similarity to it, becomes an 'open class' with an 'infinite number of elements', so that: 'In these circumstances (i.e. being "breast-oriented") it is out of the question that something may be included in the list . . . and have at the same time the possibility of either being or not being a breast for the unconscious' (ibid., p. 316). Structural repression is guaranteed by the fact that the 'quality' of being unconscious is a consequence of the different logical structure of unconscious processes, with the result that 'this mode of being cannot directly enter consciousness: consciousness does not have the dimensions to contain it' (ibid., p. 69). According to Matte Blanco, there is no need for a dynamic process to keep something out of consciousness, because *there is an intrinsic impossibility of it entering directly into consciousness, and this seems to be a point which has never been clear in psychoanalytic thinking* (ibid., p. 84, italics in original).

But this version of the systematic unconscious and structural repression fares no better than the previous one, because the operations identified by Matte Blanco as belonging to the 'symmetrical mode of being' are merely relationships between propositions (which are the objects of the propositional attitudes held by the person), such that the reasoning which moves from one such proposition to another is logically invalid. To believe that if A follows B then B follows A is simply to reason invalidly. And it is not 'the unconscious' which reasons thus, but the *person*. Furthermore, such reasoning is not *distinctive* of, because it is manifestly not restricted to, unconscious thinking. A considerable body of literature in psychology attests to the ubiquity of the conscious drawing of invalid inferences, and the prevalence of the failure to observe the law of non-contradiction. These objections reveal that the structural account of repression, according to which the unconscious cannot become conscious by virtue of its nature or structure, must also fail, for that structure turns out not to differ from the structure of the conscious.

The unconscious consists of 'pre-propositional' mental states

The most recent version of Freud's 'system unconscious', developed by Gardner (1993), presents the unconscious as consisting of 'pre-propositional' mental states, in contrast to the propositional mental states of the conscious system. Briefly, Gardner's proposal is an attempt to defend, in the face of Sartre's (1956) critique of mental plurality and dynamic repression, the ability of psychoanalytic theory to explain human irrationality. He argues that the only defence is a structural account of repression and a systematic account of unconscious mentality. This means that unconscious mental states cannot be assimilated to conscious mental states, since the two are different *in kind*. Thus, the 'widespread view of the nature of Freud's postulation of unconscious motives – as simply transposing ordinary psychology into an unconscious key' (1993, p. 7) is erroneous. Instead, unconscious mental states, being pre-propositional, are *not* species of, or combinations of, beliefs or desires (since these latter are propositional, and so belong to the conscious system), but they *are*, nevertheless, *psychological*. There is, therefore, 'a psychological stratum intervening between bare behaviour and complex attributions of belief and desire' (ibid., pp. 232–3). From this, the structural account of repression follows naturally. What is repressed is 'repressed' because '*the thought itself can not be manifested* in consciousness' (ibid., p. 103, italics in original). Within this context, Gardner provides an account of symbolism which avoids the notorious problem of the censor, and depends, instead, on the notion of unconscious, pre-propositional 'seeing-as'. This process does not involve belief (and so, *a fortiori*, does not involve belief in the identity of symbol and symbolised), but is, rather, a 'non-cognitive' kind of Humean symbol/symbolised 'association'. Thus, the substitution of the symbol for the symbolised occurs 'on the border of the propositional and the pre-propositional', where 'the relevant symbolic substitution does not require an act of thought' (ibid., p. 134). Sublimation is identified by Gardner as 'an important specific form of unconscious seeing-as', in which the seeing-as is 'correlated with the acknowledgement of psychic reality'. Taking Segal's (1958) distinction between 'symbolic representation' and 'symbolic equation', exemplified in the difference between a man who sublimates his masturbatory phantasy in dreaming that he is playing a violin duet with his lover, and a schizophrenic who cannot play the violin in public because that would be equivalent to masturbation, Gardner says:

What distinguishes sublimation is a negative belief, expressing the Reality Principle, to the effect that S ≠ X: a realisation that S is only a symbol. When the unconscious seeing of S-as-X is brought up against an appreciation of their real non-identity, that structure is not abolished, but rather robbed of its irrational coercive power . . . The corrective belief constitutive of sublimation need not, of course, take an explicit form . . . (Gardner 1993, p. 168)

Now, this account appears to involve a contradiction, produced by the claim that 'seeing-as' does not involve a belief in identity. If sublimation is to be distinguished from ordinary symbolism via a 'corrective' belief in the *non*-identity of S and X, such a belief can only be 'corrective' if, after all, there *is* a belief (albeit unconscious) in identity. Thus, the use of the term 'seeing-as', which is supposed to indicate a kind of mental process different from believing, is merely a way of saying that the person 'believes but does not really believe'. The term 'seeing-as' is attractive because it can disguise the contradiction involved, and so evade the problematic implication of mental plurality. More importantly, it suggests that the unconscious *does* include propositional mental states such as beliefs. Indeed, this conclusion is borne out by a consideration of Gardner's own examples. I do not have the space here to argue the case in the necessary detail. But, briefly, it is based on the following points. Firstly, it is quite unclear what Gardner's candidates for pre-propositionality are. In his explicit statement of his thesis, they are wish-fulfilment and phantasy (as expounded by Klein), but he also nominates 'ideas' (the components supposedly left behind in the unconscious after repression), on other occasions 'thoughts' ('the thought itself can not be manifested in consciousness'), and, on yet other occasions, emotions. When each is considered in turn, it is not clear how any of them can escape propositionality. Indeed, there are serious difficulties with the notion of pre-propositional *mental* content, of the idea of a level between 'bare behaviour' and 'propositional attitudes' which is nevertheless mental. But, even if that notion were salvageable, it appears not to serve Gardner's purpose. Either his examples (such as the Rat Man's unconscious hatred of his father) actually betray a content which is fully propositional (and so no different from conscious content), or, even if it were granted that the propositional status of the mental contents in those examples *is* uncertain, these contents are demonstrably not distinctive of unconscious mentality, and so cannot illustrate the *difference* between unconscious and conscious states.

These criticisms all point to the same conclusion. The failure of attempts to show that unconscious mentality differs from conscious mentality in non-epistemic, qualitative respects, suggests that the 'structure' of unconscious mentality (whether in terms of the relationship between propositions, i.e., in terms of the validity or invalidity of the reasoning involved, or in terms of the status of the objects as propositional or not) is not, and cannot be, different from the 'structure' of conscious mentality. Thus, the 'system unconscious' cannot be independently, intrinsically, characterisable. There is, therefore, no such system.

Yet all is not lost. We are by no means forced to agree with Varela

(1995) that the concept of the unconscious should be abandoned. There is a solution at hand – ironically, in Freud's own writings. It has not been generally recognised that Freud actually presents *two* basic (but incompatible) views of the unconscious, and *two* basic (but incompatible) views of repression. Alongside the qualitative or systematic unconscious (whose complement is the structural account of repression) is a second view, one which has been overshadowed and largely neglected, both by Freud and by post-Freudian theorists. This second approach may be called the relational (or 'epistemic') view of unconscious mentality, and its complement is a 'dynamic' approach to repression.

The relational ('epistemic') view of unconscious mentality

This alternative view is seen in Freud's characterisation of unconscious mentality in what he calls the 'descriptive' sense (Freud 1912c, 1915c, 1923d, 1933). It includes both the repressed unconscious (the 'dynamic' unconscious), and the unrepressed unconscious (or 'pre-conscious'). On this account unconscious mental states are claimed to differ from conscious mental states only by the fact of their being unconscious, which fact is *relational*, not qualitative (although Freud, misleadingly, talks of unconsciousness as a 'quality' in this context, and does not explicitly identify and emphasise the relational nature of his 'descriptive' characterisation. This inappropriate use of the word 'quality' is adopted by many post-Freudians.). So, a mental state is unconscious if it is *unknown*. While this may not be so clear from the English word 'unconscious', it is in keeping with the passive participal force of the German word used by Freud, whether in its adjectival form (*unbewusst*), or in its substantival form (*das Unbewusste*). This view of unconscious mentality is crystal clear in the following statements from Freud:

> Now let us call 'conscious' the conception which is present to our consciousness and *of which we are aware*, and let this be the only meaning of the term 'conscious'. As for latent conceptions, if we have any reason to suppose that they exist in the mind . . . let them be denoted by the term 'unconscious'.
>
> Thus an unconscious conception is one *of which we are not aware*, but the existence of which we are nevertheless ready to admit on account of other proofs or signs. (1912c, p. 260, italics mine)

all the categories which we employ to describe conscious mental acts, such as ideas, purposes, resolutions and so on, can be applied to them [i.e., unconscious mental acts]. Indeed, we are obliged to say of some of these latent states that the only respect in which they differ from conscious states is precisely in the absence of consciousness. (1915c, p. 168)

large portions of the ego and super-ego can remain unconscious and are normally unconscious. That is to say, the individual knows nothing of their contents. (1933, pp. 69–70)

We call a psychical process unconscious whose existence we are obliged to assume . . . but of which we know nothing. (ibid., p. 70)

In accordance with this view, Freud is acknowledging a logical point when he asserts that every mental process must begin as an unconscious one. This is because it requires a second mental act in order for the first to become conscious – that is, a mental act becomes 'conscious' (i.e., known) only when it becomes the object of a further mental act:

every psychical act begins as an unconscious one, and it may either remain so or go on developing into consciousness. (1912c, p. 264)

every mental process . . . exists to begin with in an unconscious stage or phase. (1916/17, p. 295)

there is no choice for us but to assert that mental processes are in themselves unconscious, and to liken the perception of them by means of consciousness to the perception of the external world by means of the sense-organs. (1915c, p. 171)

Psycho-analysis regarded everything mental as being in the first instance unconscious; the further quality of 'consciousness' might also be present, or again it might be absent. (1925d, p. 31)

This approach to unconscious mentality is consistent with the view of mentality (conscious or unconscious) which regards mental processes (knowing, believing, perceiving, remembering, etc.) as *relations* between a cognising subject and a state of affairs cognised. Such a relational account has a long tradition and can be traced historically in a number of separate ideas: Aristotle's notion of the πρός τι ('towards something') of mentality, which was developed, via medieval scholasticism, into Brentano's identification of the 'intentionality' of mental states; Thomas Reid's alternative to the intermediary 'ideas' in Locke's account of mind; and William James's functionalist rejection of 'mind stuff'. It also forms a central part of the realist, relational account of mentality developed in the school of 'Andersonian Realism' (see Baker 1986) by Anderson (1927, 1929, 1930) and, for example, Passmore (1962), Maze (1983, 1991), and Michell (1988). This account emphasises the distinction between relations and qualities, arguing that any reification of mental relations (including 'being aware of' or 'being conscious of') is logically incoherent. Accordingly, the substantive 'consciousness' and 'unconsciousness', being just such reifications, must be rejected.

This view of unconscious mentality is also consistent with Freud's rejection of the Cartesian notion of consciousness as transparent to itself. If my knowing that p (or being conscious that p, or being aware of p), is a relation, then, for that knowing to be conscious (i.e., known) it must itself become the object of a separate knowing relation. In that case, the object of the second relation (i.e., my knowing that p) is plainly different from the object of the first relation (i.e., p). Further, although the second act often does occur, it is clear that such an occurrence is not entailed by the first act, and so is not a necessary or automatic accompaniment, as Descartes claimed. This is exactly the point made by James when he suggests that the stream of *cons*ciousness is more accurately described as a stream of '*Scious*ness pure and simple', because the 'knowing is not immediately *known*. It is only known in subsequent reflection', and so the stream of thought must not be conceived as 'thinking its own existence along with whatever else it thinks' (James 1890, vol. 1, p. 304).

To identify a particular mental act as unconscious, then, is not to say anything about its intrinsic nature, but only to say something about its relations (i.e., that it is not known). Naturally, the relational view must include as unconscious any mental state which is unknown for any reason; that is, it incorporates both the repressed unconscious, and the 'latent' unconscious (or pre-conscious). The fact of a particular mental state's being unconscious does not imply anything about why it is so:

the distinction between conscious and unconscious is in the last resort a question of perception, which must be answered 'yes' or 'no', and the act of perception itself tells us nothing of the reason why a thing is or is not perceived. (Freud 1923d, pp. 15–16)

Implications for the concept of repression: the 'dynamic' approach

The relational or epistemic view of unconscious mentality is compatible with a 'dynamic' account of repression, according to which an unconscious process is blocked or prevented from becoming conscious by a part of the mind which finds the content unacceptable: '*the essence of repression lies simply in turning something away, and keeping it at a distance, from the conscious*' (Freud 1915b, p. 147, italics in original). This is the account of repression which appears throughout Freud's writings. According to this view, the repressed unconscious is unconscious *because* it has been repressed, and can become conscious as a result of the 'lifting' of repression. Of course, this may be a complex process:

Freud himself commented on the apparent paradox, according to which informing the patient that he or she holds unconsciously a particular belief does not necessarily lead to the lifting of repression. An explanation of this fact would require sophisticated working out, would probably incorporate the thesis of mental plurality, and would certainly require a major overhauling of Freud's discussion of 'thing presentations' and 'word presentations', and their relationship to the dissociation and re-combination of 'idea' and 'affect'. However, the important point here is that, if the repression is lifted, the unconscious states will become conscious, but, since this is a relational change, the nature of those states will not change: 'we are inclined . . . to forget too readily that repression . . . in fact interferes only with the relation of the instinctual representative to one psychical system, namely to that of the conscious' (Freud 1915b, p. 147). The integration of this view of repression with the relational view of unconscious mentality is clear:

Psycho-analysis leaves no room for doubt that the repulsion from unconscious ideas is only provoked by the tendencies embodied in their contents . . . every psychical act begins as an unconscious one, and it may either remain so or go on developing into consciousness, according as it meets with resistance or not. (Freud 1912c, p. 264)

With respect to Freud's theory of symbolism, the extension of this stance is seen in what Todorov (1982) calls Freud's 'anti-romantic', 'realist' insistence that, insofar as the symbol is the manifest, and the symbolised the latent, content, what the symbol stands for in symbolism, what is disguised, is not 'ineffable' or in any way essentially different from what might, given different conditions of socialisation and repression, not be disguised. Herein lies a major distinction between Freud and Jung, a distinction which is necessarily eroded if the dynamic view of repression is abandoned.

That the dynamic account of repression requires some kind of mental plurality is obvious. Freud himself recognised this:

a dreamer in relation to his dream-wishes can only be compared to an amalgamation of two separate people who are linked by some important common element. (1919a, n. p. 581)

We should long ago have asked the question: from *what part of his mind* does an unconscious resistance like this arise? (1933, p. 68)

It is this view of repression which was subject to the famous critique by Sartre (1956), whose attack is considered by Gardner (1993) to be successful enough to warrant abandoning the thesis of mental plurality. However, if the structural account of repression fails, and the dynamic account is adopted, and if mental plurality is in any case necessitated by other considerations, then the supposed implications of Sartre's criticisms would require re-examination.

Clarifications and answers to criticisms

The adoption of the relational view of unconscious mentality and the dynamic account of repression allows us to reply to a number of hitherto unanswered criticisms, and to clarify several important aspects of the Freudian material. This clarification is necessary if the Freudian theory of symbolism is not to be left open to certain difficulties, which have arisen as a result of adherence to the notion of the systematic unconscious. Both the critics and the supporters of Freud fail to appreciate that these problems originate in the concept of the unconscious as a separate system, and, as a result, their attempted solutions are unsatisfactory, sometimes serving only to exacerbate the initial problems.

The supposed failure of disguise

To begin with, we can rebut Hall's (1953) attack on Freud's concept of disguise in a dream. Hall insists that he objects not to the idea that the dreamer uses symbols in the dream but, rather, to Freud's theory that the symbols hide something objectionable. One of Hall's reasons for this rejection is that the dreamer may one night have a disguised incestuous dream, and the next night have an open, undisguised dream on the same theme; in other words, for any particular person, what is latent content on one occasion may be manifest (more accurately, undisguised) content on another. Hall comments: 'What is the sense of preparing an elaborate disguise in one dream when it is discarded in another dream? I have not been able to find a convincing answer to this question in Freudian theory' (1953, p. 94).

As a matter of fact, Freud does address this question, pointing to Jocasta's remark to Oedipus that many young men dream undisguisedly of lying with their mother. True, says Freud, but 'I can say with certainty that *disguised* dreams of sexual intercourse with the dreamer's mother are many times more frequent than straightforward ones' (Freud 1909c, p. 398). Now, according to the relational view of unconscious mentality, since there is nothing about the content *per se* which requires that it be unconscious, the occurrence of openly incestuous dream content is not ruled out. Further, according to the dynamic account of repression, whether or not a particular content is subject to repression depends on motivational forces, which are liable to vary. Such variation is perfectly familiar to us in the non-psychoanalytic phenomenon of desensitisation: a person may be desensitised to a particular objection-able content, as a result of which the resistance to that content is (temporarily or permanently) decreased or removed. Since objecting to something is a relation, and nothing can be objectionable in itself, what is affected by the process of desensitisation is the person's relation to the mental content, not the content itself. Psychoanalytic theory does not hold that the same content is always equally objectionable and equally repressed, so a dreamer may very well have a disguised Oedipal dream one night, and on the next night an undisguised Oedipal dream. Rather than undermining the psychoanalytic theory, such facts under-score the contribution of that theory, which lies in elucidating both the general processes by which particular mental contents become repressed, and the reasons for variation on different occasions. In fact, the interchangeability of disguised and undisguised content keeps faith with Freud's realism with respect to the latent content (it is not intrin-sically different from manifest content, and so not incapable of consti-tuting the manifest content).

Freud's 'illegitimate' parallel between conscious and unconscious processes

Another major criticism which can be answered is the attack by Macmil-lan (1991) on Freud's supposedly illegitimate 'playing on' the 'postu-lated resemblance' between unconscious and conscious mental pro-cesses. Macmillan argues that we accept Freud's theory of the unconscious because we are seduced by his claim that irrational, inex-plicable mental processes may be understood by analogy with rational, explicable processes:

A further aspect of the appeal of the irrational is what Wittgenstein called the charm of psycho-analysis, a charm coming from the resemblance which Freud's unconscious motivational explanations have to ordinary ones. For all Freud's talk of a chaotic and irrational primary process, the unconscious wishes and motives with which he explains dreams or slips of the tongue seem just like ordinary ones, acting in exactly the same way as their conscious counterparts. (Macmillan 1991, p. 605)

The arguments presented earlier indicate that Macmillan is correct to doubt the supposedly distinctive 'chaotic and irrational' processes in the unconscious, but he fails to appreciate the evidential weight of this for the soundness of Freud's parallel. Instead:

Coming to Freud for the first time, we find we already understand the purely conscious instances of motivated forgetting and have little difficulty with the preconscious ones. It is then but a short step to accepting Freud's examples of unconscious motives along with the rest of the theory. When, in turn, we come to supposed unconscious lusts and hatreds, we have been readied to find they, too, resemble our conscious drives. Our self-applications, now easily made, produce a high level of conviction. (ibid., p. 606)

Thus, according to Macmillan, Freud fabricates the similarity between conscious and unconscious mentality:

Freud may have been aware of the charm and power of his conceptualisation of unconscious processes. Certainly he frequently capitalised on the postulated resemblance between them and conscious processes . . . As Freud set it out, slips of the tongue varied between those supposedly produced by counter-intentions of which we are aware at the time to those produced by repressed unconscious impulses. In between are those produced by the preconscious motives or counter-intentions we can fairly readily bring back to consciousness. But, whatever their type, and wherever they are located, these counter-intentions act on the primary intention in exactly the same way. We also find Freud playing on the conscious-unconscious parallel in the *Introductory Lectures*. (ibid., p. 606)

But on the relational view of unconscious mental processes, this resemblance and parallelism is exactly what should be expected. Macmillan simply asserts that 'the appeal of Freud's parallel is inversely related to the strength of its logical foundations' (ibid.), and he points to observations by others that 'many of Freud's interpretations of parapraxes depend on a verbally competent unconscious and so contradict his basic postulate that unconscious processes are irrational and non-verbal' (ibid.). True; there is a contradiction here. But it suggests that the 'basic postulate' is false, and that there is, after all, a parallel between conscious and unconscious processes. The recognition of a verbally competent unconscious is evidence against the 'systematic' difference between conscious and unconscious. For, once again, a 'verbally competent' unconscious is exactly what would be expected (consider, for example, the famous case of 'Bridey Murphy' (Bernstein 1956), who knew certain linguistic expressions and their meanings, yet had come to forget that she knew them).

Clarifying the 'characteristics' of unconscious thinking

Adopting the relational view of unconscious mentality does not prevent us from accommodating some of the insights offered by Freud in his discussion of the 'special characteristics of the system unconscious', even if those characteristics cannot be special to the unconscious. It will be recalled that Freud lists these as: exemption from mutual contradiction, primary process (displacement and condensation), timelessness, and replacement of external by psychical reality.

Firstly, 'exemption from mutual contradiction' arises in the context of two related observations. Instinctual drives, representing conflicting interests, coexist in the organism and simultaneously press for gratification. These *drives*, of course, are not contradictory, but the results of their conflicting interests can sometimes be expressed in terms of pairs of contradictory assertions such as 'I hate my father' and 'I do not hate my father'. Similarly, the explanation of behaviour in terms of the causal efficacy of repressed, unconscious mental processes often includes the person's maintaining contradictory propositional attitudes, at least one of which is typically unconscious. Secondly, the so-called 'primary process' mechanisms of condensation and displacement, while not peculiar to unconscious processes, are undoubtedly involved in the complex of conscious and unconscious processes which produces substitute formations of the kind on which psychoanalysts focus. Thirdly, 'timelessness' can be taken to refer to two separate facts. The first is that the instinctual drives themselves are, so to speak, timeless; they are continuous forces pressing always for gratification (not necessarily in the sense that one is always, say, hungry, but more in the sense that one's hunger drive is always alert to, and capable of reacting to, information which is relevant to its own gratification, present or future). The second fact is that what is important in early childhood, particularly if it has been subject to repression, remains important in later life, and, further, is typically not acknowledged as belonging to the past. For example, in the phenomenon of transference, the patient does not realise that he or she is re-enacting the past in the present. Finally, 'replacement of external by psychical reality' is a general statement regarding the importance and causal efficacy of wishful thinking, phantasy, delusion, hallucination, etc., which may replace veridical perception of reality, and, typically, do so unconsciously. One way of summarising these observations is that it is not that the unconscious is 'timeless', 'exempt from contradiction', etc., but simply that the inexorability of time, the fact of contradiction, etc., are often unconsciously ignored or denied.

Implications for the distinction between primary and secondary processes

Adopting the notions of the relational unconscious and dynamic repression also provides a framework for dispelling some of the confusions, and answering some of the criticisms, surrounding the supposed distinction between 'primary' and 'secondary' processes, both as they apply to thinking in general, and to symbolism in particular. This distinction is the one which Jones (1953) identified as Freud's 'revolutionary contribution to psychology' (p. 436). On examination, however, the distinction is, at best, misleading.

Freud claims that the unconscious (or the id) is characterised by the 'primary process', which is 'irrational', and whose 'mobility of cathexes' is provided by the mechanisms of condensation and displacement. These two processes are 'distinguishing marks of the so-called *primary psychical process*' (1915c, p. 186). The term 'primary process' is also used to refer to primitive, infantile, hallucinatory attempts at instinctual gratification (in accordance with the Pleasure Principle), before the Reality Principle comes to prompt the infant to engage in the 'secondary process' of 'reality testing', i.e., to search the environment for real objects which will provide real gratification. In contrast to primary processes, secondary processes are 'rational', 'bound' (i.e., instinctual cathexes are less mobile), and involve the 'replacement of psychical by external reality'.

This characterisation of the primary/secondary process distinction, related as it is to the systematic unconscious, fails on two counts. Firstly, as has already been shown, whether we are considering the mechanisms of condensation and displacement, or whether we are referring to the irrationality of certain mental processes, the characteristics of the unconscious (and so of its primary process *modus operandi*) are not distinctive of it. Secondly, wishful thinking and hallucinatory attempts at gratification cannot occur without prior experience both of real, gratifying objects and of the loss or absence of those objects. In other words, primary process thinking, insofar as it consists of hallucinating objects of gratification, must *follow* secondary process thinking; one needs to have perceived the real object in order to be able to hallucinate it, and one needs to be experiencing real loss or frustration, in order for the hallucinatory wish to be set in motion. Therefore, the type of thinking identified in psychoanalysis as 'primary' is primary neither logically nor temporally.

There *is*, however, a genuine aspect of early (and so infantile) mental life which is included in the notion of primary process thinking. This is the infant's initial inability to tolerate frustration (whether in the form of the absence of gratification, or in the form of delayed gratification). The infant's immediate response to this frustration is the formation of hallucinatory wish-fulfilments (false beliefs). Naturally, such a response is insufficient, and the infant is eventually forced to abandon phantasy in favour of reality. However, if the characteristics which are supposed to distinguish 'primary processes' from 'secondary processes' are *not* distinctive, and if the epithets 'primary' and 'secondary' are inappropriate in all but this last sense, the best way to avoid the confusions would be to abandon the use of these terms.

These observations lead to a number of clarifications. One of the major confusions engendered by the distinction between primary and secondary processes has been a forced gulf between the id and the ego, which are typically taken to be co-ordinate with the two kinds of processes. Jones, for example, takes Freud's distinction between the wish-fulfilment of the primary process and the reality-orientation of the secondary process, and parallels that with the difference between a reflex action and more complex reactions which involve cognitions. This is dangerously misleading; it fuels the widespread misunderstanding that cognition belongs properly to the secondary, but not to the primary process. The id, which is characterised by primary processes, is typically represented as not involving thoughts and cognition, not involving 'cognitive transactions with the external world'. Instead, such transactions, secondary processes, are held to be the function of the ego. Many 'ego psychologists' are then faced with two problems. Firstly, they object to what they perceive to be the overly strong focus by 'classical' Freudians on the id, supposedly composed of unconscious, non-cognitive, purely biological instinctual drives, and they accuse these theorists of neglecting secondary (ego) processes, of treating the ego as a later development from the id (rather than as something present at, or even before, birth). Secondly, they are puzzled by the mystery of how the non-cognitive, purely biological id can interact with the cognitive ego. These concerns and accusations rest on misunderstandings of Freud's theory, for which, admittedly, Freud may to some extent be responsible (for example, in his later characterisation of the ego as a set of control functions interfacing cognitively with the external environment). But, as Maze (1983) has argued, this theoretical change was unsound and unwarranted. Freud's sound distinctions between unconscious and conscious mentality, reality and wish-fulfilment, rationality and irrationality, ability and inability to tolerate frustration, are not captured by his particular version of a primary/secondary process distinction, and in fact are obfuscated by the way that distinction is presented. If, however, we take the relational view of unconscious mentality, together with the genuine distinctions listed above, there is an interpretation of Freud's observations which does not lead to such misunderstandings. The interpretation consists of three points. Firstly, given that the infant can perceive, feel, etc., it is, from the very start, engaged in cognition. Thus, insofar as Freud's critics take (mistakenly) 'cognitive transactions with reality' to be the essential core of the ego, they are correct to locate the origins of the ego alongside the origins of the id, for these cognitive transactions appear at (or before) birth. Secondly, before an object can be hallucinated, it must have been perceived. At least part of what it is to hallucinate an object is to believe falsely that the object is present, and such a false belief requires a prior true belief. Error is dependent on knowledge, as it logically must be, and the implication for psychoanalysis is that psychic life does not begin with hallucination but with veridical apprehension. Thirdly, the mystery of id–ego interaction, how a non-cognitive drive can interact with a cognitive thought, disappears once it is understood that instinctual drives are from the very beginning capable of cognising (or of being in contact, in some sense, with the infant's cognitive apparatus); thus, they are all engaged in cognitive interchanges with the environment. This is not at all to suggest, however, that the Freudian distinction between the 'primary' and the 'derivative' (in terms of a distinction between original objects of desire and their substitutes) be abandoned.

Resolution of tensions in the treatment of repression

All this takes us several steps closer to clarifying a number of significant, hitherto unresolved, tensions in psychoanalytic theory. These tensions can be attributed to a failure to see that dynamic and structural repression, stemming from two incompatible approaches to the unconscious, are incompatible. This failure has led to futile attempts by Freud's supporters to accommodate those incompatibilities within a single theoretical framework.

Amongst Freud's supporters, Wollheim (1971), for example, remarks on the apparent inconsistency between the treatment of condensation and displacement as methods of distortion used by the censor, and those same mechanisms as inherent characteristics of unconscious mental activity:

However, there is, on the face of it, a difficulty in putting these two views together. For how can condensation and displacement be imposed on unconscious mental processes by the censor if such processes inherently exhibit these characteristics? And, if they do, what need can there be for censorship? (Wollheim 1971, p. 164)

Wollheim's response is to say that the dilemma is not serious, since it depends on the 'point of view from which we regard the unconscious' (ibid., p. 165), i.e., whether we are considering the unconscious as it impinges on the conscious, or whether we are considering the unconscious in itself. This will not do; apart from the fact that condensation and displacement are manifestly not *peculiar* to unconscious processes, the contradiction can only be resolved by rejecting one of the competing assertions.

Amongst Freud's critics, Macmillan (1991) draws attention to the same problem, and he correctly locates this within the wider context of Freud's inconsistencies regarding the characterisation of unconscious and conscious, and primary and secondary, processes. Of the way in which censorship is supposedly related to condensation and displacement, Macmillan observes:

Both processes form part of the dream-work, seemingly contributing equally to dream distortion . . . both reflect primary-process thinking . . . yet only displacement was said to be a function of the censorship . . . What the inconsistency reflects is Freud's difficulty in reconciling an explanation of dreams in terms of a regressive flow of excitation, where distortions are produced automatically, with an explanation in terms of wishes, psychological forces, and counter-forces. (Macmillan 1991, p. 269)

The confusion to which Macmillan is pointing leads to further problems for Freud, especially, as we shall see shortly, in his account of symbolism. No wonder Freud had difficulty in 'reconciling' these two accounts – the dynamic and the structural approaches to repression are simply incompatible. But the evidence suggests that Freud, for the most part, opted for the conceptually sound dynamic account, particularly when dealing explicitly with repression. Indeed, as Wollheim points out:

though Freud had thought it important to recognize that there were unconscious as well as conscious mental processes, he had never thought that, simply by paying attention to this distinction, we could arrive at . . . a dynamic, as opposed to a descriptive, view of mental life. In other words, the distinction between the two types of process could not be invoked to explain the difference in their roles. At times Freud gave different explanations of inner conflict, but he never suggested that it arose between conscious and unconscious ideas *as such*. On the contrary, from the very beginning there was implicit in his thinking a view that ran totally counter to any such facile account of the matter. For Freud's preferred explanation was in terms of incompatibility: the incompatibility lay between certain ideas, which in consequence underwent repression, and a mental agency, which exerted repression. (Wollheim 1971, pp. 174–5)

Furthermore, it seems not to have been appreciated that the elision of the dynamic approach to the Freudian concept of repression would not only remove the 'cornerstone on which the whole structure of psychoanalysis rests', but also close the gap between Freud and Jung, leading to the Jungian demolition of the notion of motivated disguise, in favour of the intrinsic ineffability of the contents of the unconscious:

The form that dreams take is natural to the unconscious because the material from which they are produced is retained in the subliminal state in precisely this fashion. Dreams do not guard sleep from what Freud called the 'incompatible wish'. What he called 'disguise' is actually the shape all impulses naturally take in the unconscious. Thus a dream cannot produce a definite thought. If it begins to do so, it ceases to be a dream because it crosses the threshold of consciousness. (Jung 1964, p. 53)

Freud's resistance to this was based on his appreciation that any such assimilation with the Jungian position would change the whole character of psychoanalytic theory.

Resolution of tensions in the treatment of symbolism

The tensions in Freud's treatment of symbolism arise from the intersection of the two general confusions already illustrated, that is, from the attempt to accommodate two incompatible approaches to repression, and adherence to the distinction between primary and secondary processses.

The 'presenting problem' for the theory of symbolism is, *prima facie*, serious. On the one hand, Freud describes symbolism as belonging to an unconscious, archaic, primitive mode of expression (the natural mode of expression of the 'system unconscious'), an essentially 'primary process' phenomenon. On the other hand, despite the 'distinctive' characteristics of that system, the unconscious is also 'continued into what are known as its derivatives', which may be 'highly organised, free from self-contradiction, have made use of every acquisition of the system Cs. and would hardly be distinguished in our judgement from the formations of that system' (Freud 1915c, p. 190). Symbolism, like other substitute formations such as neurotic symptoms, falls into this latter category. The potential difficulties of the tension between these two characterisations did not escape Freud:

Study of the derivatives of the *Ucs.* will completely disappoint our expectations of a schematically clear-cut distinction between the two psychical systems. This will no doubt give rise to dissatisfaction with our results and will probably be used to cast doubts on the value of the way in which we have divided up the psychical processes. Our answer is, however, that we have no other aim but that of translating into theory the results of observation, and we deny that there is any obligation on us to achieve at our first attempt a well-rounded theory which will commend itself by its simplicity. (ibid., p. 190)

The tension here is basically the same as that produced by Freud's inconsistent claims that symbolism depends essentially on displacement, that displacement in the dream is 'entirely the work of the dream-censorship' (Freud 1916/17, p. 174), but that symbolism is not the work of the censorship, and is already present in unconscious thinking. Even without the dream-work, says Freud, and without the operation of censorship (whose characteristic techniques are condensation and displacement), the manifest dream would not be understandable because of the symbolism present. Freud's confused characterisation here is not borne out by his own evidence. Symbols may be already present in the unconscious in the sense I suggested earlier, that is, the similarity between potential symbol and symbolised has been perceived, but symbols do not appear in the dream *unless* there is censorship. Freud's examples of dreams illustrate that, in the absence of repression/censorship, the manifest dream is equivalent to the latent dream, containing images to be 'read' at face value only. But Freud, wishing to combine dynamic repression with the systematic unconscious, attempts to reconcile the irreconcilable – the two versions of repression. He merely asserts that the twofold characterisation of symbolism is no problem:

The copious employment of symbols, which have become alien to conscious thinking, for representing certain objects and processes is in harmony alike with the archaic regression in the mental apparatus and with the demands of the censorship. (Freud 1933, p. 20)

It is not surprising that Freud's supporters are confused, wondering and arguing about whether symbolism is strictly a primary process phenomenon, or whether it is a secondary process phenomenon, part of healthy ego development, and necessary for sublimation. They too accept the systematic unconscious, and then engage in futile attempts to reconcile the two incompatible versions of repression.

Ehrenzweig (1953), for instance, distinguishes two forms of repression: 'structural repression' which is 'inherent in unconscious form processes', and 'the superego's repression directed against the archaic or infantile contents symbolised in them'. Ehrenzweig relates this to the 'deep' and the 'surface' mind, and to the two different characterisations of symbolism:

Symbols are understood by the depth mind because they still fit into its wide frame of undifferentiated reference, but the symbols themselves – i.e. the substitution of one object for the other – would be wholly the work of the surface mind; only for the differentiating surface mind is the symbolic object differentiated from the original object which it now merely 'symbolizes'. (Ehrenzweig 1953, p. 113)

Ehrenzweig's formulation is similar to Fenichel's (1946) insistence that there is no need to feel that we must make a choice between symbolism which is the result of censorship, and symbolism which is a characteristic mode of 'archaic thinking':

> Another strange characteristic of archaic thinking is represented by symbolism. In adults a conscious idea may be used as a symbol for the purpose of hiding an objectionable unconscious idea; the idea of a penis may be represented by a snake, an ape, a hat, an airplane, if the idea of penis is objectionable. The symbol is conscious, the symbolized idea is unconscious. The distinct idea of a penis had been grasped but rejected. However, symbolic thinking is vague, directed by the primary process. It is not only a method of distortion; it is also a part of the primary prelogical thinking. Again, the censoring ego uses regressive methods. Again, when distorting through symbolism, the ego in its defensive activities makes use of mechanisms that previously operated automatically without any intent. The use of symbols is a falling back into an earlier primary stage of thinking, by means of which intended distortions are brought about. In dreams, symbols appear in both aspects, as a tool of the dream censorship and also as a characteristic of archaic pictorial thinking, as a part of visualizing abstract thoughts. (Fenichel 1946, p. 48)

Fenichel goes on to argue that the 'regressive' nature of symbolic distortions explains two facts: firstly, 'that the symbols, being a residual of an archaic way of perceiving the world, are common to all human beings, like affective syndromes' (ibid.); secondly, 'that symbolic thinking occurs not only where distortions have to be made but also in states of fatigue, sleep, psychosis, and generally in early childhood, that is, in all states where archaic ego characteristics are in the foreground' (ibid.):

> it is an essential part of archaic thinking with insufficient apperception to experience the world in symbols. However, *archaic symbolism as a part of prelogical thinking and distortion by means of representing a repressed idea through a conscious symbol are not the same.* Whereas in distortion the idea of penis is avoided through disguising it by the idea of snake, in prelogical thinking penis and snake are one and the same; that is, they are perceived by a common conception: the sight of the snake provokes penis emotions; and this fact is later utilized when the conscious idea of snake replaces the unconscious one of penis.
>
> Primitive symbolism is a part of the way in which conceptions are formed in prelogical thinking: comprehension of the world radiates from instinctual demands and fears, so that the first objects are possible means of gratification or possible threats; stimuli that provoke the same reaction are looked upon as identical. (ibid., pp. 48–9, italics mine)

The distinction to which Ehrenzweig and Fenichel are pointing is genuine, but it does not depend on two different accounts of repression. If we accept the dynamic, and reject the structural account of repression, the matter begins to become clear.

To begin with, the notion of 'prelogical' thinking is misleading, insofar as it suggests a kind of thinking which is not fully propositional. In that regard, all thinking, whether rational or irrational, is of the same structure. We might sensibly label rational thinking 'logical', and irrational thinking 'illogical', but neither can sensibly be called 'prelogical'. However, what Fenichel is identifying here when he talks of 'symbolism as part of prelogical thinking', what Ehrenzweig sees as the 'understanding of symbols' by the 'depth mind', and, it is suggested, what Freud is pointing to when he claims that symbols are 'already available' in the unconscious, is that aspect of the so-called 'primary process' which was argued earlier to be the only genuine aspect, namely, a particular failure of the Reality Principle (in terms of a false belief in the identity of symbol and symbolised). This is a failure to see that something (i.e., that symbol and symbolised are not identical) is the case. It is undoubtedly produced by what might be called the 'interested perceiving' of the instinctual drives, operating according to what Freud terms the Pleasure Principle. Thus, it may be a characteristic of infantile thinking, driven by wish-fulfilment, to be subject to particular motivated false beliefs, namely, that certain objects are identical when they are in fact not. It may also be the case that, as a result of external pressures during development, the child is forced to appreciate the real differences (the development of the Reality Principle). However, the result can be described in terms of the infant's predisposition to retain the 'archaic equation' in the id, and to make use of it by the ego in the case of the substitute symbolic formations which are described by Freud as the organised 'derivatives of the unconscious'. Furthermore, in this account one can make sense of the claims made by Ehrenzweig (1953), and by Gombrich (1963), that the pleasure derived from metaphors and symbols comes not, as Aristotle claimed, from the way in which they establish new linkages and make us see new resemblances, but from the way in which they indicate linkages never broken, reminding us of what are simply 'very wide pigeon-holes' (Gombrich 1963, p. 44).

Summary and conclusions

A number of difficulties with which Freud's material on symbolism is faced are attributable to his treatment of the unconscious as a separate system, and to the attempts to combine its complementary structural account of repression with his preferred, but incompatible, dynamic approach. Once it is accepted that a systematic unconscious is untenable, that there is no way of *qualitatively* characterising unconscious processes as different from conscious processes, the assertion that symbolism is the natural mode of expression of the system unconscious must be rejected; there is no such 'system'. With that rejection, and with the adoption of the relational view of unconscious mentality, comes clarification of several hitherto unresolved issues which have important implications for the theory of symbolism. (1) The accusation by certain critics, that the mechanisms of condensation and displacement cannot be restricted to unconscious processes, is no longer damaging. (2) The attempt to falsify the theory of disguise via the observation that, for the same person, what is disguised on one occasion may be undisguised on another occasion, fails; such variability is to be expected. (3) The 'criticism' that Freud illegitimately 'plays on' the 'postulated resemblance' between conscious and unconscious processes is not a criticism at all, since, once again, this also is to be expected. (4) The insights provided by Freud's 'special characteristics of the system unconscious' may be retained, provided that they are revised, and are divorced from their supposed connection with the notion of the unconscious as a separate system. (5) When the traditional formulation of the primary/secondary process distinction (i.e., in terms of the 'systems' unconscious/conscious) is abandoned, the gulf between id and ego, with all of its attendant confusions, disappears. (6) When the structural view of repression is abandoned, the explanatory power of Freud's (dynamic) theory of repression (particularly in contrast with the Jungian position) becomes clear. (7) The contradiction between the two different characterisations of symbolism to be found in Freud's material is resolved, and the genuine insights offered by that material can be identified. The post-Freudian insistence that symbolism should not be restricted to id or primary processes, that it is part of healthy ego-development, sublimation, etc., can then be accommodated.

While these conclusions can be drawn only after some revision of Freud's material, this revision does not alter the major tenets of his theory, and is consistent with his own maxim: 'we must always be prepared to drop our conceptual scaffolding if we feel that we are in a position to replace it by something that approximates more closely to the unknown reality' (Freud 1900, p. 610).

The second of the two propositions to be rejected is that symbolism is a *language* whose universality is confirmed by linguistic evidence. Variants of this proposition occur often enough in Freud's material for the assertion to be perceived as central to his theory of symbolism, and for it to have had considerable influence on later developments. The proposition also intersects with the concept of the 'system unconscious'; Freud typically presents symbolism as an essential part of the 'language of the unconscious' – an inherited, archaic, primitive, regressive mode of expression, a 'primary process' phenomenon. The constancy of the symbolic relation can be traced back (he tells us) to an original identity between word and thing, and symbolic connections are therefore 'residues' of a 'basic language' (Freud 1916/17, p. 166). Of course, if the notion of the unconscious as a separate system is untenable, this (FN) version of the connection between symbolism and language must be rejected. But the proposition is not so easily dismissed. Freud's treatment of the theme of language has ramifications and implications which seriously jeopardise his account of symbolism. The problems must therefore be addressed before the way can be cleared for presenting the theoretically sound FB theory.

The role of language has, admittedly, received more attention than has the notion of the 'system unconscious'. Much of that attention, however, has amounted either to relatively uncritical acceptance, or to a consideration of issues not specifically connected with the aim here of developing a defensible account of symbolism. As I pointed out earlier, a number of scholars (e.g., Ricoeur 1970; Edelson 1972; Foulkes 1978; Forrester 1980; Todorov 1982) have remarked on Freud's persistent preoccupation with language and linguistic material. Of these scholars, Forrester (1980) has provided the most extensive critical examination of some of the problems associated with Freud's linguistic focus. In the course of a general investigation of the relationship between psychoanalysis and language, Forrester explores the importance of language to Freud, documenting Freud's penchant for linguistic speculation, and illustrating how, in seeking to bring about a harmonious relationship between psychoanalysis and philology, Freud often preferred philological to non-philological argument; witness his frequent attempts to anchor his symbolic interpretations in linguistic evidence at the expense of more obvious connections. Forrester's analysis of the reasons for these manoeuvres, and of the resulting tensions, can be strengthened by a number of additional observations.

Briefly, I shall argue that Freud's reasons for focusing on language stemmed from theoretically sound considerations, but he was mistaken to believe that the particular role which he allocated to language was necessary; he failed to see that the tenets of his theory make such linguistic manoeuvres unnecessary. This mistaken belief, combined with other motivations, led to his over-enthusiastic excursions into language along paths which led inevitably to confusions. In failing to distinguish clearly between conventional and non-conventional symbolism, he over-extended the analogy between symbolism and language. But symbolism is *not* a language, and treating it as one leads to serious difficulties. It might be retorted, in view of Freud's inconsistencies on the subject, that his claim is not that symbolism *is* a language, but, rather, that symbolism is *like* a language. However, this (even if justified) objection does not really alter the issue or its problems; it serves merely to identify the focal question, which is whether Freud correctly identified the ways in which symbolism is like, and the ways in which it is unlike, a language – and whether he succeeded in adhering consistently to those distinctions. On the evidence, he did neither. This failure had both immediate and long-term consequences; Freud's account of symbolism became exposed to attack on a number of fronts, and his confusions about language spread into many post-Freudian developments of psychoanalysis and language, effectively obscuring several distinctions which are crucial for a proper treatment of symbolism.

Freud's reasons for focusing on language

The material presented earlier in the chronological examination of Freud's writings on symbolism allows us to answer the question why he came to devote so much attention to language. That material reveals a growing number of concerns and external pressures which gradually led to his focus on language, especially as part of his movement towards the FN position. Some of these concerns were merely practical, but it is possible to identify three major theoretical reasons, each of which is sound.

Firstly, Freud was aware of the potential charge of arbitrariness in his interpretation of symbols, and he sought to find an independent and stable foundation for symbolism which would rebut such a charge; language, in the form of a basic, archaic, inherited mode of communication was, in his view, the answer. Freud's concern, and his proposed solution, are indicated in the way he contrasts his own method of dream interpretation with that of the 'symbolic' method which he rejects: 'In the case of symbolic dream-interpretation the key to the symbolization is arbitrarily chosen by the interpreter; whereas in our cases of verbal disguise the keys are generally known and laid down by firmly established linguistic usage' (Freud 1900, pp. 341–2).

Secondly, Freud wished to maintain his realism with respect to the symbol's meaning, in the face of the Jungian idealist notion of its essential ineffability. The phenomenon to be explained was the failure, on the part of the patient, to provide verbal 'associations' to elements that were to be understood as symbols. Jung claimed that the symbol occurs, and associations fail, because what is symbolised belongs to a special ontological order, that of the 'ineffable', or unspeakable. Freud, opposing this, clearly felt that the obvious reply was to insist that the symbolised was 'effable' after all. As Forrester (1980) points out, 'For Jung . . . the silence of the symbol was to be welcomed as an opening onto the ineffable. Freud took the silence of the symbol, just as he took the silence of the transference, as creating a practical exigency: the necessity of connection' (p. 111). The appeal to language to provide that connection was reinforced by Freud's realist approach to unconscious latent content:

Freud is antiromantic . . . when he affirms that latent thoughts are in no way different from any other thoughts, in spite of their symbolic mode of transmission: for the romantics, on the contrary, the symbol's content differs from that of the sign, and that is why the symbol is untranslatable. (Todorov 1982, p. 251)

Freud's persistent efforts to avoid this romantic notion of the ineffable, untranslatable symbol played a major part in his over-extending the analogy between symbolism and language, and prompted his numerous appeals to linguistic evidence to support his interpretations.

The third of Freud's reasons for the focus on language was his appreciation of, and attempt to accommodate, the obvious hermeneutical aspect of symbolism. Hermeneutics, as the art or science of 'interpretation', originated in the translation and exegesis of texts (i.e., language). In the case of symbolism, the task of the dream interpreter (to discover the 'meaning' of the symbol) can equally be described as one of 'translating' the symbol. Freud recognised that the fact of the original 'substitution', i.e., the appearance of the symbol in place of the symbolised, allows the work of interpretation (via discovery of the symbolised and its subsequent 're-substitution' for the symbol in the otherwise unintelligible dream or symptom) to proceed analogously to the work of the translation of a text. This legitimises the approach to symbolism and to other unconscious substitute formations as if they were a kind of language. As a result, the presentation of psychoanalysis as an 'art of interpretation', and the treatment of symbolism as a language, appear to fit neatly together:

in the first resort, this psycho-analysis was an art of *interpretation*. (Freud 1923a, p. 239)

the work of analysis involves an *art of interpretation*. (1925d, p. 41)

The dream-thoughts and the dream-content are presented to us like two versions of the same subject-matter in two different languages. Or, more properly, the dream-content seems like a transcript of the dream-thoughts into another mode of expression, whose characters and syntactic laws it is our business to discover by comparing the original and the translation. (1900, p. 277)

These three concerns of Freud about the potential weaknesses in his treatment of symbolism were sound. But he was mistaken in thinking that he needed to appeal to language in order to allay them. As will be seen, his linguistic manoeuvres were unnecessary and confused. As a result, his claims about the role of language in symbolism produced two unfortunate consequences.

Exposure of the theory of symbolism to direct attack

One consequence was that Freud's account of symbolism was left directly vulnerable to attack on a number of fronts. Specifically, critics have successfully called into question: (i) the notion of symbolism as an inherited, innate language; (ii) the grounding of the meaning of symbols in the origins of language, via a claimed original identity between word and thing; (iii) the (supposedly conclusive) force of (actually weak) linguistic evidence; and (iv) the 'finalist' nature of Freud's supposedly unbiased interpretative strategy.

Firstly, in his mistaken belief that appeals to language are the way to avoid arbitrariness in the translation of symbols, Freud over-extends the analogy between symbolism and language, and treats the dreamer's unconscious knowledge of symbols as if it were unconscious knowledge of an innate language. Even without attributing to symbolism the status of a language, the thesis of the inheritance of knowledge of symbolic meanings (particularly when the 'archaic heritage' putatively consists of cognitive *content*, and not mere 'predispositions') would be, at best, implausible and unnecessary. Freud himself insists that it is 'a methodological error to seize on a phylogenetic explanation before the ontogenetic possibilities have been exhausted' (1918, p. 97), a principle to which he did not adhere consistently. But when innateness is proposed for something *linguistic*, the result is particularly anomalous, precisely because the symbolism of language is *conventional*. It is not surprising that Freud, assuming the linguistic status of symbolism, is uneasy about the *innateness* of such knowledge, which (i.e., knowledge of linguistic elements and their referents) is otherwise acquired only through learning. In fact, Freud's proposal that symbols belong to a phylogenetically acquired archaic language is easily rejected. This, however, leaves open the possibility that symbolism is indeed a language, although not one that is innate. Thus, the validity of this first criticism lies in its attack on the notion of phylogenetic inheritance (i.e., on one of the distinctive characteristics of the FN theory of symbolism).

The second attack has been directed at Freud's attempt to trace the origins of symbolism back to the origins of language, and his claim that conceptual and verbal identity once united the symbol and the symbolised:

things that are symbolically connected today were probably united in prehistoric times by conceptual and linguistic identity. The symbolic relationship seems to be a relic and a mark of former identity. (Freud 1914a, p. 352)

This theory is fraught with unclarities and confusions, and critics have been justifiably scornful. Ricoeur (1970) correctly points out that it is no solution at all, since it 'assumes everything by making identity prior to similarity' (p. 503), and Forrester (1980) says: 'In order to gain a foothold on the universal, a nominalism has been sneaked in round the back door, into the language of the unconscious, from which all other languages derive' (p. 129). But, as pointed out earlier (in Chapter 5), conceptual and linguistic identity cannot in any case do the job which Freud requires. 'Conceptual identity', as opposed to factual identity, can only mean that two things are thought to be identical, when in fact they are not. Such a mistaken belief must be attributed to at least one part of the mind, and must underlie all unconscious, defensive substitution of the kind dealt with by Freud – including symbolism. 'Linguistic identity' can only mean that the same word is used both for the symbol and for the symbolised; that is, the same labels may be used for certain things which share certain perceptible characteristics. This requires that the similarities, and the perceiving of them, are logically and empirically prior to their reflection in the linguistic terms chosen.

Once the 'identity' of the symbol and symbolised is clarified in this way, it is obvious that it need not be, and is not, restricted to 'prehistoric times', it is not dependent on an inherited, archaic language, no real identity is involved, and linguistic connections are logically dependent on non-linguistic ones.

A third attack has been directed at Freud's reliance on linguistic 'evidence'. As Forrester (1980) observes, 'a reference to language, albeit only to its history, was felt to be necessary for psychoanalytic interpretation to retain its character, even when dealing with putatively universal symbols' (pp. 80–1). If, then, historically determined linguistic usage is seen as providing evidence for 'paths along which all humanity passed in the earliest periods of civilization' (Freud 1900, p. 347), it is not surprising to find the (intolerable) burden of explanatory power falling on such linguistic 'evidence'. Thus, part of Freud's focus on language consists of his often allowing linguistic evidence to take precedence over other, more obvious and conclusive, evidence. Forrester shows how Freud was constantly engaged in a search for a connection between instinctual desire and speech, and how this concern with linguistic usage spread to others. For example, Ferenczi justifies the gun as a phallic symbol by pointing out that the Hungarian slang word for coitus is 'shoot'. Forrester remarks that 'Ferenczi did not think to base his argument upon the "similarity" seemingly so obvious to the "post-Freudian" eye, of the shape of a gun and a penis' (ibid., n. p. 230), or, one may add, upon the similarity of the ejaculatory function of each.

The fourth attack has been directed at Freud's method of interpretation. His linguistic efforts leave his theory of symbolism open to the charge of 'finalism'. Todorov (1982) argues that, because 'the desires of early infancy close the symbolic circuit' (p. 253), Freudian explanation is 'finalist' in character; it masquerades as an unbiased journey of discovery, yet it is actually based on an 'a priori codification of the results to be obtained'. That is, the 'free play' of the language of symbolism is unjustifiably limited by specifying certain final referents which are symbolised (primary objects), and which, Todorov says, 'are no longer convertible in turn into symbolisers' (ibid.). Now, of course, in a *conventional* symbolic system, such as a language, there is no justification for limiting the field of the signified, or, indeed, of the signifier. Any sign whatever can be used to symbolise anything whatever. However, Todorov's objection would be applicable to symbolism only *if* symbolism *were* a language. Once it is recognised that symbolism is *not* a language, that it is not a conventional system, it is clear that the criticism of 'finalism' is being directed at what is actually a *strength* of Freud's theory, since both the 'drivenness' of unconscious symbolism and the determination of the symbolised cannot be explained without the kind of further detail which Freud's theory supplies.

The obscuring of real distinctions

A more far-reaching consequence of Freud's linguistic manoeuvres is that insights about the genuine relationship (similarities and differences) between symbolism and language have become obscured, not only in Freud's material, but also in post-Freudian extensions. Just as in the case of the 'system unconscious', the seeds of confusion which appear in Freud's own writings have grown in reformulations of Freudian theory. Freud's own focus on language encouraged an intensification of interest in the topic, and, in some developments, language became even more important than it had been for Freud. Also, instead of extracting from Freud's inconsistent treatment those parts which are conceptually sound, many theorists have adopted the unsound ideas, no doubt partly because of their own, additional, reasons for focusing on language. The ensuing problems are especially evident in semiotic and hermeneutical treatments of symbolism (in the broader context of current postmodernist approaches to language). In semiotics, there is widespread acceptance of the Lacanian view that, since 'the unconscious has the structure of a language' (Lacan, in Lemaire 1977, p. 118), and since 'what the psychoanalytic experience discovers in the unconscious is the whole structure of language' (Lacan 1966, p. 147), language is *the* subject matter of psychoanalysis. In hermeneutics, there are persistent attempts to assimilate psychoanalysis into the hermeneutical paradigm which, for some time now, has been set in opposition to scientific, causal explanation; psychoanalysis, it is claimed, is an exclusively hermeneutical or semiological system *rather than* a general scientific theory of motivation and behaviour. The confusions which have led to such assertions centre on three, interrelated, topics: (i) the distinction between conventional and non-conventional symbolism; (ii) the relationship between language and thought; and (iii) the separation of the hermeneutic and the non-hermeneutic aspects of symbolism. Only if these distinctions are clearly and consistently maintained can Freud's concerns be allayed, and the theory of symbolism adequately supported.

(i) The distinction between conventional and non-conventional symbolism

It was observed in Chapter 1 that the distinction between conventional symbols (e.g., the symbols of logic, mathematics, or language) and non-conventional symbols (e.g., the symbols which appear in dreams, symptoms, rituals, myths, etc.) seems to stand out from the otherwise confused mess of definitions and classifications to be found in the literature, notwithstanding variations in the terms used to identify the two classes (signs versus symbols; discursive versus non-discursive symbols; referential versus condensation symbols; logical versus non-logical symbols, etc.). It was also suggested that a major source of confusion and controversy in theories of symbolism lies in the failure to make that distinction explicit, and to adhere consistently to it, particularly where non-conventional symbols are under discussion. The paradigm case of conventional symbolism, language, is a system of arbitrary or 'freely chosen' signifiers, the learning of which requires seeing that one thing is used to refer to, or represent, another; it requires perceiving two independent (and usually quite unlike) things, and perceiving also that someone is using one to refer to the other. The essence of language is conventional reference (which is not to deny that it has other functions – expressive, performative, etc.). Also, it is typically used for communication. Non-conventional symbolism, on the other hand, such as occurs in dreams, myths, rituals, symptoms, etc., is not 'freely chosen'; symbolic substitution depends on a mistaken belief (often based on perceived similarities) that one thing (which an interpreter subsequently identifies as the 'symbol') is another (which an interpreter subsequently identifies as the 'symbolised'). This implies, of course, that symbolism is not verbal, and can precede language. Symbolism is a case of motivated mistaken identity (although not just *any* kind of mistaken identity), in which (one part of) the symbol user or producer takes the symbol to be the symbolised (hence, Saussure excludes symbols from semiology on the grounds that they are 'motivated', not arbitrary). The symbol does not 'refer to' the symbolised, nor is it used, either by the dreamer or by the interpreter, to refer to the symbolised, nor is its purpose communication, as Freud acknowledged. This is what Grünbaum appears to have in mind when he rejects Ricoeur's linguistic interpretation of the kinds of substitute formations dealt with by Freud:

In a further futile effort to hermeneuticize psychoanalysis, Ricoeur offers a 'semiotic' construal of the various outcroppings of repressed ideation as linguistic communications, with the clinical theory providing a 'semantics of desire'. In psychoanalytic theory, both full-fledged neurotic symptoms and minineurotic ones (e.g. manifest dream contents, Freudian slips, jokes) are seen as *compromise-formations*, products of the defensive conflict between the repressed ideas and the repressing ones ... As such, symptoms have also traditionally been viewed as 'symbols' of what is repressed. But they are 'symbols' in the nonsemantic sense of being substitutive formations affording replacement satisfactions or outlets, not linguistic representations of their hypothesized unconscious causes. (Grünbaum 1986, p. 219)

It is clear that the attempt to present psychoanalysis as a hermeneutic or semiotic system on the grounds that the symbolic phenomena dealt with are, by virtue of having 'meaning', referential, communicative, acts (albeit unconscious) is based on a confusion. The same confusion, I would suggest, underlies Sartre's (1956) approach, to which Gardner's (1993) response is that we must play down 'the assimilation of psychoanalytic symbolic meaning to the kind of meaning that we find in natural language' (p. 133), since the latter depends on rational, conscious substitution of the symbol for the symbolised.

There is, however, a residual problem. The signifiers in a language are, in at least two senses, not 'freely chosen'. Firstly, the infant is born into a language-using community and has no choice of language; it must accept the already established signs and their referents if it is to understand and be understood. Secondly, as the example of Zamenhof's Esperanto attests, natural language is less like an artificial system, and more like a living, evolving system, over which the community has incomplete control. This is related to the controversial question of the origins of language, and of its relationship to non-conventional symbolism. As noted in Chapter 1, the consensus of those who speculate about this question is that non-conventional symbols have ontogenetic priority over conventional ones, and that the latter develop from the former via a gradual erosion of affective connections:

the less primary and associational the symbolism, the more dissociated from its original context, the less emotionalized it becomes, the more it takes on the character of true reference. (Sapir 1959, p. 493)

when we seek to follow language back to its earliest beginnings, it seems to be not merely a representative sign for ideas, but also an emotional sign for sensuous drives and stimuli. The ancients knew this derivation of language from emotion, from the pathos of sensation, pleasure and pain. In the opinion of Epicurus, it is to this primal source, which is common to man and beast and hence truly 'natural', that we must return in order to understand the origin of language. Language is not the product of mere convention or arbitrary decree; it is as necessary and natural as immediate sensation itself. (Cassirer 1955, p. 148)

Nevertheless, whatever the evolutionary relationship between conventional and non-conventional symbolism, the distinction between them is real and important.

(ii) The relationship between language and thought

The second problem, the conflation of language and thought, is illustrated in Edelson's (1972) doubts concerning the ontological status of a thought 'unclothed' in language:

> Is a thought – an abstraction or conception – without any manifest symbolic form to represent it, actuality or fiction? Do we suppose a naked thought waiting indifferently to be clothed in the form of one symbolic system or another, or do we suppose a thought to be always represented by the form of some system? (p. 251)

The impression which Edelson is wanting to convey, in the description of an unexpressed or unsymbolised thought as 'naked', is that it somehow requires symbolisation to *be* a thought. But, of course, a 'naked' thought is still a thought. This confusion about the relationship between thought and language is not restricted to psychoanalytic thinking. In contemporary philosophy of mind, the widespread treatment of mental states (beliefs, desires, etc.) as 'propositional attitudes' is accompanied by an almost equally widespread acceptance that such states are *thereby* linguistic (typically, consisting of internal mental representations or symbolic tokens). Heil's (1981) competent dismissal of Fodor's (1975) influential thesis of the 'language of thought', according to which thinking always requires a linguistic medium in which to occur, seems to have made little impact. What underlies this confusion is the mistaken belief that propositionality is equivalent to linguisticality. This belief leads Fodor, for example, to reject the relational view of mental processes, on the grounds that, although the objects of cognition are propositions, relations to propositions 'aren't plausible candidates for ultimate stuff' (Fodor 1985, p. 95). Nor would they be, if propositions were, as many seem to conceive them, insubstantial linguistic entities mediating between us and the world. Fodor is then left with the 'problems' of the 'productivity' and 'constituency' of propositional attitudes, i.e., 'what it is about organic states like believing and desiring that allows them to be (roughly) as differentiated as the propositions are' (ibid., p. 89). The conflation of propositionality and language is also used by Gardner (1993) to argue that the very propositionality of conscious mental states is what distinguishes them from unconscious states; since the unconscious is 'non-verbal', it cannot be propositional:

> The explanations advanced by psychoanalytic theory for the incoherence and indeterminacy of unconscious content discourage a view of it as propositional. There is, first, the pre-verbal nature of unconscious content, a feature which it shares with the mental contents of infants and animals, and indicates that the

important factor of language in fixing propositional content is missing. (pp. 154–5)

But language does *not* fix propositional content, if what is meant by this is that there is no propositionality without language. Firstly, on the question of the relationship between language and thought, one cannot learn a label for an object (the most basic form of language-learning) without being aware of (knowing, perceiving) the object; one cannot describe the world without first being aware of the world. Awareness (i.e., cognition) must precede language. Knowing that something is the case cannot then require knowledge of, or use of, language, nor, of course, does a linguistic expression of knowledge follow automatically. Secondly, while the objects of so-called 'propositional attitudes' are indeed propositional, these objects are external states of affairs. Thus, the propositionality lies in the structure of the *state of affairs in the world.* To say that p is true is simply to say that a certain state of affairs obtains. Putting these two together, it follows, as Armstrong (1973) points out, that propositions are not fundamentally linguistic, being logically prior to linguistic expression – 'there is no necessary connection between having beliefs and having the capacity to express them linguistically' (p. 28). Conversely, contrary to what Gardner (1993, p. 89) suggests, failure to articulate beliefs does not make them *not* beliefs. If, as is generally recognised, the pre-verbal infant is capable of perception, and if, as is also generally acknowledged, the objects of perception are states of affairs, then pre-verbal thought, like all thought, is propositional. Therefore, insofar as the kinds of substitutive formation dealt with by Freud are based on the unconscious taking of one thing to be another, prompted by perceived similarities, symbolism is not linguistic, and need have nothing to do with language. A similar conclusion has been reached by Lakoff and others (e.g., Lakoff and Johnson 1980; Johnson 1987; Lakoff 1993) with respect to the concept of metaphor; according to their proposed 'contemporary theory of metaphor', which rejects the classical treatment of metaphor as a strictly linguistic device, 'the locus of metaphor is not in language at all, but in the way we conceptualize one mental domain in terms of another' (Lakoff 1993, p. 203); thus metaphor, like (non-conventional) symbolism, is 'fundamentally conceptual, not linguistic in nature' (ibid., p. 244).

(iii) The hermeneutic aspect of symbolism

This leads us to the final distinction which is obscured by Freud's treatment of language – the hermeneutic versus the non-hermeneutic aspects of symbolism. Freud's assertion that psychoanalysis is an 'art of interpretation' identifies psychoanalysis as a hermeneutical enterprise. The hermeneutical question is: what is the *meaning* of . . . (the dream, the symbol, the behaviour, etc.)? The major difficulty within the hermeneutic literature is that 'meaning' is attributed to conventional symbols, non-conventional symbols, and non-symbolic phenomena, without any clear understanding or exposition of the differences between these three groups. In particular, hermeneuticists (heavily influenced by phenomenological and existentialist thinking) typically support their claim that all human action is 'semantic' or 'textual', by shifting back and forth between 'linguistic' or 'referential' meaning, and another kind of meaning which they call 'experiential'. When these two kinds of meaning are scrutinised, the first, 'linguistic' meaning, can be identified as a three-term relation holding between a signifier, a signified, and a subject. The person (the subject) uses the word (the signifier) to refer to the object (the signified). On this analysis, 'meaning' is the *relation between the three terms*, and not any single one of the terms. This important fact is obscured by the common practice of using the word 'meaning' to refer to just one of the terms of the relationship, the signified. In the case of conventional symbols, then, the question of the 'meaning' of the signifier is answered by identifying the signified. 'Experiential' meaning, however, is quite different. On examination of the literature, this new kind of 'meaning' turns out to be constituted by a person's *psychological states* (beliefs, feelings, etc. about an event or situation, together with his or her motivational state). While one cannot legislate about usage, the use of the term 'meaning' here can be misleading; the questions of what a particular action or event 'means' to a person, and of what 'interpretation' that person places on the action or event, are used to replace a combination of more straightforward, comprehensible questions: What (true and/or false) beliefs does the person have about the event? How does the person feel about it? What is his or her psychological reaction to it? And so on. If we reject the application of the term 'meaning' to this second case, we are left, so far, with the legitimate three-term concept of 'linguistic' meaning. What, then, of non-conventional symbolism? Since we are dealing with symbolism, there is a three-term relation between symbol, symbolised, and person. However, because the symbolism is non-conventional, the three-term relation is not one of reference. The dreamer, for example, does not use the symbol to 'refer to', or to 'stand for', the symbolised in the dream. Rather, it is a case of mistaken identity; the dreamer (or, at least, some part of the dreamer) treats the symbol as if it were the symbolised. The appropriate question, then, is: 'what is the dreamer mistaking the symbol for?' However, in the task of interpretation, that question can be replaced by the question 'what does this symbol stand for in this person's dream?', or 'what must I substitute in place of the symbol in order to make the dream intelligible?' The hermeneutical aspect of symbolism lies in the applicability of this question. Only here do symbolism and language converge; as with language, the question of the 'meaning' of the symbol is answered by identifying the symbolised.

One of the outcomes of the failure to appreciate exactly what the hermeneutical question does, and does not, ask is confusion about the relationship between hermeneutic and causal explanation. Those who claim that psychoanalytic explanation does not fit the standard causal model of science, but is *instead* a hermeneutic system, set up a dualism: the world of causes versus the world of meanings. But causes and meanings, while different, belong to the same world. To take a classic Freudian example, the operation of a dreamer's instinctual drives in terms of, say, incestuous wishes, may cause the dreamer to dream – to hallucinate being involved in an incestuous act with his mother, under the guise of climbing a staircase with a queen. Now, the 'meaning' of one of the symbols here (i.e., the answer to the hermeneutic question 'what does the queen stand for?') is mother. Once this is discovered, the hermeneutic question has been answered. But there are other (separate) questions, which are not hermeneutic but causal: why does the dreamer dream of his mother, and why is his mother replaced in the dream by a queen? The answers to *these* questions, which are questions about causes, and which are answered (in Freud's theory) in terms of the primary objects of instinctual drives, repression, etc., are just as necessary for an explanation of symbolism as are the answers to the hermeneutic questions. To be sure, the answer to a hermeneutic question may play a role in the answer to a causal question; it is partly *because* the queen means mother that the queen appears in the dream. It was suggested earlier (in Chapter 4) that, when Freud distinguishes between tracing a symptom back 'historically' and tracing it back 'symbolically', his use of the word 'historically' is not simply an acknowledgement of determinism, but includes the requirement to identify the psychological causes, usually conditions of motivational conflict, which have produced the symptom. On the other hand, tracing the symptom back 'symbolically' consists of finding answers to the hermeneutic question of what this object or action (or its elements) 'represents' or 'substitutes for' in the mind of the patient. Hermeneutic and causal explanation in psychoanalysis are complementary, and the apparent dichotomy, according to which psychoanalysis must be either a hermeneutic system or a scientific theory providing causal explanations, is a pseudo-dichotomy.

Clarifications and conclusions

Allaying Freud's concerns

It is clear that Freud's appeals to language to allay his concerns about potential weaknesses in his theory of symbolism were misguided and unnecessary. He already had the means to avoid arbitrariness in the translation of symbols; the theory of instinctual drives and of their gratification via objects which might be termed 'primary' allows both for the identification of symbols, and for the explanation of their meanings. The biological factor of the long period of infantile dependence, the universal primitiveness of the body and early experiences, and the deflection of desire on to available and acceptable substitutes (normally as a result of repression) via the CRS formula (see Chapter 3), is the foundation not only of an explanation of what is symbolised, and why, but also of the universality of symbolism. Freud's failure may have been induced, in part, by the isolation of the treatment of symbolism from the rest of the theoretical structure of psychoanalysis, which may also explain why he persisted in his misconception even when his material points in a direction other than the one he took. For example, the adequacy of the non-linguistic parts of his theory is already adumbrated and exemplified in his criticisms of Scherner's approach to dream symbolism, and in his rejection of the Jung/Silberer approach on the grounds that it 'seek[s] to disguise the fundamental circumstances in which dreams are formed and to divert interest from their instinctual roots' (Freud 1919a, p. 524). However, as Forrester notes, Freud appears not to have appreciated the adequacy of the grounding of symbolism in 'biological facticity':

An empirical demonstration of the convergence of all these facts upon such primary meanings, a conceptual dissection of the inadequacy of a conception that tried to orient symbols towards a less sordid and less bodily future was not enough: the psychoanalysts seemed to need a foundation of symbolism both in language and in biology. (Forrester 1980, p. 129)

To make matters worse, this foundation was supposedly not in language and biology separately, but in the original convergence of the two (viz. Sperber's theory of the sexual origins of language). As we shall see, the untenability of this position was clear to Ernest Jones, who, in his seminal (1916) paper on symbolism, manages to make a number of subtle but significant modifications to Freud's linguistic assertions.

With respect to Freud's second concern, the desire to retain realism in the face of Jung's idealism can be satisfied not, as Freud thought, via language, but via the adoption of the relational approach to mentality (including unconscious mentality), and via an appreciation of the relationship between language and thought. Jung's view was that the symbol expresses something which cannot be expressed in any other way. Freud rightly rejected this. What is symbolised is not 'ineffable', since it can be identified, and since, given other conditions, it may appear in undisguised form. To say that it is 'effable' is just to say that one can specify what it is that the symbol replaces, and, in so doing, represent it not by unconscious symbolism, but by conscious language. But this does not mean that the symbol is a linguistic entity, or that symbolism is a language.

Finally, with respect to Freud's desire to accommodate the hermeneutical aspect of symbolism, it now becomes clear that he was quite correct to feel that, *vis-à-vis* one particular aspect of the work of interpretation, the interpreter can legitimately approach the task in the same way as he or she might a language. To understand a dream, for example, the interpreter needs, among other things, to substitute the symbolised for the symbol, and is misled if the symbols are 'read at face value'. Without the work of substitution, the dream can be as unintelligible as a text containing foreign words whose meanings have not been identified. However, this is true only for *one* aspect of the method of interpretation. The analogy does not hold for other aspects: the use of symbols by the dreamer; the investigation of the causes and production of symbolism; and the fact that a symbol 'read at face value' is an intelligible entity which is simply not being regarded as a symbol, whereas the signifying function of an unintelligible foreign word in a text does not vanish just because the word is not translated. For these reasons, the distinction between conventional and non-conventional symbolism is important, since the phenomenon under investigation is not a language; the relationship between symbol and symbolised is not one of conventional reference, the use of symbolism does not involve intentional reference, and the symbolism is not designed to serve the purpose of communication. Freud, in contrasting the dream with ancient languages, recognises this last point:

It must, of course, be admitted that the system of expression by dreams occupies a far more unfavourable position than any of these ancient languages and scripts. For after all they are fundamentally intended for communication: that is to say, they are always, by whatever method and with whatever assistance, meant to be understood. But precisely this characteristic is absent in dreams. A dream does not want to say anything to anyone. It is not a vehicle for communication. (1916/17, p. 231)

Yet Freud, like many after him, did not adhere consistently to the distinction between language and non-conventional symbolism.

The genuine role of language

Given that the role which Freud allocated to language in symbolism was unnecessary and, in any case, untenable, what is the place of language and of linguistic material in the overall theory of symbolism?

In separating 'true symbolism' from all other types of indirect representation, Jones (1916) adopts the six characteristics of symbolism listed by Rank and Sachs (1913), following Freud. Of these characteristics, the two which relate specifically to language are 'evolutionary basis' and 'linguistic connections'. However, Jones makes significant (but subtle) modifications to Freud's claims. On the question of 'evolutionary basis', Freud's remarks about the 'conceptual and linguistic identity' of the word and thing are explicitly interpreted by Jones thus: 'Just as the simile is the base of every metaphor, so is an original identification the base of every symbolism' (Jones 1916, p. 105). Jones here converts the unacceptable Freudian 'identity' into the acceptable 'identification', supporting it with observations about the infantile, unconscious 'general primitive tendency to identification'. On the question of 'linguistic connections', Jones points out that 'the study of etymology, and especially of semantics, reveals the interesting fact that, although the word denoting the symbol may have no connotation of the idea symbolised, yet its history always shows some connection with the latter' (ibid., p. 99). Jones cites a number of examples (for instance, the etymological origins of the words 'king' and 'queen' in the Sanskrit words for father and mother), but he does not draw from these observations the kinds of invalid conclusion drawn by Freud. This sound approach to the role of language has been pursued by others. For example, Baker (1950) surveys several languages belonging to the Polynesian group (Maori, Samoan, Hawaiian, etc.), in an attempt to examine whether Freud's dream symbols are mirrored in these languages. Baker justifies his choice of languages on two grounds. Firstly, examining primitive forms of language allows the best chance to catch language at its most spontaneous, before it has become subject to taboos and formalised repressions. Secondly, the presence of dream symbols in those languages would show that Freud's discoveries were not confined to just one section of the world. Baker documents an impressive number of connections between words for sexual and other symbolised things and the words used for the symbols themselves. For example, in all of these languages, the word for 'penis' is also the word for a number of phallic symbols like 'pole', 'tail', 'wedge', etc. The Maori word for vagina or womb is *werewere*, and the word for spider (*pungawerewere*) means 'mother-vagina'. Baker observes that the Polynesian dialects 'are found to contain linguistic associations which directly parallel dream symbolism' (1950, p. 177). In a similar investigation, Minturn (1965) claims to find cross-cultural support for Freudian symbols in his analysis of the relationship between grammatical gender and the sex of what is symbolised in French, German, Russian, Greek, Irish, Maharata, Arabic, Tunica, Nama, and Hausa, the strongest relationships occurring in the last three, indicating that such connections are not restricted either to Christian cultures or to Indo-European languages. As for the conclusions which are drawn from this kind of work, Baker allows that 'There is a question, of course, whether this linguistic evidence is adequate in itself' (1950, p. 171), and, although his observations are offered as support for Sperber's views on the sexual origins of language, the support is not extended to the more extreme claims made by Freud:

We are certainly led to pay greater respect to Sperber's view that language has sexualised origins. If one is not mistaken, it would seem that infantile or primitive experiences focus attention on pleasure-giving functions and that the exterior world is then arranged in terms of those functions. (ibid., p. 177)

This same point is made by James (1890):

My own body and what ministers to its needs are thus the primitive object, instinctively determined, of my egoistic interests. Other objects may become interesting derivatively through association with any of these things, either as means or as habitual concomitants; *and so in a thousand ways the primitive sphere of the egoistic emotions may enlarge and change its boundaries.* (vol. 1, p. 324, italics in original)

Thus, what Wollheim (1982) calls the 'bodily ego' forms the basis for our initial categorisation of the world, which is indicated in primitive languages, or in primitive forms (e.g., slang) of sophisticated languages, before the forces of repression have taken over in the form of taboos which affect the choice and use of terms.

   In general, then, where linguistic material provides evidence, it is not evidence for the assertion that symbolism is a language, but evidence for pre-linguistic and non-linguistic connections. Such a conclusion was, on occasion, drawn by Freud himself. As has been reiterated, Freud is inconsistent, and it may be argued that this inconsistency is attributable, at least partly, to the failure of linguistic material to carry the explanatory load allotted to it. Often, Freud either uses language merely to provide a final connection, a kind of icing on the cake, or, having spent considerable effort on accumulating linguistic connections, he suddenly falls back on non-linguistic connections, as though realising that something more conclusive is required. Forrester cites, for example, Freud's inconsistency in adhering to the primacy of linguistic data in his analysis of Leonardo's 'memory', in which the vulture = mother connection, despite circuitous philological speculations, is finally assumed to have been made on the basis of Leonardo's acquaintance with the classical texts, in which he must have found the equation. This kind of last-minute manoeuvre is reminiscent of Freud's appeal to associative connections which ultimately validate the linguistic connections in the 'symbolization' of hysteria. As I noted in Chapter 3, despite Freud's assertion about the autonomy of that mechanism of symbolization, in which the explanation turns on taking literally a verbal, metaphorical expression, the mechanism can always be traced back to an original non-linguistic phenomenon – an original pain, or physical state of some kind, which provides the basis for the metaphor. This grounding of the linguistic in the non-linguistic, despite the manoeuvres to the contrary, is typical of Freud. In addition, the many examples of Freud's unrealistic faith in linguistic material can be set against numerous other examples of his uncertainty about the strength of such material. Freud's own discussion of the *tertium comparationis* of the symbolic relation, which he claims to be primarily shape or form, then function, and so on, and his specification of 'similarity' as the key relationship between manifest and latent content, illustrate his grounding of symbolism in non-linguistic factors.

Implications for the theory of symbolism

The foregoing considerations have the following implications for the theory of symbolism:

(1) The symbolism which is the focus of psychoanalytic interest is not a primitive, archaic language, nor is it a sophisticated, modern language; it is not a language at all. It is a non-conventional, not a conventional, form of symbolism. It is not linguistic, nor does it depend on language; rather, it is an outcome of a mistaken belief in the identity of symbol and symbolised, a belief whose juxtaposition with a true belief in the *non*-identity of symbol and symbolised allows (via a process which is not properly understood) for the satisfaction of the repression-driven search for substitutes via compromise formations.

(2) Contrary to the Lacanian semiotic programme, then, language is not *the* subject matter of psychoanalysis. With respect to the language/thought distinction, the focus of psychoanalytic inquiry is thought – particularly the role of unconscious mental processes in the explanation of human behaviour. Thought precedes language, and is logically independent of it. One of the implications of this for psychoanalytic theory is that, contrary to Edelson (1972),

dreaming does not depend on language; dreaming depends on, or rather is, thought. Dreams are hallucinations, sequences of false beliefs about what is being 'seen', 'heard', etc. As Freud says: 'we appear not to *think* but to *experience*; that is to say, we attach complete belief to the hallucinations' (1900, p. 115). As has been pointed out, latent thoughts cannot be qualitatively different from manifest ones, since thoughts are the same everywhere; they may be conscious or unconscious, and they may be represented in different symbolic systems, but this cannot change their (relational) nature, nor the propositional nature of their objects.

(3) When critics accuse Freud of presenting a 'finalist' system, of specifying beforehand what the elements are which will be found to be symbolised by the symbol, they reveal that they do not appreciate the implications of the conventional/non-conventional distinction. Only in the case of conventional symbolism would such a criticism be justified. In the case of non-conventional symbolism, something other than arbitrary agreement determines the symbolised. This is what is recognised in Freud's theory, and what he sets out to explain.

(4) However, in one aspect of the task of interpretation, symbolism may properly be approached as a language. The difference between conventional and non-conventional symbolism, and the recognition that the kind of symbolism with which Freud deals is non-conventional, allows clarification of the hermeneutical aspect of psychoanalysis, a clarification often obscured in the hermeneutic literature.

(5) Once the place of hermeneutical questions in psychoanalysis is understood, we can see how the psychoanalytic approach to symbolism clarifies the complementary relationship between hermeneutic and causal explanation, and we can see that this relationship is not an incompatible, either-or, dichotomy. In the psychoanalytic explanation of symbolism, the question of the meaning of the symbol is separate from the question of the cause of the symbol's occurrence. But each question must be answered before any particular case of symbolism can be fully explained.

The second of the two propositions presented at the beginning of Part Two, that symbolism is a language whose universality is confirmed by linguistic evidence, can, then, be rejected. With that rejection, certain weaknesses of Freud's account of symbolism vanish, and a number of currently widespread misconceptions about language and thought, conventional and non-conventional symbolism, and hermeneutics and causal explanation, can be dispelled. With the adoption of the relational approach to unconscious mentality and the dynamic approach to repression, and with the clarification of the role of language, the way is almost cleared to present an account of the FB theory of symbolism. There remains only one step – to identify and incorporate the contribution to be found in Ernest Jones's treatment of the Freudian material.

9   Ernest Jones's contribution

Jones's paper 'The theory of symbolism', published in 1916 during the core years of Freud's presentation of the FN theory, is, apart from Freud's own writings, the most substantial contribution to the psycho-analytic account of symbolism. Systematic and focused, it reveals a perceptive appreciation of the unity of Freud's material on symbolism. Yet its real value, which goes beyond this, has not yet been recognised. Rodrigué's (1956) assessment, that it is 'the limitations of our basic theoretical assumptions on symbolism' which explain why symbolism 'has had a strange and disappointing fate', and why so little 'has been added since Jones wrote his comprehensive essay' (p. 147), is as relevant today as it was forty years ago. Without the kind of extensive exegesis of Freud's writings on symbolism which has been offered in the first part of this book, without the thesis that a broad theory of symbolism is to be found in those writings, and without the revisions to Freud's material which are necessary to support that theory, the genuine contribution of Jones's paper remains hidden; instead, it is generally considered to be little more than a comprehensive summary of Freud's views.

In the context of the present thesis, however, Jones can be seen to make two significant contributions. His main claim is that it is possible to distinguish 'one fundamental type of indirect representation' (what he calls 'true symbolism') from all other types (collectively labelled 'metaphor'), and that, although there are similarities between the two categories, the distinction must be recognised. Jones's first contribution can be described as the achievement of an FN/FB synthesis, by demonstrating how the FN theory can be assimilated into a broader approach (in this case, into the category of 'true symbolism'). That Jones effects this synthesis with only minor modifications to Freud's FN assertions supports my earlier claims about the prevalence in Freud's writings of the FB theory, and about the weakness of the support for the three FN characteristics of symbols. Jones's second contribution is that, in his account of the distinction between 'true symbolism' and 'metaphor', he provides some grounds for answering a number of post-Freudian critics of the FB theory, who insist on the continuity of the symbolic function through so-called primary and secondary processes, and who accuse Freud of neglecting the role of symbolism in sublimation and in healthy ego-development. However, in order to answer these critics successfully, an adjustment must be made to Jones's treatment, and the FB theory presented as incorporating, as well as Jones's 'true symbolism', a part of his category of 'metaphor'. This adjustment, I shall argue, is warranted by Jones's own account of the psychodynamic basis of the relationship between the two.

The assimilation of the FN position into 'true symbolism'

It was argued earlier that the three supposedly distinctive characteristics of symbols (according to the FN view) are only weakly (if at all) supported in Freud's material, are not consistently adhered to by Freud, and are undermined by the greater part of Freud's material. The untenability of a theory of symbolism which restricts the term 'symbol' to that special, narrow, case implies that a broader view is required.

The collapsing of the FN position into such a broader view is well illustrated in Jones's treatment. In presenting his own definition of 'true symbolism', Jones makes significant (but in most cases subtle) modifications to five of the six characteristics of symbols listed by Rank and Sachs (1913), following Freud. These characteristics are:

Representation of unconscious material, constant meaning, independence of individual conditioning factors, evolutionary basis, linguistic connections, phylogenetic parallels in myths, cults, religion etc. (Jones 1916, pp. 96–7)

In Jones's hands, these (largely FN) characteristics are remoulded to form the core of the FB position. The first characteristic ('representation of unconscious material') is the only one left unchanged. For Jones, it is 'perhaps the characteristic that most sharply distinguishes true symbolism from the other processes to which the name is applied' (p. 97). Here, Jones is isolating a major aspect of the FB theme: the symbol as substitute for something which is unconscious (because repressed). With respect to the second characteristic ('constant meaning'), Jones says that this claim 'needs some modification' (ibid.); it is not that the meanings of symbols are constant, but that they are very restricted. If, for example, a symbol has two or more possible meanings, 'the interpretation will depend on the context, the associations, and other material available' (ibid.). However, a striking feature of symbols is indeed their relative constancy of meaning in different fields (dreams, myths, etc.), and in different kinds of people. Thus, even with some variation, 'there is little scope for arbitrariness in the interpretation of symbols' (ibid.). The third characteristic ('independence of individual conditioning factors') also needs modification. Jones claims that the language used here is misleading, since:

'Independence of' should be rather 'non-dependence on', the point being that the symbolism is not conditioned by individual factors only. The individual has not an unlimited range of choice in the creation of a given symbol, but on the contrary a very restricted one, more important determining factors being those that are common to large classes of men or, more often, to mankind as a whole. The part played by individual factors is a much more modest one. While the individual cannot choose what idea shall be represented by a given symbol (for the reason just mentioned), he can choose what symbol out of the many possible ones shall be used to represent a given idea; more than this, he can sometimes, for individual reasons, represent a given idea by a symbol that no one else has used as a symbol. (ibid., p. 98)

This move towards the FB view (acceptance of individual, as well as universal, symbols) simply repeats assertions which are to be found in Freud's own writings. When Jones rejects the explanation of symbolism via the inheritance of ideas, it is Jung (rather than Freud) whom he opposes as the proponent of that view:

This curious independence of symbolic meanings raises in another form the old question of the inheritance of ideas. Some writers – *e.g.,* Jung – hold that anthropological symbolism is inherited as such, and explain in this way its stereotyped nature . . . I adhere to the contrary view that symbolism has to be re-created afresh out of individual material, and that the stereotypy is due to the uniformity of the human mind in regard to the particular tendencies that furnish the source of symbolism – i.e., to the uniformity of the fundamental and perennial interests of mankind. (ibid.)

Clearly, Jones's alternative to the Jungian approach can successfully account for both individual and universal symbols. The fourth characteristic ('evolutionary basis') concerns the 'genetic' aspect of symbol formation, which centres on 'the evolution, in both the individual and the race, from the original concrete to the general, and from this to the abstract', an evolution which involves 'an increasing inhibition of feeling' (ibid., p. 143):

Our point of departure is that in symbolism a comparison between two ideas, of a kind that is alien to the conscious mind, is established unconsciously, and that then one of these – which for the sake of convenience may be called the secondary idea – may unknowingly be substituted for, and so represent, the first or primary idea. (ibid., p. 104)

The requirement which is of genetic importance for the substitutive process is a certain amount of 'affective inhibition' with respect to the primary idea, which then leads to the transfer of attention on to the secondary idea. On the question of the original symbolic equation, the unconscious belief in the identity of symbol and symbolised, Jones rejects the FN version of this process (the Sperber theory), and draws support for this rejection from Freud's own words. To begin with, Jones says: 'Just as the simile is the base of every metaphor, so is an original identification the base of every symbolism' (ibid., p. 105). He then immediately adds: 'as Freud puts it . . . "what today is symbolically connected was probably in primaeval times united in conceptual and linguistic identity. The symbolic relationship seems to be the remains and sign of an identity that once existed" ' (ibid.). But, of course, since there is a crucial difference between the concept of *identification* and that of *identity*, this quote from Freud requires a particular interpretation for it to illustrate Jones's much milder point, that of the 'general primitive tendency to identification'. As I mentioned earlier, Jones has, sensibly, taken Freud to mean 'identification' when he uses the word 'identity'. Jones continues:

If, as is here maintained, the individual child recreates such symbolism anew – *i.e.,* if he (largely unconsciously) perceives these comparisons which are alien to the adult conscious mind – then it is plain that we shall have radically to revise our conception of the infantile mind, and especially in regard to sexuality. This has already been done by Freud on other grounds. (ibid., pp. 111–12)

Here Jones camouflages his rejection of Freud's notion of the inheritance of ideas, by shifting the focus onto Freud's recognition of the importance of infantile sexuality. With respect to the fifth characteristic ('linguistic connections'), I have already drawn attention to the fact that Jones's treatment avoids the Freudian linguistic extremes. Finally, the sixth characteristic ('phylogenetic parallels') is treated in a similar way. Jones again merely comments on 'the remarkable ubiquity of the same symbols, which are to be found, not only in different fields of thought, dreams, wit, insanity, poetry, etc., among a given class and at a given level of civilisation, but among different races and at different epochs of the world's history' (ibid., p. 101). We know that Jones later persistently and explicitly rejected Freud's Lamarckian version of the 'archaic heritage'. What Jones is illustrating here is that there is a respectable way in which the concept of 'phylogenetic parallels' can be accommodated.

These transformations of some aspects of the FN claims have been effected by Jones unobtrusively. It is not clear whether this was the result of conscious policy, or whether it was simply the result of an implicit acceptance of the FB approach he found in Freud's writings. Two things, however, are clear: firstly, Jones appreciated the necessity of the basic tenets of Freud's theory for grounding the theory of symbolism; and, secondly, there is nothing in Jones's modifications which cannot be found in Freud. This brings us to a consideration of Jones's second contribution.

The distinction between 'true symbolism' and 'metaphor'

The main thesis of Jones's paper is that:

it is possible usefully to distinguish, under the name of symbolism, one funda-mental type of indirect representation from other more or less closely allied ones, and that consideration of the points of distinction throws a light upon the nature of figurative representation in general and of symbolism in particular. (ibid., p. 137)

In Jones's description of 'true symbolism', whose core is the six charac-teristics described above, the term 'symbolic' can be applied to any unconsciously formed substitute used in the service of defence. Thus, there is a connection between symbols and symptoms:

when a strong affective tendency is repressed it often leads to a compromise-formation – neurotic symptoms being perhaps the best known example – in which both the repressed and the repressing tendencies are fused, the result being a substitution product. From this it is a very slight step to infer that sym-bols are also of this nature, for it is known that they, like other compromise formations, are composed of both conscious and unconscious elements . . . That symbolism arises as a result of intrapsychical conflict between the repressing tendencies and the repressed is the view accepted by psycho-analysts. (ibid., p. 115)

Furthermore, in the central concept of repression lies the justification for the 'unidirectional' nature of symbolism:

All psycho-analytical experience goes to shew that the primary ideas of life, the only ones that can be symbolised – those, namely, concerning the bodily self, the relation to the family, birth, love, and death – retain in the unconscious throughout life their original importance, and that from them is derived a very large part of the more secondary interests of the conscious mind. As energy flows from them, and never to them, and as they constitute the most repressed part of the mind, it is comprehensible that symbolism should take place in one direction only. *Only what is repressed is symbolised; only what is repressed needs to be symbolised.* This conclusion is the touchstone of the psycho-analytical theory of symbolism. (ibid., p. 116, italics mine)

This category of 'true symbolism' is marked off by Jones from all other forms of indirect representation, which he collectively (and somewhat misleadingly) labels 'metaphor'. The unifying aspect of 'metaphor' is the conscious (and non-repressed) nature of what is represented.

Jones acknowledges that there is a similarity and a continuity between the two groups. The similarity lies in the fact that the common essential element for *all* symbolism (including metaphor) is 'affective inhibition':

> In so far as a secondary idea B receives its meaning from a primary idea A, with which it has been identified, it functions as what may be called a symbolic equivalent of A. At this stage, however, it does not yet constitute a symbol of A, not until it replaces A as a substitute in a context where A would logically appear. There is an overflow of feeling and interest from A to B, one which gives B much of its meaning, so that under appropriate conditions it is possible for B to represent A. According to the view here maintained, the essential element of these conditions is an affective inhibition relating to A. This holds good for all varieties of symbolism, in its broadest sense. (ibid., p. 139)

The continuity between the two groups is illustrated in the opacity/ transparency dimension of the symbol:

> The wider and more diluted the sense in which the word 'symbol' is used, the more easily is its meaning perceived and the more readily is the interpretation accepted. With a symbol in the strict sense, on the contrary, the individual has no notion of its meaning, and rejects, often with repugnance, the interpretation. (ibid., p. 90)

However, despite acknowledging the continuity between the two categories, Jones insists that '*true symbolism, in the strict sense, is to be distinguished from other forms of indirect representation*' (ibid., italics in original).

Now, on the question of the tenability of this distinction between 'true symbolism' and 'metaphor', it seems that, with the concept of repression and the unconscious, Jones has identified a genuine basis for the distinction, in contrast to the criteria typically offered by others. The difference between the two groups cannot be established by appeal either to peculiar 'mechanisms' or to peculiar 'content'. This was one of the conclusions of the earlier examination of the 'system unconscious'. On the one hand, it cannot be shown that 'true symbolism' operates via distinctive 'mechanisms' (condensation and displacement), since those same mechanisms operate equally in conscious symbolism, metaphors etc. On the other hand, the distinction cannot be maintained by claiming that the content (what is symbolised) is somehow different in kind in the case of 'true symbolism', since what has been repressed can, on other occasions, remain unrepressed. The failure of the systematic approach to unconscious mentality (with the concomitant structural view of repression), and the adoption, instead, of the relational approach to mentality (both conscious and unconscious) and of the dynamic view of repression, all lead to the conclusion that the distinction between Jones's two categories can be made only in terms of the unconscious, repressed nature of the symbolised material in the first category.

However, a new factor enters the picture when Jones goes on to explore the relationship between the two groups, illustrating how the production of 'metaphor' is often a response to, and elaboration on, the process of 'true symbolism'. This account forms the basis of Jones's rejection of the Jung/Silberer approach to the interpretation of symbols, in which, according to Jones, the relationship of 'collateralism' is confused with that of 'descendence'. 'True symbolism' involves 'descendence', which is a kind of 'vertical' relationship between symbol and symbolised, in which the symbolised is replaced unconsciously, as a result of repression, by the symbol. 'Metaphor', in contrast, is based on 'collateralism', which is a 'horizontal' relationship between a symbol and associations made consciously to it. The error of the Jung/Silberer approach is to fail to appreciate the differences between these two kinds of relationship, and to endow them with equivalent explanatory power:

According to the Jung-Silberer school, the image of a serpent in a dream will symbolise the abstract idea of sexuality more often than the concrete idea of the phallus, whereas to the psycho-analytical school it only *symbolises* the latter, though of course it is commonly *associated* with the former . . . to say that a serpent may 'symbolise' *either* a phallus or wisdom is to confound two entirely different psychological processes. (ibid., pp. 127–8)

Thus:

what Silberer . . . calls the passing of material symbolism over into functional I should prefer to describe as the replacement of symbolism by metaphor – *i.e.,* by an associative connection between collaterals – and the difference is a great deal more than one of words. (ibid., p. 126)

But the major contribution of Jones's account is the elucidation of the psychodynamic causal relationship between these two processes – such cases as the supposed symbolisation of wisdom by the serpent are, he says, *reactions to* 'true symbolism':

in the psycho-analytical sense the symbol is a substitute for the primary idea compulsorily formed as a compromise between the tendency of the unconscious complex and the inhibiting factors, whereas the functional interpretation is mainly concerned with *the more conscious reactions to and sublimations of the unconscious complex.* (ibid., p. 131, italics mine)

If this is true, the material produced by these reactions and sublimations must form a part of a theory of symbolism, since its production is analogous to the original formation of 'true symbolism', insofar as the associations (supposed symbolisations) are made in defensive response to the true meaning of the symbol:

The observation is that after a patient has discovered the meaning of a (true) symbol he often strives to weaken and explain away the significance of this by trying to give it some other 'functional', or more general (and therefore more harmless) interpretation. These abstract and metaphorical interpretations do, it is true, bear a certain relationship to the fundamental meaning of the symbol ... but the patient's strong preferences for them is merely a manifestation of his resistance against accepting the deeper meaning, against assimilating the unconscious ... Some patients become exceedingly adept at this method of protecting themselves from realisation of their unconscious; when they interpret their dreams, every boat-race becomes the ambition to succeed on the river of life, the money they spill on the floor is a 'symbol' of wealth, the revolvers that are fired in front of women and behind men are 'symbols' of power, and, finally, even openly erotic dreams are desexualised into poetic allegories. If, now, the psycho-analyst allows himself to be deceived by these defensive interpretations, and refrains from overcoming the patient's resistances, he will assuredly never reach a knowledge of his unconscious, still less will he be in a position to appraise the relative importance of unconscious trends and those of the surface. By this I do not in any sense mean that the latter are to be neglected, or in their turn under-estimated, but simply that one should not put the cart before the horse and talk of something secondary and less important being *symbolised* by something primary and more important. (ibid., p. 125)

Jones goes on to explain why the defensive associations should not be classed with cases of 'true symbolism':

What I shall call a *levelling* of this sort does, it is true, go on, but the all-important point is that it does so only in the more conscious layers of the mind, so that to describe the process of symbolism in terms of it represents only a very partial truth. The order of events is rather as follows: The ideas or mental attitudes unconsciously represented in true symbols yield, of course as the result of repression, a great many other manifestations besides symbolism. These may be either positive in kind, as the result of sublimation and other modifications, or negative, such as reaction-formations. They, like symbols, are conscious substitutes for, and products of, unconscious mental processes. From this consideration it is intelligible that many of these other conscious products stand in an associative connection with various symbols, both being derived from the same sources. But the connection is collateral, not lineal; to speak of one conscious idea symbolising another one, as the post-psycho-analytical school does, is very much like talking of a person inheriting ancestral traits from his cousin. (ibid., p. 126)

The question to be considered here, however, is whether, if Jones's analysis is correct, those things which 'like symbols, are conscious sub-stitutes for, and products of, unconscious mental processes' must be accounted for by a theory of symbolism.

The difference between Jones's account and the FB theory

Since the core of the FB theory is the CRS (conflict-repression-substitution) 'formula', Jones's 'true symbolism' captures that core, and so is consistent with the central part of that theory. However, the FB theory of symbolism is broader than 'true symbolism'; it encompasses those cases of symbolism which Jones categorises as 'metaphor', but which he subjects to the analysis presented above. Because Jones's analysis is accepted, the difference between his account of symbolism and the FB theory is, largely, one of terminology. There is no dispute with Jones over the nature of the processes which he describes, or over the causal relationship between those processes. The FB theory takes up Jones's account of the psychodynamics of the development of certain cases of 'metaphor' out of 'true symbolism', and includes those in the category of symbolism; they belong to the controversial group of non-conventional symbols and symbolic phenomena which Freud's theory attempts to explain. But in the FB theory, these are separated from other, non-controversial cases of 'metaphor', so that the line is drawn between those cases of 'metaphor' which are the defensive products of the processes described above, and those which are not. Thus, with 'descendence' relations, the FB theory of symbolism encompasses those relations of 'collateralism' which *appear* to be independent of 'descend-ence', but which in fact are not, being produced *because* there is an intrapsychic need to disguise the relation of 'descendence'.

The reason for this adjustment is that, while Jones's analysis is generally sound, a complete theory of symbolism cannot leave out of the category of 'symbolism' those cases which are reactions to uncon-scious meanings of the symbol, for there is, as Jones remarks, an important connection between the unconscious meaning of the symbol (which, of course, is known by one part of the mind), and the substitute, conscious, meaning offered by the person. For example, with respect to the supposed symbolisation of 'wisdom' by the serpent, Jones comments: 'Serpents are, in fact, not wiser than most other animals, and the false attribution of wisdom to them is secondary and due to a process of true symbolism' (ibid., p. 142). The products of sublimation, the conscious symbolism of religious rituals, the surface justifications of superstitions and obsessive-compulsive acts, and so on, must all be components of a theory of symbolism which makes clear what these phenomena *really* mean. Such symbolism is to be differentiated from those cases of 'metaphor' (such as the use of various literary figures of speech, or the vast range of conventional metaphors of which ordinary language, according to Lakoff (1993), is composed) which are conscious, but which are not defensive productions and do not mask other, unconscious, meanings.

In summary, although an adjustment must be made to Jones's demarcation, the distinction, and the elucidation of the psychodynamic basis of the distinction, between 'true' symbolism and certain cases of 'metaphor', is a major contribution by Jones to the FB theory. But the value of this adjustment extends well beyond terminological revision. A significant consequence is that post-Freudian psychoanalysts' criticisms of components of the FB theory can now be answered.

Implications for post-Freudian psychoanalysts' criticisms of the FB theory

In Chapter 2, the focus was on post-Freudian criticisms directed specifically at the FN theory. But when Rodrigué (1956) claimed that 'the strange and disappointing fate in the development of psychoanalytic thought' was the result of 'the limitations of our basic theoretical assumptions on symbolism', which 'have remained unchallenged for so long' (p. 147), the theoretical assumptions to which he referred were not restricted to those of the FN position; Rodrigué and others have raised a number of objections to Freud's broader approach. These criticisms (of the FB theory) centre on the perceived failure of Freud to give adequate consideration both to the importance of symbolism in so-called healthy ego-development, and to the role of conscious (ego) processes in the development and use of symbolism. That is, Freud is accused of neglecting the interdependence of symbolism and ego functioning, and of illegitimately restricting symbolism to the unconscious, and to archaic, infantile, regressive, defensive functions. Some symbolism, the critics argue, may indeed be amenable to that kind of explanation, but psychoanalysis will provide only an incomplete theory of symbolism so long as it ignores the implications for symbolism of later developments in 'ego-psychology'.

The role of symbolism in ego-development

The major criticism is that Freud does not sufficiently appreciate that symbol formation is necessary for the development of the ego.

According to Rycroft (1956), the classical theory of symbolism was rendered untenable by Freud's own claim that the concept of a conscious opposing the unconscious should be replaced by the concept of the ego as 'that part of the id which has been modified by the direct influence of the external world'. Thus, says Rycroft, 'analysts in their thinking about symbolism have not always fully appreciated the implications of ego-psychology and have tended to think of symbolism and ego functioning as being two entirely unrelated fields of psycho-analytical study' (1956, p. 141). As a result, 'it is not only misleading to restrict, as some writers do, the concept of symbolism to the use of symbols by the primary process, but also incompatible with Freud's later views on the nature and development of the ego' (ibid., p. 137). This view is based on Melanie Klein's insistence that symbol formation is crucial for the development of the ego, and lies at the heart of the process of sublimation:

Symbolism is the foundation of all sublimation, and of every talent, since it is by way of symbolic equation that things, activities and interests become the subject of libidinal phantasies . . . not only does symbolism come to be the foundation of all phantasy and sublimation but, more than that, upon it is built up the subject's relation to the outside world and to reality in general. (Klein 1930, pp. 25–6)

The role of conscious processes in symbolism

The second criticism is closely related to the first; this is that Freud neglected the role of conscious processes in symbolism. According to Rycroft, Freud's restriction of some of the so-called 'characteristics of the system Ucs.' (namely, symbolisation and displacement) to the unconscious and to the primary process is illegitimate, for it 'implies two things that are, I believe, untrue: (i) That the modes of unconscious and conscious thinking are qualitatively absolutely different, and, in particular, (ii) that symbolization is a feature of unconscious mental activity and does not occur in conscious thinking' (Rycroft 1956, p. 140). This view is shared by Kubie (1953), who points out how obvious it is that symbolic processes occur both unconsciously and consciously, so that 'not to have one generic name for them would obscure the essential continuity of all "symbolic functions" from one end of the spectrum to the other' (pp. 67–8). The conclusion is that Freud's theory requires 'reformulation', to take these points into account. Accordingly, Rycroft announces: 'I have attempted to reformulate the theory of symbolism on the basis of the assumption that symbolization is a general capacity of the mind which is based on perception and which may be used either by the primary or the secondary process' (1956, p. 137).

Replies to the criticisms

The material presented in earlier chapters, together with the account I have just given of Jones's contribution, reveals that neither of these criticisms is justified. The rebuttal is provided by the revisions of some of the Freudian material, particularly of the concept of the system unconscious and the distinction between primary and secondary processes, and by the taking of the FB theory as that whose core is Jones's 'true symbolism', but which includes certain extensions into 'metaphor'. It can be shown that the criticisms rest on ignorance, confusion, and anti-psychoanalytic sentiment: some aspects which the critics claim are neglected in the theory of symbolism are not in fact neglected, some of the criticisms rest on the confounding of conventional and non-conventional symbolism, and some involve a concession to the Jungian position (in which 'collateralism' is confused with, and presented as always causally independent of, 'descendence').

Firstly, while Rycroft is correct in saying that there is no qualitative difference between conscious and unconscious thinking, and that symbolism is not a peculiar mode of operation of the unconscious, he is wrong in claiming that Freud neglected either the role of the ego in symbolism, or the role of symbolism in ego-development. Even in cases of the use of unconscious symbolism via the CRS formula, the unconscious equating of the symbol with the symbolised leads to the replacement of one by the other only if there is conscious recognition of their non-identity. In psychoanalytic terms, the replacement of the symbolised by the symbol is the work of the ego, in the sense that it is censorship, the repressing part of the mind, which does not allow the unacceptable symbolised to remain conscious. As Jones, quoting Rank and Sachs, says: 'symbolization essentially belongs to the unconscious, though, in its function as a compromise, it in no way lacks conscious determining factors, which in varying degrees condition both the formation of symbols and the understanding for [sic] them' (1916, p. 96). This point is supported on numerous occasions when Freud discusses the purpose of repression and substitution. As is well known, Freud first located the repressing part of the psyche in the ego, later, in the super-ego, even though the discovery that repression operates unconsciously necessitated the abolition of the equation of the ego with consciousness. Symbolism, therefore, is not restricted to the id, which, as the repressed part of the psyche, is the source of the need for symbolism only insofar as it is in conflict with the ego, this conflict motivating the search for acceptable substitutes – acceptable to the ego. Even in the case of Jones's 'true symbolism' (in which only what is repressed is symbolised), the ego plays a part, and it is not true that Freud ignored the place of the ego and of conscious processes in the theory of symbolism.

But this is only the beginning. When ego-psychologists talk of the role of symbolism in 'healthy ego-development', they actually have in mind two processes. The first is the ability to understand and use symbols as symbols, as exemplified in the use of language. The second process is sublimation, as indicated in Klein's assertion above that symbolism 'is the foundation of all sublimation, and of every talent', and this process is exemplified in artistic and other cultural productions. Because these two processes often occur together, they are easily conflated. But they have very different psychodynamic origins, and serve different economic functions. The development of language, the ability to use symbols and other representational systems, the ability to understand and appreciate literary figures of speech, and so on, are not, of course, denied in Freud's theory. But those uses of symbols belong to the uncontroversial class of conventional symbolism. It may be granted that psychoanalysis can throw light on the breakdown of this process, and explain why, for example, the schizophrenic cannot (or does not) use conventional symbols conventionally, but treats them as if they belonged to the non-conventional group of symbols. However, the FB theory, while acknowledging the occurrence of conventional symbolism, recognises the crucial difference between it and non-conventional symbolism, and focuses on the latter. Again, in accordance with the adjustment made here to Jones's demarcation, the role of symbolism in, and the psychodynamic origins of, sublimation are a major part of the FB theory. Freud neither denies nor ignores these processes. When Freud is accused of neglecting them, the accusation is directed rather at the Freudian explanation of the dependence of these processes on unconscious processes of defensive substitution; in other words, the criticism is based on confounding what Jones refers to as 'descendence' and 'collateralism', and rejecting the Freudian account of the relationship between the two. In fact, the insistence that symbolism is the basis of adjusting to reality, of sublimation, and of every talent is, in many critics' hands, driven by a humanistic idealism according to which Freud failed to acknowledge the positive, 'progressive', anagogic function of symbolism, which stands as a testament to our higher, divine, spiritual side; the Jungian position. Psychoanalysis, it is argued, is 'interested in symbolism solely in its morbid manifestations: symbolic behaviour as substitute satisfaction for those who (for example, sexually) couldn't get the real thing' (Hacker 1965, p. 73). This complaint, so often associated with the appeal for a greater emphasis on the ego and on conscious processes, is commonplace in the field of aesthetics, where psychoanalysis is accused of a 'reductionist bias', because it treats art as:

one variety of defence against reality, rather than a celebration or recreation of it . . . Art as defence, as refuge, as illusion, as renunciation, as substitute, as reparation: nearly all psychoanalytically oriented scrutiny of art, even from writ-ers as diverse and sensitive as Ernst Kris and Adrian Stokes, still assumes the loss, and not the satisfaction to be the basic reason for creating. (Reviewer A 1972, p. 817)

Psychoanalysts have been disappointingly reductionist and evaluative in respect of creativity. When they have not ignored it they have seen creativity in a nega-tive way; as a tombstone above drive impulses inscribed 'Here lie wishes now put to "better" uses'. This has seemed to outsiders to be a mechanistic and materialist reduction, a debasing of spontaneous impulse and a determinism ignoring the positive force of qualities which have their own autonomous life. (Reviewer B 1971, p. 1579)

These remarks reveal that criticisms of Freud's failure to focus on subli-mation and conscious ego processes are based on a denial of the fact that some cases of what Jones calls 'metaphor' are developments from 'true symbolism', defensive reactions to true symbolism.

In summary, then, the post-Freudian psychoanalysts' criticisms turn out either to be insisting that conscious symbolism does occur (which Freud does not deny), or to be focusing on conventional symbolism (which is relatively uncontroversial and not the focus of Freud's inquiry), or to be insisting that the particular Freudian account of non-conventional symbolism is unacceptable because it focuses only on its unconscious, defensive, regressive function, or, finally, to be denying that conscious, avowed symbolism is ever a reaction to underlying unconscious, unavowed symbolism. The FB theory does not deny the role of conscious processes or of the ego, nor does it deny the continuity of the symbolic function through conscious and unconscious, 'primary' and 'secondary', conventional and non-conventional symbolism. However, part of the FB theory is that many cases of apparently innocent, conscious symbolism are related in important psychodynamic ways to underlying unconscious symbolism, which is disguised by the surface symbolism. What many of the post-Freudian critics wish to maintain is that there is no such cate-gory, and no such process.

Summary

Jones's contribution to the FB theory, though hitherto unrecognised, is substantial, and the opportunity it provides to reply to some of the major and influential psychoanalytic criticisms of Freud's treatment of symbolism is no small matter. Hence, I have presented the arguments of this chapter in summary form in Figure 2. The starting point is Jones's distinction between 'true symbolism' and 'metaphor'. By considering what is involved in 'true symbolism', it can be shown that the FN theory of symbolism is untenable. Jones's first major contribution to the FB theory is to demonstrate how smoothly the FN theory can be assimilated into a broader position, via the simple modification of one or two of the more extreme aspects of the FN characteristics of symbols. The FN/FB distinction thus collapses, as a first step, into what Jones calls 'true symbolism'. This leads to a consideration of Jones's major thesis, the necessity to keep separate 'true symbolism' from 'metaphor'. It is clear, as was shown by the evaluation of the 'system unconscious', and as is pointed out by some of the post-Freudians themselves, that this distinction cannot be made by appeal to different content or different mechanisms. What is symbolised in 'true symbolism', as a result of repression, can when not repressed be symbolised consciously. And condensation, displacement, etc. are as much the basis of conscious symbol formation as of unconscious symbol formation. The distinction can only be made, therefore, in terms of the conscious versus unconscious nature of the symbolism. This is, indeed, what Jones maintains; that 'true symbolism' includes only what is unconscious because it has been repressed. In these cases, the relationship between symbol and meaning can be described as one of 'descendence'. Now, however, the way seems open for post-Freudian critics to step in and accuse Freud of presenting a theory which ignores the ego and conscious processes, and which fails to recognise the obvious continuity of symbolism through conscious and unconscious, primary and secondary, processes. These criticisms can be answered by a modification to Jones's account, a modification which makes use of Jones's perceptive analysis of the psychodynamic basis of certain cases of 'metaphor'. As a result, instead of a division of symbolism into two categories, and the restriction of the theory of symbolism to one of those categories, the FB theory recognises three categories (labelled A, B, and C), and restricts its focus to two of these (A and B). Category A consists of Jones's 'true symbolism'; for example, the serpent symbolises the penis, via a relationship of 'descendence', in which the CRS (conflict–repression–substitution) 'formula' plays a central role. Category B consists of conscious reactions to, and sublimations of,

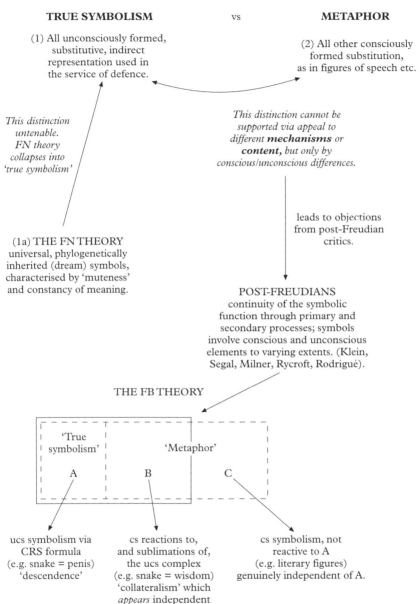

TRUE SYMBOLISM   vs   **METAPHOR**

(1) All unconsciously formed, substitutive, indirect representation used in the service of defence.

(2) All other consciously formed substitution, as in figures of speech etc.

This distinction untenable. FN theory collapses into 'true symbolism'

*This distinction cannot be supported via appeal to different **mechanisms** or **content**, but only by conscious/unconscious differences.*

(1a) THE FN THEORY
universal, phylogenetically inherited (dream) symbols, characterised by 'muteness' and constancy of meaning.

leads to objections from post-Freudian critics.

POST-FREUDIANS
continuity of the symbolic function through primary and secondary processes; symbols involve conscious and unconscious elements to varying extents. (Klein, Segal, Milner, Rycroft, Rodrigué).

THE FB THEORY

'True symbolism'   'Metaphor'

A   B   C

ucs symbolism via CRS formula (e.g. snake = penis) 'descendence'

cs reactions to, and sublimations of, the ucs complex (e.g. snake = wisdom) 'collateralism' which *appears* independent of A but is not.

cs symbolism, not reactive to A (e.g. literary figures) genuinely independent of A.

Figure 2 Jones's contribution to the FB theory

the unconscious complex; for example, the serpent is now taken consciously to symbolise wisdom, via a relationship of 'collateralism', which *appears* to be independent of the serpent–penis relationship in A, but which is in fact a defensive reaction to it. A and B are thus related psychodynamically. Category C consists of those cases of 'metaphor' which are not reactions to 'true symbolism' but are cases of conscious, non-defensive symbolism, such as the use of literary figures of speech. The post-Freudian critics can now be answered. Firstly, it is clear that the ego, conscious processes, sublimation, and so on, are an important part of the FB theory. Secondly, the existence of cases of C cannot be used to deny the existence of cases of A and B (although, naturally, a major task of the FB theory is to identify cases of each category, and to justify that identification). One significant result of the adjustment to Jones's classification is to highlight the *genuine* disagreement between Freud and some of the post-Freudian ego-psychologists; it is not so much a disagreement about whether the ego and conscious processes are involved in symbolism; rather, it is a disagreement about the dynamic origins and functions of those ego processes.

The FB theory of symbolism is, then, among other things, a theory about the relationship between what Jones calls 'true symbolism' and some cases of what Jones calls 'metaphor'. It seeks to separate those cases of 'metaphor' which *are* secondary elaborations and developments from those which are not. In giving an account of the development of 'metaphor' from 'true symbolism', and of the masking of 'descendence' by 'collateralism', the FB theory is also a theory of the origins and development of our cultural world of symbols. While this is clearly indicated in Jones's paper, it is also a main conclusion of Freud's general theory.

10   The 'Freudian Broad' (FB) theory of symbolism

I argued earlier that the weakness of the FN theory is partly the result of its having progressively become isolated from the rest of psychoanalytic theory. This isolation was reinforced by a focus on the symbol as substantive entity, and neglect of the adjectival notion of symbolic as applicable to events, actions, relations, and other phenomena more complex than a single entity. While Freud did continue to refer to these more complex phenomena in his writings, the connection between them and symbolism was not made explicit. The FB theory, in contrast, is not at all isolated from the rest of psychoanalytic theory; indeed, it is so well embedded that considerable effort is required to extract it from Freud's writings. Because it is derived from Freud's general theory, and depends for its coherence and explanatory power on the theoretical assumptions and empirical claims of that theory, understanding of the context is a prerequisite for understanding the FB theory.

That alone would be sufficient justification for including here an outline of Freud's general theory, but there are three other reasons for presenting such an outline. Firstly, it is well known that the numerous expositions of Freud's theory, even those given only in summaries and brief sketches, differ (often radically) in their 'readings' of the theory, and the reader must be told which of many (sometimes incompatible) versions of Freud's theory is being adopted. Secondly, while the main purpose here is to provide a context for the FB theory, rather than to mount a defence of a particular version of Freud's general theory, the two tasks are, *ex hypothesi*, linked. Finally, this outline is selective; it focuses on aspects of Freud's general theory which are particularly relevant for the theory of symbolism.

The context: Freud's general theory

The best contemporary philosophical approach to Freud's theory is that (e.g., Hopkins 1982, 1988, 1992; Gardner 1993; Wollheim 1993) which presents it as an extension of what is referred to in the literature as 'ordinary psychological' or 'folk-psychological' explanation, at whose centre is the 'desire plus belief' model. As Wollheim (1993), for instance, rightly claims, the view that Freud's theory is a radical reconceptualisation of the mind lends itself, paradoxically, to the eventual trivialising of Freud's contribution, to the conclusion that psychoanalysis is merely a new 'notation' or alternative 'set of metaphors'. Instead, Freud should be seen as one who inherited the 'desire plus belief' explanatory schema, and who expanded that schema in the following ways: 'He *deepened* the schema: he *elaborated*, or *produced variations upon*, it: and he *contextualized* it' (Wollheim 1993, p. 94). The deepening of the schema, Wollheim says, was effected by introducing into it, as explanatory factors, non-conscious beliefs and desires – 'factors which common sense either completely overlooks or invokes with less than total conviction' (ibid.). Elaboration of the schema was provided by Freud's addition of the explanatory role of such events as chains of associations, displaced actions, etc. The contextualisation was provided by locating explanatory psychological factors within developmentally salient constellations of beliefs and desires, with the result that labels like 'oral', 'anal', 'phallic' etc. become explanatory by virtue of 'particular desires, particular chains of association, particular mechanisms of defence, specific phantasies associated with the developmental phase that the label picks out' (ibid., p. 102).

This presentation of Freud's contribution, however, is fruitful only when that contribution is shown to be solidly founded. As Maze (1983) has pointed out, because of the widespread assumption that cognition implies purpose, and the equally widespread acceptance of teleological explanation in psychology, the 'desire plus belief' model is, in the hands of most theorists, empty and non-explanatory. In particular, while 'desire' is supposedly a causally efficacious internal state, it is presented always as a desire *for* something, i.e., as intrinsically relational, and has built into it the notion of self-generated movement. Therefore:

> even the analysis of teleological explanations into the actor's desire for something and belief in how to get it does not go far enough towards an acceptable causal theory, because for that the concept of desire must be turned round from 'striving towards' something to 'being driven by' something else, and the nature and number of these driving engines be discovered, if we are to avoid that instantly available and completely trivial form of pseudo-explanation, 'Because he wanted to'. (Maze 1983, p. 7)

it is the lack of any suggestion, however schematic, of what desires consist of, where they come from, and how their existence produces the movements they are said to cause, which turn the 'desire or intention plus belief' model . . . into something that is not much more than a distant and polite nod towards a causal theory. (ibid., p. 27)

Maze goes on to present a strong case for the thesis that Freud's deterministic theory of motivation, based on the concept of primary drives as physiological mechanisms with inbuilt, though modifiable, ways of working under internal and external conditions, is 'the only way to give empirical content to the notion of the inherently desirable' (ibid., p. 9), and is the most promising foundation for fleshing out the skeletal 'desire plus belief' model in a way which avoids the conceptual traps which have ensnared other versions of this schema. I agree entirely with Maze's thesis, and my outline of the context for the FB theory of symbolism owes a great deal to his exposition.

The foundations of that context comprise two theoretical commitments which are responsible for the value of Freud's deepening and elaborating the 'desire plus belief' model: these commitments are to determinism and to realism.

Determinism

Despite an occasional looseness of expression, which has encouraged some to present him in a different light, Freud was always an uncompromising determinist. He recognised that, for psychology, the most important implication of determinism is the illusory nature of free will, an illusion which is based on our ignorance of certain causes of our actions, and which testifies to the causal efficacy in mental life of unconscious processes. Thus, psychoanalytic theory rests on 'the necessary assumption of *unconscious yet operative* mental processes' (Freud 1901b, p. 272, n. added 1924). Since the causal relation is independent of the knowing relation, it is plain that a mental state within us, of which we are unaware, does not thereby lose its causal efficacy:

Many people, as is well known, contest the assumption of complete psychical determinism by appealing to a special feeling of conviction that there is a free will . . . it is precisely with regard to the unimportant, indifferent decisions that we would like to claim that we could just as well have acted otherwise: that we have acted of our free – and unmotivated – will. According to our analyses it is not necessary to dispute the right to the feeling of conviction of having a free will. If the distinction between conscious and unconscious motivation is taken into account, our feeling of conviction informs us that conscious motivation does not extend to all our motor decisions. *De minimis non curat lex.* But what is thus left free by the one side receives its motivation from the other side, from the unconscious; and in this way determination in the psychical sphere is still carried out without any gap. (Freud 1901b, pp. 253–4)

I ventured to tell you that you nourish a deep-rooted faith in undetermined psychical events and in free will, but that this is quite unscientific and must yield to the demand of a determinism whose rule extends over mental life. (1916/17, p. 106)

Although Freud's determinism is accepted by most Freudian scholars as relatively uncontroversial, the implications of that determinism are, as will be seen, not as readily appreciated.

Realism

The second of Freud's commitments was to realism, that is, to the independent existence of an objective physical world. Furthermore, his realism was a scientific realism: materialist and empiricist. He denied dualism or Platonic idealism, with its postulation of entities beyond the laws and scrutiny of physical science, and he insisted that the foundation of science is observation. Psychoanalysis, according to Freud, is not speculative, but 'is on the contrary empirical – either a direct expression of observations or the outcome of a process of working them over' (1916/17, p. 244). Freud is quite clear about the distinction between what is central, and what is peripheral, in his theory. For example, when proposing a number of ideas concerning narcissism, he says: 'these ideas are not the foundation of science, upon which everything rests: that foundation is observation alone. They are not the bottom but the top of the whole structure, and they can be replaced and discarded without damaging it' (1914d, p. 77).

Freud's scientific outlook is given its clearest and most extended expression in Lecture XXXV of the *New Introductory Lectures*. Here, Freud argues that psychoanalysis does not construct its own *Weltanschauung*, but accepts the scientific one, based on observation: 'It asserts that there are no sources of knowledge of the universe other than the intellectual working-over of carefully scrutinized observations' (Freud 1933, p. 159). Thus, although the main contribution of psychoanalysis lies in its extending scientific observation to unconscious mental life, nevertheless 'no new sources of knowledge or methods of research have come into being' (ibid.). In addition, Freud rejects the philosophical relativism which is designed to protect dualism, and which masquerades as intellectual liberalism:

It is not permissible to declare that science is one field of human mental activity and that religion and philosophy are others, at least its equal in value, and that science has no business to interfere with the other two: that they all have an equal claim to be true and that everyone is at liberty to choose from which he will draw his convictions and in which he will place his belief. A view of this kind is regarded as particularly superior, tolerant, broad-minded and free from illiberal prejudices. Unfortunately, it is not tenable ... It is simply a fact that the truth cannot be tolerant, that it admits of no compromises or limitations, that research regards every sphere of human activity as belonging to it and that it must be relentlessly critical if any other power tries to take over any part of it. (1933, p. 160)

Thus, religion and philosophy cannot remove themselves from scientific scrutiny, which must extend to every sphere of human activity. Further, science aims at objective truth: 'Its endeavour is to arrive at correspondence with reality – that is to say, with what exists outside us and independently of us and, as experience has taught us, is decisive for the fulfilment or disappointment of our wishes. This correspondence with the real external world we call "truth" ' (ibid., p. 170).

As for the notion of 'degrees of truth', which is indispensable to the idealist, Freud points out its incoherence. 'The ordinary man', he says, 'knows only one kind of truth, in the ordinary sense of the word. He cannot imagine what a higher or highest truth may be. Truth seems to him no more capable of comparative degrees than death' (ibid., p. 172). This objective view of truth is contrasted with the subjective or relativist approach:

Acording to the anarchist theory there is no such thing as truth, no assured knowledge of the external world ... Since the criterion of truth – correspondence with the external world – is absent, it is entirely a matter of indifference what opinions we adopt. All of them are equally true and equally false. And no one has a right to accuse anyone else of error. (ibid., pp. 175–6)

Freud's reply is to point out that, despite what relativists may assert, they inevitably betray their lack of commitment to relativism:

If what we believe were really a matter of indifference, if there were no such thing as knowledge distinguished among our opinions by corresponding to reality, we might build bridges just as well out of cardboard as out of stone, we might inject our patients with a decagram of morphine instead of a centigram, and might use tear-gas as a narcotic instead of ether. But even the intellectual anarchists would violently repudiate such practical applications of their theory. (ibid., p. 176)

Finally, because of its objectivism, psychoanalysis, unlike religion, cannot be consolatory, for 'A *Weltanschauung* erected upon science has, apart from its emphasis on the real external world, mainly negative traits, such as submission to the truth and rejection of illusions' (ibid., p. 182).

These two tenets, determinism and realism, are fundamental to Freud's theory and, as will be seen, they have significant implications for various aspects of the theory.

Psychobiological constants: instinctual drives and infantile dependence

Freud's commitment to determinism finds its most important expression in his theory of motivation. In psychoanalytic theory, the motivators are the innate 'biological engines', as Maze (1983) calls them, the instinctual drives:

> the deepest essence of human nature consists of instinctual impulses which are of an elementary nature, which are similar in all men and which aim at the satisfaction of certain primal needs. (Freud 1915d, p. 281)

However, Freud differs from other theorists in his approach to the two questions: (i) what is the nature of these drives, and (ii) how many drives are there? For Freud, although the exact nature and number of the drives is a matter for empirical investigation, the answer to the first question places constraints on the answer to the second. In a deterministic system, the instinctual drives must be identified, he insists, in terms of their physiological *sources*, even if, in mental life, we know them only by their aims. 'What distinguishes the instincts from one another and endows them with specific qualities is their relation to their somatic sources and to their aims' (1905c, p. 168). The postulation of drives *ad libitum* is an unsound move which is typically prompted by the failure to maintain a deterministic approach, and falling into the teleological trap of defining drives in terms of their aims:

> You know how popular thinking deals with the instincts. People assume as many and as varied instincts as they happen to need at the moment – a self-assertive instinct, an imitative instinct, an instinct of play, a gregarious instinct, and many others like them. People take them up, as it were, make each of them do its particular job, and then drop them again. We have always been moved by a suspicion that behind all these little *ad hoc* instincts there lay concealed something serious and powerful which we should like to approach cautiously. (1933, p. 95)

Although there seems to be nothing to stop us from postulating an instinct of play, of destruction, of gregariousness, and so on:

> Nevertheless we should not neglect to ask ourselves whether instinctual motives like these, which are so highly specialized on the one hand, do not admit of further dissection in accordance with the *sources* of the instinct, so that only primal instincts – those which cannot be further dissected – can lay claim to importance. (1915a, p. 124)

Freud puts this principle into practice when he is considering the psychology of group behaviour:

it is easy to regard the phenomena that appear under these special conditions as being expressions of a special instinct that is not further reducible – the social instinct ('herd instinct', 'group mind'), which does not come to light in any other situations. But we may perhaps venture to object that it seems difficult to attribute to the factor of number a significance so great as to make it capable by itself of arousing in our mental life a new instinct that is otherwise not brought into play. Our expectation is therefore directed towards two other possibilities: that the social instinct may not be a primitive one and insusceptible of dissection, and that it may be possible to discover the beginnings of its development in a narrower circle, such as that of the family. (1921, p. 70)

Although we do not know exactly how many drives there are, still, in order to accommodate the fact of mental conflict, of a conflict of interests within a single mind, there must be a plurality of drives – at least two. Freud's treatment of the instinctual drives is typically described as 'dualistic'. This does not, of course, mean that there are only two drives, nor that they are part of a Cartesian dualistic world, but, rather, that they tend to be organised in two opposing groups. In Freud's words: 'The mind has wishes at its disposal whose fulfilment produces unpleasure. This seems self-contradictory; but it becomes intelligible when we take into account the presence of two psychical agencies and a censorship between them' (1900, p. 235). In Freud's early theorising, the two groups are the ego instincts and the sexual instincts. In his later theorising, the opposition is between Eros (the life instincts) and Thanatos (the death instinct). However, because the concept of Thanatos is an example of an instinct defined in terms of its aim, a forsaking of Freud's own insistence that instinctual drives be defined in terms of their sources, the earlier grouping is sounder, and is the one accepted here.

As for the nature of the instinctual drives, defining them in terms of their physiological sources is the first step. Freud's discussion of the primary objects and the vicissitudes of the instinctual drives is the basis of the amplification presented in Maze's (1983) account. The instinctual drives come with innately 'programmed' consummatory activities which are, nevertheless, highly plastic and modifiable, partly because they are subject to the influence of the information which they can seek and acquire via the perceptual systems, partly because they are connected to the muscles which control motility:

The concept of drive . . . must include not only that of an internal mechanism which when activated impels the organism to action, but also that of *the innately provided specific actions which it impels, and whose performance is a necessary condition of the termination of the drive state.* (Maze 1983, p. 142, italics in original)

the history of a person's mental life will be the history of her or his biologically determined drives as they work towards consummation, collecting information and arguing their own justification as they do so. These drives are brain structures with ancillary sensory and motor mechanisms. (ibid., p. 130)

Further, adopting the relational view of mental processes, and a materialist approach to the mind–brain question, Maze shows how the use of the concept of instinctual drives to identify the subject term of those mental relations enables us to explain other phenomena:

> If mental processes are relations into which brain processes enter, as central state materialism proposes, then on the instinctual drive theory it is specifically the drive structures which, through their connections with the perceptual system, enter into those cognitive relations. Freud's theory, if his mentalistic terminology were purified, would reveal itself as a psychologically more detailed version of the mind-brain identity theory. Each instinctual drive accumulates information and misinformation about the location and means of acquisition of the objects necessary for its specific actions to be performed. It is only from a pluralistic view of this sort that one can begin to make sense of the facts of internal conflict and of repression, of the situation in which one part of the psychological apparatus knows something that another part does not know. Also, it makes possible an understanding of the fact that cognitive processes are always motivated, never perfectly disinterested or rational, even when they are clinging to the reality principle because of its generalised practical utility. (ibid., p. 162)

In this more expanded sense the instinctual drives can be viewed as constant forces, and in this sense they are not, as many of the ego-psychologists believed, cut off from psychology and 'intentionality' by being blind, biological, directionless, non-cognitive urges, a view which is nevertheless understandable, given Freud's later formulations on the ego. Thus, through their characteristic of having objects (the things via which the aim is achieved), and through their ability to cognise, and thus be the subject term in psychological processes, the drives are more accurately characterised as *psycho*biological. Amongst these, the sexual drive warrants special attention, for it is special in a number of ways; its sources are many and varied, it is extremely plastic and modifiable, and it is subject, more than any other drive, to repression. When discussing the ubiquity of erotic wishes underlying dreams, Freud says:

> There is no theoretical necessity why this should be so; but to explain the fact it may be pointed out that no other group of instincts has been submitted to such far-reaching suppression by the demands of cultural education, while at the same time the sexual instincts are also the ones which, in most people, find it easiest to escape from the control of the highest mental agencies. Since we have become acquainted with infantile sexuality, which is often so unobtrusive in its manifestations and is always overlooked and misunderstood, we are justified in saying that almost every civilized man retains the infantile forms of sexual life in some respect or other. We can thus understand how it is that repressed

infantile sexual wishes provide the most frequent and strongest motive-forces for the construction of dreams. (1911a, p. 682)

In particular, of all the instincts, the sexual instincts are most able to change their objects and aims, so that 'they are capable of functions which are far removed from their original purposive actions – capable, that is, of "sublimation" ' (1915a, p. 126).

The second of the psychobiological constants which form the deterministic basis of Freud's theory is the long period of infantile dependence (which Freud occasionally refers to as 'the biological factor'):

the long period of time during which the young of the human species is in a condition of helplessness and dependence . . . it is sent into the world in a less finished state. As a result, the influence of the real external world upon it is intensified and an early differentiation between the ego and the id is promoted. Moreover, the dangers of the external world have a greater importance for it, so that the value of the object which can alone protect it . . . is enormously enhanced. The biological factor, then, establishes the earliest situations of danger and creates the need to be loved which will accompany the child through the rest of its life. (1926a, pp. 154–5)

It is this second factor which is the major determinant of the superego:

It follows from what we have said about its origin that it presupposes an immensely important biological fact and a fateful psychological one: namely, the human child's long dependence on its parents and the Oedipus complex, both of which, again, are intimately connected. (1933, pp. 66–7)

The long period of childhood, during which the growing human being lives in dependence on its parents, leaves behind it as a precipitate the formation in his ego of a special agency in which this parental influence is prolonged. It has received the name of *super-ego*. (1940, p. 146)

The confluence of the innate characteristics of the instinctual drives and the long period of infantile dependence determines the vicissitudes of those drives, and certain contingent regularities follow: incestuous object choice for the sexual drive, frustration and deprivation as the inevitable results of socialisation and repression, the establishment of the superego, ambivalent object relations, and the search for, or deflection of drives onto, substitute objects and activities. Among these processes, the instinctual renunciation which is the inevitable result of socialisation is particularly relevant for the theory of symbolism.

Socialisation: instinctual renunciation

Since Freud's motivational theory is grounded in a determinism based on drives, the socialisation of the individual via external forces, which establishes the superego, and which leads to the development of culture – aesthetics, morality, and so on – must be explained in terms of the responses of the drives to external controlling and inhibiting influences, and must be achievable only by means of the setting of drives against each other, which results in compromise formations. During the process of socialisation, the basic demand is for instinctual renunciation. 'We learn to value being loved', says Freud, 'as an advantage for which we are willing to sacrifice other advantages ... Civilization has been attained through the renunciation of instinctual satisfaction, and it demands the same renunciation from each newcomer in turn' (1915d, p. 282). But, as Freud suggests here, renunciation of one instinctual satisfaction is always in exchange for another (usually, this is couched in terms of the need for the love of those on whom we depend), and this process is responsible for the acquisition of ethical value terms:

What is bad is often not at all injurious or dangerous to the ego; on the contrary, it may be something which is desirable and enjoyable to the ego. Here, therefore, there is an extraneous influence at work, and it is this that decides what is to be called good or bad. Since a person's own feelings would not have led him along this path, he must have had a motive for submitting to this extraneous influence. Such a motive is easily discovered in his helplessness and his dependence on other people, and it can best be designated as fear of loss of love. If he loses the love of another person upon whom he is dependent, he also ceases to be protected from a variety of dangers ... At the beginning, therefore, what is bad is whatever causes one to be threatened with loss of love. (1930, p. 124)

This implies a reversal of the typical approach to conscience and ethical feeling:

The situation is usually presented as though ethical requirements were the primary thing and the renunciation of instinct followed from them. This leaves the origin of the ethical sense unexplained. Actually, it seems to be the other way about. The first instinctual renunciation is enforced by external powers, and it is only this which creates the ethical sense, which expresses itself in conscience and demands a further renunciation of instinct. (1924c, p. 170)

According to Freud, the substitution which underlies apparent renunciation is what ties together obsessional neurosis and its cultural counterpart, the development of religion:

The most essential similarity would reside in the underlying renunciation of the activation of instincts that are constitutionally present ... A progressive renunciation of constitutional instincts, whose activation might afford the ego primary pleasure, appears to be one of the foundations of the development of human civilization. (1907b, p. 127)

The important point is that one thing is only ever given up *in exchange* for something else. 'Actually', says Freud, 'we can never give anything up; we only exchange one thing for another. What appears to be a renunciation is really the formation of a substitute or surrogate' (1908b, p. 145). This is what Jones appears to have in mind when he describes human behaviour as the process of seeking satisfaction via ever-widening symbolic substitutes. The subject of symbolism, according to Jones, 'is seen to comprise almost the whole development of civilisation. For what is this other than a never-ending series of evolutionary substitutions, a ceaseless replacement of one idea, interest, capacity or tendency by another?' (Jones 1916, p. 87)

Sublimation and the origins of culture and values

Socialisation is not just based on renunciation of instinct; it also depends on this renunciation being falsely believed to be 'principled', i.e., the process is based on the acquisition of beliefs about 'values' (cf. Maze 1973), beliefs which constitute the superego, and on the simultaneous denial and repression of the knowledge of the real economic basis of the process:

whereas instinctual renunciation, when it is for external reasons, is *only* unpleasurable, when it is for internal reasons, in obedience to the superego, it has a different economic effect. In addition to the inevitable unpleasurable consequences it also brings the ego a yield of pleasure – a substitutive satisfaction, as it were. The ego feels elevated; it is proud of the instinctual renunciation, as though it were a valuable achievement. (Freud 1939, pp. 116–17)

In this process, the concept of 'sublimation' plays a central role. Because of their special characteristics, the sexual instincts are peculiarly adapted for diversion into cultural pursuits; they have a great capacity for changing their objects:

This displaceability and readiness to accept a substitute must operate powerfully against the pathogenic effect of a frustration. Among these protective processes against falling ill owing to deprivation there is one which has gained special cultural significance. It consists in the sexual trend abandoning its aim of obtaining a component or a reproductive pleasure and taking on another which is related genetically to the abandoned one but is itself no longer sexual and must be described as social. We call this process 'sublimation', in accordance with the general estimate that places social aims higher than the sexual ones, which are at bottom self-interested. Sublimation is, incidentally, only a special case of the way in which sexual trends are attached to other, non-sexual ones. (1916/17, p. 345)

Now, sublimation apparently lies at the heart of artistic and other cultural activity. Yet, again and again, Freud distinguishes between neuroses and cultural products like art and religion, not in terms of intrinsic differences, but in terms of whether they are individual or collective responses, and in terms of society's estimation of them, its judgement of the latter as 'higher' or 'finer':

neuroses are asocial structures; they endeavour to achieve by private means what is effected in society by collective effort. (1913d, p. 73)

the forms assumed by the different neuroses echoed the most highly admired productions of our culture. Thus hysterics are undoubtedly imaginative artists . . . the ceremonials and prohibitions of obsessional neurotics drive us to suppose that they have created a private religion of their own . . . It is impossible to escape the conclusion that these patients are, in an *asocial* fashion, making the very attempts at solving their conflicts and appeasing their pressing needs which, when those attempts are carried out in a fashion that is acceptable to the majority, are known as poetry, religion and philosophy. (1919b, p. 261)

The motive forces of artists are the same conflicts which drive other people into neurosis and have encouraged society to construct its institutions. (1913e, p. 187)

The dynamic bases of obsessive actions and religious observances are the same; it is just, according to Freud, that the latter have been mitigated by being collectivised. The history of civilisation is the history of human efforts to find the most successful compromises for instinctual gratification, whether in the form of individual neurosis, or artistic achievement, or in the form of social practices and cultural institutions:

The whole course of the history of civilization is no more than an account of the various methods adopted by mankind for 'binding' their unsatisfied wishes, which . . . have been met by reality sometimes with favour and sometimes with frustration . . . Myths, religion and morality find their place in this scheme as attempts to seek a compensation for the lack of satisfaction of human wishes . . . the neuroses themselves have turned out to be attempts to find *individual* solutions for the problems of compensating for unsatisfied wishes, while the institutions seek to provide *social* solutions for these same problems. (ibid., p. 186)

The significant point about sublimation, then, is that, if this is true, the 'sublimity' of the products of sublimation is illusory. The lure of the concept of 'value', and of notions of the 'higher' and 'superior', derives its force from a complex process of renunciation, self-delusion and substitute gratification.

Compromise formations: the unconscious and the primary/ derivative distinction

From the notion of compromise formations produced as outlined above, two important consequences follow: the first, generally recognised, is the necessity, in explaining behaviour, of appealing to unconscious processes; the second, which is less adequately appreciated, is a distinction between the 'primary' and the 'derivative' (or 'secondary'), in which the primary, the primitive, is logically and temporally, and so of course *psychologically*, prior to the derivative. These two explanatory concepts work together, because the primary is usually what is repressed, what is unconscious, and what is transformed into, or represented by, the derivative.

Throughout Freud's writings there is constant reference to the 'primary' objects of the instinctual drives. These are primary in a temporal sense (they are the first satisfying objects), in a motivational sense (they remain the most important), and in a logical sense (they are the ones for which substitutes are sought):

If an infant could speak, he would no doubt pronounce the act of sucking at his mother's breast by far the most important in his life. He is not far wrong in this, for in this single act he is satisfying at once the two great vital needs. We are therefore not surprised to learn from psycho-analysis how much psychical importance the act retains throughout life. Sucking at the mother's breast is the starting point of the whole of sexual life, the unmatched prototype of every later sexual satisfaction ... I can give you no idea of the important bearing of this first object upon the choice of every later object, of the profound effect it has in its transformations and substitutions in even the remotest regions of our sexual life. (1916/17, p. 314)

We call the mother the first *love*-object. For we speak of love when we bring the mental side of the sexual trends into the foreground and want to force back the underlying physical or 'sensual' instinctual demands. (ibid., p. 329)

A human being's first choice of an object is regularly an incestuous one, aimed, in the case of the male, at his mother and sister; and it calls for the severest prohibitions to deter this persistent infantile tendency from realization. (ibid., p. 335)

Freud's biological approach which characterises human development by the length of dependence ... implies the idea not only of the unique role of the love object in human development but also the extent to which the influence of this object determines later behaviour. (Hartmann et al. 1951, p. 246)

The importance of primary objects and object relations is partly guaranteed by the original anaclitic relationship between the sexual and the ego instincts:

The sexual instincts are at the outset attached to the satisfaction of the ego-instincts; only later do they become independent of these, and even then we have an indication of that original attachment in the fact that the persons who are concerned with a child's feeding, care and protection become his earliest sexual objects: that is to say, in the first instance his mother or a substitute for her. (Freud 1914d, p. 87)

The primary/derivative distinction, and the dependence of the derivative on the primary, bear on two related phenomena. Firstly, they explain the unidirectional nature of the symbolic equation:

> All psycho-analytic experience goes to shew that the primary ideas of life, the only ones that can be symbolised – those, namely, concerning the bodily self, the relation to the family, birth, love, and death – retain in the unconscious throughout life their original importance, and that from them is derived a very large part of the more secondary interests of the conscious mind. (Jones 1916, p. 116)

Secondly, they underpin the claim that everything we do, under any conditions, is a form (albeit sometimes a very elaborated and apparently far-removed form) of the consummatory activity of one or another of the fundamental instinctual drives, and thus they can give empirical content to the notion of 'basic' actions, when we are looking for an answer to the question: 'but what is he/she *really* doing?'

> the import of this version of instinctual drive theory is that *everything one does throughout one's life, however obviously acquired, sophisticated or culture-bound it is, is some modified form or instrumental elaboration of one of the innate consummatory actions.* To put it more radically still, nothing is ever done but a consummatory action in some guise. This basic nature of learned behaviours is often heavily disguised by many layers of increasingly refined rationalisations . . . but the more one subjects such rationalisations to dispassionate logical scrutiny, the more the shape of the basic consummatory action underlying the surface behaviour reveals itself. (Maze 1983, p. 152)

This account is supported by Gardner (1993):

> Through the assumption that propositional desires are causally dependent on motivational states, and that these consist in biological need and other kinds of instinctual demand, psychoanalytic interpretation is given a definite direction: however sophisticated the content of a propositional attitude, the extended possibilities of interconnection between mental states discovered in psychoanalytic interpretation mean that it is related, at least potentially to an instinctual condition. This brings the entire extent of the mind within the orbit of bodily determination: even the most 'angelic' mental states are haunted by instinctual conditions. (p. 124)

Further:

> The assumption that satisfying desire is the business of those mental processes that are developmentally prior accords with the fact that we start off as creatures with biological needs, and only later become artists. Also, it opens up the possibility that some forms of expression in human life, such as artistic activity, may be explained as developments, albeit highly sophisticated ones, out of wish-fulfilment. (ibid., p. 127)

Another point about the primary/derivative distinction is that, in some cases, it is Freud's commitment to realism which allows the distinction to be made, and allows what is primary to be identified. This is exemplified in his discussion of the origins of taboo. In response to Wundt's assertion that taboo is explained as fear of 'demonic' power, Freud says:

> Neither fear nor demons can be regarded by psychology as 'earliest' things, *impervious to any attempt at discovering their antecedents*. It would be another matter if demons really existed. But we know that, like gods, they are creations of the human mind: they were made by something out of something. (1913d, p. 24, italics mine)

Clearly, Freud's injunction here to discover 'antecedents' is not simply a call to accept determinism, or to embark on the task of identifying an infinite sequence of causal antecedents. Rather, the discovery of antecedents is a discovery of what it is that the person concerned is *really* afraid of. The derivative is always identifiable negatively, in that it is not one of the primary objects or actions of the instinctual drives. However, in cases where the derivative is not real, the recognition of the derivative *as* derivative is made particularly easy. Since there are no such things as gods or demons, fear of them must be fear of something else which *is* real.

The explanatory importance of the unconscious and of the primary/derivative distinction in psychoanalytic theory is clear. Because of our ignorance of the motivating force of our unconscious mental processes, we tend, in our cultural products, to project these into other phenomena:

> In point of fact I believe that a large part of the mythological view of the world, which extends a long way into the most modern religions, *is nothing but psychology projected into the external world*. The obscure recognition (the endopsychic perception, as it were) of psychical factors and relations in the unconscious is mirrored ... in the construction of a *supernatural reality*, which is destined to be changed back once more by science into the *psychology of the unconscious*. One could venture to explain in this way the myths of paradise and the fall of man, of god, of good and evil, of immortality, and so on, and to transform *metaphysics* into *metapsychology*. (1901b, pp. 258–9, italics in original)

The process to which Freud refers here, transforming metaphysics into metapsychology, is completely at odds with the Jungian approach; by adhering to the primary/derivative distinction, and to the reality of the primary, Freud contradicts Jung's position, which is based on a denial of both. Freud unmasks Jung's procedure as one of cutting off the moorings of the derivative from the primary, so as to deny the instinctual bases of 'higher' activities. According to Freud, both Jung and Adler:

> court a favourable opinion by putting forward certain lofty ideas, which view things, as it were, *sub specie aeternitatis*. (1914c, p. 58)

All the changes that Jung has proposed to make in psycho-analysis flow from his intention to eliminate what is objectionable in the family-complexes, so as not to find it again in religion and ethics. For sexual libido an abstract concept has been substituted, of which one may safely say that it remains mystifying and incomprehensible to wise men and fools alike. The Oedipus complex has merely a 'symbolic' meaning: the mother in it means the unattainable, which must be renounced in the interests of civilization; the father who is killed in the Oedipus myth is the 'inner' father, from whom one must set oneself free in order to become independent . . . The truth is that these people have picked out a few cultural overtones from the symphony of life and have once more failed to hear the mighty and primordial melody of the instincts. (ibid., p. 62)

But all the evidence suggests that we must reject the independence of 'higher' activities:

It may be difficult too, for many of us, to abandon the belief that there is an instinct towards perfection at work in human beings, which has brought them to their present high level of intellectual achievement and ethical sublimation and which may be expected to watch over their development into supermen. I have no faith, however, in the existence of any such internal instinct and I cannot see how this benevolent illusion is to be preserved. The present development of human beings requires, as it seems to me, no different explanation from that of animals. What appears in a minority of human individuals as an untiring impulsion towards further perfection can easily be understood as a result of *the instinctual repression upon which is based all that is most precious in human civilization* [italics mine]. The repressed instinct never ceases to strive for complete satisfaction, which would consist in the repetition of a primary experience of satisfaction; and it is the difference in amount between the pleasure of satisfaction which is *demanded* and that which is actually *achieved* that provides the driving factor which will permit of no halting at any position attained. (1920b, p. 42)

This is also responsible for the fact that substitute gratification is never as good as the original:

At present we can only say figuratively that such satisfactions seem 'finer and higher'. But their intensity is mild as compared with that derived from the sating of crude and primary instinctual impulses; it does not convulse our physical being. (1927, pp. 79–80)

In consequence, Freud rejects emphatically the attempt to remove these supposedly 'higher' areas from scientific scrutiny:

Moreover, it is quite unscientific to judge analysis by whether it is calculated to undermine religion, authority and morals; for, like all sciences, it is entirely non-tendentious and has only a single aim – namely to arrive at a consistent view of one portion of reality. Finally, one can only characterize as simple-minded the fear which is sometimes expressed that all the highest goods of humanity, as they are called – research, art, love, ethical and social sense – will lose their value or their dignity because psycho-analysis is in a position to demonstrate their origin in elementary and animal instinctual impulses. (1923a, p. 252)

Now, Maze is quite correct to point out that:

it is obviously insufficient to assert in a merely *a priori* way that actions of the order of aesthetic and ethical actions are just elaborated forms of the basic consummatory actions of the physiological drives . . . what is required is some indication of how the connections come about, of how the one action actually functions as an elaborated form of the other. . . to justify the assertion that behaviours of this elevated kind are not simply what they claim to be, and conceal earthier motivations, it will be necessary to show in each case some objective ground for disputing the validity of the rationalisation; then to show how the activities so rationalised may plausibly be related to drive satiation. (Maze 1983, pp. 166–7)

Accordingly, Maze presents a number of examples of human behaviour typically described as 'higher', and offers analyses of them of the kind which he suggests is necessary.

However, there is also much theoretical support for the basic position, and anyone who disputes it must dispute many of the elements of the theory presented above. In other words, the claim of the connection is not merely *a priori*; a complex theoretical structure supports it. It is clear how the components of the theory interlock. In the context of determinism and realism, Freud argues that the confluence of two psychobiological constants, the innate instinctual drives and the long period of infantile dependence, explains the influence and effects of socialisation, thus connecting our mental infantilism with the predisposition to religion and culture. The demands of socialisation (particularly that of instinctual renunciation) lead us to seek gratification via ever broader symbolic substitutes, in the form of the partially satisfying compromise formations of neurosis, culture, religion, and so on. Freud is correct when he complains that psychoanalysis is unjustly reproached for ignoring the higher, moral side of human nature. The concept of the superego explains this aspect, and, because it is an expression of instinctual drives, it shows how 'what has belonged to the lowest part of the mental life of each of us is changed, through the formation of the ideal, into what is highest in the human mind by our scale of values' (Freud 1923d, p. 36).

In accounting for human behaviour, the appeals to the unconscious and to the primary/derivative distinction converge; they combine in the claim that what is sought and repressed (renounced) is primary, and therefore that what is symbolised is primary, and that the behaviour is explicable by appeal to the causal efficacy of the unconscious belief that the derivative (the secondary) is really the primary. Here we arrive, in terms of symbolism, at the unconscious belief of part of the mind that the symbol is the symbolised.

The FB theory of symbolism

Clearly, the FB theory of symbolism is integral with the general theory of psychoanalysis. The specific claims of the FB theory may be summarised by the following points:

(1) There are two general classes of symbolism: conventional and non-conventional. While there are problems concerning the former, and concerning the relationship between the two, the latter class is the focus of inquiry here, because it contains those symbols (occurring in dreams, myths, art, rituals, folklore, symptoms, etc.) which are controversial and especially in need of explanation. These are symbols which, in the literature, are called variously 'non-discursive', 'condensation', 'non-logical', and even, sometimes, 'psychoanalytic'. Non-conventional symbolism differs from language and conventional symbolism in that the non-conventional symbol is not used primarily to refer or to communicate. Rather, it is a substitute produced via displacement, and can be used normally or pathologically, consciously or unconsciously. It includes not just isolated entities, but actions, events, and complex combinations.

(2) Given a normal/pathological continuum, rather than a dichotomy, the term 'normal' is applicable in a variable way, and cannot be relied on to isolate and identify a distinctive category of symbolism. For instance, there can be conscious and deliberate employment of non-conventional symbols whose meanings have become known (e.g., a writer of a fairy story may deliberately use the queen to stand for the mother). Alternatively, some symbols may be regarded as normal either because the substitution occurs consciously (the knight who fights for his lady's glove knowing that it stands for her), or because, although the process may be unconscious and defensive, it is socially acceptable and not regarded as neurotic (the old spinster who keeps a pet as a companion-substitute on which to bestow her love). 'Normal' symbol formation and use includes particularly the vast field of cultural symbolism, which is the product of socially acceptable 'sublimation'. Conversely, the term 'pathological' is not for Freud restricted to the products of mental illness; it can be used in connection with various phenomena typically regarded as normal, including

dreams, the symptoms of normal defence mechanisms, myths, and so on.

(3) The concept of the symbol as substitute produced via displacement is illustrated in Freud's early notions of the mnemic symbol and symbolization in hysteria, which are special cases of the more general schema (see Chapter 3, Figure 1, p. 46). Within this schema, the psychoanalytic focus on the controversial, non-conventional class of symbols is highlighted, the theme of the symbol as defensive substitute produced via the conflict–repression–substitution 'formula' being central. Once again, it is emphasised that, despite the use of the substantive 'symbol', this process includes more complex actions, relations and events. The queen in a dream may be a symbol, but an elaborate sequence of ritualistic performances in obsessive compulsive neurosis may be equally symbolic, serving the same kind of economic function, and being explicable via the same psychodynamic principles.

(4) The basis of (non-conventional) symbolism lies in four empirical facts: (i) the initial primary objects and consummatory activities of the innate instinctual drives; (ii) the long period of infantile dependence; (iii) the connection between the drives and cognitive structures, which leads to the 'interested' perceiving of similarities between the primary objects and other, non-primary, objects; and (iv) the unavailability (to some part of the mind), mainly through repression, of those primary objects, and the inhibition, mainly through repression, of the expression of the consummatory activities with respect to particular primary objects.

(5) These four facts result in the displacement of interest from the wished for, but repressed, primary objects and activities onto partially gratifying substitutes which are compromise formations for conflicting impulses. This substitution lies at the heart of dreams, neurotic symptoms, myths, art, fairy tales, rituals, and other religious actions. The nature of these formations as partially gratifying compromises is determined by the existence within the mind of competing interests. One part of the mind unconsciously takes the symbol to be the symbolised, but for another part of the mind the symbol is simply whatever it is in itself. For the repressed impulse, symbolism is a case of motivated mistaken identity, in which the symbol is mistaken for the symbolised and treated as if it were the symbolised. For the repressing impulse, there is no such mistaken belief; the object or activity in question is acceptable. The combination in one person of these two processes results (for reasons not properly understood) in gratification which is not as

complete as would be the gratification obtained from the satisfaction, via primary objects and activities, of the unopposed instinctual impulse.

(6) Symbolism can be individual or universal, but much of the symbolism found in the manifestations of culture is universal. The uniformity of the instinctual drives in all people, the cross-cultural constants of the early infantile situation (long period of dependence, parents of opposite sexes, centrality of the body and bodily experiences, socialisation and repression in some form), and the ubiquity of objects bearing similarities to the primary objects, account for the existence of universal symbolism. In addition, the peculiarity of the sexual instinct – its multiple sources, its plasticity and modifiability, and the fact that it is particularly subject to repression, especially in its infantile pre-genital forms – accounts for the prevalence and universality of sexual symbolism, and also for sublimation.

(7) In symbolism, there is always a combination of conscious and unconscious processes, and often a complex interlacing of the two. For example, in religious practices and rituals the avowed symbolism not only overlies, but symbolically substitutes for, the unconscious symbolism. These phenomena require the inclusion of certain cases of 'surface symbolism' (Jones's 'metaphor') in a complete theory of symbolism.

(8) The concepts of the unconscious and of the primary/derivative distinction are central to symbolism. The symbolised is primary and unconscious, the symbol secondary and conscious; the belief in the identity of symbol and symbolised is unconscious, the recognition of their non-identity is conscious. Instinctual renunciation is always *in exchange* for a substitute. As Freud says, we never give anything up – 'what appears to be a renunciation is really the formation of a substitute or surrogate' (1908b, p. 145). This explains the unidirectionality of the symbolic equation, and makes sense of questions like 'what is he/she *really* doing, (seeing, believing, etc.)?'

(9) Because of the primary/derivative distinction, because of a particular theoretical stance on the relationship between the two, and because of a commitment to realism, which entails that what is primary, what is symbolised, must be real, the FB theory of symbolism is opposed to theories which present the so-called 'regressive' and 'progressive' vectors of symbolism as independent of each other, and which assert that any theory of symbolism will either inform a choice between two equally legitimate interpretations, or, more typically, will insist that symbols have both vectors. The FB

theory is, in part, a theory of the nature of the relationship between the two – the development of the 'progressive' interpretation as a reaction to the 'regressive'. In many cases, 'progressive' and 'anagogic' interpretations are not primary; they refer not to real things, but to transformations and derivatives of things which are real. In Freud's terms, the anagogic approach, with its idolising of the ineffability of the symbol, and its celebration of the freedom and creativity of the human spirit, is part of Jung's programme *ad captandam benevolentiam* (Freud 1914c, p. 59), and is an attempt to disguise the origins of symbolism. It is a denial of a primary/derivative distinction, and *a fortiori*, of the relationship between the two.

(10) Thus, in contrast with those who assert that symbols belong to the higher realm of aesthetic and moral values, a realm which is inscrutable scientifically, the FB theory elucidates the psychodynamic origins and the economic function of the 'higher realm' of the cultural world of symbols. Symbolism cannot be a manifestation of free will or individual spontaneity, because there is no such thing. We are caused to symbolise, caused to treat the symbol as if it were the symbolised, and so on. Symbolism cannot indicate a 'higher' truth, because there is no such thing, and what it does indicate must be discoverable in this single (albeit complex), material, spatio-temporal world.

Explanatory application

To return to Wollheim's (1993) assessment of Freud's contribution, and in particular to his specification of the three ways in which Freud extended the 'desire plus belief' schema of ordinary psychological explanation, Wollheim's model can in turn be extended in a number of ways, and the role of symbolism in that extension clarified. The success of the deepening, elaboration, and contextualisation of the schema, to which Wollheim refers, depends on a certain amount of prior 'infilling' (to use Wollheim's term) provided by Freud's theory. Firstly, Freud elucidates the nature of the 'desire' component, fleshing out the term via the concept of instinctual drives, which, as Maze suggests, must be done if the model is not to be vacuous. Secondly, Freud's theory clarifies the relationship between desires and beliefs. If the instinctual drives are neurophysiological brain structures with ancillary sensory and motor mechanisms, then it is the instinctual drives which are, in some sense, the specific subject terms of the cognitive relations, although we do typically attribute knowing, believing, etc. to the *person as a whole*. This attribution is not problematic until we are faced with cases such as symbolism, where the person appears both to know and not to know, both to believe and not to believe, and so on. In those cases, given the multiplicity of drives, and the inevitable conflict of competing drives, the combination in one person of conflicting and often contradictory beliefs is accounted for; the explanation of any particular behaviour may require a number of simultaneous desires and beliefs.

This kind of 'infilling' is the key to the explanatory power and effectiveness of Freud's extension of the 'desire plus belief' model. It also allows us to reply to the objection which has been raised (by, e.g., Eagle 1988) that there is a *prima facie* 'lack of fit' between some (indeed, the most important) psychoanalytic explanations and that model. According to Eagle, obsessive acts, symptoms, etc. which are developed to satisfy unconscious desires cannot be seen as 'actions or quasi-actions carried out by an agent', but, rather, as events which just 'happen to' the person:

A dream or a slip is not an intentional action in the sense of following the practical syllogism in which one has a particular desire (or goal or intention), a belief that a particular set of actions will fulfil that desire, and then carries out one of those actions in order to fulfil that desire. While a slip or dream may express a wish or desire, it is not an action or quasi-action through which that desire is satisfied. (Eagle 1988, p. 99)

how one develops symptoms that appear to resolve conflicts and satisfy unconscious desires is a complete mystery. What is clear is that one does not bring that about voluntarily; rather, they just happen. (ibid., n. p. 108)

It seems to me that, properly speaking, a repressed desire does not belong to a person but is rather a subpersonal phenomenon . . . a repressed desire or wish belongs to the world (or language) of organisms rather than of persons . . . unconscious or repressed desires are extensions of and derived from (perhaps degenerate forms of) ordinary desires . . . [each] is a neurophysiological phenomenon that influences conscious experience and behaviour. (ibid., p. 101)

There are a number of confusions here, which are dissipated by an understanding of the extension of the 'desire plus belief' model outlined above. Indeed, Eagle himself provides the key to the clarifications, in his implicit recognition that the crux of the Freudian elaboration of the model lies in the combination of unconscious processes and mental division: 'inner conflict does not necessarily consist simply in having a desire that one wishes one did not have, but in having a desire on the one hand and experiencing guilt and anxiety on the other' (ibid., p. 100).

But, of course, the experiences of guilt and anxiety are, in Freud's model, as much expressions of desire as are the conscious desires. Further, Freud rejects the assumption of the kind of free-will/determinism compatibilism upon which Eagle's distinction between a voluntary action and something which 'just happens' rests; instead, the *experience* of an 'it happens to me' is simply an indication of an *unconscious* desire at work. Finally, as I have argued, unconscious desires are no less desires than conscious ones; they are not 'degenerate' or *merely* neurophysiological phenomena. *All* desires have their sources in neurophysiological structures, but they are all equally *psycho*biological.

These aspects which constitute Freud's elaboration of the standard model of action explanation are combined in any particular case of symbolism. To illustrate, Wollheim uses the example of the Rat Man's sudden furious weight-reducing efforts while on holiday in the mountains with his girlfriend (Freud 1909b). The Rat Man's behaviour consisted of adopting an extreme and dangerous regimen, according to which he would interrupt lunch suddenly to rush along the road and up the mountain slope in the hot sun:

This regime [sic] is explained, first, by appeal to the Rat Man's intense but unconscious jealousy of his lady's cousin Richard, who was staying with her at the same resort, and his instrumental belief that, with Richard out of the way, the situation would improve and his jealousy disappear. However, what this desire and this belief rationalize is the Rat Man's murdering Richard, which it was out of the question that he should do. So the explanation of the Rat Man's curious regime further appeals to a chain of association, operative in his head, which runs from murdering Richard to getting rid of his own fat, the intermediate links being supplied by Richard's nickname, 'Dick', and the German word for 'fat', that is, *dick*. The desire and the belief, which in the case of a different type of person might have caused him to kill his rival, cause the Rat Man to lose weight in this ferocious fashion: something which has a further appositeness, in that, as Freud suggests, what the Rat Man does is over-determined, for it is additionally caused by the Rat Man's desire to punish himself for having entertained murderous impulses, even if only to reject them. (Wollheim 1993, p. 97)

While accepting this analysis, we can add to it by identifying the behaviour as a piece of symbolism. By getting rid of his fat ('Dick'), the Rat Man is symbolically getting rid of Richard. A part of his mind makes the unconscious equation of his body fat with Richard (there is a linguistic similarity, each being referred to by the same word); this leads in turn to the unconscious equation of losing the weight with getting rid of Dick, and so to the unconscious equation of running up the hill with a means of killing Richard. At a deeper level, in which the question of primary objects arises, the Rat Man's jealousy is a classic case of Oedipal rivalry. What this analysis of the behaviour as symbolic supplies is the elucidation that the 'chain of association, operative in his head' and supplied with 'intermediate links' consists of derivatives of his desires, and additional beliefs. It also illustrates that the two basic categories of explanation in psychology, cognition and motivation, which are captured by that traditional model, are, when clearly formulated and given the detail provided by Freud's theory, adequate to account for psychological phenomena. Freud's psychoanalytic theory is indeed an extension, with increased explanatory depth, of 'ordinary psychological' explanation.

11 Symbolism: logical constraints and psychological requirements

The time has come to consider the question of evaluation: how does the FB theory fare in comparison with alternative approaches to symbolism? I mentioned in the introduction that, within psychology, psychoanalysis is caught between two opposing groups, each equally hostile to it, and each, ironically, locating it in the opposing movement. On one side, mainstream 'experimental' psychologists dismiss psychoanalysis as 'unscientific'. On the other side, humanistic, phenomenological, existentialist and idealist psychologists reject classical psychoanalysis as 'reductionist' and 'scientistic'. This latter group is part of a much larger movement in the social sciences generally, and it is there that the alternative material on symbolism is to be found. This material spans a number of different areas, each with its own claims on symbolism. In many general philosophical treatments, the question of 'meaning' is held to be the starting point of philosophy. Hermeneutics, the art or science of interpretation, also has 'meaning' as its central concept, and sees its task as 'untangling the symbolic'. Semiotics, dealing with all signs and signifying systems, locates theories of symbolism within *its* boundaries. Aesthetics is concerned with the question of the 'significance' and the symbolic nature of art. Anthropology and sociology deal with the symbolic nature of the phenomena which make up 'culture', especially the cross-cultural symbolism of religion, myth and ritual. Finally, psychology, despite widespread neglect of the topic, has produced some attempts (other than that of Freud) to give an account of the 'symbolic function'. These alternative treatments of symbolism often include comment on the psychoanalytic approach; some explicitly present their theories as alternatives to psychoanalysis, others identify the supposed contributions and limitations of psychoanalysis within the wider scheme of things, still others claim to provide a necessary reformulation of psychoanalysis. In this bewildering diversity of 'frameworks' disagreement and controversy are rife, but the following assertions are frequently made. There is no general, unified theory of symbolism, and this lack of unity, though regrettable, is the understandable result of the complex nature of the symbol. The contribution of psychology (specifically, psychoanalysis) to a theory of the symbol is limited. At any rate, the symbol is not amenable to the artificial constraints of scientific investigation, so cannot be studied by *scientific* psychology. Only a broader, social-science perspective, whose eclecticism can accommodate the unique, 'multifaceted' nature of the symbol, holds any promise at all for the emergence of a unified theory.

My own theme has been that it *is* possible to develop a general theory of the symbol, and that this is (as it must be) a scientific theory. In this final chapter, I shall argue that the current disorganisation and lack of unity in the literature are less attributable to the 'intrinsic complexity' and 'infinite variability' of the symbol, than to the fact that the various alternative treatments and explanations are bedevilled by confusions and inconsistencies. My case rests on the claim that there are certain logical constraints and certain psychological requirements (summarised in Figure 3) which *any* sound theory of symbolism must meet, that it is a lack of appreciation of these constraints which is responsible for the present farrago, and that, of the theories which have been proposed, the FB theory alone respects them.

The logical contraints are those by which any theory of symbolism is necessarily bound; their violation renders a theory untenable. They are not mutually exclusive; failure to respect one constraint may entail failure to respect others. The psychological requirements are those which it is reasonable to expect any theory of symbolism to meet; their neglect leaves a theory, at best, incomplete. These, too, are interrelated; an account which satisfies one requirement may simultaneously satisfy another.

The logical constraints

Notwithstanding contemporary attacks on the tyranny of logic, there are certain logical constraints which any form of informative discourse must respect (for instance, that acceptable theory must avoid contradiction, and any term which appears in the premises and in the conclusion of an argument must retain the same meaning in all of its appearances, otherwise the argument is invalid). These constraints are taken as given; they do not require elucidation or support. In contrast, the logical contraints presented here are specific to symbolism, and are marked out for special attention because they are typically overlooked or violated in so many treatments of symbolism.

A. LOGICAL CONSTRAINTS

(1) Symbolisation is a three-term relation: signifier (symbol), signified (symbolised), subject (person or knower). Hence:

    i.   No two terms can be collapsed into each other.

    ii.   Meaning cannot be a *property* of the symbol.

    iii.   The ontological status of the symbolised is no different from the ontological status of the symbol.

(2) The signified (symbolised) cannot be *ultimately* a signifier (symbol); at some stage in the chain of signification, it must be a non-signifier.

(3) A theory of symbolism must be a *psychological* theory, since one of the terms in the signifying relation is a cognising subject. Any theory which ignores or denies the subject cannot be a theory of symbolism.

(4) The required psychological theory must not be based on contradictory premises; it cannot combine (explicitly or implicitly) incompatible philosophical positions, such as realism and idealism.

B. PSYCHOLOGICAL REQUIREMENTS

(5) A complete psychological theory of symbolism will explain:

    i.   The ontogenesis of symbols: how and why they occur.

    ii.   The selection of the symbolised.

    iii.   Individual and universal symbols.

    iv.   Variations in the *tertium comparationis*.

    v.   Conscious and unconscious elements.

Figure 3 Summary of the logical constraints and psychological requirements

Symbolisation is a three-term relation

The most important logical constraint is that symbolisation (conventional or non-conventional), like any signification, is a *relationship* between three independently existing and independently characterisable terms: the signifier (in this case the symbol), the signified (in this case the symbolised), and the subject (for whom the symbol stands for, or substitutes for, the symbolised). There are three noteworthy implications of this constraint: (i) firstly, the three-term relation cannot be presented as, or converted into, a two-term relation, by collapsing any two of the terms, particularly, as does happen, by collapsing the signifier and the signified; (ii) secondly, because meaning is a relation (X 'means' Y to A – the symbol 'means' the symbolised to the person), meaning requires each of the three terms, and cannot therefore be a property or quality of any one of them; (iii) thirdly, the symbolised must exist independently of its role in signification, i.e., it must have intrinsic properties which are neither created nor changed by the signifier, or by the fact that it is signified. Its ontological status is no different from the ontological status of the symbol.

How does the FB theory of symbolism fare on this first logical constraint, and on each of its three implications? Certainly it acknowledges the three separate terms; the symbol or symbolic activity (the element which appears in the dream, the obsessive symptomatic act, etc.), the symbolised (the primary object or activity for which the symbol has been substituted), and the person whose mind is the subject of beliefs which relate the symbol and the symbolised. So far so good. What of the implications of this first constraint?

There is one case which might be taken to cause problems for Freud's theory of symbolism, by suggesting a collapsing of two of the three terms – in this case, the collapsing of the symbol and the symbolised. It concerns the psychoanalytic distinction between 'symbolic equation' and 'symbolic representation' suggested by Segal (1958) with reference to two different patients. The first, a schizophrenic, when asked why it was that, since his illness, he had stopped playing his violin, replied angrily, 'Why? Do you expect me to masturbate in public?' The second patient, during analysis of his dream of playing the violin, produced associations which prompted the interpretation that playing the violin represented masturbation. For this patient, according to Segal, playing the violin in waking life was an important sublimation. Segal says that we are faced here with two cases where, for each patient, the symbol is the violin, and the symbolised is the penis, but the ways in which the symbol functions are very different, since, for the schizophrenic, the violin has become so *completely equated* with his genitals, that to touch it in public is impossible, i.e., the two have become *identical* (hence the label 'symbolic equation'). On the other hand, for the non-schizophrenic, who continues to play the violin in waking life, the symbol and symbolised do not become identical (hence the label 'symbolic representation'). Is not the case of 'symbolic equation' a collapsing of two of the terms in the three-term relation, and thus a violation by the theory of the first logical constraint? Not at all. While it may be part of a theory of symbolism to assert that the first two terms (the symbol and the symbolised) are treated by the third term (the subject) *as if* they were identical, the theory need only recognise that they are *not* in fact so, something which the FB theory does (in the stipulated falsity of the unconscious belief in the identity of symbol and symbolised). There is no logical problem with this process; indeed, that one thing is taken to be another, when it is not in fact so, is an assertion whose intelligibility rests on the separate identities of the two things. The only point to be added is that, if there is a genuine distinction between 'symbolic equation' and 'symbolic representation', it will require an account in terms of different beliefs of the third element of the symbolising relation, the person, not an account which depends on actual identity versus non-identity.

By contrast, the collapsing of the signifier and signified is particularly prevalent in various approaches to symbolism within hermeneutics, semiotics, and aesthetics. In hermeneutics, a major outcome of the constructivism according to which any interpretation *creates* the interpreted is the belief in the so-called 'hermeneutic circle', which is characterised as the impossibility of a truly 'uninterpreted' objective reality. This notion is similar to what in semiotics is called the 'semiotic circle'. In the latter, reality consists of a chain of signifiers; in the former, reality consists only of signifieds. However, insofar as each 'circle' involves the collapsing of the signifier and the signified into a single term, the two versions are indistinguishable. This collapsing constitutes a rejection of the independent ontological status of the symbolised, a rejection which, as we shall see, leads to serious difficulties. In the field of aesthetics, the FB theory of symbolism, according to which 'All art is "image-making" and all image-making is rooted in the creation of substitutes' (Gombrich 1963, p. 9), is neo-classical, in the sense that it is committed to realism, accommodates the aesthetics of form, and rejects any idealism *vis-à-vis* the symbolised. There are two approaches in aesthetics which stand as rivals to the FB theory: formalism and romanticism, and, although there are important differences between these two, the collapsing of the signifier and signified can be found in each of them. Here, the symbol is characterised as: 'intransitive' (by analogy with the grammatical intransivity of some verbs); 'significant form' without, however, signifying anything; expressive of the 'inexpressible'; and even, sometimes, 'self-signifying' or 'autotelic'. Such contradictory characterisations have not escaped notice. Todorov (1982), for example, questions the combination of the 'intransitivity' (the *sui generis* nature) of the work of art with its supposed 'autotelic' (self-signifying) function: 'is it not a generic characteristic of every sign . . . to refer to something other than itself? . . . The work of art is "a thing which signifies itself" (but is this still signification?)' (pp. 161–2); 'symbols are intransitive – but in such a way that they do not cease to signify for all that' (p. 201); 'The symbol is the thing itself without being it even while being it (intransitivity goes hand in hand with syntheticism). The symbolic object at once is and is not identical to itself' (p. 203). Todorov's comments here point to the incoherence of any system which deliberately or inadvertently denies the *relational* nature of symbolisation and, with it, the independent existence of the symbol and the symbolised.

The second implication of the three-term relation is that 'meaning' cannot be a quality or property of the symbol. Since meaning is a relation, nothing can have *inherent* semantic properties. Under this constraint, the FB theory of symbolism must reject, as indeed it does, the FN view of the phylogenetic inheritance of symbols, a view which lends itself to (although it does not imply) treatment of the meaning of the symbol as if it were a property of the symbol. Various assertions in the non-psychoanalytic literature on symbolism reveal a failure to respect this constraint. For instance, as indicated above, in formalist aesthetics, Bell's (1914) concept of 'significant form' does not recognise the relational nature of meaning: 'the form of a work of art has a meaning of its own' which 'does not depend upon the association of the form with anything else whatever' (Fry, in Segal 1975, p. 800). But to claim that something is 'significant' while not signifying anything is incoherent. Again, in humanistic psychology, we find the claim that human values are different from biological values because the former are 'at the symbolic level' (Bertalanffy 1981, p. 43), as if 'at the symbolic level' were equivalent to 'intrinsically symbolic', and as if there were no need to say what those values are symbolic *of*. The humanists do, of course, implicitly treat meaning as a relation, locating symbols (they really mean the things which are symbolised) in the higher spiritual realm.

The third implication of the three-term relation is that the symbolised (like the symbol and the person) must exist independently of its role in symbolisation, i.e., it must have intrinsic properties which are neither created nor changed by the symbol, or by the fact that it is symbolised.

This independence is, of course, denied when the signifier and the signified are collapsed into a single term. But the ontological status of the symbolised cannot be different from the ontological status of the symbol. This constraint is clearly respected by the FB theory, according to which, since the unconscious is a relational unconscious, and not a systematic or qualitative unconscious, latent content is no different in kind from manifest content. The 'symbolised' is not qualitatively different from the object of any other thought, despite the symbolic mode of transmission or expression. There are not two different levels of reality, in which the reality of the symbolised is intrinsically different from that of the symbol, and/or is created by the symbol. In the FB theory of symbolism, the crucial difference between symbol and symbolised is that the latter, having been subject to repression, is unconscious. But to be repressed is not a quality, and the difference is not intrinsic.

By contrast, many influential approaches to symbolism are based on two proposals: (i) that the symbolised belongs to a different reality, and (ii) that it is created by the symbol or by the process of symbolisation. These theories usually involve a complex mixture of phenomenology, idealism, constructivism, and relativism, which combine in the following way. Firstly, the phenomenological treatment of the symbol results in an idealism of the symbolised; the view that, because representation requires some mediator (the symbol), this somehow constitutes evidence against epistemological realism in our access to the symbolised, leads to the claim that the nature of the symbolised is fundamentally different from that of the symbol. This then promotes ontological dualism, in which symbol and symbolised belong to different worlds, the symbolised being located in a 'higher' metaphysical realm. Additional steps are then taken into constructivism and relativism, the symbolised being supposed to be created by, and so relative to, the symbol.

To give just a few illustrations: Cassirer (1944, 1955) asserts that the symbol, forming a veil between us and the *Ding an sich*, results in the non-immediacy of our apprehension of reality. This idea is echoed in Lacan's thesis that language distances us from the 'real', as well as in many other approaches to the symbol. 'Man', says Royce (1965b), 'can never come to grips with the ultimate nature of things . . . the symbol is a necessary image or metaphor which stands between man and ultimate truth' (p. 21). This concept of the symbol is then used to consolidate the distinction between science (truth/fact) and the humanities (value/ phantasy) (cf. Whitehead 1927), a distinction which is sometimes held to rest on the division of symbols into the conventional and the non-conventional, such that the latter are excluded from the scientific realm. 'One conception of symbolism', says Langer (1942), 'leads to logic and leads to new problems in theory of knowledge; and so it inspires an evaluation of science and a quest for certainty. The other takes us in the opposite direction – to psychiatry, the study of emotions, religion, fantasy, and *everything but knowledge*' (p. 24, italics mine). Bertalanffy (1981) agrees; discursive symbols convey facts, whereas non-discursive symbols are 'experiential', convey values, and are 'at the very limits of the ineffable' (p. 50).

The problem here is a confusion which lies at the heart of any form of epistemological representationism. An image or a metaphor or a symbol cannot be understood as such without our potential to know what it is an image or symbol *of*, what it is a metaphor *for*. This requires that we have independent, direct, access to whatever is symbolised. It is fine to assert that language distances us from the real, so long as what is meant is simply that language (or any symbol or symbolic system) is logically distinct from the experience it signifies. But, of course, that distinction, far from entailing the *in*accessibility of one of the terms in the relation, actually entails the *accessibility* to the subject of *both* the signifier *and* the signified. The preclusion of 'knowledge' in the presence of the 'symbol' is, therefore, nonsensical, and the dualist distinction between the symbol and science (the 'facts') is, like any metaphysical dualism, untenable. The problems proliferate when further steps are taken into constructivism and relativism. Cassirer asserts that the symbol actually *creates* the distinction between us and the symbolised, a distinction which is not there prior to the symbolisation. It also creates the symbolised, which thus becomes relative to the symbol. What is being asserted here is not simply that the symbolised *qua* symbolised is relative to the symbol – which is obviously the case, given that symbolisation is a relation. Something much stronger is being claimed: that the symbolised as *existent* or *object* is relative to the symbol.

Take, for example, Ricoeur's (1965, 1970) hermeneutic treatment of symbolism, according to which the necessary multiplicity of different interpretative systems for symbolism can only be accommodated within a relativist, perspectivist approach, which denies realism and rejects the separation of truth from method. Since existence is always an interpreted existence, ontology is inseparable from, and dependent on, the so-called 'movement of interpretation' – truth is inseparable from method; the symbolised has no existence prior to symbolisation. These assumptions allow Ricoeur to present a tripartite system in which the psychoanalytic approach to symbolism represents just one ('regressive' or 'archaic') movement of interpretation, limited to a 'semantics of desire' and to a 'demystification of discourse', but without allowing for a 'remythicising of discourse', for 'revelation', for 'access to the sacred'.

Since these latter are represented by the (Jungian) 'progressive' or 'anagogic' movement of interpretation, a complete theory of symbolism must, according to Ricoeur, combine both; it must be 'subject to two modes of exegesis, one along the lines of the Freudian erotics, the other along the lines of a phenomenology of the spirit' (1970, p. 507) – the latter actually further divisible into a 'teleology' and an 'eschatology'. In proposing this tripartite system as a unified theory of symbolism, Ricoeur is oblivious to the theoretical incompatibility between the Freudian archaeology and the other two movements. This is because he engages in two illegitimate manoeuvres. The first is to assume that, in the concealing and revealing aspects of symbolism, the disguise and the disclosure must be directed at different contents in the symbolised (this also allows him to accuse Freud of dealing only with the former, of belonging, together with Nietzsche and Marx, to the iconoclastic 'school of suspicion', of not being interested in the 'recovery of meaning'). The second manoeuvre is to assimilate Freudian theory into constructivism by claiming that, since each movement of interpretation constructs its own ontology, the truth of any interpretation is created by, dependent on, the method: 'it is in deciphering the tricks of desire that the desire at the root of meaning and reflection is discovered. I cannot hypostatize this desire outside the process of interpretation; it always remains a being interpreted . . . I cannot grasp it in itself without the danger of creating a mythology of instinctual forces, as sometimes happens in coarse conceptions of psychoanalysis' (Ricoeur 1965, p. 253). Again, the teleology, 'just like the Freudian archaeology, is constituted only in the movement of interpretation' (ibid., p. 254), so that 'The ontology proposed here is in no way separable from interpretation' (ibid., p. 255). Now, apart from the incoherence of the constructivist position (if the desire is *discovered* through the decipherment of its tricks, there must *be* some desire there in the first place), Ricoeur's thesis here rests on a quite mistaken characterisation of the Freudian 'archaeology'. In psychoanalytic theory, desire and its objects *do* exist prior to the 'movement of interpretation'; realism and determinism, the postulation of instinctual drives as real, existing, causally efficacious physiological structures, are fundamental in the theory, and not something which 'sometimes happens in coarse conceptions of psychoanalysis'. Ricoeur's reluctance to 'hypostatize this desire outside the process of interpretation' is ill-founded. As Bleicher (1980) points out, psychoanalysis cannot be assimilated into that kind of idealism: 'The materialist-naturalist basis of such a science is guaranteed by its emphasis on the drive structure – thereby preempting its fusion with an idealist oriented approach to social phenomena' (p. 169).

Constructivism and relativism in theories of symbolism exploit the fact that 'meaning' is indeed 'created by man'; but it is created only in the sense that, since meaning is a relation, it cannot exist without the terms of that relation. This by no means entails the relative existence of what is meant or symbolised. On the contrary, the relation *requires* the *independent, prior* existence of the symbolised.

The chain of signification must be grounded in a non-signifier

The second logical constraint, which is derived from the first, concerns the nature of what is symbolised. The signified (symbolised) cannot be ultimately *nothing but* a signifier (symbol); at some stage in the chain of signification, it must be grounded in a non-signifier. When Freud recognises this in his theory of symbolism, and grounds his symbolism in reality, he is accused of illegitimately 'closing the semiotic circle'. The FB theory provides a structure which justifies the claim that certain elements which are ultimately symbolised do not, in turn, themselves become symbols. Now, Freud's assertions that 'a dream does not symbolise every possible element of the latent dream-thoughts but only certain definite ones' (1916/17, p. 152), and 'The range of things which are given symbolic representation . . . is not very wide' (ibid., p. 153) must be understood as empirical, not logical, claims. However, while the particular selection is empirical and, as will be seen, requires for its support a meeting of the psychological requirements which will be discussed later, it rests on the logical point that, even if these 'final' referents were themselves to become signifiers (as, logically, they could), and even if what they signified were to be, in turn, other signifiers, at some stage in the chain of signification or symbolisation, some signified must be a non-signifier. That is, everything cannot be, from the beginning and simultaneously, a signifier. Reality cannot consist of signifiers only.

In contrast, many approaches to symbolism, particularly in the fields of semiotics and hermeneutics, are based on just the opposite claim. 'A symbol', according to Zentner (1980), 'is the relation of a signifier to another signifier and its interpretation should not be understood as the relation between a signifier and a signified' (p. 107). Any 'signified' is only another signifier, and so on *ad infinitum*, resulting in an endless chain of significations known (anomalously) as the 'semiotic circle'. In this circle, the signifier is king, for 'it is the signifier that produces the signification. This priority of the signifier implies the sequence of signifier first and then signification' (Safouan 1982, p. 103). The semiotic cult of the signifier, in which the moorings to the signified, to reality, are severed, amounts (we are triumphantly told) to a critical revolution which 'frees the sign from its subservience to the "reality" (or *presence*) which it was supposed to serve' (Hawkes 1977, p. 149), and allows us to realise 'that meaning arises from the *interplay* of signs, that the world we inhabit is not one of "facts" but of signs *about* facts which we encode and decode ceaselessly from system to system . . . We live in a world, the argument concludes, which has no "pure", no "innocent" contexts to offer us' (ibid., p. 122). In the jargon of deconstructionism, there is nothing beyond the text.

But the notion of the 'semiotic circle' (or of the 'hermeneutic circle') is self-contradictory. Any 'reading', that is to say, interpretation, requires that there be *something* to be interpreted; and to a hermeneuticist who claims that 'there is no reality; only an interpretation of reality', the reply is: 'an interpretation of . . . *what*?' Likewise, the claim that all reality is symbolic of something else which is, in turn, symbolic, is no more coherent than the Hindu concept of *Maya*, in which all reality is an illusion. Just as illusion, or error, is dependent on reality, or truth, so representation is dependent on something to be represented, interpretation on something to be interpreted, sign on something to be signified. Hawkes's assertion, that we inhabit a world, not of facts, but of signs pointing to facts, implies that we *do* inhabit a world of facts. The signifier is presented as *something*, and its signifying another signifier is presented as a *fact*. More than that, since 'signifier' would lose its meaning without the correlative 'signified', it is a rhetorical absurdity to refer to a signifier's signifying something as 'subservience to' that something, and to attempt to 'rescue' it from that something. In adhering to the semiotic maxim that the signified is created by the signifier, Safouan is adhering to a confusion between the intrinsic nature of the signified as pre-signified object, and the creation of the relation of that object as 'signified' in the act of signification. The latter, of course, is indeed a relation into which the pre-signified object enters. But the fact that it becomes signified when the act of signification occurs does not affect its existence prior to that act. Furthermore, since being signified is a relation, becoming signified does not change the nature of the signified. Finally, since whatever is to be signified, and whatever is to be used as a signifier, must exist prior to that use, the logical priority of existence over the signifying relation holds equally for both of the correlative terms of the relation; the signifier is no more privileged than is the signified.

Clearly, then, the accusations that Freud (e.g., Safouan 1982; Zentner 1980) is 'closing the semiotic circle', and the criticisms of his 'finalism', are misguided. They are effectively criticisms of the psychoanalytic commitment to the existence of a real signified, and to the need for a theory which explains the selection of the symbolised. Todorov (1982) paraphrases Freud as saying that 'there exist ultimate symbolised elements, which are no longer convertible in turn into symbolisers', which, says Todorov, means that 'The desires of early infancy close the symbolic circuit' (p. 253). But this is the semiotic construal of Freud's comment that 'The range of things which are given symbolic representation . . . is not very wide' (1916/17, p. 152), which is not at all the same as claiming that symbolised elements are not convert*ible* into symbols. In Freud's system the limitation is empirically confirmable and theoretically defensible, as it must be. For a complete theory of the symbol, the *psychological* (as opposed to logical) constraints on signification require an account of the psychology of the signifying subject, an account which explains the particular symbolic equations made by that subject.

A theory of symbolism must be a psychological theory

This brings me to the third logical constraint. A theory of symbolism must be a psychological theory, because one of the terms in the signifying relation is a cognising subject. A person, or at least a knower, is a necessary part of the symbolic relation. Any theory which denies the subject cannot be a theory of symbolism. Any theory which acknowledges the existence of the subject, but which ignores that subject in the details of the theory, must justify such a move; it must show that the nature of the subject, and the existence of individual differences in subjects, are irrelevant to symbolism.

There is no need to illustrate the claim that the FB theory of symbolism is a psychological theory; indeed, as I argued in the previous chapter, part of its success (compared with the FN theory) rests on its derivation from, and dependence on, the rest of the theoretical structure of psychoanalysis.

In contrast, there is widespread violation of this constraint in alternative approaches to symbolism. In the field of hermeneutics, for all the emphasis on the subjective construction of meaning, it is mainly via an ignoring of the subject that the interpretation of symbols is allowed what is typically regarded as the strong point of the hermeneutical approach – unrestricted 'free play' in interpretation. Semiotics, as we have seen, also neglects the subject, dealing only with the relation between signifier and signified (reformulated as the relation between two signifiers). Where the subject *is* acknowledged, it is treated in one of three ways: as the *product* of linguistic constructivism; as an irrelevant kind of Husserlian constant; or as the mere 'point of intersection' in a network of signi-

fiers. The semiotic attack on the 'autonomy' of the subject is an attack
not on free will but on realism, on the existence of the subject independently of language and discourse. In the history of semiotics, there has
been only one significant attempt to reverse this trend and re-establish
the signifying subject at the centre of the field, where it belongs. Not
surprisingly, this attempt draws on Freud's theory. Nearly three decades
ago, Kristeva (1969, 1973) advocated the union of psychoanalysis and
semiotics (leading to a science she called 'semanalysis') not, as Lacan
does, by subsuming the unconscious under the all-important paradigmatic conception of language, but, rather, by bringing back into the
centre of symbolism the Freudian conception of the independently
characterisable signifying subject, particularly as motivated by a set of
instinctual drives. Kristeva (1973) criticised the increasing formalism of
semiotics, its abandonment of historical and psychological approaches,
and its neglect of a theory of a 'speaking subject' in favour of 'a *transcen-
dental ego*, cut off from its body, its unconscious, and also its history'
(p. 1249). Instead, semiotics must 'attune itself to the theory of the
speaking subject as a divided subject (conscious/unconscious) and go
on to attempt to specify the types of operation characteristic of the two
sides of this split; thereby exposing them to those forces extraneous to
the logic of the systematic; exposing them, that is to say, on the one
hand, to biophysiological processes (themselves inescapably part of the
signifying process – what Freud labelled "drives"), and, on the other
hand, to social constraints' (ibid.). Kristeva's warnings have gone
unheeded. Even those modern semiotic treatments which attempt to
give due recognition to the subject, via an assimilation of psychoanalysis
and semiotics, cannot shake themselves free from linguistic constructivism, which is incompatible with psychoanalysis. For instance, Silverman
(1983) claims that, unlike standard semiotic approaches, hers 'maintains the centrality of psychoanalysis to semiotics; it proposes, that is,
that the human subject is to a large extent the subject of semiotics'
(preface). Yet she also insists 'that signification occurs only through discourse, that discourse requires a subject, and that the subject itself is an
effect of discourse' (ibid.). If we move away from hermeneutics and
semiotics, into the fields of sociology and anthropology, we find there
too a violation of the logical constraint requiring a theory of symbolism
to be a psychological theory. For example, Durkheim's (1915) seminal
attempt to account for the products of culture (rituals, social practices,
religious belief systems, etc.) without recourse to psychology or to the
individual, by claiming that they are symbolic of aspects of society, in
particular of the social and moral forces embodied in the group, results
in incompleteness and cannot be consistently maintained. With respect

to incompleteness, Durkheim is content to stop at society, whereas psychoanalysts ask the further question: if moral and social forces are symbolised, why and how? For psychoanalysis and the FB theory of symbolism, the moral forces embodied in society derive from the earlier power, first physical and only subsequently moral, of the parent, a process which *explains* both the existence and the efficacy of the moral power of the group. With respect to inconsistency, Durkheim runs into difficulties in his analysis of the moral function of religion, where he allows that the moral ideal, whose function is to strengthen the bonds attaching the individual to society, is bought at the price of renunciation of individual needs. Durkheim's position shows that recognition of the symbolic nature of cultural phenomena is not always accompanied (as it should be) by the recognition that such phenomena are psychological. Durkheim's legacy takes an extreme form in the approaches to culture known as 'cultural materialism' or 'culturology', whose advocates insist that human psychology has nothing to do with the cultural process. Instead, society, ideology, and social relations, all subordinated to techno-environmental factors, have autonomous explanatory status. But, as Langness (1974) points out, 'Symbolization is fundamentally a psychological phenomenon, not a technoenvironmental feature', so that any attempt to study cultural phenomena without considering symbolic processes 'must be limited to a passing glance rather than a full view' (p. 107). The full view is provided in the work of Róheim (1941, 1943), who agrees with Malinowski that 'The birth and development of symbolism always occur under the control of organic drives', because 'symbolism was born with the first deferred and indirect satisfaction of any and every bodily need' (Malinowski 1963, p. 237). In examining the origin and function of culture, Róheim isolates sublimation of instinct as 'an especially conspicuous feature of cultural evolution; it is this that makes it possible for the higher mental operations, scientific, artistic, ideological activities, to play such an important part in civilised life' (1943, p. 95). Thus, 'psychoanalysis as a psychology is in harmony with a biological theory that would attempt to explain human nature on the basis of a specific infantile situation' (Róheim 1941, p. 39). The implications of this theory for anthropology and sociology are that, 'we must explain human institutions as based on human nature and not human nature as based on human institutions' (ibid., p. 47). That is to say, in any account of the symbolism which makes up culture, psychology must be fundamental. This is because the existence of symbolic phenomena presupposes the processes of symbolism, and these processes must be psychological, since logically they require cognition (representation), and empirically they require motivation.

The (psychological) theory of symbolism cannot combine
incompatible philosophical premises

The final logical constraint is that the required psychological theory must not be based on contradictory premises; it cannot combine (explicitly or implicitly) incompatible philosophical positions, such as realism and idealism. This constraint is a form of the logical law of non-contradiction.

The FB theory of symbolism is based on a consistent determinism and a consistent realism, and, as I have argued, only those parts of Freud's material which do not conflict with this stance are acceptable and can be incorporated into the theory of symbolism.

There are, however, many other approaches to symbolism in which a combination of incompatible philosophical positions is seen not as contradictory, and so theoretically untenable, but rather as particularly liberal and open-minded; in order that justice may be done to the 'infinite variability' of the symbol, idealism is combined with realism, and free will is combined with determinism. It is not surprising that, in these attempts, the study of symbolism is located outside science. But the confusions and contradictions which are entailed by such combinations lead, once again, to the untenability of explanations founded on them. We have already seen how, in Ricoeur's hermeneutic treatment of symbolism, the assertion that a complete theory of symbolism must acknowledge, as Freud's does not, that symbols carry both regressive and progressive vectors is a resurrection of the Jungian position, in which there is an attempt to wed the unweddable, to dissolve the opposition between realism and idealism, and between determinism and teleology. This is also the case with the treatment of symbolism from a humanistic perspective in psychology, such as that developed by Bertalanffy (1981). The humanistic rejection of psychoanalytic 'reductionism' is only partial, and so leads to inconsistencies. According to Bertalanffy, 'human values cannot be derived from and ultimately reduced to biological values' (1981, p. xvii), because 'specific human values may be distinguished from general biological values . . . by the fact that they are at the symbolic level' (p. 43); the whole of human culture, art, literature, etc. simply has nothing to do with biological values. Indeed, 'There are many realities which are neither physical nor mental, but which are beyond and outside the Cartesian synthesis' (p. 102). Yet, despite the supposedly independent higher realm, Bertalanffy confesses that existential symbols present special difficulties 'because of their connection with processes at the unconscious level' (p. 55), and because they can distort reality and create illusions:

The evolution of symbolism . . . warns us that the highest rational forms of symbolism (language, science) must not mislead us into assuming that creative symbolism is principally a process at the conscious or, in psychoanalytic language, at the 'secondary' level . . . creative intellectual work is also largely based upon 'inspiration', that is, on primary processes in the unconscious. (ibid., p. 69)

The inconsistencies and lacunae here are evident. It appears that the higher realm *is*, but after all is *not*, independent of 'primary processes in the unconscious', and that values *are*, but after all are *not*, independent of facts. Moreover, to distinguish human values from biological values by claiming that the former are 'at the symbolic level' is vacuous unless we are told what those values are symbolic *of*, which, of course, is impossible, if they are ineffable. As an example of a 'quasi-need', Bertalanffy selects the need for 'keeping up with the Joneses', a need which arises in the symbolic world, and is independent of the kinds of need dealt with by Freud. But we are given no explanation of the origin of such teleologically defined needs, and the use of the qualifier 'quasi' suggests that they are not needs at all, but derivations from genuine (now unconscious) needs, whose identification is necessary to explain their origins. Such tensions result from the doomed effort to rescue the 'higher' realm from dependence on the 'regressive' and 'archaic', and from the inevitable confronting of that dependence in any genuine explanation.

The psychological requirements

Given that any theory of symbolism must be a psychological theory, there are a number of aspects of symbolism which a complete psychological theory of symbolism will explain. Since these aspects concern the third term of the relation, the signifying subject, it is not surprising that those theories of symbolism which deny or ignore the subject do not meet the psychological requirements. However, there are other theories which do acknowledge the subject, but which fail to appreciate the psychological requirements, and consequently provide a very inadequate account of certain important aspects of symbolism.

The ontogenesis of symbols

Firstly, the theory will explain the ontogenesis of symbols: how and why they occur. In the FB theory, the account of the ontogenesis of symbols depends on the category of symbolism under discussion. Conventional symbolism is acknowledged, but, as is the general consensus, it is recognised to be relatively uncontroversial. Instead, the focus of inquiry is non-conventional symbolism, including those cases identified in Jones's treatment (see Chapter 9) as 'metaphor', but which, because of their psychodynamic origins, are categorised as defensive reactions to 'true symbolism'. The FB account of the ontogenesis of symbols has already been presented in some detail (particularly in Chapter 10), and it is clear that the theory answers both the 'how?' and the 'why?' of symbolism.

By contrast, in the extensive literature on symbolism there is very little on the question of the ontogenesis of symbols. In the field of psychology outside psychoanalysis, some attention is paid to it, but usually only to deny the 'biologically determined' nature of symbolism, and instead to promote the view of symbols as 'freely-chosen' (e.g., Bertalanffy 1965, 1981). This claim confuses conventional and non-conventional symbolism; the explication of the ontogenesis of *conventional* symbols is relatively unproblematic; they are, in a sense, freely chosen; but that is not true of non-conventional symbols. The only other psychological theory which offers any account of the ontogenesis of symbols is that of Piaget (1920, 1927, 1966). However, without the psychoanalytic concepts of the unconscious and repression, which he rejects, Piaget cannot explain some obvious facts about the development of the 'symbolic function', such as its relation to conflict and affect, and its apparent role in the compensation of unsatisfied needs.

The selection of the symbolised

The second psychological requirement is that there be some explanation of the selection of the symbolised. Since, logically, anything can be used to symbolise anything else, the first step here is to acknowledge, again, the distinction between conventional and non-conventional symbolism. Because the symbol–symbolised connection in non-conventional symbolism is not determined by convention, any claim about what the symbol stands for requires support. As Ricoeur (1970) says, 'the puzzling thing about symbols is not that ships stand for women, but that women are signified' (pp. 500–1).

In the FB theory, the focus on the psychology of the signifying subject and the account of the ontogenesis of symbols provide the basis for meeting this requirement, via the concept of primary objects and repression, followed by the deflection of interest onto substitutes. In terms of the selection, the list of things which are symbolised (the self, the body, immediate blood relatives, birth, love and death), and which 'represent the most primitive ideas and interests imaginable' (Jones 1916, p. 102), is relatively small. But:

The actual number of ideas is rather greater, however, than might be supposed from the briefness of this summary – they amount, perhaps, to about a hundred – and a few supplementary remarks are necessary. The self comprises the whole body or any separate part of it, not the mind; perhaps twenty different ideas can here be symbolised. The relatives include only father, mother, brothers and sisters, and children; various parts of their bodies also can be symbolised. Birth can refer to the ideas of giving birth, of begetting, or of being born oneself. The idea of death is in the unconscious a relatively simple one, that of lasting absence; it always refers to the death of others, for the idea of one's own death is probably inconceivable as such in the unconscious, being always converted into some other one. Love, or more strictly sexuality, comprises a very considerable number of distinct processes, including some, such as excretory acts, that are not commonly recognised to have a sexual bearing; it would lead us too far to enumerate and describe them all here, but it may be said that the total conception thus reached closely corresponds with Freud's theory of sex. The field of sexual symbolism is an astoundingly rich and varied one, and the vast majority of all symbols belong to this category. (Jones 1916, pp. 102–3)

To Jones's list it must be added that, in keeping with the FB use of the term 'symbolic' to describe not just single entities, but events, actions, etc., the consummatory activities of the instinctual drives involving these primary objects can also be symbolised. Most importantly, in the FB theory the symbolic equation is 'unidirectional': the selection of the symbolised always operates in accordance with the primary/derivative distinction, and so it is always, ultimately, the primary which is symbolised. When a church spire in a dream is identified (given supporting indications) as a phallic symbol, the method of identification is based on a theory which grounds symbolism in the privileged primacy of the body and its early experiences, because of the instinctual drives as motivators, and which supports that grounding via an account of the processes of socialisation, repression, substitution etc., along lines indicated earlier.

By contrast, the alternative theories not only betray a tendency to misunderstand and misrepresent the Freudian position, they also fail to provide any explanatory foundation of their own. Misunderstanding is, for instance, evident in the attacks by anti-realist semioticians (e.g., Zentner 1980; Safouan 1982) on Freud's theory of the selection of the symbolised. In 'closing the semiotic circle', by fixing an end point (viz. primary objects and activities) to the series of substitutions uncovered by interpretation, Freud's explanation becomes a 'finalist' one, one which masquerades as an unbiased journey of 'discovery', yet is directed by an 'a priori codification of the results to be obtained' (Todorov 1982, p. 253). Todorov sees the 'finalist' nature of Freudian interpretation as analogous to that other great finalist strategy, Patristic exegesis, wherein

Christian hermeneutics invariably found, for it was established *a priori* that it *would* find, Father, Son, and Holy Ghost. But there is a crucial difference between these two different 'finalist' accounts; one is realist and empiricist, the other idealist and rationalist. The body and its products, parents, siblings, etc., are a good deal more tangible and empirically verifiable than the Father, Son, and Holy Ghost. A limitation of possible meanings is theoretically defensible to the extent that it is empirically discoverable and supportable, and this is made possible by meeting the third logical requirement, that a theory of symbolism must be a psychological theory. It is not logic which produces ultimate symbolised elements but psychology, a theory of the cognising subject which explains the selection of the symbolised; and the logical arbitrariness is avoided by discovering what Jones (1916) describes as 'the uniformity of the fundamental and perennial interests of mankind' (p. 98). Provided these are given independent validation, their discovery via the interpretation of symbols is not a question-begging exercise (as it is in the case of the 'discovery' of the Holy Trinity via Patristic exegesis). Other theorists accuse Freud of narrowness, in illegitimately restricting the *direction* of the symbolic equation. Surely, they insist, symbolism can go both ways. Munz (1973), in support of Ricoeur, claims that the two 'contradictory' movements of thought about symbols (to demystify versus to remystify – or, as Ricoeur puts it, to find the *logos* behind the *mythos*, and vice versa), are equally valid; it just depends on which direction one takes. Because symbols have both a 'concealing' and a 'revealing' function, Jones's (1916) stock example of the church spire in a dream has the following interpretation: the church spire *conceals* the phallus, but '*reveals* that the phallus *means* the spire . . . Travelling upwards we are destroying the illusion that a spire is a spire. Travelling downwards we are destroying the illusion that a phallus is a phallus' (Munz 1973, p. 90). Apart from the unclarity of the notion of moving 'upwards' or 'downwards' in the interpretation, Munz's attempt to have it both ways is based on his failure to move past his recognition that, while there must be a symbol and a symbolised, there are no logical constraints on which is which. That is true, but since one of the terms in the symbolic relation is a signifying subject, there are *psychological* constraints which require an explanation of the *selection* of the symbolised and the *direction* of the symbolic equation. While the phallus can *logically* symbolise a church spire, the onus on anyone who claims that it does is to offer a characterisation of the signifying subject which provides a psychologically plausible explanation of such an occurrence. This Munz does not do. Indeed, such an account would be required only if the phallus were to appear in the manifest content of a dream, and if the supposed interpretation of the dream required the phallus to be taken as a symbol of a spire. This is not the case in the example. In claiming that 'the phallus means the spire', Muntz ignores the fact that it is the spire, not the phallus, which appears in the dream; the spire is the symbol, the phallus the symbolised.

In sum, these criticisms of Freud rest partly on a confusion of non-conventional with conventional symbolism (only in the latter is the logic of the symbolic equation free from any psychological requirement), and partly on a failure to appreciate that, for non-conventional symbols, an independent justification of the selection of the symbolised is what is required in a theory of symbolism.

Individual and universal symbols

A theory of symbolism must be able to account both for individual and for universal symbols. In rejecting the FN characterisation of symbols (which precludes individual symbols), the FB theory meets this psychological requirement. Individual and universal symbols are both formed in the same way; each person acquires the 'raw material' for symbols through perception, especially early in life, and a symbol's 'universality' (or other degree of prevalence) is explained by common early experiences and by the ubiquity of certain kinds of object. Apart from Jung's notion of the collective unconscious (which amounts to a version of the FN position), other theories of symbolism appear not to hold the individual/universal distinction worthy of serious consideration.

Variations in the tertium comparationis

A complete psychological theory of symbolism will not only specify what connects the symbol with the symbolised, but also explain why this often varies from one symbol to another, or why it changes over time. In the FB theory of symbolism, the most common 'third (term) of comparison' is, not surprisingly, similarity of shape or form. As Freud says: 'The imagination does not admit of long stiff objects . . . being used as symbols of the female genitals, or of hollow objects being used as symbols for the male ones' (1900, p. 234). Another element of comparison is function, which Gombrich (1963), for instance, considers more important than shape or form: 'substitutes reach deep into biological functions that are common to man and animals – a child . . . will reject a perfectly naturalistic doll in favour of a monstrously abstract dummy which is "cuddly"' (p. 4). One determinant of variations in degree of similarity is variation in strength of the impulse; according to Gombrich, the stronger the drive, the less stringent the requirement for formal similarity between symbol and symbolised. In addition, if the much-noted balance between the concealing and the revealing aspects of the symbol reflects its nature as a defensive compromise, then shifts in this balance can be explained by either decrease in interest, or increase in anxiety. For example, one psychoanalytic approach to aesthetic interest (e.g., Gombrich 1960, 1963, 1979; Ehrenzweig 1953) suggests that art which symbolically displays tabooed objects too obviously is reacted to with aesthetic repugnance: hence we uphold as ideal the sublimity and restrained grace of classical art, whose surface form allows us to react to the more primitive, gratifying symbolism contained at a deeper level. Also, Freud argued that dream symbolism in neurotics, because of stronger censorship, is often obscure and hard to interpret. In support of Freud's point, there is reason to believe that dream symbols change during psychoanalysis; as repression is gradually lifted, leading to confrontation and acceptance of hitherto repressed impulses, and then to resolution of conflicts, symbols increasingly become 'transparent', i.e., more obviously similar to what is symbolised, a fact which any theory which rejects the concept of defence would find difficult to explain.

In contrast, other theories do little more than comment on the 'sliding scale' of opacity/transparency in symbolism: sometimes the meaning of the symbol is obvious, sometimes it is obscure. However, no theory of symbolism other than psychoanalysis attempts to give any account of this, except to attribute it to the mysterious complexity and infinite variability of the symbol. This, of course, is simply *petitio principii*, and non-explanatory.

Conscious and unconscious elements

Finally, in a complete psychological theory of symbolism, some account will be given of the relationship between conscious and unconscious elements in symbolism, i.e., of when symbolism is conscious, when unconscious, when conscious symbolism masks, or is a rationalisation of, unconscious symbolism, what the particular conscious and unconscious elements in any complex symbolic formation are, and so on.

Clearly, the FB theory of symbolism devotes considerable attention to this question, since the combination of unconscious and conscious elements not only lies at the heart of symbolism, but is also what is distinctive about the Freudian approach to mentality and psychological explanation (see, e.g., Smith 1970). Details of this part of the theory have been presented extensively in earlier chapters. For example, Jones's discussion of the function of 'abstract, metaphorical' symbolism as a defensive reaction to the true unconscious meaning of the symbol (i.e., the relationship between 'descendence' and 'collateralism', which was examined in Chapter 9) is summarised by him thus:

> We are concerned with three groups of psychical material: (1) the unconscious complexes, (2) the inhibiting influences (Freud's ethical censorship) that keep these in a state of repression, and (3) the sublimated tendencies derived from the unconscious complexes. In my judgement, the relation of symbolism to these three groups is this: Like the third group, symbols are the product of intrapsychical conflict between the first two groups. The material of the symbol is taken from the third group. The second group, which prevents the first one from coming to direct expression, is to some extent represented in the formation of the symbol; but the dynamic force that creates the symbol, the meaning carried by the symbol, and the reason for the very existence of the symbol, are all derived from the first group, from the unconscious complexes. (Jones 1916, p. 141)

In Freud's own writings, one particularly clear example of the complex interplay of conscious and unconscious elements and processes appears in his account of the psychodynamic basis of rituals and ceremonies in neurosis and primitive religions, involving ambivalent attitudes towards the father or father-substitute:

> the strongest support for our effort to equate taboo prohibitions with neurotic symptoms is to be found in the taboo ceremonials themselves ... These ceremonials unmistakably reveal their double meaning and their derivation from ambivalent impulses, as soon as we are ready to allow that the results which they bring about were intended from the first. The taboo does not only pick out the king and exalt him above all common mortals, it also makes his existence a torment and an intolerable burden and reduces him to a bondage far worse than that of his subjects. Here, then, we have an exact counterpart of the obsessional act in the neurosis, in which the suppressed impulse and the impulse that suppresses it find simultaneous and common satisfaction. The obsessional act is *ostensibly* a protection against the prohibited act; but *actually*, in our view, it is a repetition of it. The 'ostensibly' applies to the *conscious* part of the mind, and the 'actually' to the *unconscious* part. In exactly the same way, the ceremonial taboo of kings is *ostensibly* the highest honour and protection for them, while *actually* it is a punishment for their exaltation, a revenge taken on them by their subjects. (Freud 1913d, pp. 50–1)

In contrast, there are a number of theories of symbolism in anthropology and sociology, or in the more humanistic, phenomenological, and existentialist movements in psychology, which treat the relationship between conscious and unconscious factors unsatisfactorily. Some deny unconscious processes altogether, but as a result are left making inconsistent claims. For instance, the anthropologist Beattie (in Skorupski 1976), in his account of ritual symbolism, claims (a) that the person *knows* the symbol is *merely* a symbol and that his action is 'purely' symbolic, and *yet* (b) that he is convinced of the instrumental efficacy of his ritual. But, as Skorupski observes, these two claims are inconsistent, and can be made consistent only by postulating some unconscious identification of the symbol with the symbolised. Others choose to ignore unconscious processes, proclaiming that the meaning of symbols lies in their conscious social functions and roles. As a consequence, these theories are left with glaring lacunae, which are replaced by contradictions as soon as any attempt is made to examine the origins of those all-important social functions and roles. For example, Skorupski himself, supporting the 'literalist' (as opposed to the 'symbolist') position on religion, ritual, and magic, argues that the notion of unconscious symbolism is unnecessary, because the feelings tied to a postulated unconscious level of symbolic awareness 'are explained perfectly well in terms of consciously held, literally expressed beliefs' (1976, p. 39). The rituals of the Catholic Church are perfectly 'literalist' *given* the actors' beliefs in God, and 'Anyone who wants to take the further, Marxian or Feuerbachian, step of seeing the theistic framework itself as a reification must explain what it is a reification of' (p. 113). Of course. But anyone who does not take this further step is sidestepping the issue, ignoring the question (pertinently asked by Freud) why and whence such beliefs arise in the absence of any evidence that gods exist. Durkheim does ask this question, but his attempt to give an account of the origins and function of symbolism without recourse to the psychology of the individual fails, as we have seen. Still others insist that symbols which are unconsciously formed, 'driven' and not 'freely chosen' are not deserving of the label 'symbolic', but their treatment of the foundations of what they assert to be genuine symbols is riddled with inconsistencies and unclarities. Bertalanffy (1981), for instance, asserts both that genuine symbols have nothing to do with the biological drives central to Freud's theory, and that these symbols nevertheless present special difficulties 'because of their connection with processes at the unconscious level' (p. 55). Finally, a few accept the role of unconscious and conscious elements in symbolism, but their treatment of the relationship between the two is confused and contradictory. Turner's (1967) work in symbolic anthropology illustrates the problems with a theory of symbolism which recognises the psychodynamic relationship between conscious and unconscious aspects, but which, at the same time, is influenced by the anti-psychological legacy of Durkheim. Turner argues that the meanings of ritual symbols are polarised into a 'sensory pole' (psychobiological and physiological constants such as blood, genitalia, semen, urine and faeces, which arouse desires and emotions), and an 'ideological pole' (components of the moral and social order, unity of groups, norms and values of groups, etc.). Now, when it comes to the question of the relationship between these poles, Turner's account vacillates wildly between what amounts to a psychodynamic position (which identifies the relation as one of 'descendence'), and what amounts to a Durkheimian position, the latter accompanied by various versions of the charge of 'reductionism' against psychoanalysis. According to Turner, the essential quality of ritual symbols with respect to the two 'poles' is their juxtaposition of the grossly physical (the organic) and the normative (the social), the 'low' and the 'high':

> We do not need a detailed acquaintance with any of the current depth psychologies to suspect that this juxtaposition of opposites in the symbol is connected with its social function . . . Ritual, scholars are coming to see, is precisely a mechanism that periodically converts the obligatory into the desirable . . . Norms and values on the one hand become saturated with emotion, while the gross and basic emotions become ennobled through contact with social values. The irksomeness of moral constraint is transformed into the 'love of virtue'. (Turner 1967, pp. 29–30)

This is so close to the FB view that only a small step is required to elucidate the connection between the social function and the other aspects of symbolism, by showing that the 'obligatory' is founded on the 'desirable' via socialisation, and so uncovering the notion of 'value' as based on renunciation of instinctual gratification. Indeed, in many places Turner's account is strongly psychoanalytic. For instance, he suggests that what places limits on anthropological interpretation at the sensory pole is the latter's reaching into the unconscious, so that 'We often become aware that the overt and ostensible aims and purposes of a given ritual conceal unavowed, and even "unconscious", wishes and goals . . . a complex relationship exists between the overt and the submerged, and the manifest and latent patterns of meaning' (ibid., p. 46). In Turner's analysis of colour symbolism, the universal appearance, in initiation rituals, of the basic colour triad (black, white, red) is explained by pointing to the fluids, secretions, and waste products of the human body, whose emission, spilling, or production is associated with a heightening of emotion. The colours 'epitomize the main kinds of universal human organic experience' (ibid., p. 88), and thus 'culture, the superorganic, has intimate connections with the organic in its early stages, with the awareness of powerful physical experiences' (ibid., pp. 88–9). Turner expands these observations into what amounts to an endorsement of the FB theory, and a rejection of Durkheim:

> Not only do the three colours stand for basic human experiences of the body (associated with the gratification of libido, hunger, aggressive and excretory drives, and with fear, anxiety and submissiveness), they also provide a kind of

primordial classification of reality. This view is in contrast to Durkheim's notion that the social relations of mankind are not based on the logical relations of things but have served as the prototypes of the latter . . . against this I would postulate that the human organism and its crucial experiences are the *fons et origo* of all classifications. Human biology demands certain intense experiences of relationships . . . the colour triad white-red-black represents the archetypal man as a pleasure-pain process. The perception of these colours and of triadic and dyadic relations in the cosmos and in society, either directly or metaphorically, is a *derivative* of primordial psychobiological experience . . . biologically, psychologically, and logically prior to social classifications by moieties, clans, sex totems and all the rest. (Turner 1967, p. 90, second italics mine)

In all this, there is nothing incompatible with the FB theory, and much which strongly supports it. Turner's account recognises the necessity of a psychological theory, and offers an explanation of the genesis of symbolism and of the relationship between conscious and unconscious elements in those symbolic phenomena whose social function makes them central to culture.

However, this clear psychoanalytic treatment is interlaced with a remarkable series of complete about-faces and contradictions, epitomised in Turner's claim that 'it is theoretically inadmissible to explain social facts, such as ritual symbols, by the concepts of depth psychology' (ibid., p. 56). The psychoanalysts Reik, Jones, and Bettelheim are criticised for treating interpretations at the ideological pole almost as rationalisations, and thus as irrelevant:

all those things with which the social aspect of ritual symbolism is concerned – are surely of at least equal importance with biopsychical drives and early conditioning in the elementary family. After all, the ritual symbol has, in common with the dream symbol, the characteristic, discovered by Freud, of being a compromise formation between two main opposing tendencies. It is a compromise between the need for social control, and certain innate and universal human drives. (ibid., p. 37)

Naturally, but one has to ask where the 'need for social control' comes from. That social relations are real is not denied by Freudian theory, and, if they are symbolised, one must explain why (as Turner himself begins to do). But Turner's account is incomplete; socialisation cannot be achieved via social 'forces' which appear *ex nihilo*. Thus, the claim that symbols embody the moral values and ideals of the group is only a first step; an account of these ideals is required – what are they, where do they come from? It is not enough simply to point to the revelation in symbolism of 'values' and to insist that values are sociocultural facts. Values are indeed facts (sociocultural *and* psychological), but only in the sense that someone or some group values something, and not in the sense that there are intrinsically valuable things. An examination of the origins and ontological status of values is required and, as revealed in Turner's own analysis, only Freud's theory attempts that. The core of Turner's inconsistency seems to be the result of the tension between, on the one hand, an ideology in which the independence of anthropology as a separate discipline is mistakenly believed to depend on a rejection of Freud, and, on the other hand, the inevitability of the Freudian approach whenever a genuinely explanatory account is embarked upon. In order to keep faith with his fellow social anthropologists, Turner appears to feel constrained to pay lip service to the dismissal of psycho-analytic 'reductionism', but, in his attempt to give an explanatory account of ritual symbols, he cannot avoid the very stance which he has rejected. Many other theories of symbolism are likewise marred by inconsistencies produced by the tension between the effort to rescue the 'higher' realm from its dependence on the 'regressive' and 'archaic', and the inevitable confronting of that dependence in any genuine explanation.

Conclusion

My brief contrasting of the FB theory with alternative approaches to symbolism has perforce been sketchy and incomplete, but I trust I have made clear the general lines which a detailed treatment would follow. In sum, any theory of symbolism must respect certain logical constraints and, because one of these constraints is that the theory be a psychologi-cal one, it must fulfil certain psychological requirements. The FB theory appears to satisfy all of these requirements. The alternative material on symbolism, extensive though it is, contains no serious challenge to the FB theory, because it displays little appreciation of the logical and psychological requirements, and so is inevitably flawed. If one were to nominate a single recurrent theme which encapsulates the various viol-ations of these constraints, it would be the dualist setting of the symbol in opposition to science, such that the two are incompatible. Science (we are told) has to do with the 'sign', with facts, with theory, with causal explanation, with objectivity, with specifiable and discoverable meaning, with cognition, and with a unitary perspective ('univocality'). When we are dealing with the symbol, either the possibility of knowl-edge is excluded, or, if knowledge is allowed, it is not the ordinary, scientific, kind of knowledge, which 'flees away from existence into the world of concepts' (Palmer 1969, p. 10). By contrast, the symbol (we are told) belongs to a separate world; it has to do with values, with the humanities, with interpretation and expression, with subjectivity, with elusive, perpetually shifting meaning, with emotion, and with a dialectical perspective ('plurivocality'). It is this mistaken dualist attitude towards symbolism and science which has fuelled, again and again, the current chaotic state of the field of symbolism, and has encouraged the mistaken belief that no general unified theory is possible.

Epilogue

The case I have made here for a general theory of the symbol is, of course, far from closed. Doubtless there will be those who will not be persuaded by it, perhaps because they still believe that no general theory is possible, or because they favour one or another of the alternative approaches, or because they see flaws in the FB theory which I have failed to identify. Whatever objections there may be, however, it seems to me that they would need to be organised along one of two possible lines. The first would be to challenge my claim that only the FB theory meets the criteria for an adequate account of symbolism. Critics would need to demonstrate either that some particular alternative approach *does*, after all, meet those criteria, and does so more adequately than the FB theory, or that *no* theory, not even the FB theory, meets them. A second possibility would be to dispute the criteria, showing that a general theory of the symbol is *not*, after all, bound by the requirements which I have stipulated. Such objections would at least take the debate about symbolism into appropriate and hitherto unexplored territory.

As for that territory, it is clear to me that much remains to be done in support of my own case. In particular, there are three obvious directions to take.

Firstly, a detailed treatment is required to fill in the sketchy lines of argument presented in the last chapter, contrasting the FB theory with alternative approaches. Only a more substantial, thorough examination of those alternatives would completely expose their lack of clear overall vision with regard to the requirements for an adequate account of symbolism, and would fully reveal the confusions and inconsistencies which result from ignoring those requirements. Such a detailed examination would also help to identify existing valuable contributions, consistent with the FB theory, which have already been made in a number of different areas dealing with symbolism (philosophy, aesthetics, semiotics, hermeneutics, anthropology, and sociology) but which have never been systematically coordinated into a single theory.

Secondly, the FB theory is embedded in Freud's general psychoanalytic theory, and stands or falls with it. Given the long history of attacks on psychoanalysis, particularly those concerned with the question of its scientific status (notably from Popper 1963; Eysenck 1985; Grünbaum 1984, 1993; Macmillan 1991), it would seem that the FB theory is vulnerable. True, I have proposed some revisions to Freud's material, which, I have argued, go a considerable way towards overcoming serious difficulties for psychoanalytic theory in general. Others (e.g., Hopkins 1982, 1988, 1992; Wollheim 1971, 1982, 1993; Maze 1983; Gardner 1993) have contributed substantially towards the development of a sound, coherent, and scientific version of psychoanalytic theory. Even so there is still more that could be achieved. Crews's recent (1993, 1996) reiteration of what he earlier (1988) had termed the 'scientific bad faith of the entire Freudian enterprise' (p. 236) is a reminder that no psychological theory has been subjected to more criticism because of its putatively unscientific status than has psychoanalysis, and that no other theory in psychology is so widely and often automatically dismissed on those grounds. But the question of the scientific status of psychoanalysis, although debated *ad nauseam*, has not been given the kind of rigorous, systematic, synoptic treatment which it requires. Instead, a tangled mixture of argument and rhetoric has been emitted in scattered form from both sides of the debate, revealing that psychoanalysis lacks not only effective critics (which explains why their charges, like prophecies of Armageddon, keep resurfacing), but also competent defenders. In the face of a barrage of heterogeneous accusations, supporters of psychoanalysis often become disorientated, respond in misguided and inappropriate ways, seize upon one point while ignoring the rest, or simply shrug off the whole issue and refuse to be drawn into the debate, so lending specious support to the critics. But if the material of the last several decades is carefully analysed, it becomes clear that what at first sight appears to be an overwhelming wealth of evidence and argument against psychoanalysis can be arranged into a few distinct categories, and that this organisation allows the separation of logical, empirical, rhetorical, and emotional issues, a necessary step in a proper evaluation of the charges. The results of such an evaluation show, I believe, that the case, far from being proven, is hardly even adequately formulated. Such a conclusion would naturally be of value to the FB theory.

Finally, there is the forced distinction to which I drew attention at the end of the last chapter, that between the symbol and science, which continues to bedevil the treatment of symbolism and to fuel psychology's exclusion of symbolism from serious scientific consideration. This distinction is not, of course, new; it is part of the age-old dichotomy between the natural and the social sciences, which still flourishes in contemporary psychology and philosophy of science, and has been bolstered by the postmodernist shift in the social sciences towards a more contextualist, hermeneutic, social constructionist approach. On one side, a traditional scientific approach to psychology is regarded as inadequate, on the grounds that it cannot cope with a number of central notions which cluster around the concept of 'meaning'. According to this view, since 'meaning' cannot be dealt with by the categories of science, and since human action is 'semantic or textual rather than abstract or causal' (Packer, 1985, p. 1086), psychology must be a hermeneutic, and not a scientific, enterprise. On the other side, a deterministic, scientific approach to psychology is regarded as the only acceptable one. Hence, 'meaning' and all that goes with it (symbols and symbolic activity in human behaviour and mental life) are simply excluded from scientific psychology. On both sides there is the barely examined assumption that the symbol is just not amenable to scientific investigation. Here, again, there is room for further development, by challenging that assumption. Already there has been movement towards exposing the postmodernist misrepresentation of science and scientific realism (see, e.g., Greenwood 1992; Bickhard 1992). What is also needed is an approach to the 'scientific' which enables (indeed, is indispensable for) a rigorous, systematic elucidation of the concept of 'meaning'. This would serve to demystify the nature and place of hermeneutical inquiry, which, as I have argued here, is perfectly compatible with a (properly understood) scientific approach.

These developments, extensions of the ideas contained in this book, might eventually have an impact on psychology. I have (re)claimed symbolism as a subject for psychology. With the revelation of the amenability of symbolism to scientific investigation, there would no longer be good reason for psychologists to avoid symbolism, or to relegate it to those parts of their discipline which they regard as lacking scientific respectability. Further, having accepted the possibility of a scientific treatment of symbolism, and simultaneously being faced with the results of a comprehensive re-evaluation of the case against the scientific status of psychoanalysis, psychologists who have been quick to dismiss psychoanalytic theory may be led to reconsider its potential contribution.

References

Anderson, J. 1927, The knower and the known, in *Studies in Empirical Philosophy*, Sydney: Angus & Robertson, 1962.
 1929, The non-existence of consciousness, in *Studies in Empirical Philosophy*, Sydney: Angus & Robertson, 1962.
 1930, Realism and some of its critics, in *Studies in Empirical Philosophy*, Sydney: Angus & Robertson, 1962.
 1936, Causality and logic, in *Studies in Empirical Philosophy*, Sydney: Angus & Robertson, 1962.
Armstrong, D. M. 1973, *Belief, Truth and Knowledge*, London: Cambridge University Press.
Badcock, C. R. 1980, *The Psychoanalysis of Culture*, Oxford: Blackwell.
Baker, A. J. 1986, *Australian Realism*, Cambridge: Cambridge University Press.
Baker, S. J. 1950, Language and dreams, *International Journal of Psychoanalysis*, 31: 171-8.
Balkányi, C. 1964, On verbalization, *International Journal of Psychoanalysis*, 45: 64-74.
Bell, C. 1914, *Art*, New York: Capricorn Books, 1958.
Bernstein, M. 1956, *The Search for Bridey Murphy*, New York: Doubleday.
Bertalanffy, L. von. 1965, On the definition of the symbol, in J. R. Royce (ed.), *Psychology and the Symbol. An Interdisciplinary Symposium*, New York: Random House.
 1981, *A Systems View of Man*, Colorado: Westview Press.
Bickhard, M. H. 1992, Myths of science, *Theory & Psychology*, 2 (3): 321-37.
Bleicher, J. 1980, *Contemporary Hermeneutics*, London: Routledge & Kegan Paul.
Cassirer, E. 1944, *An Essay on Man*, New Haven: Yale University Press.
 1953, 1955, 1957, *The Philosophy of Symbolic Forms* (trans. R. Manheim from orig. 1923, 1925, 1929), vols. I–III, New Haven: Yale University Press.
Cheshire, N. and Thomä, H. 1991, Metaphor, neologism and 'open texture': implications for translating Freud's scientific thought, *International Revue of Psycho-Analysis*, 18: 429-54.
Corradi Fiumara, G. 1992, *The Symbolic Function*, Oxford: Blackwell.
Crews, F. 1988, Beyond Sulloway's *Freud*: psychoanalysis minus the myth of the hero, in P. Clark and C. Wright (eds.), *Psychoanalysis, Mind and Science*, Oxford: Blackwell.
 1993, The unknown Freud, *New York Review*, November: 55-66.

1996, The verdict on Freud, *Psychological Science*, 7(2): 63–8.

Durkheim, E. 1915, *The Elementary Forms of the Religious Life*, London: George Allen & Unwin.

Eagle, M. 1988, Psychoanalysis and the personal, in P. Clark and C. Wright (eds.), *Psychoanalysis, Mind and Science*, Oxford: Blackwell.

Eco, U. 1973, Looking for a logic of culture, in The tell-tale sign: a survey of semiotics I, *Times Literary Supplement*, 5 Oct.: 1149–50.

Edelson, M. 1972, Language and dreams: the interpretation of dreams revisited, *The Psychoanalytic Study of the Child*, 27: 203–82.

Ehrenzweig, A. 1953, *The Psychoanalysis of Artistic Vision and Hearing*, London: Sheldon Press, 1965.

Eysenck, H. J. 1985, *Decline and Fall of the Freudian Empire*, Middlesex: Viking.

Fenichel, O. 1946, *The Psychoanalytic Theory of Neurosis*, London: Routledge & Kegan Paul.

Fingesten, P. 1970, *The Eclipse of Symbolism*, Columbia: University of South Carolina Press.

Fliess, R. 1973, *Symbol, Dream and Psychosis*, New York: International Universities Press.

Fodor, J. A. 1975, *The Language of Thought*, Hassocks, Sussex: Harvester Press.
1985, Fodor's guide to mental representation: the intelligent auntie's *Vade-Mecum, Mind*, 90: 76–100.

Forrester, J. 1980, *Language and the Origins of Psychoanalysis*, London: Macmillan.

Foulkes, D. 1978, *A Grammar of Dreams*, Harvester Press, Basic Books Inc.

Freud, S. 1893, On the psychical mechanism of hysterical phenomena: a lecture, *Standard Edition*, vol. III, London: Hogarth.
1894, The neuropsychoses of defence, *Standard Edition*, vol. III, London: Hogarth.

Freud, S. (and Breuer, J.) 1895a, *Studies on Hysteria (1893–95)*, *Standard Edition*, vol. II, London: Hogarth.

Freud, S. 1895b, *Project for a Scientific Psychology*, *Standard Edition*, vol. I, London: Hogarth.
1895c, Draft H. Paranoia, in Extracts from the Fliess papers (1892–1899), *Standard Edition*, vol. I, London: Hogarth.
1897, Letter 72, in Extracts from the Fliess papers (1892–1899), *Standard Edition*, vol. I, London: Hogarth.
1899, Screen memories, *Standard Edition*, vol. III, London: Hogarth.
1900, *The Interpretation of Dreams* (1st edn), *Standard Edition*, vols. IV and V, London: Hogarth.
1901a, On dreams (1st edn), *Standard Edition*, vol. V, London: Hogarth.
1901b, *The Psychopathology of Everyday Life*, *Standard Edition*, vol. VI, London: Hogarth.
1905a, Fragment of an analysis of a case of hysteria, *Standard Edition*, vol. VII, London: Hogarth.
1905b, *Jokes and their Relation to the Unconscious*, *Standard Edition*, vol. VIII, London: Hogarth.
1905c, *Three Essays on the Theory of Sexuality*, *Standard Edition*, vol. VII, London: Hogarth.

1907a, Delusions and dreams in Jensen's Gradiva, *Standard Edition*, vol. IX, London: Hogarth.

1907b, Obsessive actions and religious practices, *Standard Edition*, vol. IX, London: Hogarth.

1908a, Character and anal erotism, *Standard Edition*, vol. IX, London: Hogarth.

1908b, Creative writers and day-dreaming, *Standard Edition*, vol. IX, London: Hogarth.

1909a, Analysis of a phobia in a five-year-old boy, *Standard Edition*, vol. X, London: Hogarth.

1909b, Notes upon a case of obsessional neurosis, *Standard Edition*, vol. X, London: Hogarth.

1909c, *The Interpretation of Dreams* (2nd edn), *Standard Edition*, vols. IV and V, London: Hogarth.

1910a, Five lectures on psycho-analysis, *Standard Edition*, vol. XI, London: Hogarth.

1910b, On future prospects of psycho-analytic therapy, *Standard Edition*, vol. XI, London: Hogarth.

1910c, Leonardo da Vinci and a memory of his childhood, *Standard Edition*, vol. XI, London: Hogarth.

1910d, The antithetical meaning of primal words, *Standard Edition*, vol. XI, London: Hogarth.

1911a, *The Interpretation of Dreams* (3rd edn), *Standard Edition*, vols. IV and V, London: Hogarth.

1911b, On dreams (2nd edn), *Standard Edition*, vol. V, London: Hogarth.

1911c, The handling of dream-interpretation in psycho-analysis, *Standard Edition*, vol. XII, London: Hogarth.

1911d, Dreams in folklore (Freud and Oppenheim), *Standard Edition*, vol. XII, London: Hogarth.

1911e, Psycho-analytic notes on an autobiographical account of a case of paranoia, *Standard Edition*, vol. XII, London: Hogarth.

1912a, Contributions to a discussion on masturbation, *Standard Edition*, vol. XII, London: Hogarth.

1912b, On the universal tendency to debasement in the sphere of love, *Standard Edition*, vol. XI, London: Hogarth.

1912c, A note on the unconscious in psycho-analysis, *Standard Edition*, vol. XII, London: Hogarth.

1913a, An evidential dream, *Standard Edition*, vol. XII, London: Hogarth.

1913b, The occurrence in dreams of material from fairy tales, *Standard Edition*, vol. XII, London: Hogarth.

1913c, The theme of the three caskets, *Standard Edition*, vol. XII, London: Hogarth.

1913d, *Totem and Taboo*, *Standard Edition*, vol. XIII, London: Hogarth.

1913e, The claims of psycho-analysis to scientific interest, *Standard Edition*, vol. XIII, London: Hogarth.

1913f, Observations and examples from analytic practice, *Standard Edition*, vol. XIII, London: Hogarth.

1914a, *The Interpretation of Dreams* (4th edn), *Standard Edition*, vols. IV and V, London: Hogarth.

1914b, Some reflections on schoolboy psychology, *Standard Edition*, vol. XIII, London: Hogarth.

1914c, On the history of the psycho-analytic movement, *Standard Edition*, vol. XIV, London: Hogarth.

1914d, On narcissism: an introduction, *Standard Edition*, vol. XIV, London: Hogarth.

1915a, Instincts and their vicissitudes, *Standard Edition*, vol. XIV, London: Hogarth.

1915b, Repression, *Standard Edition*, vol. XIV, London: Hogarth.

1915c, The unconscious, *Standard Edition*, vol. XIV, London: Hogarth.

1915d, Thoughts for the times on war and death, *Standard Edition*, vol. XIV, London: Hogarth.

1916a, A connection between a symbol and a symptom, *Standard Edition*, vol. XIV, London: Hogarth.

1916/17, *Introductory Lectures on Psycho-Analysis*, *Standard Edition*, vols. XV and XVI, London: Hogarth.

1918, From the history of an infantile neurosis, *Standard Edition*, vol. XVII, London: Hogarth.

1919a, *The Interpretation of Dreams* (5th edn), *Standard Edition*, vols. IV and V, London: Hogarth.

1919b, Preface to Reik's *Ritual: Psycho-Analytic Studies*, *Standard Edition*, vol. XVII, London: Hogarth.

1920a, Associations of a four-year-old child, *Standard Edition*, vol. XVIII, London: Hogarth.

1920b, *Beyond the Pleasure Principle*, *Standard Edition*, vol. XVIII, London: Hogarth.

1921, *Group Psychology and the Analysis of the Ego*, *Standard Edition*, vol. XVIII, London: Hogarth.

1922, Dreams and telepathy, *Standard Edition*, vol. XVIII, London: Hogarth.

1923a, Two encyclopaedia articles, *Standard Edition*, vol. XVIII, London: Hogarth.

1923b, Remarks on the theory and practice of dream-interpretation, *Standard Edition*, vol. XIX, London: Hogarth.

1923c, The infantile genital organization: an interpolation into the theory of sexuality, *Standard Edition*, vol. XIX, London: Hogarth.

1923d, *The Ego and the Id*, *Standard Edition*, vol. XIX, London: Hogarth.

1924a, The dissolution of the Oedipus complex, *Standard Edition*, vol. XIX, London: Hogarth.

1924b, The loss of reality in neurosis and psychosis, *Standard Edition*, vol. XIX, London: Hogarth.

1924c, The economic problem of masochism, *Standard Edition*, vol. XIX, London: Hogarth.

1925a, *The Interpretation of Dreams* (8th edn), *Standard Edition*, vols. IV and V, London: Hogarth.

1925b, Some additional notes on dream-interpretation as a whole, *Standard Edition*, vol. XIX, London: Hogarth.

1925c, Negation, *Standard Edition*, vol. XIX, London: Hogarth.

1925d, *An Autobiographical Study*, *Standard Edition*, vol. XX, London: Hogarth.

1926a, *Inhibitions, Symptoms and Anxiety*, *Standard Edition*, vol. XX, London: Hogarth.

1926b, The question of lay analysis, *Standard Edition*, vol. XX, London: Hogarth.

1926c, Psycho-analysis, *Standard Edition*, vol. XX, London: Hogarth.

1927, *The Future of an Illusion*, *Standard Edition*, vol. XXI, London: Hogarth.

1929, Some dreams of Descartes': a letter to Maxime Leroy, *Standard Edition*, vol. XXI, London: Hogarth.

1930, *Civilization and its Discontents*, *Standard Edition*, vol. XXI, London: Hogarth.

1932, The acquisition and control of fire, *Standard Edition*, vol. XXII, London: Hogarth.

1933, *New Introductory Lectures on Psycho-Analysis*, *Standard Edition*, vol. XXII, London: Hogarth.

1937, Analysis terminable and interminable, *Standard Edition*, vol. XXIII, London: Hogarth.

1939, *Moses and Monotheism: Three Essays*, *Standard Edition*, vol. XXIII, London: Hogarth.

1940, *An Outline of Psycho-Analysis*, *Standard Edition*, vol. XXIII, London: Hogarth.

Gardner, S. 1993, *Irrationality and the Philosophy of Psychoanalysis*, Cambridge: Cambridge University Press.

Gergen, K. J. 1991, Emerging challenges for theory and psychology, *Theory & Psychology*, 1 (1): 13–35.

Gombrich, E. H. 1960, *Art and Illusion*, New York: Pantheon.

1963, *Meditations on a Hobby Horse: and Other Essays on the Theory of Art*, London: Phaidon Press.

1979, *The Sense of Order: A Study in the Psychology of Decorative Art*, New York: Phaidon Press.

Graubard, S. R. (ed.) 1988, *The Artificial Intelligence Debate*, Cambridge, Massachusetts: MIT Press.

Greenwood, J. D. 1992, Realism, empiricism and social constructionism, *Theory & Psychology*, 2 (2): 131–51.

Grünbaum, A. 1984, *The Foundations of Psychoanalysis: A Philosophical Critique*, Berkeley: University of California Press.

1986, Précis of *The Foundations of Psychoanalysis: A Philosophical Critique*, *Behavioral and Brain Sciences*, 9: 217–84.

1993, *Validation in the Clinical Theory of Psychoanalysis: A Study in the Philosophy of Psychoanalysis*, Madison, CT: International Universities Press.

Hacker, F. J. 1965, Psychology and the psychopathology of symbolism, in J. R. Royce (ed.), *Psychology and the Symbol. An Interdisciplinary Symposium*, New York: Random House.

Hall, C. S. 1953, *The Meaning of Dreams*, New York: Harper & Bros.

Hart, W. D. 1982, Models of repression, in R. Wollheim and J. Hopkins (eds.), *Philosophical Essays on Freud*, Cambridge: Cambridge University Press.

Hartmann, H., Kris, E. and Loewenstein, R. M. 1951, Some psychoanalytic comments on 'Culture and Personality', in Wilbur, G. B. and Münsterberger, W. (eds.), 1951, *Psychoanalysis and Culture*, New York: International Universities Press.

Hawkes, T. 1977, *Structuralism and Semiotics*, London: Methuen & Co.

Heil, J. 1981, Does cognitive psychology rest on a mistake? *Mind*, 90: 321–42.

Hopkins, J. 1982, Introduction: philosophy and psychoanalysis, in R. Wollheim and J. Hopkins (eds.), *Philosophical Essays on Freud*, Cambridge: Cambridge University Press.

   1988, Epistemology and depth psychology: critical notes on the *Foundations of Psychoanalysis*, in P. Clark and C. Wright (eds.), *Psychoanalysis, Mind and Science*, Oxford: Blackwell.

   1992, Psychoanalysis, interpretation and science, in J. Hopkins and A. Savile (eds.), *Psychoanalysis, Mind and Art*, Oxford: Blackwell.

Ibañez, T. 1991, Social psychology and the rhetoric of truth, *Theory & Psychology*, 1 (2): 187–201.

Jaffé, A. 1964, Symbolism in the visual arts, in C. G. Jung (ed.), *Man and His Symbols*, London: Aldus.

James, W. 1890, *The Principles of Psychology*, vols. I & II, Dover Publications Inc., 1950.

Johnson, M. 1987, *The Body in the Mind: The Bodily Basis of Meaning, Reason & Imagination*, Chicago: University of Chicago Press.

Jones, E. 1916, The theory of symbolism, in *Papers on Psychoanalysis*, 5th edn, London: Hogarth, 1948.

   1953, 1955, 1957, *Sigmund Freud: Life and Work*, 3 vols., London: Hogarth.

Jung, C. G. 1954, *The Archetypes and the Collective Unconscious*, in *Collected Works* (trans. R. F. C. Hull), London: Routledge & Kegan Paul.

   1964, Approaching the unconscious, in C. G. Jung (ed.), *Man and His Symbols*, London: Aldus.

Klein, M. 1930, The importance of symbol formation in the development of the ego, *International Journal of Psychoanalysis*, 11: 24–39.

Kluckhohn, C. 1960, Recurrent themes in myths and mythmaking, in H. A. Murray (ed.), *Myth and Mythmaking*, New York: George Braziller.

Kristeva, J. 1969, *Le Langage: Cet Inconnu*, Paris: Editions de Seuil, 1981.

   1973, The system and the speaking subject, in the tell-tale sign: a survey of semiotics II, *Times Literary Supplement*, 12 Oct.: 1249–50.

Kubie, L. S. 1953, The distortion of the symbolic process in neurosis and psychosis, *Journal of the American Psychoanalytic Association*, 1: 59–86.

Lacan, J. 1966, *Écrits* (trans. A. Sheridan), London: Tavistock, 1977.

Lakoff, G. 1993, The contemporary theory of metaphor, in A. Ortony (ed.), *Metaphor and Thought* (2nd edn), Cambridge: Cambridge University Press.

Lakoff, G. and Johnson, M. 1980, *Metaphors We Live By*, Chicago: University of Chicago Press.

Langer, S. K. 1942, *Philosophy in a New Key*, Cambridge, Massachusetts: Harvard University Press.

Langness, L. L. 1974, *The Study of Culture*, University of California: Chandler & Sharp.

Laplanche, J. and Pontalis, J.-B. 1985, *The Language of Psychoanalysis*, London: Hogarth (orig. 1973).

Lemaire, A. 1977, *Jacques Lacan* (trans. D. Macey), London: Routledge & Kegan Paul.

Lévi-Strauss, C. 1978, *Myth and Meaning*, London: Routledge & Kegan Paul.

Liddell, H. G. and Scott, R. 1968, *Greek–English Lexicon*, Oxford: Clarendon.

Macmillan, M. 1991, *Freud Evaluated: The Completed Arc*, Amsterdam: North-Holland.

Malinowski, B. 1963, *Sex, Culture and Myth*, London: Rupert Hart-Davis.

Matte Blanco, I. 1975, *The Unconscious as Infinite Sets: An Essay in Bi-Logic*, London: Duckworth.

Maze, J. R. 1973, The Concept of Attitude, *Inquiry*, 16: 168–205.

1983, *The Meaning of Behaviour*, London: Allen & Unwin.

1991, Representation, realism and the redundancy of 'mentalese', *Theory & Psychology*, 1(2): 163–85.

Michell, J. 1988, Maze's direct realism and the character of cognition, *Australian Journal of Psychology*, 40: 227–49.

Milner, M. 1952, Aspects of symbolism in comprehension of the not-self, *International Journal of Psycho-Analysis*, 33: 181–95.

Minturn, L. 1965, A cross-cultural linguistic analysis of Freudian symbols, *Ethnology*, 4 (3): 336–42.

Munz, P. 1973, *When the Golden Bough Breaks: Structuralism or Typology?* London: Routledge & Kegan Paul.

Packer, M. J. 1985, Hermeneutic inquiry in the study of human conduct, *American Psychologist*, October: 1081–93.

Palmer, R. E. 1969, *Hermeneutics*, Evanston: Northwestern University Press.

Passmore, J. A. 1962, John Anderson and twentieth-century philosophy, in *Studies in Empirical Philosophy*, Sydney: Angus & Robertson.

Piaget, J. 1920, Psychoanalysis in its relations with child psychology, in H. E. Grüber and J. J. Vonèche (eds.), *The Essential Piaget*, London: Routledge & Kegan Paul, 1977.

1927, The first year of life of the child, in H. E. Grüber and J. J. Vonèche (eds.), *The Essential Piaget*, London: Routledge & Kegan Paul, 1977.

1966, The semiotic or symbolic function, in H. E. Grüber and J. J. Vonèche (eds.), *The Essential Piaget*, London: Routledge & Kegan Paul, 1977.

Popper, K. R. 1963 (orig. 1957), *Conjectures and Refutations*, London: Routledge & Kegan Paul.

Rank, O. and Sachs, H. 1913, *Die Bedeutung der Psychoanalyse für die Geisteswissenschaften*, Grenzfr. Nerv.- u. Seelenleb., No. 93, Weisbaden (trans. *The Significance of Psychoanalysis for the Mental Sciences*, New York, 1916).

Reichenbach, H. 1951, *The Rise of Scientific Philosophy*, Berkeley: University of California Press.

Reviewer A. 1972, Between the wound and the work of art: the reductionist bias of psychoanalysis. Anonymous review of D. Fernandez, *L'Arbre jusqu'aux racines*, *Times Literary Supplement*, July 14: 817–19.

Reviewer B. 1971, Between the thumb and the teddy-bear. Anonymous review of D. Winnicott, *Playing and Reality*, *Times Literary Supplement*, 17 December: 1579–80.

Ricoeur, P. 1965, Existence and hermeneutics (trans. K. McLaughlin), in J. Bleicher, *Contemporary Hermeneutics*, London: Routledge & Kegan Paul, 1980.

1970, *Freud and Philosophy* (trans. D. Savage), New Haven: Yale University Press.

Rodrigué, E. 1956, Notes on symbolism, *International Journal of Psychoanalysis*, 37: 147–58.

Róheim, G. 1941, The psychoanalytic interpretation of culture, in W. Münster- berger (ed.), *Man and his Culture: Psychoanalytic Anthropology after 'Totem and Taboo'*, New York: Taplinger, 1969.

1943, *The Origin and Function of Culture*, New York: Anchor, 1971.

Royce, J. R. (ed.) 1965a, *Psychology and the Symbol. An Interdisciplinary Symposium*, New York: Random House.

1965b, Psychology at the crossroads between the sciences and the humanities, in J. R. Royce (ed.), *Psychology and the Symbol. An Interdisciplinary Symposium*, New York: Random House.

Rycroft, C. 1956, Symbolism and its relationship to the primary and secondary processes, *International Journal of Psychoanalysis*, 37: 137–46.

Safouan, M. 1982, Seminar on symbolism, in *Papers of the Freudian School of Melbourne*, Freudian School of Melbourne.

Sapir, E. 1959, Symbolism, in E. R. A. Seligman (ed.), *Encyclopaedia of the Social Sciences*, vol. XIII, New York: Macmillan.

Sartre, J.-P. 1956, *Being and Nothingness: An Essay on Phenomenological Ontology* (trans. H. E. Barnes), New York: Philosophical Library.

Segal, H. 1950, Some aspects of the analysis of a schizophrenic, *International Journal of Psycho-Analysis*, 31: 268–78.

1952, A psycho-analytic contribution to aesthetics, *International Journal of Psycho-Analysis*, 33: 196–207.

1958, Notes on symbol formation, *International Journal of Psychoanalysis*, 38: 391–7.

1975, Art and the inner world, *Times Literary Supplement*, July: 800–1.

Segal, N. P. 1961, The psychoanalytic theory of the symbolic process, *Journal of the American Psychoanalytic Association*, 9: 146–57.

Silverman, K. 1983, *The Subject of Semiotics*, New York: Oxford University Press.

Skorupski, J. 1976, *Symbol and Theory*, Cambridge: Cambridge University Press.

Smith, E. W. L. 1970, The fascinating toothpick: a study in phallic symbolism, *International Journal of Symbology*, 1 (3): 21–5.

Sperber, H. 1912, Über den Einfluss sexueller Momente auf Enstehung und Entwicklung der Sprache, *Imago*, Jahrg. i., s. 405.

Stove, D. C. 1991, *The Plato Cult and Other Philosophical Follies*, Oxford: Blackwell.

Todorov, T. 1982, *Theories of the Symbol* (trans. C. Porter), Oxford: Blackwell (Editions du Seuil, 1977).

Turner, V. 1967, *The Forest of Symbols: Aspects of Ndembu Ritual*, New York: Cornell University Press.

1968, Myth and symbol, in D. L. Sills (ed.), *International Encyclopedia of the Social Sciences*, vol. X: 576–82. New York: Macmillan.

Varela, C. R. 1995, Ethogenic theory and psychoanalysis: the unconscious as a social construction and a failed explanatory concept, *Journal for the Theory of Social Behaviour*, 25 (4): 363–85.

Ver Eecke, W. 1975, Symbol as a philosophical concept, *International Journal of Symbology*, 6 (1) March: 20–9.

Whitehead, A. N. 1927, *Symbolism*, New York: Macmillan.

Whyte, L. L. 1960, *The Unconscious Before Freud*, New York: Basic Books.

Wollheim, R. 1971, *Freud*, Glasgow: Fontana/Collins.

1982, The bodily ego, in R. Wollheim and J. Hopkins (eds.), *Philosophical Essays on Freud*, Cambridge: Cambridge University Press.

1993, *The Mind and its Depths*, Cambridge, Massachusetts: Harvard University Press.

Zentner, O. 1980, The Freudian unconscious, symbolism, and censorship, in *Papers of the Freudian School of Melbourne*, Freudian School of Melbourne.

Index

Note: page numbers in *italics* indicate a table or chart.

33099529